ULTIMATE PENALTIES

ULTIMATE PENALTIES

Capital Punishment, Life Imprisonment
Physical Torture

LEON SHASKOLSKY SHELEFF

THE OHIO STATE UNIVERSITY PRESS : COLUMBUS

Library of Congress Cataloging-in-Publication Data
Sheleff, Leon Shaskolsky.
Ultimate penalties.

Includes index.
1. Capital punishment. 2. Life imprisonment. 3. Torture. I. Title.
HV8694.S48   1987   364.6   87–5553
ISBN 0–8142–0436–8

In fond remembrance of
a good friend, Judah Landau
and a dear cousin, Joanee Fainstein Fisher

CONTENTS

PREFACE

SOME BOOKS are written to describe an author's fixed and firm thesis, and the final form of the work is often precisely envisaged in the initial stages. Other books take on a life and a quality of their own, growing and changing as the writer confronts the many faces of the problem that is his concern. This work is of the latter type.

My interest in capital punishment has been a long-standing one: from an awareness of its extensive use during my years as a law student in South Africa, through my response as an Israeli—first to the impact of the Eichmann trial, and then later to the debate over the appropriate punishment for terrorist activities—to my fascination, during sabbatical teaching and research periods in the United States, with the many intriguing facets and urgent issues of the constitutional implications of its use. Moving among three cultures and their totally different approaches has also made me more aware of the international dimensions of the problem as a primary issue of human rights, a factor that is a major aspect of this book.

I will not outline all the transformations in my ideas on capital punishment—only indicate that my move from what might be called a rigid abolitionist position to a more flexible one arises largely from my work, both academic and practical, with the issue of life and long-term imprisonment. The final dimensions of this book, as well as its very title, flow from the recognition that there are not one, but three ultimate penalties, and that discussion—legal, moral, philosophical, sociological, practical—of any one of them is dependent on attitudes to, and knowledge about, the other two.

As for capital punishment, I accept the validity of most of the arguments that have been advanced for its abolition. I respect the dedication of those who have embarked on battles for the saving of an individual's life. I object to the use of this punishment in order to further a political cause or to satisfy the base demands of a vindictive public. I reject the standard arguments that the differing aims of deterrence and retribution would be well served by the taking of life. I applaud the worldwide campaign of Amnesty International and like organizations against the death penalty. I myself have contributed to the debate, arguing against using the death penalty as a punishment for those who commit acts of terror in Israel, where I live and work.

Yet I have been unable, over the years, to ignore the gnawing doubts as to the total justification of the absolute abolitionist argument and, in particular, the unwillingness to deal with certain issues that I consider crucial to the debate. It is in the light of my own inner deliberations, the doubts that still possess me, and the dilemmas which I have been unable to resolve, that I present my own view—partly personal, partly political, partly professional, partly pragmatic—in the hope that it will help enrich the debate on what is one of the major moral issues of the modern age.

The clarification and crystallization of my ideas has been greatly facilitated by interaction with colleagues and students, to whom I am greatly indebted. Among the former who have either read or heard, and then responded to, parts of the thesis are David and Nitza Libai, Menachem Amir, Gerald Cromer, Israel Charny, Herman Goldstein, Zvi Zubin, Eliezer Ben-Rafael, Phil Harris, Alan Harland, Margaret Zahn, Steven Lukes, Marvin Wolfgang, Billy Gild, Matthew Silberman, Ilan Schiff, Peter Sevareid, Hank Richardson, Bill Woodward, Joe Passon and Bill Traylor. My thanks also to Yoram Dinstein and Dani More for their encouragement as editors of law journals at Tel Aviv University, in which earlier articles on the theme were published. Sy Dinitz and Gil Geis read a draft of the book, and I am as grateful to them for their positive response and collegial support as I am for their criticisms, always constructive, and challenges, always friendly.

Many of my ideas were first presented in a series of seminars given to law students at Tel Aviv and Temple Universities; their probing enquiries and thoughtful discussions were always a source of stimulation. At both these institutions I was given excellent research assistance by David Goren, Rina Hakamian, and Julian Gonzales. To all of them my gratitude. Similarly, I wish to acknowledge the helpful and efficient contribution of typists at both these universities, particularly Freddie Sanford, Mildred Woodson, David Bogan, Brenda Smith, Rachel Sandler, and Vera McPhilomy.

The major part of this book was written while on sabbatical leave at Temple University, as part of an exchange program between the Schools of Law at Tel Aviv and Temple Universities. My sincerest thanks to colleagues and administrative staff at Temple for the personal kindness extended to me during my stay there, with a special hearty, Hebraic "Todah Rabah" to the director of the exchange program, Burton Caine, who has helped make the cooperation between the two institutions so meaningful and pleasant.

Writing is by nature a lonely experience, and family members may not even realize how much they contribute to helping maintain social ties and a sociable disposition. So my final thank you is to Rinah, Kinor, and Ariel for the many happy interludes away from pursuing the often depressing topic of this book.

I

THE PROBLEM

■

1

BEYOND DETERRENCE
AND RETRIBUTION

F EW ISSUES in the realm of penal law theory and penological practice have aroused as much controversial debate
as that of capital punishment. The extremity of the act, the
irrevocability of its consequences, the power of its impact, have
given it both a substantive and a symbolic quality which
distinguishes it from any other sanction used by society to
punish its transgressors.

This uniqueness is nowhere more clearly noted than in
recent judicial rulings in the United States, where a special standard has been laid down according to which arbitrariness and
capriciousness must be totally eliminated from the sentencing
process in the case of capital punishment,[1] even though it is
widely acknowledged that in other areas of penal practice, such
arbitrariness and capriciousness seem well-nigh unavoidable.[2]
In other words, a constitutional standard, what has been referred to as "super due process of law,"[3] has been instituted
for capital punishment which is not applied to other forms of
punishment.

Indeed, the arguments as to punishment in general often
take on an added quality when they are applied to the specific
question of the death penalty, as noted, for instance, in the
comparative studies between jurisdictions that use the death
penalty and those that do not, or in the recent sophisticated
statistical analyses attempting to show the precise number of
subsequent murders that could be avoided in the future if capital
punishment were used.[4] Similar research projects are not
generally undertaken in respect to other punishments, com-
paring, for instance, the efficacy of compulsory imprisonment
as opposed to judicial discretion.

3

Then again, another of the major aims of punishment—
that of rehabilitation—is not applicable at all in the case of the
death penalty; although here it should be noted that there are
instances in which it is imposed on a deferred basis, the final
decision as to its implementation being determined by whether
the accused has rehabilitated himself within a specified time
period. This is used most notably in China, where legislative
injunction recognizes such procedures for political (but not ordinary) criminals, allowing them two years to be re-educated;[5]
yet similar considerations as to the reform of the condemned
person are sometimes used in other countries when the possibility of reprieve or pardon is being explored.

In recent years there has been no let-up in the spate of
writing on the subject of capital punishment.[6] In fact, in some
respects the debate has gained momentum. In the United States,
for example, a combination of factors—sparked by the ten-year
moratorium on its use in the late sixties and early seventies,
highlighted by the Supreme Court's decisions in the leading
cases of *Furman* and *Gregg,* and sustained by an ongoing struggle to delineate the impact and implications of these, and subsequent, decisions—has triggered renewed interest in the topic,
particularly in its legal and constitutional aspects.[7]

Yet beyond the specific problems encountered in any one
country, the issue of capital punishment has also increasingly
taken on international dimensions in recent years. Thus there
have been a number of international and regional conventions
dealing with the death penalty, oriented both to immediate
restrictions on its present use and the future goal of its eventual abolition; there has been increasing concern expressed by
active and articulate human rights organizations, both national
and international; there has been a greater awareness, in the
post–World War II years, of the many excesses committed
through the use of extreme punitive means for the furtherance
of political goals—an awareness that arose originally from the
knowledge of the Holocaust perpetrated by the Nazis during
the war, and that has continued by further revelations of acts

of extermination carried out by those in possession of political power, sometimes in a wholesale manner, sometimes with selective precision.

Social scientists have, from the perspective of their various disciplines, examined endlessly the background to such actions, the motivations of the perpetrators, the vulnerability of the victims. These acts have a special relevance for penology, for they are in essence a unique combination: extreme *punitive* actions by state authorities constitute also extreme acts of *criminality*. Genocide is defined as an international crime, but the act itself is, as understood by those who commit it, an act of punishment; similarly for extra-judicial executions, as carried out both in the name of and on behalf of governmental authorities or, alternatively, by organized groups seeking to obtain such governmental status through armed struggle.

A full enquiry into all the ramifications of the death penalty must thus inevitably examine such acts, both as forms of punishment, however irregular and unjust, and as acts of extreme criminality, themselves perhaps requiring extreme punitive responses.[8]

Thus it would seem that, wide-ranging as the debate on capital punishment is in scope, prolonged and ongoing as it is in time, it has been focused too much on the manifest major issues—of deterrence and retribution, of cruelty and irreversibility, of possible judicial error, and of constitutional interpretation—and has largely ignored a number of what are casually defined as peripheral issues but which may, in fact, lie at the heart of the problem.

Such latent issues are:

1. The punishment to be used as an alternative for the death penalty—generally that of life imprisonment

2. The right of a convicted person to acquiesce in the imposition of the death penalty

3. The use of pardoning and commutation power to amend the original sentence—used extensively both in capital punishment and life imprisonment
4. The use—or the abuse—of political power to carry out death penalties without the formal decision of a court, known as extra-judicial executions, political murders, or humanicide
5. The appropriate punishment to be imposed on those whose acts are so extreme as to arouse a particularly strong sense of revulsion—for example, genocide, humanicide, terrorist activities, ruthless massacres, or the use of torture against innocent and helpless persons
6. The desire to avoid torture in the implementation of any penalty—raising the questions as to what extent either death or life sentences are tantamount to torture, and, further, of how to define torture
7. The attitudes to death in general prevalent in a particular society, both in broad philosophical perspective and in respect to specific related areas of concern, such as suicide, euthanasia, and pacifism
8. The rules laid down for the protection of life in terms of overall social control—for example, the directives given to members of the police, security, and armed forces as to the circumstances in which they can open fire, and when they may justifiably shoot to kill
9. The manner in which capital punishment and other extreme punishments reflect ideological beliefs and political interests—in particular the ideological and political perceptions of human rights, state power, and international concerns.

It seems that there can be no conclusive summary of the pros and cons of capital punishment without a frontal and intense confrontation with these factors, which, although ostensibly peripheral, are, as will be argued, acutely pertinent and form, perhaps, the essence of the issue. I shall attempt to describe each of these issues, to relate them together in a meaningful manner, and, in the light of this matrix of facts and ideas, to pose anew the issue of capital punishment.

In any event, the debate is already underway, yet only in a haphazard way, as a result of isolated events that have *en passant* and momentarily focused public attention on certain of these issues. Thus, when a condemned person actively pursues a course of action designed at consummation of the death penalty, and resists attempts—by his family and by abolitionists—to save his life, a number of entirely new dimensions are introduced into the capital punishment debate, such as the right of a person (including a prisoner) to commit suicide, and the crucial question—certainly for the accused—of what is the most extreme punishment, till now axiomatically presumed to be that of death.

Interestingly enough, there have been thinkers who have in the past raised these issues, but without making any serious impact on the capital punishment debate. Twenty years ago, Jacques Barzun argued that a truly liberal approach to capital punishment would of necessity allow for a choice to be given to the accused.[9] He favored retaining the death penalty, if only to allow the accused an alternative to languishing long years in the deprived and degrading environment of a prison. His description of a life sentence suggests that it could well be considered the most severe punishment, a greater violation of human rights than that of a death sentence acquiesced in by the accused.

When Gary Gilmore adopted just such an approach, he raised a critical, almost excruciating, dilemma for those civil rights activists who are involved in the struggle for abolition of the death penalty.[10] Basically, they were faced with a choice between recognizing the right of a person to end his own life (a right to suicide, generally accepted by most liberals) or maintaining the moratorium on the use of the death penalty, especially since the longer that moratorium was maintained, the greater were the prospects of judicial recognition of the penalty as being unusual and, therefore, also unconstitutional.

The question of a society's approach to issues of suicide and euthanasia has a direct bearing on the question of capital punishment, even though such connection has been barely acknowledged in the course of the recent debate. For, if a society tolerates suicide or attempted suicide, the question arises as to whether it can then deny the right to end his life to an imprisoned person. This argument has particular impact for human rights activists, since a prisoner's desire to put an end to his life may be directly related to the stress aroused by his contemplating the meaning for him of a lengthy prison sentence. Consistency would suggest an abolitionist stance on the death penalty to be matched by a similar attitude to long-term imprisonment.

The factor of suicide was an important argument used by Cesare Beccaria, one of the forerunners of criminology, and widely recognized as a great early voice of modern liberalism. He argued that since the state did not allow a person to put an end to his own life, it would be inconsistent for the state to take a life on its own.[11] However, the liberalization of attitudes to suicide and accompanying changes in either policy or law, has undermined the force of Beccaria's arguments on this score.

Inasmuch as some of the arguments against the death penalty are based on the sanctity of life, they are affected by attitudes to suicide. No less are they affected by attitudes to euthanasia. Here, despite medical advances that ensure a prolongation of life, that may on occasion be unwanted and sometimes even demeaning, society has not acknowledged the virtue of the "easy death," which some ancient and primitive societies allowed and even encouraged.

But it is specifically the technological advances of modern society that may perforce precipitate this issue and—perhaps in the not so distant future—lead to both a changed perception of death and a changed legal approach. This, too, is liable to influence discussions on the death penalty, just as the present situation—of placing life, however painful or meaningless, above an "easy death"—affects present attitudes to capital punishment. In terms of attitudes, it may be only the committed pacifist who can sustain the total logic of an absolute abolitionist stance. For such a person there is no wavering and no ambivalence. Any deliberate taking of life is forbidden—whether voluntary individual decisions as to suicide and euthanasia, or whether imposed state decisions as to the death penalty and war; and for many they embrace also opposition to abortion or the needless killing of animals. For abolitionists on capital punishment who are less than pacifists on other issues, it would seem that there are many serious ambiguous situations to be confronted.

In prison itself, deaths may arise not only from executions or deliberate suicides; they may be the consequence of a failed act of protest such as a hunger strike. Even in this instance the issue of suicide may be relevant. This was openly, if cynically, expressed by the British prime minister, Margaret Thatcher, when, in response to the hunger strikes by several IRA prisoners, she declared that they were entitled to commit suicide if they so desired.[12] But this, of course, is no more than polemic debate, for they did not desire suicide as such, but the improvement of their conditions and the recognition of their rights as political prisoners and not ordinary criminals. Further, those who believe in the right to commit suicide presume that it will be performed in conditions that avoid pain and suffering, unlike the situation in which it is the consequence of a hunger strike, spread over many weeks, in the course of which a person gradually loses control over many of his faculties and encounters increasing pain as his life-system ebbs away and his end draws near.

Further, prison authorities generally take precautions to safeguard the life of their prisoners, even to the extent of force-feeding those who go on a hunger strike. The willingness to allow the IRA priosners to die was based primarily on political considerations and on administrative decisions not to force-feed, not on liberal willingness to acquiesce in suicide.

The issue of political prisoners is relevant for the capital punishment debate in a different perspective, for a full survey of capital punishment would indicate its extensive use in the case of political prisoners. Yet, important as this fact clearly is, it, too, has been generally ignored in the discussions of capital punishment. One aspect of the political overtones to capital punishment is the fact that many countries that abolish the death penalty for most "normal" crimes nevertheless retain it for treason and sabotage. Some countires that are known as aboli-tionist are not really entirely so, since they still have the death penalty in these limited areas.

More important is the use of political power to liquidate political enemies, done either through streamlined and trun-cated judicial procedures, as in the case of military, people's, or revolutionary courts, or through evading formal processes, when the authorities sanction liquidations either by specific prior instructions, by overall connivance, or by subsequent retrospective acquiescence.

Interestingly enough, the basic aims of such actions are the traditional ones of penological theory—those of deterrence and retribution—but they obviously acquire a different mean-ing in the context of political struggle. In the areas of political crime, it is, after all, not the welfare of the total population that is of major concern, but the narrow sectarian interests of those holding power, who are intent on ensuring that they quash any threats to that power, including the use of the full repressive apparatus of the criminal justice system or the police force.

Very few participants in the capital punishment debate pay due attention to this factor; most of the facts enunciated and analyzed revolve around the question of traditional crime—murder, rape, armed robbery, etc. Yet, in numerical terms, it is likely that more people are executed because of their political beliefs than because of their criminal acts.

In some cases, in fact, even crimes apparently of a non-political nature may be seen as having clear political overtones, and this latter consideration provides the real rationale for the use of capital punishment. Thus, for instance, in the Soviet Union a large percentage of executions are carried out for white-collar crime, from embezzlement to the theft of state property.[13] In most of the Western world, such acts are often treated as being of a minor nature, and even the increased concern in recent years over these delinquencies has led to only minimal change in sentencing patterns.[14] The different approach in the Soviet Union stems not just from the concern for the harm done to the social comity at large, but from the perception that such acts strike at the very ideological structure of the regime.

Further, the fact that most regimes in the world today are not democratically elected and have no clear-cut norms for the regular, peaceful, and accepted transference of power, lends an added thrust to the use of capital punishment in a political context. For reluctance to hand over power to an opposition group implies ineluctably the consequent need to maintain strict control over any expression of dissident opinions. Such control is often most effectively exercised through extensive use of the criminal justice system, including the use of capital punishment as the surest means of eliminating opposition and deterring others, in the present and the future.

Conversely, when a change of power is effected by usurpation, violent or otherwise, the need to cement the framework of a new power structure often leads to wholesale or selective executions in an effort to ensure the elimination of those associated with the old regime. The history of the classic French Revolution still serves as a model, unfortunately, not so much for its liberal message of "liberty, equality, fraternity," but for its authoritarian model of large-scale executions, most recently cited as a precedent by the leaders of the present regime in Iran.

In circumstances where there are no firm democratic principles, no constitutional guarantees, no independent judiciary, no legitimate opposition, then executions, or at the least the threat of using such means, become a significant means of stifling opposition and bolstering the regime. In some instances the formalities of judicial procedure will be observed; in others, military and administrative power will be used indiscriminately to liquidate opponents.

In recent years there has been a growing awareness of this latter phenomenon, termed by some as extra-judicial executions, political killings, or political murders. Reports in the mass media are far more regular and accurate than in the past; there are a number of international and regional organizations, set up in the last two decades, that are devoted to the furtherance of civil and human rights, thereby ensuring a constant monitoring of violations; there are the persistent activities of voluntary groupings, most notably Amnesty International, that have undertaken to mount worldwide campaigns against such violations.[15]

So, what was once often no more than rumored suppositions unsubstantiated by solid evidence is now carefully and consistently documented, widely and regularly publicized, and open and vigorously challenged. It is no longer only historians who pore over musty records to elicit the horrors of the past, but a coterie of journalists and jurists, human rights activists and families of the victimized, who maintain a constant barrage of attack on violations of civil rights and contribute to a heightened awareness by the public of such practices.

However, public awareness and activities in this regard have not been fully matched by parallel academic analyses. Indeed, although international human rights is a fast-growing field of academic study, the issue of capital punishment and extra-judicial executions does not figure prominently in its concerns. Similarly, in the field of criminology and penology, the issue of extra-judicial executions has been almost completely ignored.

Yet, it is a key factor, since there are countries which, though formally abolishing the death penalty, still allow executions to take place without judicial sanction, sometimes at the active instigation of the authorities, sometimes with their passive collusion. In such circumstances it might well be that the cause of human rights and the protection of life would actually, paradoxically, be better served by the existence of capital punishment. For if such were to be the case, there would always be the possibility—and the hope—that the authorities would refrain from summary executions and would prefer judicial authorization for them. The utilization of the criminal law process, however weighted against the accused, however biased the proceedings themselves, at least provides a recognized procedure within which to work and the time in which to plan a legal strategy on behalf of the accused, build up resources, and pursue to the end any chance of saving the accused, including the quest for a reprieve from an official, adjudicated sentence of death. There are thus human rights activists in some parts of the world, notably Latin America, who favor the existence of capital punishment, as it provides a better prospect for safeguarding human life than when extra-judicial executions are resorted to in lieu of a formal death penalty.

Although extra-judicial executions are generally used for political purposes, they have also been known to be used against ordinary criminals. Indeed, there is often an interconnection between their use in a criminal context and their use in a political context, the former often serving as a precedent for the latter. So it has been in parts of Latin America, where the practice by the police, acting as death squads in their off-duty hours, of liquidating criminals (as a means, as they saw it, of combating crime) has sometimes served as a model for the later persecution of political opponents.[16] Similarly, in 1983, in China there were several months of dragnet operations against criminals and undesirable elements, culminating in death penalties for several hundreds, perhaps thousands. Hardly had this operation finished than it was followed by political purges.[17]

Thus, there is a clear line linking the actions of the police against ordinary criminals to those later practiced against political dissidents; there is also a line linking the aforementioned abuses of police power with abuses of a more direct nature, perpetrated in countries where strict provisions exist for due process of law. For, despite a professed commitment to the rule of law and human rights, there is sometimes a laxity in the use of arms in the practice of law enforcement. In the United States, for instance, the number of people killed by the police in the course of affecting arrests, or in the prevention of crime, is several hundred per year.[18] Not all of those responsible for deaths are exonerated, but on the whole it would seem that the standards applied in assessing the legitimacy of police action are not always consistent with the highest demands of respect for human life. Thus, although it may be true that there is no official approval of such killings, a norm has often been applied which sanctions them in retrospect, even, occasionally, when a careful analysis of the exigencies of the situations shows that the use of deadly force was not necessarily warranted.

Whereas killings are sometimes condoned in order to prevent a suspect from escaping custody, a stricter standard that restricts the use of deadly force only to those cases akin to the normal rules for self-defense, when there is a clear and present danger to somebody's life, may be necessary. In all other instances, the threat posed by the escape does not justify the taking of the escapee's life, nor the endangering of lives of innocent bystanders, as occasionally occurs. Indeed, in recent years a number of states have been working towards stricter control; it was not until 1985 that the United States Supreme Court finally laid down constitutional guidelines limiting the use of deadly force against fleeing felons, though the rationale was related to the Fourth Amendment reference to search and seizure, and not the Fourteenth Amendment injunction as to due process.[19] It may well be argued that such police action, when subsequently condoned, amounts to a deprivation of life without due process of law. In essence, the police have often been allowed a flexibility of action which is not sufficiently circumscribed by a paramount desire to preserve life and which seems inconsistent with constitutional injunctions for maintaining due process of law.

I suggest that discussions of the death penalty must give due consideration to actions involving loss of life committed by the police, and must seek to lay down clear guidelines in accordance with overall attitudes to capital punishment. For, whereas strict control is sought over the power of judges, the dangers of the taking of life may continue to exist for those who are involved in encounters with the police. The very irreversibility of a fatal shooting should lead to a stricter rule as to when to open fire, just as the irreversibility of the death penalty has been a major factor in stricter attitudes to the death penalty. There is even the danger that the very lack of an official death penalty may lead to more severe police action.

A further factor must be examined. No discussion of capital punishment can be exhaustive without giving thought (especially from an abolitionist perspective) to the fact that there may be a certain class of extreme acts which require separate consideration. The abolitionist is obliged to consider whether there are acts so beyond the pale of ordinary human actions that, even when capital punishment is abolished, there may still be a need to reserve the use of that penalty for such special cases. Where capital punishment has been abolished in the name, *inter alia,* of the sanctity of life, exceptions may have to be made in the name of that very same principle.

In the aftermath of the Second World War, the Nuremberg trial laid down the norm that violations of international law in certain cases, such as crimes against the peace, crimes of war, crimes against humanity, and genocide, are breaches of positive law deserving punishment. However, although this trial dealt extensively with the procedural and substantive issues raised, it ignored the penological and moral question of the appropriate punishment. The sentence of death, imposed on some of the accused, was pronounced without any explanation as to the rationale behind the decision, and without providing the accused or their representatives (or, for that matter the prosecution) with the opportunity after conviction to argue the merits or demerits of various penal sanctions in a unique and precedent-setting case. In contrast, the Eichmann trial in Israel contains extensive argumentation on this issue by prosecution and defense counsel, as well as an exposition by the judges of the reasoning that led them to the death penalty.

There is a similar lacuna in the provisions of international conventions dealing with extreme acts such as genocide, crimes against humanity, crimes of war, etc. Definitions of these acts are spelled out, and their prohibition declared, but the critical questions as to the punishment is generally left in abeyance.

Yet, although it is relatively easy today to gain a worldwide consensus on the prohibition of such acts (at least in theory), the real issue relating to them may be the appropriate penalty that should be imposed. This is an issue of particular pertinence for those in favor of abolition. Simply put, even within an abolitionist perspective, is it possible to conceive of the limited use of the death penalty for certain defined acts which put their perpetrators outside of the pale of humanity? Should an abolitionist approach reserve a small defined area of exception so as to allow for an expression of utter and unmitigated revulsion at the perpetration of certain acts? Or, alternatively, is it better that such persons be sentenced to long terms of imprisonment? Witness, for instance, the case of Rudolf Hess, a survivor of the Nuremberg trials in his nineties, still being kept in Spandau Prison.

Given the fact that we live, in the modern world, in the shadow of the Holocaust, and that there have been other genocides practiced in other places since, it may well be that one of the cardinal moral issues of today is how to respond to gross violations of the most fundamental human rights. The very difficulties involved make it understandable why international groups have shirked the question. Indeed, the ultimate issue of capital punishment might well revolve around this factor. In any event, it seems clear that any comprehensive discussion of capital punishment entails earnest examination of the appropriate sanction for the vilest of acts.

THERE IS ONE FINAL FACT that forms a key focus of my discussion of capital punishment: the nature of other extreme punishments.

In any gradation of penalties, the death penalty is normally conceded to be the most severe. Most criminal law codes lay down the form of punishment that is within the power of the court to impose and indicate ascending and descending degrees of punishment; the death penalty, where it exists, almost inevitably forms the peak of the grading.

It is largely on the basis of its severity and its uniqueness that so much attention has been focused on the death penalty. Yet this focus on the death penalty has tended to distort the perspective of penal alternatives. Thus, the fight to save a condemned person from the death chamber is invariably accompanied by intense public interest, but similar forensic struggles aimed at avoiding other extreme penalties, such as long-term imprisonment or corporal punishment (where such exists), are barely noticed, not just by the public but even in academic circles.

Although there are books that deal with almost all the variegated aspects of sentencing policy—not just capital punishment but suspended sentences, probation, parole, community service orders, fines, short-term imprisonment—there is no book in the English language devoted solely to the issue of life imprisonment.[20] There are, it is true, many books that deal with the experience of long-term prisoners themselves, written in their prison cells, as well as a few notable works by others that portray the personal thoughts and feelings of those faced with a future of interminable imprisonment.[21] No real comprehensive attempt has, however, been made to address the penological, moral, legal, and constitutional issues raised by life imprisonment. In countries such as the United States and

Britain, which have, or till recently had, the death sentence, it would appear that the overwhelming concern as to this punishment—both pro and con—has led to a total disregard of the ramifications of a life sentence. This is so even though the issues raised in the capital punishment debate may be similar to, or even identical with, the problematics of life imprisonment; even more paradoxically, the very alternative to capital punishment that is often suggested, or at least presumed, is a life sentence, often a mandatory one.

Why have writers not given consideration to what should be a critical issue in the capital punishment debate? Indeed, how is it possible even to recommend the abolition of the death sentence without considering the alternatives to its use, their desirability from a general penological perspective, and the implications for the accused?

It would seem that so intent are abolitionists, in those countries where there still is a death penalty, to have it rescinded that they avoid any consideration of the life sentence in the realization—acknowledged or presumed—that this is perhaps the only acceptable alternative punishment that the public will accept. If strictures were to be placed on the desirability of life imprisonment as well, it would become all the more difficult to present a persuasive argument for abolition of the death penalty.

Yet, so many of the arguments used by abolitionists against capital punishment are applicable, in one form or another, to life imprisonment. This is shown by an examination of penological issues in countries which have no capital punishment, and which have basically resolved the issue in this regard.

A key example of a situation of this type is West Germany, which, after the Second World War and in the wake of the Nazi period, incorporated into its constitution a total prohibition of capital punishment. The German constitution also contains in its first clause an overriding commitment to human rights. A number of jurists have argued that life imprisonment is not compatible with this clause.[22] The argumentation used contains many parallels to those in the United States in capital punishment cases, where reliance is also placed on the constitutional provisions prohibiting, on the one hand, cruel and unusual punishment and ensuring, on the other hand, due process of law. In other words, it would seem that release from involvement with the issue of capital punishment has led, perforce, to an examination of the preferred alternative—that of life imprisonment—in terms that are reminiscent of arguments normally reserved only for capital punishment. In any event, one of the main reasons for the punishment of life imprisonment not being declared unconstitutional by the German court was the fact that empirical evidence indicated that almost all prisoners sentenced to life imprisonment had their sentences reduced through the pardoning power of the executive, the clear implication being that if the sentence was carried out to the full, it might indeed be considered unconstitutional.

There might well be a need for a close analysis of the two most extreme penalties to assess which is the more severe. Such an assessment would have relevance both for abolitionists and for retentionists, the former in order to determine which constitutes the greater infringements of human rights (in terms, for instance, not just of the sanctity of life in the narrow sense of physical existence, but in the broader sense of the quality of life), the latter in order to determine which, by reason of its severity, might have the better deterrent impact or give more apt expression to retributive needs.

At the outset it should be noted that there is already, albeit unnoticed, a worldwide consensus that the death penalty might not in fact be the most extreme step that a society can take against its criminals. For although there is ongoing debate as to the pros and cons of capital punishment, there is universal condemnation of torture as an acceptable form of punishment.[23] Further, many states that do retain capital punishment seek out what they claim is the most humane way of performing it.

Indeed, for those who argue for the best form of deterrence, based on severity and consequent fear for the potential criminal, or for the best form of retribution, particularly in severe cases, their arguments in favor of capital punishment contain an unnoticed flaw: they would actually be often better applied in the support of torture. This is said not facetiously, but in order to elicit a direct confrontation with the ultimate logical implications of some of the retentionist arguments.

In former times physical torture was an essential ingredient of the ritualized procedures associated with the death penalty, which was for the most part the culmination of the physical suffering. In fact, without the suffering there was no point in seeking the death. This aspect has largely undergone total transformation. Nowadays most countries take precautions to ensure that there will be no gratuitous physical suffering at the execution.

In addition, it is interesting to note the manner in which the public reacts to different forms of execution: on the one hand, a complacent acceptance of the manner in which it is performed in one's own country; on the other hand, an aversion to other means practiced in other countries and other cultures.

Thus, the English-speaking world tends to look upon the guillotine as being particularly vicious, yet, truth to tell, it may be the swiftest and surest means; much of the aversion may stem from its association with the excesses of the French Revolution, when it was used for the first time. Within the English-speaking world itself, there is no agreement as to the most desirable form of execution. In England and most of the Commonwealth, the electric chair and the gas chamber have been shunned, the latter even more so because of the odious reminder of its use by the Nazis. Conversely, the gallows, traditionally the most common form of execution in the countries of the Commonwealth, is rarely used in the United States.

Recently, the search for a painless death has led in a few jurisdictions to the use of lethal injections or drugs to end a life, but this approach is even more highly controversial; the medical profession has banned the participation of medical personnel in a role which seems to be a denial of their professional obligations to save life. Yet their involvement is not new— doctors are generally present at executions to confirm the expiry of the executed person. It is by no means clear that such action, albeit passive, is any more compatible with a doctor's humanitarian obligations than the administering of a lethal injection or drug.

There seems to be a certain paradox in this almost desperate attempt to use the least harmful form of execution, for surely this undermines part of the very arguments of deterrence and retribution that lie at the heart of the retentionist stance. For truth to tell, a strict application of deterrence and, in certain cases, of retribution (depending on the circumstances of the crime) would allow for torture. Though such sentiments are normally absent from academic discussions of capital punishment, they often find expression among the public, in letters to the editor, in anguished outbursts by family and friends of a victim, in ordinary conversation.

This aspect takes on added significance when it is noted that often there is an intermediate position adopted between pure abolitionism and pure retentionism. Arguments are sometimes advanced that, at the least, capital punishment should be reserved for those whose crimes are of a particularly vile and heinous nature. Certainly, the purest retribution arguments allows that an accused who, for example, committed murder after torturing his victim should be subjected to similar physical indignities prior to his execution.

I am obviously not advocating torture. What I am suggesting is that the *logical conclusion* of many retentionist arguments based on deterrence or retribution lead not just to capital punishment, but to torture. Deterrent or retributive aims would, in many cases, be far better furthered by exposing the condemned person to pain and suffering—even over a prolonged period of time, with or without a death penalty (and some people claim that is what happens on death row)—than a so-called humanely-administered execution. There may then be a crucial fallacy in the retentionist argument—not just in its refusal to pursue to the end the ruthless logic of its basic premises, but in its disregard for the societal price, in terms of moral values, that inevitably has to be paid in implementing *any* form of punishment, whether the death penalty or torture—or life imprisonment.

Just as society today is not prepared to countenance torture, at least in its public pronouncements and official regulations, even though it might conceivably be the most effective form of deterrence or retribution, so retentionist arguments for capital punishment may be undermined if it could be shown that this penalty constitutes a violation of the values of the society and its moral aspirations.

However, the debate cannot be limited only to the death penalty. Perceptions of what is the most severe punishment may, as has already been mentioned, be incorrect, and it is the perceptions of the accused themselves that are uniquely relevant; further, other punishments may contain overtones of cruelty, and may be tantamount to torture. This factor may be of particular significance in the case of life imprisonment, the favored alternative to capital punishment.

Simply put, the attitudes of the enlightened world at present seem to be:

1. Torture is not acceptable at all—yet the fact is that it is widely practiced, especially, but not solely, in cases of political prisoners.
2. Capital punishment is constantly debated and scrutinized—by judges and legislators, by polemicists and academicians, by the public and the press.
3. Life imprisonment is for the most part acceptable as an extreme punishment—with negligible interest in its implications.

I suggest that this tripartite differentiation is misplaced. The connection between the three is far closer than these three diverging approaches would indicate; arguments made in one context are apt and applicable in another. If torture is unacceptable for various stated reasons, then capital punishment or, indeed, life imprisonment, may be unacceptable for similar reasons. If, on the other hand, there are legitimate penological considerations for either or both of the last two, then they may be valid also for the former. It is from this perspective that there is a need for a reexamination of some of the public debate, the judicial decisions, and the academic analyses dealing with capital punishment.

The humanitarian values of an enlightened modern age have created a society which outlaws slavery, condemns racism, and acknowledges basic human rights entrenched in constitutions of nation states and conventions of the international community. It is within this framework that torture has been declared illegal, capital punishment has been declared undesirable, and life imprisonment has been seen by many as an unavoidable alternative. Yet, in fact, torture has not been eliminated, capital punishment may be on the increase as a surreptitious political weapon, and life imprisonment has its indisputable problematics. Further, modern society is obliged to confront the ultimate issue of what to do with those—genociders, mass murderers, torturers (whether isolated perverts, or official agents of the state)—who have, by their actions, placed themselves beyond the pale. What is to be done with them? Are they to suffer the tortures and indignities they inflicted on others; are they to be deprived of their life for their sins of depravity; are they to be kept in confinement till their demise? Or are they to be forgiven, while attempts are made to reform them? Till we have agonized over these issues—at length, in honesty and in humility, concerned for our own humanity, but aware also of a human desire for appropriate response to unspeakable evil—we cannot solve the perennial issue of capital punishment.

It would seem, then, that the debate on capital punishment must move beyond the standard arguments that have been traditionally presented and focus on the several issues I have tried to enumerate—of its use as a political weapon by those in authority, of its use as a punishment in special extreme cases, of overall attitudes as to the right to put an end to life, of police actions in the prevention of crime, of the wishes of the accused themselves, and of a satisfactory alternative. Generally, we must realize that the attitudes adopted represent not just perceptions of the purpose and the efficacy of punishment, but reflect larger and underlying ideological premises.

These are matters of life and death that deal not merely with sentencing policy, but with the ultimate values and professed morality of a society. At stake is not merely what is to be done with transgressors, but how society perceives itself and its commitment to human rights and social decency.

2

IDEOLOGY AND PENOLOGY

GENERAL INTEREST in capital punishment stems partly from the intrinsic severity of the punishment and partly from the public revulsion at the act to which it is generally a response. The outward focus is generally on the condemned person or his victim, yet, in another sense, the importance of capital punishment is in its expression of one of the most absolute powers of the state. From this perspective, the issue of capital punishment is more political than penological, is far more related to the perceptions of the functioning of a state than to the daily operations of its criminal justice system, and deals, in the final analysis, with a broad range of philosophical issues beyond the traditional ones of deterrence and retribution arguments for and against capital punishment.

These latter arguments may well actually serve as a convenient framework for avoiding far deeper and more complicated issues. The questions of deterrence and retribution are honored ones in penological circles, and many discussions have been woven around these ideas, but it is not certain that they are truly of the essence. Of far more importance, I would submit, are the issues, rarely articulated and sometimes inchoate, of the parameters of state power, of the role of the individual, of overall philosophies, and of personal value-systems.

In many ways, attitudes to capital punishment are a probing test of a person's deepest beliefs—for at stake is not only crime and punishment, deterrence or retribution, but the manner in which a state should use its power to maintain social control over those who pose the greatest threat to its stability and perhaps to its very security. For those, acting on behalf of the state, directly confronted with the issue—police and prosecutors preparing an indictment, judges and juries in court, executive authorities entrusted with the final disposal of a case through the pardoning power—looming over the specific fate of a particular individual are larger issues such as the sanctity of life, the meaning of death, the purposes of sovereignty, the rights of the individual, the suffering of those victimized, and the basis of the social bond.

Similarly, in the larger area of policy, whereas public debate and legislative action focus on such issues as concern about crime, the effective expression of social control, the human fallacies that lead to judicial error, the need for retribution, and the possibility of deterrence, underlying the debate are sentiments of larger philosophical issues that go far beyond the specific search for the best way to punish society's most serious deviants. An indication of the depth of the issues involved are the special arrangements that are often made when dealing with capital punishment in its various manifestations. In parliamentary debates, for instance, members are often given a "free vote," released from the normal constraints of party discipline, even in those parliamentary systems in which independence in voting is not normally practiced.[1] In the United States, people who are utterly opposed in principle to the death penalty may be systematically excluded from jury duty, on the supposition that their attitude will inhibit them from making a just and correct decision when the consequences might be a death sentence.[2]

The reasoning behind these approaches is interesting, and based, as I shall try to show, on a slight misconception—the theory being that the issue of capital punishment is the issue par excellence of a person's conscience. This emphasis on conscience in such a crucial issue is to be welcomed—but, in focusing on the individual's conscience per se and allowing it preeminence, there is a danger that a deeper dimension of the political factors involved will be missed—namely, that attitudes to punishment in general, and capital punishment in particular, are part of a larger ideological and philosophical framework, moulded in the crucible of the social, political, and ethical forces to which a person is exposed. Although it is the person's conscience that is ostensibly being expressed, in effect it is the person's total *weltanschauung* that is reflected.

Thus, whereas respect for a person's conscience in this issue is perhaps understandable, it is also to a certain extent misplaced. The focus on one's conscience is indeed justified only if there is an awareness of the larger philosophical framework which sustains the content; further, it must be recognized that those for whom conscience *apparently* does not play a part (mainly, that they do not oppose the death penalty), also have a philosophical and moral stance of their own. For instance, Supreme Court justices, such as William Brennan and Thurgood Marshall, who have been consistently abolitionist in all the decisions of the Court in the last two decades, are not expressing their personal conscience as such, but their general philosophy, a liberal philosophy that finds expression in so many of their decisions in other areas.[3] Conversely, though, judges who, at all levels, have consistently favored the death penalty are not just being retributive, but are acting in terms of their general philosophy.

It is of particular interest to note that in the recent unsuccessful bid for reelection of Chief Justice Rose Bird of California, the public debate revolved almost solely around her abolitionist stand on the death penalty; but, as several commentators pointed out, the real issue was that of her overall liberal attitude in other other areas. Her removal from office would provide the opportunity for a conservative replacement as a new Chief Justice. It was her attitude on the death penalty that aroused interest, both antagonistic and supportive; but in a sense it was correctly perceived as being reflective of her ideology (as well as being an easier issue for the electorate to focus on).[4]

This is where the idea of a "free vote" in parliament (such as in Britain) misses the point. One's attitude to capital punishment is not personal in the sense of being totally idiosyncratic and impervious to logical analysis. It is personal only in the sense of being a specific outcome on a key issue of one's overall ideology. The willingness to allow a free vote is not so much an expression of democratic tolerance by party leaders for personal conscience, as it is an escape from responsibility, an agreement to avoid potential tensions which may arise over an issue that is often felt with heightened intensity. It seems to be easier to allow the free vote than to insist on imposing the parliamentary whip.

Capital punishment may indeed be the cutting edge of the measure of a person's commitment to a comprehensive political ideology—the kind of issue which neatly distinguishes between nuances of approach. It is thus potentially liable to cause a rift between political partners which they would prefer to be left untouched. Conversely, it also is liable to reveal strange political bedfellows, who would perhaps rather be spared the embarrassment of political alignment on this issue, preferring their similar vote to be linked by a presumably idiosyncratic and neutral conscience.

In looking at the issue of capital punishment within a universal framework, outside of nation-states where convenient parliamentary solutions of free votes exist, certain interesting patterns emerge. In general terms, the lines between abolitionists and retentionists may be drawn along a traditional left-right continuum, between those, for instance, of liberal persuasion, who, in line with the emphasis on the individual and on civil and human rights, favor the abolition of the death penalty, and those of a more conservative bent, who see a need to preserve social stability by the use of an effective and, if need be, harsh penal policy, including the death sentence.

But this particular left-right continuum is clearly a limited one; there are ideologies outside of this sphere. There is a broader one which embraces a left wing of communism and socialism, and a right wing of capitalism and fascism. Prima facie, it would appear that the left-right continuum does not hold up in this particular context—if liberals are to be reckoned as to the left of center, then the more extreme left, the communists, have been prepared to use the death penalty. Somewhere between communism and liberalism is socialism, which is largely committed to an abolitionist stance. How explain, then, the difference between the groupings at the left end of the spectrum?

What seems to be at first a paradoxical situation is actually an accurate reflection of a social and political reality, the finer nuances of which are often lost. For although communism and socialism are close to each other in their professed attitudes to a whole series of economic questions such as equality, ownership of property, centralized control of the means of production and of the market, and workers benefit programs, they differ as to their professed attitudes to the rights of the individual. In fact, it is this difference that is the major distinguishing factor between these two ideologies—and this, in turn, has a major impact on their contrary positions in regard to capital punishment.

Most of the socialist and social democratic governments in Europe have been largely responsible for the abolition of capital punishment, most recently in France where, after their accession to power in 1982, the socialists acted promptly to affirm and implement their declared policy of abolishing capital punishment; similarly in England, where the ritual has been repeated of allowing a free vote on several occasions in the past century, it is the members of the Labor party who have been in the forefront of the struggle for abolition. In fact, of course, in the realm of civil and human rights, as also flowing therefrom in the realm of attitudes to punishment, the socialists are far closer to the liberals than they are to the communists. Herein lies embedded a greater truth of the overlapping and distinguishing nature of many ideologies that can in fact only be understood by appreciating the different approaches adopted to the two different key variables: of economics, on the one hand, and civil and human rights, on the other. These are almost self-contained issues allowing for separate perceptions and decision-making processes.

The proximity of socialism to liberal principles is enhanced by an inverse process in which, in the United States for instance, the liberal camp, though emphasizing the rights and the freedom of the individual, also acknowledges that certain limitations and restrictions may be imposed on the individual in the economic sphere in order to ensure the possibility of achieving social justice—admittedly not in terms of equality, but at least of equity. This partial convergence is the real underlying factor making for a similarity in approach to the death penalty on the part of both liberals and socialists, when the issue is regarded not as a pure issue of criminal justice, but as part of a larger philosophy.

This kind of analysis and reasoning, though more complicated, applies also to the nature of dictatorial regimes. Fascist regimes of the right and communist ones of the left adopt similar approaches to the death penalty—of support for it—and are generally both clearly distinguished from those of the liberals and socialists. Their similar approaches to the death penalty is not merely fortuitous but reflects a deeper convergence in their ideologies, relating mainly to the manner in which they perceive of the functions of the state apparatus and the role that they assign to the individual. Stemming from divergently opposing initial premises, they reach similar conclusions as to the paramountcy of the state; in the case of right-wing fascism, as a result of the central role that the state plays in the overall ideology, emphasizing tight control over the individual in order to ensure the fairly extensive degree of uniformity essential for the furtherance of the nation's goals; in the case of left-wing communism, as a result of the desire to control the economy in order to achieve the economic goals that are the essence of the ideology. In the latter case, the stress on the ideological factor of the economy even leads to the use of the death penalty in cases that involve economic crimes.

In a similar manner to that linking liberals and socialists, the extreme left thus sometimes finds itself in a close and strange alignment with the extreme right, the former extending its control over the economy into the realm of personal freedom, the latter expanding its control over its citizens into intervention in the economy.

The paradox of this linking of the left and the right—both the moderate groupings and the extreme polarities—requires a probing analysis beyond the scope of this book; for the purposes of this thesis, though, drawing attention to these convergences provides an explanation for the similarities and the differences in attitudes to capital punishment, and thereby enables us to be aware of the close interconnection between ideology in general and the specific issue of capital punishment.

Far from one's attitude to capital punishment being a chance expression of an intensely personal conscience, divorced from one's ideology, immune to its influences, and conceived in a vacuum, it could well be argued, in contradistinction, that one's attitude to capital punishment is the quintessence of a person's ideology, at least insofar as it deals with the realm of ideas and personal rights (i.e., in contrast to the economic sphere).

The issue of crime, its causes and control, is a key factor, not always acknowledged, in the formulation and development of an ideology. For the conservative, the issue of law and order—linked to and striving toward the stability of the social order—is of major importance and has, on occasion, become a factor in election campaigns. For liberals, in contrast, the concept of the rule of law is a crucial factor in the protection they wish to provide for individuals, for minority groups, for protagonists of unpopular causes—and for criminals, seeking to assure them of their day in court.

Apart from the effect of such issues in elections, crime has often been a factor, particularly in many developing countries, in military takeovers, when perceptions of a breakdown of social order are fostered and fueled by a high crime rate. Historically, it is more than coincidence that one of the trigger events in the French Revolution, and one of its persistent symbols, was the storming of the Bastille.

A person's attitude to crime and to punishment, his toleration or rejection of deviant behavior, his urge to punish, or his willingness to forgive, all reflect a larger ideological position.

A number of incisive works in the sociology of law and historical penology have shown how penalties originate and are implemented in terms of clear-cut sociological and historical factors relative to ideology or interests. George Rusche and Otto Kirchheimer used a Marxist framework to show how economic interests are served by penal policy and Thorsten Sellin subsequently expanded this thesis by focusing on the manner in which punitive practices applied to slaves affect the nature of subsequent penal policy; what is done to slaves in the beginning is liable, and indeed likely, to be done to citizens on the morrow.[5] The Scandinavian scholar Svend Ranulf has shown how the class interests of the middle class and its collective psychological sentiments find outlet in the penal system for their frustrations, fears, and failures, whereas more recently Stanley Cohen has described the role of ideology in the formulation of penological policy.[6]

Since the death penalty is commonly considered to be the most extreme penalty, it often reflects even more strongly basic ideological premises. Walter Berns, in a strong argument in favor of the death penalty,[7] correctly draws attention to the underlying liberal stance of the first person to favor the total abolition of capital punishment, Cesare Beccaria. The latter's classic study of penal philosophy represents an attempt to give tangible expression to the full import of incipient liberal thought in the eighteenth century as it affected the criminal justice system.[8] To refuse to acknowledge this connection (as in the free vote in a parliament) is to divest the issue of an essential component. Indeed, those whose stance on the death penalty seems to be incongruent with their overall ideological position, or with their avowed political affiliation, may be hinting at a flaw in their reasoning, a weakness in their commitment, or an error in their perceptions.

Thus Robespierre, an early advocate during the French Revolution of the abolition of the death penalty, exposed not just the evil in his character, but his lack of a true liberal belief by his later ruthless and wholesale use of the guillotine—and thereby, more than any other person, doomed the future of the original thrust of the liberal revolution.[9] Similarly, in the long run, it may well be Stalin's exploitation of the criminal justice system in the Soviet Union, and especially the death penalties handed down both in public show trials and through extra-judicial executions secretly performed, that more than any other factor destroyed the image that many perceived in the early years after the revolution of an exciting new society, one which at the beginning had even abolished capital punishment. It is perhaps no coincidence that one of the most powerful attacks on capital punishment was made by Arthur Koestler, one of those who rejected communism in the 1930s, but possessing unique qualities for assessing capital punishment as a result of having been himself a condemned prisoner for several months at the hands of right-wing forces during the civil war in Spain.[10]

One of the most interesting perspectives on the death penalty is that of John Stuart Mill, who introduced a caveat into his comprehensive and classic statements on the rights of the individual, (including penal reform) by suggesting that the desire for total abolition might be misconceived.[11] For Mill, true liberalism, a full awareness of the import of alternatives in extreme cases, and perceptive insight into the world of the condemned and the convicted, would lead to an acceptance of capital punishment as a preferred alternative to what he saw as the more severe punishment of life imprisonment. In many respects Mill's thesis serves as the underpinning for much of this work (though the basic idea preceded my acquaintance with Mill's thesis, which appears only in a marginal statement in his total works, the report of a speech that he made in the British House of Commons).[12]

Mill saw the need to protect the potential "lifer" from the overzealousness of liberal penal reformers, in order to preserve the very respect for human rights that is the essence of liberalism. His reservations as to life and long-term imprisonment maintain a certain logic and clarity that are still relevant and deserving of attention. His willingness to concede the necessity for a death penalty is firmly ensconced in his liberal philosophy, based not on deterrent, retributive, or vindictive factors, but on the infringement of human dignity entailed in lengthy confinement.

M O S T   O F   T H E   A R G U M E N T S in the recent debate about the death penalty revolve around the traditional penological questions of retribution and deterrence; although, even here, there is an imbalance as the bulk of the material relates to the issue of deterrence. Comparisons are made between abolitionist and retentionist states with similar population characteristics, most notably in the United States, where a federal system allows for differing criminal justice policies among states.[13] Countries, such as Britain or Canada, that have undergone several reversals of policy in the past few decades have been used to measure the rate of major crime at the periods when there was a death penalty and when there was not.[14] Other research focuses on the period immediately before or after a key event takes place, such as the imposition of a death penalty or an actual execution, to test whether there is any change in the rate of murder or other crime being punished.[15] For some of this research the issue is not just of deterrence, but of brutalization, in which the death penalty is seen not as minimizing crime, but as attracting further crime.

Work on retribution is less empirical and more philosophical. For some time, in fact, penologists were reluctant to directly address the issue of retribution since it seemed for the most part far too close to the negative idea of revenge. But in recent years Kantian[16] and Hegelian[17] approaches have been resuscitated, and in the light of the many admitted failings of the penal system—achieving neither rehabilitation nor deterrence—

the trend in much thinking today is toward a retributive approach. This approach is attuned far more to philosophical arguments than empirical research, since it is more an attitude of mind than a consequence.

Whether retribution is desirable is again based generally on larger philosphical or ideological premises. The social contract theory lends itself neatly, for instance, to retributive arguments. By receiving the benefits which a stable society is supposed to confer, members of that society are presumed to have agreed a priori (through a hypothetical social contract) to accept the known punishment which they, by their criminal act, have brought upon themselves. In committing a major crime they are presumed to have submitted themselves to the appropriate penalty, whatever that might be.

Often those who provide convincing data and arguments as to the ineffectiveness of the death penalty as a deterrent ignore the fact that there is an alternative philosophical base to punishment and that those whose stance is retributive will not be unduly impressed by the proof of a lack of deterrence.[18] On the contrary, the failure of deterrence is liable to provide extra force to the retributive arguments; if deterrence is not working, it should not be a factor in sentencing, and thus it becomes so much easier to achieve retributive aims, which are based on a simpler analysis of doing justice through ensuring that the criminal gets his just desserts—his *own* just desserts irrespective of any impact that his punishment may or may not have on him or on others in the future.

Whether Ehrlich is right that many future murders could be saved by using the death penalty or Sellin is correct that abolitionist and retentionist states show no difference in rates for major crime, is of little importance if the framework for measuring punishment is retributive.[19] In any event, the less deterrence seems to work the more retribution seems to make sense. Or put differently, if the death penalty, as an ultimate penalty, does not deter, then perhaps *no* sentence deters extreme crimes. Thus, if we continue to punish those who commit these extreme crimes—and there is very little disagreement as to the need for some punishment—the justification for so doing would seem to be retribution. Under such circumstances, the death sentence would become a viable option, at least in the case of murder, "a life for a life"—which is the basic position in the United States today in the retentionist states, since the death penalty may not be imposed unless a life is taken.

As for Kant and Hegel, they had no sophisticated data as to the effectiveness or otherwise of penal policies at their disposal; and thus they did not address the question of capital punishment as a deterrent. They expounded their own ideas on criminal justice, both from a pure retributive perspective and within the context of a larger philosophical framework that emphasized the importance of the society and the state, and that de-emphasized, even for that period, the importance of the individual. The key to understanding their penal philosophy is in their larger political and moral philosophy. This is so, also, for others who have addressed penological questions; even if they have not spelled out a philosophy of their own, they, too, work within some philosophical and ideological framework that moulds their ideas.

The basic retributive approach is simply and succinctly presented by Kant, based on direct proportionality: "Whoever has committed murder, must die." So important is this needed balance that in an oft-quoted statement Kant argues that in a society which wished to dissolve, "the last murderer lying in jail ought to be executed before implementation of the agreement. This ought to be done, in order that everyone might receive his dessert."[20]

In recent years the retributionist approach has been reinvigorated by the works of criminologists Andrew Von Hirsch and Ernest van der Haag, the philosopher Walter Berns, and the lawyer Frank Carrington.[21]

Whereas the retributive argument is generally acknowledged to be a conservative approach to punishment, the deterrence argument is generally seen as being a typical liberal approach. It has been used most extensively by thinkers, such as Jeremy Bentham, who justify punishment only in terms of the future advantages to be derived by society in general. A criminal should be punished if by so doing similar criminal acts in the future could be avoided—whether by the criminal himself (individual deterrence) or by society at large (general deterrence). This argument applies, of course, not just to capital punishment but to all punishment.[22]

What many modern liberals have done is to show that the deterrence argument does not hold in the case of capital punishment, and therefore argue that it should be abolished, completely ignoring retributive factors or whether life imprisonment also fails to deter.

However, the general deterrence argument has other weaknesses from a purely liberal approach, for it accepts the punishment of one individual in order to achieve larger societal results at his expense. In essence, the criminal pays the penalty not just for his own crime, but for the likelihood that others will do likewise if he is not severely dealt with. Were it not for the impact that his punishment would have on others, he could have received a far lesser punishment. This is to use the criminal as an object to achieve other aims, which is essentially a denial of his autonomy and a violation of basic liberal principles. The liberal argument should not be that a particular penalty does, or does not, deter, but that general deterrence should not be considered an aim of penology at all.

It is however also true that, in the last century, liberals have used arguments other than deterrence to analyze punishment, most notably the prospects for rehabilitation. This certainly fits in far better with the basic liberal approach of stressing the needs and the rights of the individual. For some time reform of the criminal became the acme of liberal aspirations in the area of criminal justice; and so it also became easier to criticize the lack of success of the traditional liberal approach of deterrence. But in recent years there has been rising disillusionment over rehabilitation, reaching its peak with several research projects reporting findings of recidivism.[23] The liberals have now found both their major philosophical stands undermined; with the search now on for alternatives and, particularly, the replacement of the emphasis on the prison.[24]

A possible alternative exists in the growing area of victimology. By focusing on the plight of the victim, there is ample scope for liberal solutions—in seeing to the victim's need as a harmed citizen, in helping when necessary in his physical or emotional rehabilitation, in seeking compensation for him, and perhaps even in seeking a reconciliation between him and the criminal.[25] The last is a particularly new and interesting possibility; but it has been tried mainly in the cases of petty crime, not major crimes with their ultimate penalties.[26]

Basically, the liberal approach today has no feasible solution or concerted approach to the problem of major crime. Reform is under attack; deterrence is used as part of the philosophy, but mainly to argue a negative—that there has been no deterrence. Liberal thinkers are active in showing what does not work—for example, the attacks against the death penalty—but are less persistent or creative in suggesting what should be done.

At the least, there is a need to spell out the principles which must serve as the guiding directives. It is the task of the liberal to ensure that the basic human rights of those accused of major crimes are safeguarded. It is nowhere easier to forego some of the protections which are so insistently implemented in other cases than in dealing with someone who has committed a reprehensible crime. It is even possible that the process by which the final result emerges is no less important than the outcome of what penalty is imposed.[27]

In fact, there may be no "liberal" way, or at least no ideal liberal way, of solving the problems created by murderers, rapists, torturers—but there may be a liberal way of ensuring that the solution, whatever it is, is arrived at justly. The liberal must see that the basic rights of the individual are respected, that society exerts its resilience in acting toward the presumably depraved brought before its courts with fairness and justice, that the individuality of the accused or condemned criminal is respected, and, most of all, that the punishment itself, whatever its nature, is implemented in such a way as to ensure the essential dignity of the person being punished.

The liberal has one further task. To take up the cudgels of behalf of the condemned everywhere. All human rights struggles must be blind to the artifical imposition of geographic boundaries. The question of ultimate punishments can no longer be limited to the confines of one particular nation-state. This is a prime issue of universal human rights. It is the most absolute expression of state power, more so than the right to levy taxes or to draft the young.

It is this, I submit, that is no less important than, let us say, the oft-quoted abolitionist argument, as to the irreversibility of the penalty in the event of judicial error. In so many countries it is not human error that is the issue, but deliberate falsehood; not judicial fallibility, but political exploitation; not deterrence of potential criminals, but intimidation of total populations; not the carnival of public executions, but the terror of secret tortures and killings; not retribution for the proven criminal, but elimination of the political rival; not the need only to ensure consideration for the victim, but the need also to prevent victimization of the suspect.

In the United States, the issue may no longer be arbitrary decisions by juries, but illogical application of the simple and straightforward rule as to arbitrariness by some of the very judges who laid it down. Although my approach involves general and universal issues, several chapters in this book deal specifically with the situation in the United States.[28] Many reasons underly this approach, not the least that this book was largely written and then published in America. The availability of research material was a further factor, as was the intriguing nature of many of the unique issues that the courts in the United States have addressed in recent years, when they have been inundated with a series of innovative and creative arguments brought forward by lawyers and groups seeking determinedly to save the life of a condemned person; but mainly because the outcome of the abolitionist struggle in the United States is liable to have far-reaching consequences beyond its border. Certainly for as long as it retains the death penalty, right-wing dictatorial societies, directly or indirectly supported by the United States, will have little incentive to eliminate the death penalty or to curb its use in politically motivated executions, whether by regular court procedures or extra-judicial actions.

Today the United States is one of the few countries that maintains democratic institutions and subscribes partially to a liberal ethos yet which still retains the death penalty; and not only does the United States retain it, but, after some initial hesitation in the years immediately after the moratorium was broken, seems intent on maintaining a constant march from the death cell to the execution chamber, with the last months of 1984 marking a conscious change in the climate of opinion and practice toward the death penalty.

Almost alone among the Western democracies, the United States uses the death penalty in a manner reserved normally only for nondemocratic societies, whether of the left or the right. In fact, in contrast to many of these latter countries, it still allows the death sentence for minors.[29] From a worldwide perspective, the position in the United States thus becomes crucial. If a worldwide campaign against the death penalty is to succeed, the battle must be engaged first and foremost in the United States. It is perhaps no coincidence that the increase in the number of death penalties actually carried out occurred during a period in which the liberal ethos of American life was under attack and when its advocates seemed to be on the retreat in so many areas, or no coincidence that strong representations made by the United States to a political ally, the Sudan, in 1985, to refrain from executing a political dissident, a highly respected man in his seventies, failed—since in that very same week three executions occurred in the United States.[30]

An examination of the death penalty in the United States becomes important for another reason. In seeing the manner in which it is applied in this country, where evidence is freely available, one is given a hint of the kind of illogic, obtuseness, and cruelty that doubtless characterizes the judicial and administrative processes in countries where access to such information is limited or even barred.

Finally, it is intriguing and disturbing to see the arbitrary and capricious manner in which the Supreme Court justices have monitored their own directive that death penalties must not be handed out in an arbitrary and capricious manner.

In the course of this book I shall argue from a liberal perspective that capital punishment is not necessarily the most serious punishment, and that there may be circumstances in which it would be applicable. Yet there may be no stronger argument against the death penalty than the blatantly arbitrary pattern of executions currently being performed in the United States. It is almost a prototype of the arbitrariness that the Court assailed in its original historical *Furman* decision, and an example of the kind of situation the Court was trying to avoid in laying down the guidelines for the resumption of the death penalty in the 1976 *Gregg* case.[31] Indeed, inasmuch as there is any pattern at all, it may be one of discrimination, more subtle than that originally divulged in the *Furman* case (for instance, the race of the victim), but nonetheless ever so real for those condemned. When the Court itself acknowledges the possibility of this pattern but refuses to intervene without direct proof of personal bias by judge or jury, and when the Court foregoes its own initial insistence on proper proportionality review to ensure that a death penalty is not inconsistent with other penalties given in that same jurisdiction, then the wheel has indeed come full circle.[32]

So the final evidence may be at hand that, even under the optimum conditions of judicial guidelines, activist defense lawyers, and intense public scrutiny, unfairness and illogic still reign supreme. It might be possible, theoretically, to utilize the death penalty in a fair manner. But the United States has seemingly failed to do so; and given the existence of optimum conditions for making it work fairly, this failure suggests that in other countries, too, where in some cases no clear constitutional protections or judicial guidelines exist, there is likely to be a similar inability to implement this ultimate punishment in a just manner.

For those of liberal persuasion, however, the issue of life imprisonment remains a haunting presence. For though it serves as a convenient alternative to capital punishment, often aggressively and enthusiastically touted by abolitionists, it contains many disturbing elements clearly inconsistent with the very values sustaining the liberal philosophy. The demands of the internal logic of liberalism and the aspirations for a humane penal policy necessitate a frontal confrontation with the issue of life imprisonment, even though aspects of such a confrontation may affect aspects of the abolitionist position.

Unfortunately, the arbitrariness and unfairness may not be unique to capital punishment cases. It may reflect the problematics and the malaise of the criminal justice system as a whole. It certainly seems to apply, as will be shown, to the other ultimate penalty, that of life imprisonment—indeed, the arbitrariness and unfairness may be even more acute in this area because the courts have failed to provide even minimum mandatory guidelines. And so people are being sentenced to life imprisonment with disregard for constitutional standards of due process, for judicial directives as to the avoidance of arbitrariness, and for liberal tenets as the dignity of the individual.

What advantage is there for the accused to be saved from the penalty of death if he is then consigned to a penalty of life, when the adjudication may be arbitrary, the conditions of confinement a violation of his dignity, and a likely end-result, his death while yet in confinement?

3

FOR LIFE

THERE IS PERHAPS no more difficult issue confronting abolitionists than deciding on the penalty that they wish to offer in place of the death penalty. Yet, for the most part, their attitude to this issue is, unfortunately, not one of earnest confrontation in an attempt to seek a viable solution, but—perhaps understandably—careful evasion in an attempt to avoid some of the implications of their position. On the rare occasions when abolitionists do address this issue, they generally do so in a way calculated more to deflect potential criticism or to disarm their opponents than to express their own deepest beliefs, those very humanistic beliefs that largely motivate them in the first place in their abolitionist stance, and which underlie most of their premises.

The most generally offered alternative is of life imprisonment, but very rarely is any effort made to probe the full import of such a sentence, its manner of adjudication, its method of implementation, its meaning for the convicted, or its compatibility with humanitarian principles. One of the most prominent abolitionists in the United States, Hugo Bedau, has acknowledged this weakness in the abolition argument, conceding that "abolitionists have often been silent on the alternative they would substitute for the death penalty, or they have embraced the somewhat ambiguous idea of 'life imprisonment.' . . . It is neither sensible nor serious to advocate abolition of the death penalty without reasonably precise answers" to questions as to whether parole should be allowed, or the conditions of imprisonment, such as solitary confinement, etc.[1]

When abolitionists do deal with the alternative, often in their eagerness to prevent the death penalty, they are even prepared to countenance policies and practices that seem to be inconsistent with their legitimate concerns, part of their abolitionist stance, as to the assurance of human dignity, and the avoidance of unnecessary pain, suffering, and humiliation.

From Cesare Beccaria, who integrated a ban on capital punishment into his influential treatise on criminal law, through Albert Camus in his passionate polemic against the guillotine, to Justice Thurgood Marshall, acknowledged as one of the most determined, consistent, and articulate abolitionists of modern times, the refrain of the severity of a proposed alternative punishment recurs. In Beccaria's case, penal servitude was his explicitly formulated proposal as the most suitable punishment to be meted out; indeed, as preferred specifically because, by virture of its severity, it seemed to posses superior deterrent qualities. Camus argued similarly using the phrase "hard labor," but not defining it. For Justice Marshall it was solitary confinement that was the casually offered suggestion for guaranteeing the future impotence of any violent-prone offender, those who occasion the most concern of moderate retentionists.

Thus Beccaria: "Perpetual slavery, then, has in it all that is necessary to deter the most hardened and determined, as much as the punishment of death. I say it has more. There are many who can look upon death with intrepidity and firmness; some through fanaticism, and others through vanity . . . but fanaticism and vanity forsake the criminal in slavery, in chains and fetters, in an iron cage; and despair seems rather the beginning than the end of their misery."[2]

Thus Camus: "Capital punishment would then be replaced by hard labor—for life in the case of criminals considered irremediable." Presumably, he here refers to habitual criminals, not just murderers.[3]

And thus Justice Marshall: "Life imprisonment and, if necessary, solitary confinement would fully accomplish the aim of incapacitation."[4]

Let me stress that I do not wish to impugn on the outstanding credentials of the great Italian thinker, the great French writer, or the great American jurist. On the contrary, it is specifically their unquestioned contribution to liberal legal ideas that is the cause for alarm; for whatever the depths of their abhorrence of the death penalty and the sincerity of their convictions as to the abolitionist cause, these can surely not serve as a justification for proposing penal policies whose ultimate consequences may constitute a denial of—or, at least, a serious derogation from—the very values they claim to uphold.

In fairness, it should be noted that some abolitionists accept harsh alternative measures more because of the tactical advantages to be derived therefrom (as, for instance, a means of convincing others that no danger lurks at the end of the abolitionist road) than because of any eagerness to have a "real" life sentence with additional severe conditions actually implemented. Indeed, they probably presume both that the added severity, for example, solitary confinement, will not in fact be carried out, and that even the life imprisonment as such will be mitigated, through commutation, in the course of time.

This reservation is not, however, applicable in the case of Beccaria, as he certainly wished for what emerged, a form of punishment—penal servitude—the horrors of which were revealed in all their extremity after some of his ideas were implemented.[5] But for modern abolitionists, one may presume that some of their more harsh suggestions are no more than polemical argumentation, not intended for serious consideration (as, for instance, in the case quoted of Justice Marshall, where it was mere *obiter dicta,* of no pertinence to the legal issues at hand in the judgment).

It would appear indeed that there is an unacknowledged constant assumption that a life sentence is simply not what it is stated to be, and that "lifers" are generally released from prison before their demise—an assumption that hovers over and directly affects penological debate. It placates liberal abolitionists and influences judges called upon to determine the various legal and constitutional issues that arise in life imprisonment cases. At the same time it also affects retentionists, who are often so adamant as to the importance of capital punishment specifically because they fear that the full degree of retributive or deterrent value of a severe sentencing policy will not be achieved, since the life sentence will likely be mitigated by subsequent executive intervention.

There are occasional reports in the mass media of individual releases of an inmate once involved in a sensational case or well known because of some legal or constitutional issue associated with his name, or of general statistical summaries showing an overly generous approach on the part of commutation or pardoning authorities.[6] Such reports add, on the one hand, to the sense of complacency of abolitionists, encouraging their acceptance of life imprisonment as an alternative to the death penalty, and, on the other hand, to the indignation of retentionists, and their rejection of any alternative to the far more certain and final penalty of death. However, the fact of the matter is that very little is known of the ultimate fate of lifers. Although some, no doubt, are the beneficiaries of a generous commutation policy and are released from prison early, others become the forgotten people of penology, locked away in penitentiaries, removed both from the awareness of the public and from the focus of academic research.[7]

Indeed, it is the leniency adopted toward some that adds an extra poignancy and urgency to the fate of the others, making them the victims—either randomly or deliberately discriminatory—of arbitrary decision-making as to who shall be released and who shall end their days in confinement. Sentencing policy is notoriously erratic, with minimum guidelines to assist judges and juries in what is a decision of monumental significance for the accused. Yet often—and particularly for long-term imprisonment and life sentences—the actual sentence imposed is itself only the outer framework within which penal policy takes shape. For the most part, the definitive decision as to the length of sentence is made at the post-trial stage—in commutation and pardoning decisions.

In some countries an awareness of the inability to give factual meaning to a life sentence has led to a recognized ritual of commutation to a fixed term (ranging around twenty years). Then under normal circumstances of good behavior, of partial remission of that sentence, the life sentence in effect becomes a sentence of about fifteen years.[8] In the United States, however, no such standardized procedures apply. The resultant picture is of a haphazard situation with large discrepancies in the periods served by those originally sentenced to life.[9]

It is clear that the actual decision as to the final fate of a life prisoner is generally made far from the spotlight of public scrutiny, at some unknown time in the future, often without the benefit of legal counsel, under circumstances vastly different from those pertaining at the time of the trial, and almost totally beyond judicial review (though, in recent years, some state and federal laws have provided protective procedures at least for parole). This loose framework may sometimes work to the advantage of the inmate, leading to an early and unexpected release; but, on other occasions, it can work to the disadvantage of those confronting an almost Kafkaesque situation, when one of the most important decisions of their life—release or continued incarceration—is made in an arbitrary and capricious manner, with far less consistency even than in sentencing.

Now it is true that a decision for pardon, commutation or early release is clearly a privilege—no prisoner is by right entitled to such consideration.[10] But it is this situation that leads to the inevitably haphazard nature of the decision-making process. Though legally unassailable as a doctrine which accords to the executive and specified administrative bodies, the power to manifest society's sentiments of grace and mercy (as also utilitarian considerations in regard to rehabilitation), practically it makes for tension, frustration, and resentment on the part of those denied the benefits of this benevolence.

For all prisoners, parole, originally a progressive step aimed at allowing a personalized approach to release procedures, has taken on increasingly problematic perspectives—leading to constant uncertainty, recurrent surges of sanguine expectations, and, when unfulfilled, negative reactions to justice denied and a sense of increasing hopelessness. This is inevitable in a system a priori designed to be flexible and attuned to individualized justice; but even if one were to presume that the system was working flawlessly (which is doubtful) one cannot ignore the consequences of negative decisions on inmates, particularly on those serving the ultimate penalty of life, which decrees, absent benevolent executive or administrative intervention, that they shall die in prison.

Further, it is likely that those self-same deficiencies which exist in the commutation process for the death penalty, making the final recipients of the executioner's power no more than a small minority of chance, are at work also in the realm of the life sentence. It is even possible that there is a pattern extant of racial discrimination. Arising out of the legitimate concerns of those abolitionists who struggled to do away with the death penalty because of the underlying pattern of racism that determined the sentencing policy in many jurisdictions, a new punishment structure for the most serious crimes may have been set up in which racism is still prevalent, but much more difficult to detect, because it is connected to the commutation stage and not the sentence itself, which is often mandatory.

I pose these facts as a working hypothesis—there is, to the best of my knowledge, no research on this specific topic.[11] There is a real need for pioneering work of the type carried out by Marvin Wolfgang, Arlene Kelly, and Hans Nolde in tracing out the final outcomes of capital punishment sentencing. Their work—an analysis of some 400 cases of capital punishment imposed in Pennsylvania between 1914 and 1958—suggests the strong possibility of racist influences as one of the factors making for differentiation between those whose execution is carried out and those who have their sentence commuted.[12] It is of interest to note that this research article was

quoted in the *Furman* case[13] as evidence of discriminatory practices, but the Court did not appreciate the fact that the data
did not relate to sentencing but to the pardoning stage. Similar
research on the commutation and pardoning practices for the
thousands of life prisoners might well reveal that the discrimination once practiced in capital cases at the sentencing stage is
now being practiced in life imprisonment cases at the posttrial
stage.

There is an urgent need to know what happens to those
sentenced to life or given a life sentence after commutation
of a death sentence by the executive. How many of these are
thereby condemned to serve out to the full, unto death, their
lives in confinement? How many are released before their
demise, and what are the key reasons for differentiating between the two groups?[14] Is there any pattern, beyond that of
possible racial discrimination? Within the framework of those
who are released, what sort of time differences are there, and
what rationale underlies this?

Is there even any meaning to the restriction sometimes
stipulated in which the life sentence is imposed without the
possibility of parole? Does this restriction retain its efficacy
or does the passage of time allow for a flexibility that a more
immediate justice could not tolerate? Yet if these restrictions
are generally retained, what have we here if not a deferred
death penalty? Even if death in these cases is not deliberately
caused by active agency of the state, it occurs passively while
the person is in state control, deprived of that ready access
to family, friends, and perhaps even adequate medical services,
all of which an individual is entitled to and are the mark of
an autonomous being.

The whole nature of the life imprisonment sentence is one
of the most difficult problems of penology. I have defined it
as an ultimate penalty, even though such designation is generally
reserved only for the death sentence. Yet, as I shall try to show,
whatever the differences between these punishments, they contain sufficient similarities to warrant similar consideration,

whether in empirical research, in judicial decisions, or in public awareness.

Which is the more severe penalty is, I would submit, a matter of dispute, one which perhaps cannot be resolved even in general terms, but only on an ad hoc basis, that is, with empirical reference to each case, taking into account the particular circumstances such as the age of the criminal and his prospects of parole. In the final analysis, it may even be beyond the capacity of neutral, objective observers to determine definitively the question of severity—this may be a uniquely individual decision which can only be decided by those actually confronted by the possibility of being subject to one of these penalties.

This is not a hypothetical or academic issue. It is a real matter of life and death, not only, as is so often assumed, for those who determinedly fight for their very lives by constant appeals or pleas for pardon. It is no less a matter of prime personal importance for those who wish to die[15]—for any of several reasons, one of which might well be because life itself would be intolerable under conditions of perpetual confinement. Some prisoners (admittedly not just lifers) seek their own means of indicating their preference, by committing or attempting suicide.[16] Others, those sentenced to death, likewise indicate their choice by the simple legal expedient of refusing to take their case on appeal, or even by explicitly, and sometimes even flamboyantly, challenging the authorities to promptly implement the death sentence that the court, in its wisdom, has seen fit to impose.[17]

Now it is true, and it has been forcefully argued, that those who choose death over life are a small minority, clearly acting under distress, many of them suffering from severe emotional problems (perhaps related to the crime). The decision to forego an appeal and to insist on the performance of the punishment imposed forthwith is not, then, the decision of a free rational human being, flowing from informed consent and attuned to a wide range of options. It may even be that at least some of these people have suicidal tendencies which fit in well with society's penal structure, and that they may even have been attracted to the idea of committing a capital crime as a means of finding an outlet for these tendencies.[18]

No less problematical are the cases in which the condemned person seeks the implementation of the death sentence specifically because of the severe conditions of the prison, often exacerbated in death row because of its especially harsh conditions, imposed partly to ensure the tight control that will prevent attempts at "cheating" the executioner, and partly because normal standards of control might seem inadequate to prevent the excesses of those already subject to the death penalty. It has been argued that these special segregated conditions undermine the inmate's will to live and to fight to avoid the death penalty. Furthermore, it should be noted that recently a number of abolitionists have lodged the charge that the harsh conditions are not merely for the oft-stated reason of security, but are manipulatively so designed to "facilitate" the inmate's acceptance of his sentence, as has been argued in several issues of *Lifelines,* the newsletter of the National Coalition for the Abolition of Capital Punishment.[19] But if these grave charges are true, the real issue emerging from them, of course, is not the desire of some condemned prisoners to choose an early death over prolonged posttrial proceeding, but an unconscionable abuse of power by the prison authorities, which prima facie constitutes a violation of basic human and constitutional rights, and which requires immediate eradication.[20] Aside from this abuse, the issue of prisoner's choice remains.

The classic case of a condemned person preferring the implementation of the death penalty over the struggle to have the sentence changed to one of imprisonment was that of Gary Gilmore. This case took on added dimensions because in his desire to have the death penalty implemented lay the key to the continuation or termination of the moratorium on the death penalty. When such an issue—of a prisoner's desire—arises, it transforms fundamentally the whole nature of the capital

punishment debate. In a word, it is no longer possible to ignore the meaning—for the prisoner—of a sentence of life imprisonment. As Hugo Bedau asks: "What is to be done with
the Gilmores of this world?"[21]

In Gilmore's case—as also in a few subsequent cases—
abolitionists fought to avert the death sentence and, in so
doing, to impose their desires, their penological value-systems
and their overall strategy, upon him.[22] Gilmore's desire to be
executed was also strenuously opposed by his family and his
legal representatives. There was in any case the possibility
that the law under which Gilmore had been sentenced was
unconstitutional since it did not conform to all the guidelines
laid down in the *Gregg* and related cases. Further, it is clear
that there was a larger societal need at stake, of maintaining
the moratorium; each passing year gave added weight to the
arguments that the death penalty constituted cruel and certainly unusual punishment. The larger picture also involved
the fact that much of the efforts of abolitionists at that time
were oriented to saving the many blacks on death row, some
of them considered to be the victims of continuing patterns
of racial discrimination, whereas Gilmore was a white; for
their fate was inextricably bound up with his, and a consummation of his desire to be killed would directly affect their
own struggles to live.

Yet even so, the desperate attempts made to intervene on
Gilmore's behalf, against his will, raise many serious issues,
for in the final analysis they are based—and are largely
justified—on the affirmed consensus that the death penalty is
the most severe punishment, and unquestioningly and uniquely
so. However, if this assumption is false, then those who wished
to intervene on behalf of Gilmore or any other condemned
person of similar attitude, are liable, in the name of human
rights and progressive penology, to implicate the supposed
beneficiary of their efforts in an alternative punishment that,
to him, is cruel, and which he must then live with for the rest
of his life, absent commutation and pardon.

Penological philosophies do not arise in a vacuum, but are intricately linked to the overall principles which guide and mold a society. Abolitionist principles stem normally from some of the deepest and finest sentiments of human nature, expressing the full flower of those humanistic principles considered to be the hallmark of modern civilization. Conversely, harsh penal measures often reflect the value-system—and serve the needs—of authoritarian regimes. In contrast, the struggle for greater public participation in the political process, for extending the rights of the individual, for developing and concretizing the concepts of freedom, equality, and justice, has been accompanied by attempts to moderate and mitigate the kinds of penalties that society is willing to tolerate; and a diminution in the use of the death penalty is one clear expression of such a process.

At the same time, one of the recognized features of the modern age is the degree of autonomy it accords to the individual. Here the paradox is that in instituting imprisonment as a major alternative to prior forms of punishment, society has created a framework that is a denial of this value. A prison is characterized by its deprivation of the right to autonomous decision-making by the inmates. Whereas such an infringement of the rights of the individual might be of only marginal meaning in societies (modern or of earlier times) that are basically authoritarian in nature, the implications are, I would submit, substantively different in societies based on democratic liberal principles.

It seems to be a matter of prime importance when the full power of the state is used in order to deprive a person of his freedom in a society devoted to, characterized by, and proud of, its liberal ethos. Any punishment based on such deprivation must be considered severe—when that deprivation is for life, it must surely rank as an ultimate penalty. It is precisely a liberal society's emphasis on the nature and quality of the individual life, each individual life, and not on mere physical existence, that gives to life imprisonment an emotional meaning and ideological connotation that spells out unique severity. As Judge Sneed of Nevada wrote in the *Bishop* case, a condemned person should be free to decide on his own whether to pursue an appeal. "To deny him that would be to incarcerate the spirit—the one thing that remains free and which the state need not and should not imprison."[23] Melvin Urofsky neatly poses the paradox facing a liberal struggling with the meaning of life and death in legal and medical situations. "It is certainly ironic," he writes, "that in the Gilmore case, the American Civil Liberties Union passionately sought to prevent the execution of a convicted murderer who wished to die, claiming that Gilmore had no right to do so. It then turned around and argued that a right to die existed for Karen Ann Quinlan who was unable to express her wishes one way or the other."[24]

Although the death penalty is almost always automatically designated as being a uniquely severe penalty, it is clearly not the most severe penalty that human ingenuity is capable of devising. The various forms of torture inflicted as punishment at different times in human history serve as a reminder of the indignities and privations that is possible to impose on the human body and spirit.[25] The fact is that, in earlier times, the death penalty alone was not even considered a sufficiently harsh punishment, unless preceded by torturous procedures. The more suffering and pain undergone by the condemned person prior to breathing his last, the more satisfaction was evoked at the retributive or deterrent capacities of the punishment. It was specifically the cruelty prior to death that was considered an essential ingredient of capital punishment. Thus drawing and quartering, bending on the wrack, dismemberment, mutilation, and other lingering painful procedures were of the essence of the penalty, and death would often come as a merciful release. The later constitutional protections were largely designed to curb or eliminate these excesses. Today one of the proclaimed (though often disputed) aspects of the death penalty is that the execution itself be performed speedily and painlessly.

In international law, it has been possible to gain the agreement of the world community as to a total, recognized prohibition on torture.[26] In contrast, the world community is still far from a similar total prohibition on capital punishment.

Thus, of the three ultimate penalites—capital punishment, life imprisonment, physical torture—it would seem that the last is the most severe; indeed, human decency has decreed that it is so severe that it shall not be used. No such similar consensus exists, for the moment, as to the death penalty. The widespread *sub rosa* practice of torture[27]—to punish as well as to intimidate or extract information—is further proof of its extreme harshness, for those who use it illicitly do so in the sure knowledge that whatever aim—political or penological—that they wish to attain will well be served by torture, and not necessarily by death.

There is a further aspect that should be borne in mind. For all the extremity associated with the death penalty—its finality and irreversibility, its arrogation to society of some divinelike power, its power, its impact on those near and dear to the condemned person—the fact is that death alone of the three ultimate penalties is an inevitable concomitant of life. Death itself comes in many forms—in some cases, as after an illness, it may come as a welcome release; in other cases, as in suicide, it comes as an act of deliberate choice; in yet other cases, as in euthanasia, it is purposively sought; in war it may be considered heroic (for a soldier) or an unfortunate unintended consequence (for innocent citizens). When it comes at a predetermined moment, as in an execution, there are certain distinct aspects, but these do not necessarily make for its unique severity as a punishment.[28]

It is true that a significant part of the uniqueness of the death penalty relates to its irreversibility (preventing reversal of error or mitigation in the course of time), but this is a fact linked more to the nature of death, and shared indeed with other forms of death, than with its nature as a punishment. Thus, a strong argument may, just as in the case of capital punishment, be made against suicide, based on its irreversi-bility—how can we know if the person who commits suicide would not, at some future date, have wished to have changed his mind? But despite this, most liberals do not oppose suicide. Or an argument against war, where ex post facto reassess-ment indicates unnecessary, but irreversible, political and mili-tary errors, resulting, perhaps, in loss of life.

Furthermore, in contrast to death, which is the inescapable lot of all human beings, subjection to physical hardship, as in torture, or deprivation of freedom, as in imprisonment, are not inevitable. In this sense they contain a uniqueness and a severity of their own; in this sense, they may well constitute a greater violation of human dignity. Inasmuch as the battle for abolition of capital punishment is engaged in pursuit of human dignity and couched in the language of human decency, it seems only logical to apply similar criteria in an analysis of other ultimate penalties. It may even be that it is a universal fear of death that confronts all of us that makes for the special concern over capital punishment (whether abolitionist or reten-tionist) as contrasted with indifference to imprisonment which most people do not have to fear or consider as a possibility which they themselves may personally encounter.

When a person is doomed to spend his final years impri-soned, with no (or few) prospects of release, then in terms of his human dignity, his individuality, his freedom, and his autonomy, one could well argue that the oppressive confines of a prison constitute as great an infringement of his basic human rights as a death sentence. In fact, when a prisoner is sustained emotionally by the hope of his eventual release, then the con-tinued denial of such release serves only to add a touch of macabre psychological strain, a Tantalus-like situation of recur-rent hope met by repeated rejection. It is to avoid just such a situation that some countries provide for ritualistic, almost automatic reduction in the life sentence. Generally abolitionist in nature, these countries have also applied some of the focus on life imprisonment—its human meaning, its constitutional implications, its penological rationale—that in the United States has been reserved only for the death penalty.[29] Probing questions as to the rights of prisoners and their human dignity have been posed in these countries.

In terms of severity, life imprisonment may certainly be considered more akin to the death penalty than to other defined and shorter periods of incarceration. A strong connecting link between capital punishment and life imprisonment is that in both cases death comes while under the control of state authority—whereas in the first instance it is predetermined and cuts a life short, in the second instance it is deferred to a future unknown date, which, because of the harsh conditions, may also be earlier than the prisoner's normally anticipated life-span.

However, when death does take place in prison—a few years later or many years later—the inmate has been deprived of one of the main qualities of a human being: his freedom. Death, the inevitable, when it comes, takes place in conditions of confinement which are not inevitable and which can only emphasize the extremity of the lack of freedom. For those who die while incarcerated—theoretically the aim and the meaning of a life sentence in contrast to other deaths in confinement— imprisonment must surely have special connotations of its own.

Until we know more of the meaning of life imprisonment as perceived by those who are so sentenced, we cannot determine the nature of its severity, or of its impact on the inmate's sense of personal dignity. For as long as life imprisonment is casually held as an acceptable alternative to what is perceived as the far more serious penalty of death, we shall be lacking in the required data and the insightful perceptions that are essential for a reasoned judgment of these issues.

Much of the imbalance in societal perceptions may stem from the frightened fascination that people have with the whole idea of death. In fact, it may be possible to appreciate the background to the penological debates on the ultimate penalties only when seen in the light of attitudes to death in general.

Thus, for instance, modern medical technology has created a new pattern of medical practices in which what are termed "heroic" measures are used to try to save the life of terminally ill patients, even against their will or, in the case of comatose patients, against what those closest to them presume to be their wishes or, at least, their interests. These determined medical practices are, in a sense, related to the efforts of civil rights activists to save the life of a condemned person—including those situations in which a condemned person does not wish to be saved, and for whom life, in its alternative form of perpetual confinement until death, would be worthless and painful. The similarity most pertinent for the purposes of our discussion is that the heroic medical measures, which sustain life, often cause intense physical suffering, and deprive the patient of the dignity of the quiet and early death that he perhaps seeks and is entitled to. It is indeed a strange phenomenon that doctors will go to extremes to maintain a person on life-supporting mechanisms when for that particular person, life, in its normal connotation, has ceased to have any meaning.

It is further interesting to note that one of the reasons occasionally used for fighting to keep a person alive is the hope that, in the course of time, a cure will be found—just as civil rightists hope that, for as long as the inmate is still alive, there is always the prospect of later commutation and release. Yet, just as some patients would rather forego these potential but dubious breakthoughs, so some prisoners would rather forego their potential but dubious chances of later release. I doubt whether, in the name of humanistic principles, it is permissible to impose on reluctant patients life-supporting mechanisms;[30] and I doubt whether, in the name of humanistic principles, it is permissible to impose on reluctant prisoners a life sentence only because it is widely perceived to be more lenient than death, even though at least some of these condemned prisoners believe otherwise.

Since Gilmore, a number of other condemned prisoners have indicated their preference for the death penalty. Their situation is slightly different from that of Gilmore since there is no longer any nationwide moratorium at stake. Yet there may well still be localized issues (for instance, when a particular jurisdiction has had no death penalty) which could again complicate the issue, by creating a confrontation between the rights and desires of an individual and the overall strategy of liberal abolitionist groups.

IN ARGUING for the severity of life imprisonment per se, in arguing for the right of prisoners to choose which ultimate penalty they perceive as the more amenable, I am echoing similar contentions that have been made by philosophers and penologists, including those who have often been most eloquent and persuasive in espousing the liberal cause and in carving out the contours of such a society. Yet the consideration and arguments advanced by them have not been given sufficient attention.

The great English liberal John Stuart Mill, in a speech in Parliament in 1868, during a debate on abolition, referred specifically to the fact that he was reluctantly forced to part company with many of those with whom he had fought together in so many other liberal causes. Acknowledging the great contribution that many of these abolitionists had made to a reform of the criminal law—including limiting the death sentence mainly to extreme crimes such as aggravated murder—yet affirming also that criminals convicted of such crimes deserved an extreme punishment, he expressed his fear that "by an exaggerated application of some just and highly important principle" incorrect conclusions could well be deduced. Referring to the most extreme cases of criminals for whom reform seemed unlikely and therefore later release well-nigh impossible, he stated,

> I defend this penalty [the death penalty] when confined to atrocious cases, on the very good ground on which it is commonly attacked—on that of humanity to the criminal; as beyond comparison the least cruel mode in which it is possible adequately to deter from crime. If, in our horror

of inflicting death, we endeavour to devise some punishment for the living criminal which shall act on the human mind with a deterrent force at all comparable to that of death, we are driven to inflicting less severe indeed in appearance, and therefore less efficacious, but far more cruel in reality. Few . . . would venture to propose, as a punishment for aggravated murder, less than imprisonment with hard labour for life; that is the fate to which a murderer would be consigned by the mercy which shrinks from putting him to death. But has it been sufficiently considered what sort of mercy this is, and what kind of life it leaves to him? . . . What comparison can there really be, in point of severity between consigning a man to the short pang of a rapid death, and immuring him in a living tomb, there to linger out what may be a long life in the hardest and most monotonous toil, without any of its alleviation or rewards—debarred from all pleasant sights and sounds, and cut off from all earthly hope, except a slight mitigation of bodily restraint, or a small improvement of diet?

In contrast, he claims that "there is not, I think, any human infliction which makes an impression on the imagination so entirely out of proportion to its real severity as the punishment of death."[31]

Mill goes on to argue that "it is not human life only, not human life as such, that ought to be sacred to us, but human feelings. The human capacity of suffering is what we should cause to be respected, not the mere capacity of existing."[32] It is true that much of Mill's criticism is directed at harsh penal policies, such as hard labor, which are not inevitable, and which are not necessarily applied at present. But the essential thrust of his argument is surely valid—that it is the quality of life, not mere physical existence, that should affect our penological deliberations.

Mill doubtless knew whereof he spoke, for the initial attempts to do away with the death penalty were sometimes accompanied by the harshest penal provisions—not just life imprisonment, but acts that bordered on, or constituted, torture. When some of Beccaria's reforms were implemented,[33] many of those thereby saved from an immediate death penalty were subject to a most torturous form of penal servitude, which, for most of them, ended in their early death some years later, with death itself providing often a welcome respite from the agonies and hardships of their final years. Thorsten Sellin notes that Beccaria's "advocacy of penal slavery encouraged the invention of horrid forms of imprisonment believed to be more deterrent than death," the consequence of which was that many convicts "actually were subjected to a prolonged death penalty," with many dying in an emaciated state.[34]

George Bernard Shaw, too, was of the opinion that the death penalty need not necessarily be considered the most severe.[35] He had participated in a penological project under the auspices of the renowned Howard Penal Association, which has done, and continues to do, so much to foster humane practices in the prison system in Britain. Shaw subsequently published his views separately, and conveys in his statement a sense of a probing attempt to understand, at the deepest level, the meaning of ultimate penalties. He claims that the issue is not just one of the severity of a punishment, but the way it is perceived. According to Shaw, "imprisonment is at once the most cruel of punishments and the one that those who inflict it without having ever experienced it cannot believe to be cruel."[36]

Similar severe strictures against imprisonment in general, and life imprisonment in particular, were voiced by other experts in penology. William Tallack, who was the secretary of the Howard Association, was one of the few writers on criminology and penology to devote a whole chapter to the problem of what he termed "Perpetual or Life Imprisonment."[37] He noted the unmitigated despair and despondency of the prisoner committed for life. "Perpetual imprisonment is accompanied by the darkness of despair," he writes, adding that "almost the only possible justification for the horrors of life imprisonment, is that it has been regarded as constituting a substitute for Capital Punishment, which many persons consider to be a still greater evil."[38] He is, however, basically critical of the stance that capital punishment is the greater evil.

> Very few, comparatively, of the persons who advocate the abolition of capital punishment, have been able, or have taken the trouble, to make themselves acquainted with the extreme practical difficulties attendant upon the provision of an effectual substitute for that penalty. Very few of them have ever devoted their personal attention to the actual features of prolonged imprisonment. . . . Some of the advocates of that abolition have been remarkably ignorant of matters connected with prisons or criminal treatment. It is to be desired that those, as a class, who oppose capital punishment, could have devoted much more serious and practical consideration to the substitutes, proposed or imagined, for that infliction, than has hitherto been given. Especially should the real nature and evils of life-imprisonment be more studied and weighed.[39]

"The more this matter has been investigated by the writer," he adds, "the more he has become convinced that, in at least a large proportion of instances, absolute life-imprisonment is not so much a substitute for capital punishment, as a slower and more disadvantageous method of inflicting it." According to Tallack, under certain circumstances the death penalty "may be mercy itself, compared with the prolonged injury inflicted upon the spiritual and mental powers, extended over many years. . . . A process thus continued may ultimately be *as real* an execution of death, but by slow operation, as the more visible and instantaneous deprivation of life."[40] Tallack's own opinion was that about twenty years should be the maximum period of time spent in prison by any offender.

In more recent times, the philosopher Sidney Hook and the educationist Jacques Barzun have also argued that a liberal

approach to penal problems might well necessitate a willingness
to accept capital punishment.[41] They have suggested that, in
matters of this nature, a feasible solution would be to offer
a convicted person the choice.

Even Camus, considered one of the most articulate and
convincing opponents of the death penalty, has conceded such
a possibility, when the prisoner might not wish to accept his
suggested solution of hard labor. Seeking to avoid also the "vile
death" of the guillotine, he suggests that "an anesthetic that
would allow the condemned man to slip from sleep to death
(which would be left within his reach for at least a day so that
he could use it freely and would be administered to him in
another form if he were unwilling or weak of will) would ensure his elimination."[42]

Although this might, at first glance, be considered a Hob-
son's choice, once society has determined guilt for a serious
offense and decided that an ultimate penalty should be imposed,
it seems to be in the true liberal tradition that the definitive
decision of which penalty should be imposed might be left to
the person who has to bear the consequences. In general, the
idea of alternative punishments being at the discretion of the
convicted person is an integral part of normal penological practice, such as when imprisonment is given in lieu of payment
of a fine, or when certain conditions are stipulated in order
for probation or parole to take effect. Of course, the choice
between life and death is a much more crucial one to make
than are these other examples, but then this unavoidably results
from the more serious nature of the crime. In any event, if
it is a terrible choice to offer the accused, it is no less terrible
a choice to impose on a judge or jury.

It should be stressed that for such a change the whole penal
structure will have to be carefully analyzed so as to ensure that
only the most heinous crimes would elicit an ultimate penalty;
for as long as petty criminals are subject to draconian habitual
criminal laws with life imprisonment (as is the case in some
states) or, for example, drug trafficking entails an ultimate

penalty, then any system of alternate choices, including also a death penalty, would be problematical.

The mere fact of a choice would in fact obligate an overdue reassessment of all those life penalties now being handed down for less than the most serious crimes. Indeed, it may well be that the seemingly lax figures for release from prison of lifers are partially affected by the fact that at least some of these prisoners should never have received such a harsh penalty in the first place.[43]

THE WHOLE MANNER in which society perceives imprisonment per se is also in need of serious consideration. It seems that we are still bound by the positive approach adopted toward imprisonment in general when it was first introduced into the penal system within the last two hundred years. Imprisonment was welcomed as a means of minimizing the almost total reliance on other extreme penalties, ranging from a long list of capital offenses, through various forms of torture, to the relics of the Middle Ages in the form of the humiliations of the stocks and the pillory, or the later innovation, made feasible by colonial expansion, of transportation.

Michel Foucault notes that prior to the French Revolution the hierarchy of penalties used in France was "death, judicial torture rendering proof, penal servitude, flogging *amende honorable,* banishment."[44] Similarly, writing of historical developments in Britain, Michael Ignatieff notes that "before 1775, imprisonment was rarely used as a punishment for felony. At the Old Bailey . . . imprisonment accounted for no more than 2.3% of the judges' sentences in the years between 1770 and 1774. These terms of imprisonment were short—never longer than three years and usually a year or less—and they were inflicted on a narrow range of offenders."[45] In fact, initially "only minor offenders" received imprisonment—the punishments for the more serious felonies continued to be execution or transportation.

Negley Teeters writes of the Walnut Street Jail in Philadelphia. Erected in 1773, it was designated a full-scale penitentiary in 1789, becoming, according to Teeters, "the first penitentiary in the world."[46] Teeters stresses the historic significance
of this penitentiary; it served as a model for prisons elsewhere,
sparked a fundamental transformation in approaches to punishment, and acted as a catalyst for "a larger movement that was
to change completely the prevailing attitudes of society toward
the treatment of criminals." According to Teeters, "this movement envisaged the concept of imprisonment for convicted
felons to supplant the barbaric types of corporal punishment
that, for so many centuries, had been the lot of those who
wronged society. Imprisonment has been taken for granted for
so long that it is difficult for those living today to appreciate
how novel and even radical it seemed during the colonial
period" in America.[47] And it was humane. Even for the worst
offender there was, as Foucault writes, "one thing, at least,
to be respected when one punishes: his 'humanity.'"[48]

The concept of imprisonment was thus, in its time, a major advance in penology. It provided an alternative to the many
forms of corporeal punishments that were attracting increasing criticism, and that were also indirectly undermining the
working capacity of the criminal justice system, since the harshness of the punishments was fostering a leniency in convictions. Confronted with the range of severe punishments—death,
mutilation, humiliation, or banishment—for crimes that were
often minor, judges and juries preferred to bend their interpretation of the law in favor of the accused rather than contemplate the consequences of conviction. The stories are legion
of the efforts made to avoid meting out the full measure of
punishment provided by law. Benefit of clergy (providing for
adjudication in ecclesiastical courts in which there was no death
penalty) was extended not just to the clergy, but to all who
were literate, with the test of literacy undergoing constant erosion of standards to allow for easier qualification in the category.
Factual evidence was deliberately misinterpreted to favor the

accused, as when the value of stolen goods was deliberately misinterpreted to avoid the extreme penalty linked to the real value of the theft. Jury nullification was used to acquit when the evidence warranted a conviction, and an extravagant pardoning mechanism was used by the executive to frustrate any harsh penalty.[49]

The possibility of imposing a prison sentence opened up new punishment possibilities: justice could be meted out in more precise fashion, and the evasive fictions of judicial practice could be ended.

Not all the harsh penalties were removed—sentences such as death and transportation continued to be applied, but were now reserved for the more serious offenses. For the lesser offenses, the flexibility of differing durations allowed for a penal system attuned more closely to the nuances of the offense and the nature of the offender. It must be stressed that initially sentences were generally for short periods of time since resort was had still to the older penalties for the more serious crimes.[50] Under these circumstances the idea of imprisonment was widely and warmly welcomed, particularly by those in the forefront of the struggle for penal reform, as well as leading thinkers of liberal sentiment, active in many areas of seeking societal advance.

It was only in the continuation of the struggle for penal reform that reformers began to see in imprisonment a more comprehensive solution to the perplexities of punishment and the possibility of it becoming the critical axis around which almost all penal punishment would revolve. It was under these circumstances that longer terms of imprisonment were introduced and that the idea of life imprisonment was put forward as an alternative to the death penalty for some of the more serious crimes; indeed, imprisonment was seen as an alternative which would finally allow for the total abolition of the prevailing harsh penalties, including those of death and transportation.[51]

It was at this point that a sensitive liberal, such as Mill, would express his reservations as to the need for further penal reform. Indeed, just as today, there were those who were supposed to be the beneficiaries of the leniency in sentencing who gave vent to their opposition. According to Ignatieff, at least some of the prisoners preferred the supposedly more drastic measure of transportation over the innovative idea of imprisonment. He writes that prisoners "did not endure the change from transportation to long-term imprisonment with Heep-like masks of contrition. For them, the change abruptly ended the chance of a new start in Australia."[52] He also notes the added consequence of increased severity in sentences, resulting, mainly, from a stricter commutation policy than was applied in Australia because the public's fear of recidivism was focused more on those imprisoned in England than those transferred halfway across the world to Australia.

As a result of dissatisfaction with imprisonment, "from 1853 to 1858, the convict prisons were swept by strikes, sit-downs, group assaults on wardens, and escape attempts, all designed to bring pressure on the convict prison directors to eliminate sentence anomalies and restore transportation in place of imprisonment."[53] A key factor motivating many of the prisoners was their awareness of the terrible stigma attached to any person who had served a prison term, their subsequent difficulties in finding employment, their harassment by the police, and their rejection by the public.

It was in the middle of the nineteenth century before imprisonment became the focus of the penal system.

> Between 1848–1863, imprisonment which had once been used for summary offenses and petty felonies, was transformed into a punishment for all the major crimes, except murder. . . . As a result, the authorities were for the first time faced with the task of administering long-term sentences. Until the late 1840s, the longest sentences in English prisons were three years. Most offenders served six months or less. Lord John Russell was only repeating a commonplace when he said in 1837 that a ten-year

imprisonment would be "a punishment worse than death."
By the mid 1850s sentences of such a length had become
common as replacements for the abandoned sentences of
transportation.[54]

In order to understand the reason for the increasing
popularity of imprisonment, two key factors must be borne
in mind. First, imprisonment reflected the growing belief in
the possibility of rehabilitation. It was felt that if judicious use
could be made of the control that society exercised over the
prisoners in confinement, then they could be inculcated with
those values—fear of God, pride in work, respect for law, consideration for others—that would enable them to undergo a
deep-seated change in their nature and to fit them for the role
of law-abiding citizens that awaited them on discharge. A subtle change came over the perception that people had of the
prison system—prisons were to be places not just for punishing
criminals, but, in line with both liberal humanitarianism and
rigorous science, places for reforming the inmates. Prayer and
work in the early stages, and therapy and counselling later on,
were to provide a rationale for the extensive use of prisons;
a positive purpose lay behind any outwardly harsh conditions.

Thus in the Pennsylvania prison system, the influence of
the Quakers led to conditions of solitary confinement, best
suited to the prayers, meditation, and reflection considered
essential prerequisites in the rehabilitation process. Perceived
harshness in the prison system could always be explained as
an integral part of the framework required to reform the
prisoners prior to their return to society. Not pain for the body,
but solace for the soul, was the underlying philosophy of
penology.[55]

Second, a more subtle and complex process was at work,
which related to the intertwining manner in which inverse
developments took place simultaneously in the process of adjudication on the one hand and punishment on the other.
Whereas formerly the court system operated largely *in camera,*

beyond the scrutiny of the public, and the punishment took place openly—in the form of stocks and pillory, branding and mutilation, and public executions—in the early modern age, it was the court system that was increasingly exposed to public view, and the punishments that were assigned to the hidden intercises of societal institutions, particularly the prison. Prevailing liberal sentiments found expression both in the open operation of the court and in the prohibition on the public expressing its baser side in vengeful and vicious conduct at the scene of the punishment. Foucault describes how punishment ceased to be the "spectacle" it had been and became

> the most hidden part of the penal process. This has several consequences; it leaves the domain of more or less everyday perception and enters that of abstract consciousness. . . . As a result, justice no longer takes public responsibility for the violence that is bound up with its practice. . . . Now the scandal and the light are to be distributed differently; it is the conviction itself that marks the offender with the unequivocally negative sign; the publicity has shifted to the trial. . . . It is ugly to be punishable, but there is no glory in punishing. Hence that double system of protection that justice has set up between itself and the punishment it imposes. Those who carry out the penalty tend to become an autonomous sector; justice is relieved of responsibility for it by a bureaucratic concealment of the penalty itself.[56]

Foucault in fact merges the two trends—of a desire for rehabilitation and a prohibition on public spectacle—into a mutually reinforcing process. He writes of a "theoretical disavowal" by judges:

> Do not imagine that the sentences that we judges pass are activated by a desire to punish; they are intended to convert, reclaim, "cure"; a technique of improvement represses in the penalty, the strict expiation of evil-doing, and

relieves the magistrate of the demeaning task of punishing. In modern justice and in the part of those who dispense it there is a shame in punishing, which does not always preclude zeal. This sense of shame is constantly growing; the psychologists and the minor civil servants of moral orthopaedics proliferate on the wound it leaves.[57]

Just as in the death penalty the intent becomes to eliminate all extraneous pains, so, in the prison system, the emphasis is not on the infliction of pain, but the deprivation of rights; not on the torment of the body, but the reflections of the soul; not on the humiliation of the condemned person, but on the reform of the future citizen—and so "a whole army of technicians took over from the executioner, the immediate anatomist of pain: wardens, doctors, chaplains, psychiatrists, psychologists, educationalists; by their very presence near the prisoner, they sing the praises that the law needs; they reassure it that the body and pain are not the ultimate objects of its punitive action."[58]

Let me sum up these interlocking trends in order to assess how they affect our attitude to, and our knowledge of, life imprisonment today.

At the outset, imprisonment was a significant breakthrough in penology, providing an alternative to harsh corporeal punishments, including death and torture, for a host of crimes, including the most petty. It was specifically for these latter crimes—the lesser felonies—that prison was, for the most part, originally used. The continuation of reform of the penal law led to the most serious crimes being eventually incorporated into the reform process, and the flexibility of a prison system allowed for what seemed to be a mere quantitative increase in the length of imprisonment. Yet, at some point—certainly when life imprisonment was introduced—this became a *qualitative* difference. The difference was, however, little noted, the increment of extra time being casually absorbed, particulary in the light of the desire to diminish the use of capital and corporal punishments, the hope that increasing scientific knowledge of human behavior provided for reform, and the ignorance of prison conditions arising out of the diminution of public participation in the "spectacle" of punishment. The unique aspects of life imprisonment were basically ignored. It was, for the most part, considered merely a form of imprisonment, not uniquely severe, nor similar in its severity to the forms of punishment it had replaced.

These factors are not of historic importance alone, for they continue to affect the manner in which the life sentence is perceived, whether by the public at large, by judges and juries, by legislative and executive bodies, or by academic researchers and theoreticians.

A S N O T E D , official statistics showing the number of life prisoners released are often greeted with dismay, and tend to foster further calls for the death penalty. But what happens to the majority of those sentenced to life? Some die in prison, some commit suicide, some go insane. Official figures on these categories are not readily available, and almost no research has been done in this area.

In 1924 Lewis Lawes, a former warden of Sing Sing Prison and president of the American Prison Association, wrote that "the number of prisoners under sentence of life or twenty years to life who have become insane is astonishingly large. In New York during the period of eight years more prisoners of this class were declared insane than were commuted or pardoned."[59] (11.32% were declared insane, 10.29% were commuted or pardoned.)

More recent studies of the prison system, both research projects and theoretical presentations, have ignored these issues. There is an urgent need for accurate and updated material on the final fate of those serving life sentences. How many of them undergo deterioration—physically, emotionally, mentally— to the extent that their incarceration constitutes a real violation of their dignity, of their individuality, of their sanity, of their will to live? If many in fact do, why should a life sentence be so facilely accepted as being more lenient, more desirable, more humane, than an early death sentence?

What little is known in the United States is also extremely confused, and depends to a large extent on speculative interpretations of incomplete official figures. In the absence of solid academic research, it is the formal figures provided by governmental organizations, such as the Department of Justice through its Bureau of Justice Statistics, that provide the basis of the information which forms the perception of both the general public and the professionals involved in the administration of criminal justice. These statistics should be submitted to careful scrutiny, for the actual picture conjured up by a superficial reference to them may be vastly different from empirical reality. The statistics themselves are often a unique and valuable mine of information, but they are also circumscribed by the limitations of inadequate knowledge.

In 1984 and 1985, the Bureau of Justice Statistics submitted separate reports, entitled *Prison Admissions and Releases,* covering the years 1981 and 1982, respectively. The statistics given cover about two-thirds of the states, the other third not having supplied the requested information.

The report for 1981 discusses the time served. It states that "murderers served a median of 63 months. About two-thirds of the murderers released served seven years or less. Approximately one of every seven murderers . . . served more than ten years."[60] Discussing release figures for those serving life sentences, the report states that "1,996 offenders were admitted with a life sentence and 1,165 were released from prison after having served time on a life sentence. Of the 1,165 releases, 844 were first releases." ("First releases" are described as those "experiencing their first exit from prison," and are contrasted with those "who may have served prior prison time on the same sentence," presumably, those having returned for a parole violation. In essence, then, the latter, smaller figure, is the key figure, and the figure which the report uses for some of its more important calculations.)

For 1982, the report states that the median time served for murder was 69 months. Focusing on life sentences and actual time served, the report concludes that "a life sentence rarely means that the offender will spend the rest of his life in prison." During 1982, among reporting jurisdictions, there were 2,223 persons with a life sentence admitted to prison and 980 released. "Of those released, 612 were first releases for whom time served data were available. . . . The median time served on a life sentence was 5 years and 9 months and the mean time served was 7 years and 4 months. Nearly a quarter of those released for the first time on a life sentence served 3 years or less and nearly three-fifths served 7 years or less."[61]

These figures, at face value, seem to indicate an extremely lenient approach on the part of pardoning and parole authorities, to the extent that life imprisonment seems to be no more than a mere shallow outer shell. However, the figures are very deceiving and distort the true picture. The deception and the distortion arise from a number of factors. First, the averages given pertain only to those who are released and *do not take into account the period of imprisonment of those who are not released.* Of course, the report purports to deal only with those released, not with all prisoners, but this not so subtle difference is not always recognized, especially in short reports by the mass media. And it is such reports that lead to complacency about life imprisonment by so many concerned for a moderate sentencing policy and, alternatively, anger by those calling for more severe sentencing. The conclusion of the report, that life sentences are rarely served to the full, also fuels this sentiment. The figures cited simply do not support this conclusion. The figures on which it is based refer only to those released, and not to the whole population of life prisoners.

On the contrary, the figures seem to raise a prima facie presumption that about one thousand life prisoners who enter the prison system each year will never be released. Assuming that the figures remain more or less constant over the years, it seems that about 2,000 persons are admitted for life per year and less than a thousand are released. The discrepancy in the numbers raises a strong possibility that about half of the lifers are not released. Even if there has been a likely increase in the number of admissions for life imprisonment over the years, which would make the difference between the numbers of intake and exit much less, the discrepancy would still be several hundred.

Thus, although it is true that for those who are released the average period of time served is very short, the key fact for understanding the nature of life imprisonment is the data that suggests that as much as half of the life prisoners do not enter into these calculations at all. They will, it seems, die in prison. The announced figures of release create the false impression that most lifers are released after only a few years. The reality is vastly different.

The short time served for most of those who are released inevitably raises further questions. Why were people who were given life sentences released so soon? Or, perhaps, if the question is asked in a different form, its answer becomes more apparent: Why were people who were released after just a few years given life imprisonment in the first place? Was it because of a mandatory punishment scale the court was unable to avoid? Was it because of an overly severe sentencing policy by the trial judges? The differential between the sentence imposed by the court and time served by the prisoner raises serious questions as to either the sentencing policies of the courts or the release policies of the parole board, or both.

Part of the discrepancy can certainly be attributed to the fact that life sentences were given for a number of nonviolent offenses, such as burglary, larceny, auto theft, and forgery. These, however, amount to less than three percent of the total of life sentences. More significant is the slightly more than thirteen percent of life sentences that were imposed for drug offenses. Unfortunately, although the report provides a breakdown of figures by offense for admissions, it does not do so for releases of those originally sentenced to a life term. Despite this lack of information, by educated guess it certainly seems likely that most of those released after short periods of time had been sentenced for nonviolent crimes, certainly not for crimes for which the death penalty might have been considered as an alternative.

A further problem in understanding the data on releases is that the more precise categorization by period of time done for 1981 stops at those who served over ten years. Although fifteen percent of all murderers were released after serving ten years, there is no further breakdown indicating what period of time they actually served—which might involve periods of twenty, thirty, forty, or fifty years.

In any case, figures that are available for two large states, California and Pennsylvania, reveal a picture vastly different from the superficial one presented in the aggregate by the report of the Department of Justice. In a recent article, John Conrad describes the situation in two maximum security prisons in California:

> At San Quentin there are 1,075 men serving life terms, with 112 more who are serving life without possibility of parole, in a total population of 3,081. The situation is about the same at Folsom; there are 820 lifers, and 124 Life Without Possibility of Parole Convicts, in a total population of 3,276. No one can compute a median time-to-be-served for such populations. Under new California laws, murder in the first degree requires a life sentence without parole, eligibility beginning at year 16 after commitment. Life Without Possibility of Parole is supposed to mean Life Without Possibility of Release and in past years it has meant just that.[62]

In Pennsylvania official sources provide a similar description of the situation. Of a total of 14,400 prisoners in state prisons at the end of 1985, the number of life prisoners was

1,700. During the seven years of the present administration, Governor Thornburgh had granted release from prison to only seven prisoners who had once been serving a life sentence, one of whom had spent 42 years in prison. As of the end of 1984, there were two prisoners who had spent more than 40 years in prison, four more who had spent more than 35 years, a further six who had been confined for more than 30 years, and another four confined for over 25 years. The next two categories showed 28 prisoners having spent 20–24 years in prison, and 84 having spent 15–19 years.[63] The drop in the numbers for the longer period of time is not a consequence only of release, but also of death. It is believed that about five to ten life prisoners die each year while in prison in Pennsylvania.

Of course, it could be argued that the present increase in lifers in Pennsylvania prisons is a consequence of the strict policy adopted by the present Governor, who is at the end of his second term and ineligible for reelection. Possibly a new governor will act to reduce the number of life prisoners, but, of course, there can be no guarantee of such a policy in the future. In any event, a drastic change in policy would be further proof of how arbitrary the whole system has become, how much dependent on personal decisions, and how capriciously a person's fate, in a matter as serious as his future liberty is concerned, is handled.

Given the vast numbers of people sentenced to life imprisonment (over twenty times as many as are given the death penalty, and over ten times as many as are convicted of murder), and given the fact that some of them do in fact die in prison, one would have imagined that both the severity of the sentence and the numbers involved would have led to academic research, public concern, and legal challenges.

It seems to me that the legal challenges here range from unconstitutionality per se (perhaps far-fetched for the moment, but a possibility in the future), through the issue of disproportionality (as already decided in one case in West Virginia, based on its own state constitution) and mandatory (even as an alternative to capital punishment) to discriminatory and arbitrary practices (as might emerge from a closer analysis of the figures than the extant reports of the Bureau of Justice Statistics provide).[64]

What has prevented such a critical approach till now are the perceptions of most people that the death penalty is uniquely severe and that nearly all life prisoners are paroled, perceptions that are shared by both proponents and opponents of the death penalty. These attitudes have had direct and far-reaching implications for legislative enactments and judicial decisons. In the United States, they have created an anomalous situation. On the one hand, the Court has been at pains to stipulate that there should be no mandatory capital punishment, but at the same time has placed rigorous strictures on any judicial discretion that might be considered arbitrary or capricious. On the other hand, the Court has complacently accepted mandatory life imprisonment, not only in cases where it is an alternative to capital punishment, but in other instances as well in which arbitrariness is rife, such as its use in "habitual offenders statutes," which require life imprisonment for a third conviction, often regardless of the type of violation or the time span between them.

Although the U.S. Supreme Court has laid down strict rules against any arbitrary decision-making in respect to the death penalty, it has failed to lay down any similar guidelines with regard to life imprisonment, which, even if not considered unique, is still widely regarded as being a severe penalty.

Of no less significance is the fact that civil rights activists and lawyers representing defendants in life imprisonment cases have only rarely attempted to raise constitutional issues similar to those used to attack the death penalty.[65] Even then, the range of issues is limited, for instance, to the punishment's disproportionality relative to the offense committed (as in habitual offender cases), or when it involves a denial of the prospects of parole (the very condition sometimes adopted when capital punishment is abolished); rarely, however, in the context of the punishment, in and of itself, being cruel, nor of the arbitrariness in its imposition constituting an infringement of due process of law, nor of discriminatory practices. In particular, little attempt has been made to at least try to apply some of the logic of the rationale in capital punishment cases to life imprisonment cases.

The Supreme Court's approach to these issues presents a further paradox. On the one hand, in capital cases the Supreme Court is adamant in its refusal to investigate whether capricious and arbitrary decisions characterize the total criminal justice system, outside of the trial itself (from police and prosecutorial discretion through the pardoning and commuting power). It has limited its scrutiny only to the actual trial. On the other hand, though not concerning itself with capriciousness and arbitrariness as to the manner and the occasions in which life imprisonment is meted out, the Court has not hesitated, in several judgments, to refer to the pardoning machinery in order to reflect on the prospects of a long-term prisoner being released through a commutation of his sentence, using data of a type that it has shunned outright in the case of the death penalty. In fact, it may well be argued that the casual complacency evinced so often in regard to life sentences may well be based on the assumption that these are generally not fully implemented, but are reduced through the intervention of some sort of pardoning or commuting mechanism, "facts" which are often brought to the knowledge of the courts.

Generally, this willingness to consider postconviction remedies works to the disadvantage of the prisoner, since the courts often operate on the assumption that he will eventually be released, though this is often more a case of a casual acceptance of the conventional wisdom than a precise evaluation of empirical data. Even so, this is possibly a preferable situation to that pertaining in capital punishment cases, for which the Supreme Court has outright refused to give consideration to the postconviction stage.

Any analysis of either of these penalties should give attention to the other. In the next two chapters, the legal position of these two ultimate penalties in the United States will be discussed, and, when relevant, examples from one area will be used to illuminate and evaluate approaches adopted in the other. If both are ultimate penalties, similar standards should apply. In reality, the existing inconsistencies in each area seem only to be magnified when viewed from the perspective of the other area.

II

MATTERS OF
LIFE AND DEATH

■

4

THE ARBITRARY
"ARBITRARY" RULE

I N 1 9 6 8 , for the first time in the modern history of the
United States, not a single execution took place.[1] That same
year, the Supreme Court heard for one of the first times in
its history a case in which the unique nature of the death penalty was the key issue, *Witherspoon* v. *Illinois*.[2] The specific
question was whether abolitionists could be excluded from a
jury in a capital murder case, and the guarded answer was that
they could not unless they would refuse under any circumstances to vote for a death penalty.

Several years before, Gerald Gottlieb had written a pioneering article in which he had suggested that a strong case could
be made for declaring the death penalty unconstitutional;[3] and
several years later, in 1972, the Supreme Court, in the momentous *Furman* v. *Georgia* decision, held that the death penalty,
as applied in an arbitrary and capricious manner, was unconstitutional.[4] This factor—of arbitrariness and capriciousness—has
become a key to the Court's interpretation of the Eighth Amendment's proscription against "cruel and unusual" punishment,
and the Fourteenth Amendment's prescription for "due process of law."

The *Furman* case culminated a well-planned campaign by
abolitionists to extend the civil rights benefits attained in the
1960s, both in the realm of the rights of minorities (it was
claimed that the death penalty was being imposed and applied
in a discriminatory manner), and the rights of criminals.[5] The
case serves till this day as a legal precedent. Although originally hailed as a definitive decision which would end the death
penalty in the United States, within four years, in the *Gregg*
v. *Georgia* and related cases, it had been reinterpreted in a

manner which allowed for the reintroduction of the death penalty under certain specified conditions.[6] Two years later, the moratorium on executions was over.

Since the *Furman* and *Gregg* decisions, the opposing camps of abolitionists and retentionists have carried on ceaseless battle, besieging the courts with an array of innovative and imaginative arguments. But running through the litigation are the themes of the uniqueness of the death penalty and the need to prevent arbitrary and capricious decision-making because of this uniqueness. I have already suggested that the first theme is inaccurate; it would seem that the second is either inadequate or unattainable.

One of the classic critiques of the death penalty in the United States is the work of Charles Black, who has suggested that one of the chief deficiencies in the imposition of the death penalty is the inevitability of its capricious and arbitrary implementation.[7] Yet the Supreme Court, in dealing with this issue, has done so without due regard for the many examples that Black gives of how inevitable these factors are at *all* stages of the criminal proceedings.

Starting with *Furman,* the judicial scrutiny of capital punishment has focused on some of the issues that Black deals with. Yet whereas Black regards arbitrariness and capriciousness as constituting an inevitable concomitant preventing any just disposition of capital cases, the Supreme Court has sought to lay down guidelines for how capital punishment may be applied in a manner compatible with due process of law, in addition to complying with the cruel and unusual provision.

A perusal of some of the leading cases will show the complexity of the issue as well as the unwillingness of the Court to confront the ultimate implications of its own emphasis on avoiding arbitrariness.

One of the paradoxes of the approach of the Supreme Court to the death penalty is that, though focusing on the need to avoid arbitrariness in the use of the death penalty, its decisions have often been so ambiguous as to lead to inevitable arbitrariness, which the Court is almost powerless to control despite initial efforts to hold the line.

Part of the confusion arises from the fact that there is a clear gap between the desire of the various legislatures giving expression to what is often perceived as the people's will (as reflected in public opinion polls and, occasionally, referenda) to have capital punishment, and the demands of expert opinion expressed by professional people—criminologists, penologists, and the like—who seem to be largely, though certainly not unanimously, against capital punishment.[8] A pattern of judicial pronouncement and legislative reaction has developed, with each leading Supreme Court decision being greeted by a spate of legislation as the various state legislatures attempt to mold a legal framework to satisfy the conditions laid down by each latest ruling. Some of this legislation has then, in turn, been subjected to the critical scrutiny of the Supreme Court to determine whether it has abided by the ground rules laid down by the Court in its earlier decisions. This process is further complicated by the fact that some of the key decisions have been rendered by a divided Court, making it difficult to know the *ratio decidendi,* since the majority justices often agree only on the ultimate result but not on the reasoning that occasioned it. This is especially so in the first case, *Furman* v. *Georgia,* in which the essential rationale behind the Court's decision was lost in the competing views of five concurring and four dissenting opinions, without any plurality decision to balance the disarray.

There were many who felt then that the Supreme Court had taken a firm stand for total abolition of the death penalty. Thus, a leading opponent of capital punishment, Hugo Bedau, optimistically declared: "We will not see another execution in this nation in this century."[9] However, others believed that the overall thrust of the Court's decision was merely to avoid the unfairness of the way in which the death penalty had been operating till then. Indeed, some legislatures took the severe strictures on arbitrariness and capriciousness in the implementation of the death penalty to be an open invitation to lay down a mandatory death sentence as the best way of avoiding an unfair sentencing policy. Others adopted the approach of spelling out the specific aggravating and mitigating factors which the court of first instance was to consider before imposing a penalty.

Some, but not all, of the uncertainties of the *Furman* decision were resolved a few years later, when, in the *Gregg, Woodson, Roberts, Profitt,* and *Jurek* cases,[10] the Court found, again in split decisions (though this time with clearer groupings), that the approach of mandatory punishment was unconstitutional, but that of specified aggravating and mitigating factors was acceptable.

The law in Georgia incorporated basic provisions which seemed the most accurate in satisfying the Court's aims.

> In short, Georgia's new sentencing procedures require as a prerequisite to the imposition of the death penalty, specific jury findings as to the circumstances of the crime or the character of the defendant. Moreover, to guard further against a situation comparable to that presented in *Furman,* the Supreme Court of Georgia compares each death sentence with the sentences imposed on similarly situated defendants to ensure that the sentence of death in a particular case is not disproportionate.[11]

Basically, the Court strongly suggested that future legislation should contain the four provisions of the law in Georgia: a two-stage hearing (allowing evidence and argument in regard to the penalty), an automatic review of sentence in an appeal court (allowing comparison of the punishment with other similar cases), a consideration of a clearly delineated list of aggravating and mitigating factors, and directions to the jury.

Since a key aspect of the *Furman* case had been the criticism of the biased manner in which the death penalty was being used to the disadvantage of deprived minority groups, the Georgia statute was considered to have eliminated the possibility of a deliberately selective or highly capricious application, by means, *inter alia,* of a postconviction sentencing stage during which mitigating and aggravating factors could be adduced in evidence, and which would be subject to review of a higher court.

In contrast, the North Carolina and Louisiana statutes were struck down, on the same day and in parallel judgments, as they provided for a mandatory death penalty. The fact that in Louisiana the jury was informed of the alternative possibilities of a conviction for lesser offenses was not considered a sufficient ground for recognizing flexibility in the jury's decision; on the contrary, it was seen as a potential source of arbitrary decisions.

The Court seems to have been seeking a golden mean between arbitrary and capricious decisions, without any guiding principles, and a uniform, obligatory penalty, without any discretion. Thus, in *Gregg,* the Court, speaking through the plurality of Justices Stewart, Powell, and Stevens, held that where discretion is afforded a sentencing body on a matter so grave as the determination of whether a human life should be taken or spared, that discretion must be suitably directed and limited to minimize the risk of wholly arbitrary and capricious action.

Yet controlling arbitrary actions has not been easy. The Supreme Court has not been able to maintain a consistent pattern of decision-making within its own judgments, let alone satisfactorily monitor the daily operations of the lower courts, all of them working under different laws.

Some decisions are arbitrary in that they result in different sentencing for the very same crime. Occasionally, because of plea bargaining, an accomplice turning state's evidence is given a lighter sentence than his fellow criminals. It is true that it is sometimes possible to apportion responsibility in a differential manner, for instance, assigning major blame to the trigger-person in an armed robbery, and lesser blame to the accomplices, especially when an accomplice was not physically present at the moment the killing was committed and was not aware of the intention to use armed force. Such a situation arose in the *Lockett* case;[12] only the differential sentencing led to the trigger-person being given the lighter sentence! On appeal the Supreme Court did vacate the death sentence given to the accomplice Sandra Lockett, who had been waiting in the getaway car, but did so without addressing the specific problem of a minor accomplice; for the Court held that the law under which she was sentenced was unconstitutional as it did not sufficiently hew to the guidelines set out in the *Gregg* decision. It was some years later, in the *Enmund* case, that the Court dealt directly with a similar situation of a death sentence received by a minor accomplice.[13] In this case, however, the trigger-person also received the death penalty. The Court held, in a five-to-four decision, that in a case of felony murder (a killing committed in the course of a robbery) the death sentence should not generally be imposed on a minor accomplice, such as the driver of a getaway car in a robbery, which had been Enmund's role.

There have also been cases in which the Court has allowed different sentences for several defendants, even though their responsibility seemed to have been substantially the same.[14] If the Court is unable to avoid arbitrariness in sentencing accomplices in the same case, how can it possibly control for arbitrariness in different cases with different judges, within different jurisdictions, in different states?

Indeed, after years of trying to hold the line, the Court seems finally to have relented and, in the most recent cases, to have foregone any serious attempt to impose strict standards or to prevent arbitrary differences as to who receives the death penalty. In *Pulley* v. *Harris,* for instance, the Court allowed the death penalty to stand despite a lack of proportionality review.[15]

Nevertheless, despite the Court's stance in these latest cases, the precedents of *Furman* and *Gregg* still hold; they have not been overruled or rejected. The aim of avoiding arbitrariness and capriciousness, the idea of enforcing super due process, because of what the Court holds to be the unique severity of the death penalty, is still its reigning philosophy and the essential thrust of its operating guidelines. It still wishes to avoid the two extremes of mandatory death sentences on the one hand, and unfettered and unfair discretion on the other.

Several articles have been written in recent years spelling out the increasing failure of the Court to maintain its own standards.[16] Perhaps, as some have suggested, it has failed because of being inundated with appeals, raising a host of new and innovative interpretations of constitutional rights, and being involved in the unpleasant business of frantic, last-minute pleas for stays of execution, in a manner which it did not foresee and cannot accept with equanimity. The frustration of the Court is best expressed in the intemperate language of Chief Justice Burger when castigating the lawyers for unflinchingly pursuing every legal possibility to save their clients' lives.[17]

In effect the trials and tribulations of the Court may have been foreseen, for although the Court is clearly capable of ensuring the one aim—by the simple process of striking down any statute that has mandatory punishment or what seems to it, as in the *Lockett* case, to be akin to a mandatory rule—the position in regard to reasoned discretion is far more difficult; for here the Court is permitting a pattern of behavior that is notoriously difficult to control.

I do not intend to go into all the vicissitudes of the Court's decisions—others have traced out the zig-zag patterns—but to focus on a few key examples. Although the tenor of some of the recent articles suggests that the Court did valiantly attempt to maintain control until about 1983, when the *Zant, Pulley,* and other cases exposed its inability and unwillingness to enforce its standards,[18] the fragility of its logical position was apparent from the beginning.

However, it seems that it was the *Lockett* case where the framework started to pull at the seams and come apart. Faced with a relatively straightforward case in which a minor accomplice had, on the evidence of the major accomplice, received a death penalty, the Court ignored this issue completely, and instead held the statute itself unconstitutional; whereas, in many respects, the law actually seemed to have been a satisfactory attempt by the Ohio legislature to adapt their law to the *Gregg* guidelines. More important, in doing so the Court was drawn into emphasizing the need for individualized analysis of the defendant—an individualization that seemed to be in conflict with the *Gregg* guidelines, and which seemed to be exactly what, for that very reason, the Ohio law was trying to avoid.

The need for an individual approach was actually well put by Chief Justice Burger.

> Given that the imposition of death by public authority is so profoundly different from all other penalties, we cannot avoid the conclusion that an individual decision is essential in capital cases. The need for treating each defendant in a capital case with that degree of respect due to the uniqueness of the individual is far more important than in non-capital cases. . . . There is no perfect procedure for deciding in which cases governmental authority should be used to impose death. But a statute that prevents the sentencer in all capital cases from giving independent mitigating weight to aspects of the defendant's character and record and to circumstances of the offense preferred in mitigation creates the risk that the death penalty will be imposed in spite of factors which may call for a less severe penalty. When the choice is between life and death the risk is unacceptable and incompatible with the commands of the Eighth and Fourteenth Amendment.

He concluded that

> The Ohio death penalty statute does not permit the type of individualized consideration of mitigating factors we now hold to be required by the Eighth and Fourteenth Amendments in capital cases.[19]

It would seem that this emphasis on individualized consideration (however hedged and hemmed in by legislative guidelines) undermined the very rule of avoiding arbitrary and capricious decisions which the Court had been at such pains to spell out in the earlier *Furman* and *Gregg* decisions. One could go further and claim that the Ohio legislative approach actually accorded closely with the principles laid down in these cases, by insisting that any discretion would be within clearly-defined limits that avoided capriciousness (viz., that, firstly, the murder was committed in aggravating circumstances, and secondly, that three individual factors had to be considered to see if there were mitigating factors to offset the aggravating circumstances). In fact, the Ohio legislature had changed an earlier draft of the death penalty in order to make it amenable to what it considered to be the essence of the *Gregg* decision, which was handed down while the Ohio legislature was still in the midst of its debate.

This approach was actually forcefully stated by Justice White in a separate judgment in *Lockett*. Noting that he personally saw no objection to a mandatory sentence when "the defendant had been found guilty beyond a reasonable doubt of committing a deliberate, unjustified killing," he went on to forecast that

the effect of the Court's decision today will be to compel constitutionally a restoration of the state of affairs at the time *Furman* was decided, where the death penalty is imposed so erratically. . . . By requiring as a matter of constitutional law that sentencing authorities be permitted to consider and in their discretion to act upon any and all mitigating circumstances, the Court permits them to refuse to impose the death penalty no matter what the circumstances of the crime. This invites a return to the pre-*Furman* days when the death penalty was generally reserved for those very few for whom society has least consideration.[20]

Justice White concurred in the reversal of the conviction for other reasons, namely, that the petitioner had not actually killed and had only been an accomplice in a felony-murder. He noted that in an investigation of the 363 reported executions for homicide submitted to the courts since 1954 "only eight clearly involved individuals who did not personally commit the murder. Moreover, at least some of these eight executions involved individuals who intended to cause the death of the victim. Furthermore, the last such execution occurred in 1955."[21]

Justice White's criticism of the plurality decision seems apt. The facts of the case in *Lockett* (the unusual situation of an accomplice being sentenced to death in a case where one of the principal offenders had turned state witness) provided an opportunity to overturn the conviction without negating the Ohio law *in toto*. The *Lockett* case was particularly disturbing in that the differential between the accomplices stemmed not from a considered deliberation by the jury, but from a prosecutorial decision to enter into a plea bargaining arrangement.

The principal accused, who had handled the gun and used it fatally in the course of an armed robbery, plea bargained for a noncapital offense; his evidence was then used as the basis for incriminating his three fellow accomplices, one of whom—the defendant, Sandra Lockett—had only been sitting in the getaway car. Indeed, even this fact was in dispute, as the defendant claimed not to have had any knowledge that a robbery was about to take place. She claimed that she had presumed that the other occupants of the car had merely gone shopping. However, she failed to provide any evidence to support this contention, firstly, because the two other accomplices (who were called to the witness-box) refused to testify to this fact, on the basis of their Fifth Amendment right against self-incrimination; and secondly, because she herself had been dissuaded by her mother, against the advice of her lawyer, from taking the witness stand. The reasons for Lockett's attitude are not known, but it might be noted that one of the accomplices was her brother, who had been at the scene of the crime; he, too, was found guilty and sentenced to death. The question of plea bargaining as violating the Supreme Court standards of disproportionate arbitrariness was not raised in the *Lockett* case.

However, it would be difficult to find another case where disproportionate, arbitrary, and unfair sentencing was so blatant as in this one. The problematic nature of the plea bargaining system emerges even more clearly in the light of the fact that Lockett herself turned down three offers of a plea bargain by the prosecutor, the final one when the trial was already in progress. (The legal problem of criminal intent, in which a lesser accomplice is found guilty of a crime for which the actual culprit was not even charged, also raises serious questions which lie outside the ambit of this chapter but have been adequately discussed by others elsewhere.)[22]

It is true that several years later the Court, in *Enmund*,[23] directly addressed a similar set of facts and overthrew the death penalty imposed on the lesser accomplice. But larger questions still remain. How did Sandra Lockett ever reach the stage where she was condemned to die? What was the nature of the deliberations of the jury in reaching such a conclusion? And beyond that, and prior to that, what was the nature of the considerations of the prosecution in making such a deal? Did they insist perhaps on the death penalty out of anger at her, occasioned by her refusal to enter into a plea bargain, thereby causing the forfeiture of a conviction of the major accomplice?

Further, how often has prosecutional power been used to make a plea bargain, which a priori undermines any possibility of avoiding overall arbitrariness? This very argument was raised in the *Gregg* case by the defense, but was rejected out of hand, together with related arguments that arbitrariness was inherently inevitable because of the total inability to control for discretionary practices at three key stages: when the prosecutor decides at the pretrial stage whom to indict for a capital offense (in contrast to others who are charged with a lesser offense), when the jury at the sentencing stage debates, in secret deliberations, the desired penalty, and, at the posttrial stage, when the executive decides whether or not to exercise its pardoning and commutation power.

The plurality opinion, consisting of Justices Stewart, Powell, and Stevens, responded to these weighty arguments, but did so, almost disdainfully, partly in a short footnote. The dissenting justices, Marshall and Brennan (who oppose the death penalty in principle and *in toto),* ignored the issue, perhaps because they did not wish to discuss what they considered extraneous issues. It seems to me that the Court's reasoning in the plurality opinion requires further examination, and that the defense arguments, particularly concerning the posttrial stage, contain basic ideas that deserve further utilization. The arguments themselves and the footnote responses have, in any case, been almost totally ignored in the many academic responses to the *Gregg* decision.

The plurality opinion held that "the existence of these discretionary stages is not determinative of the issues before us," since in no case was a specific decision to impose the death penalty being made. All that was happening was that an "actor in the criminal justice system (prosecutor, jury, governor) makes a decision which may remove a defendant from consideration as a candidate for the death penalty."[24] Any discretion exercised by anyone other than judges was seen as being irrelevant to the question of whether the punishment had been imposed in an arbitrary manner.

The essence of the defense argument in *Gregg* is succinctly set out in the plurality decision of Justices Stewart, Powell, and Stevens.

> The state prosecutor has unfettered authority to select those persons whom he wishes to prosecute for a capital offense and to plea bargain with them.

> At the trial the jury may choose to convict a defendant of a lesser included offense rather than find him guilty of a

crime punishable by death, even if the evidence would support a capital verdict.

A defendant who is convicted and sentenced to die may have his sentence commuted by the Governor of the State and the Georgia Board of Pardons and Paroles.[25]

The Court held that none of these examples of discretion was relevant, for the key decision being made in these examples was not whether to impose the death penalty, but, through using discretion, whether to remove a person from possible subjection to the death penalty. Specifically, the plurality opinion argued that "*Furman,* in contrast, dealt with the decision to impose the death sentence on a specific individual who had been convicted of a capital offense."[26]

What the plurality opinion seems to have failed to appreciate is that arbitrary decision-making cannot be assessed in a vacuum, but only in relation to other decisions being made in similar cases. Capriciousness and arbitrariness are determined not only by examining who is sentenced to death, but also who is *not,* including when the latter outcome is a consequence of a prosecutorial decision to remove the defendant *ab initio* from the purview of a possible death sentence. Capriciousness in imposing the death penalty can only be gauged by looking also at those on whom it is *not* imposed—whatever the reason, at whatever stage.

Further, the Court stressed that it had never intended to deny the chance of a condemned person's receiving mercy. But this also was not the defense argument; what the defense *was* arguing was that the consequences of dispensing mercy through commutation could well be to create an arbitrariness that might have been originally controlled for at the trial stage.

The issue the court was asked to address on this score was whether in the exercise of mercy through clemency, it might transpire that the only people actually being executed were members of a capriciously selected group, the very result that the Court was determined to avoid at the trial stage. And, of course, the issue is not whether or not people get condemned to death (important as this factor is), but *whether or not people get executed.*

A reading of the Court's reasoning here suggests that its conern was limited to the operation of trial proceedings at the sentencing stage, without displaying any interest in the final consequences. Otherwise, how could the Court claim that it had avoided the evils of arbitrariness and capriciousness merely by requiring clear rules for sentencing, if its efforts at fairness and the avoidance of discrimination were to be frustrated by racist district attorneys arbitrarily and capriciously deciding who was to be subjected to a capital trial, or prejudiced governors arbitrarily and capriciously deciding who was to have their sentence commuted?

But the real thrust of the attitude of Justices Stewart, Powell, and Stevens is to be found not in the text of their judgment, but in a footnote reference, where they casually note that "the petitioner's argument is nothing more than a veiled contention that *Furman* indirectly outlawed capital punishment by placing totally unrealistic conditions on its use."[27] Precisely—and there can be no more convincing way of substantiating this defense argument than by examining the unsatisfactory manner in which the plurality judgment rejects each of the three examples provided from the pretrial, trial, and posttrial stages. In effect, what the defense lawyer in *Gregg* did was to carry the arbitrary rule in *Furman* to its inevitable conclusion— something that the Court itself was manifestly reluctant to do.

The Court claimed that it would not be possible to impose restrictions on the discretion of the prosecutor, as this would compel him, in every case that seemed to contain the possibility of a capital murder, to proceed to so charge the accused. Why not, one might well ask? Why should the prosecutor, in a case involving a possible death sentence, be free to act without guidance as to when to activate the possibility of such a sentence? How can such unfettered discretion avoid arbitrariness? The Court seemed particularly worried that restrictions might inhibit the prosecutor's capacity to enter into plea bargaining. In effect, the Court here seemed more concerned with preserving the controversial system of plea bargaining than with safeguarding its own path-breaking principle of ending arbitrariness in the specific instance of the death penalty.

Yet, clear as this approach seems, it was abandoned by one of the judges, Justice Powell, when it was raised in a life imprisonment case, *Bordenkircher* v. *Hayes.*[28] Here he was strongly critical of prosecutorial behavior in the plea bargaining stage. The prosecutor, having failed to convince the accused to plead guilty (to a charge of issuing a forged check for eighty-eight dollars), went back to the grand jury and served a new indictment (as he had threatened to do during the plea negotiations) in which he invoked the state's Habitual Offenders Act, with its provision for a mandatory life imprisonment. Though a 5–4 majority of the Court upheld the mandatory life sentence in this case, Justice Powell, filing a dissenting opinion, argued that "although I agree with much of the Court's opinion I am not satisfied that the result in this case is just or that the conduct of the plea bargaining met the requirements of due process."[29]

Yet it was specifically this issue of the manner in which plea bargaining was carried out and whether the strictest standards of due process could be observed which, in principle at least, the Court had been asked to address in the case of *Gregg.* However, the defense counsel's suggestion that what happened at this stage was a key factor in determining whether arbitrariness could be avoided was rejected.

If Justice Powell was concerned about due process in a life imprisonment case, why did he reject outright the hypothetical situation posed in the *Gregg* case? As hypothetical as the argument was, its reality was shown only two years later in the *Lockett* case, and has been repeated in several other cases that have been challenged in the courts.

But, of course, most plea bargaining cases never come to the attention of the higher courts mainly because the bargain normally leaves both sides satisfied. This is exactly what the defense was challenging in the *Gregg* case—that such satisfaction was the consequence of arbitrary decisions, and was often gained at the expense of those for whom there was no plea bargain—either in the very same case (as in *Lockett)* or in general, and sometimes in arrogant use of power to punish the "stubborn" who refuse to negotiate (*vide* the life imprisonment case—and also probably *Lockett* as well, as I have suggested).

At the second stage, the trial itself, a similar inconsistency is apparent in the rejection of the defense argument in the *Gregg* case and its basic acceptance in another case. Yet here the conflict between the two cases is even more stark—for the decision in the other case was handed down on the very same day as *Gregg,* in the *Roberts* case,[30] in which the law in Louisiana was declared unconstitutional since it allowed too much discretion to the jury, even though this discretion was to be based on clearly articulated judicial directions.

In *Gregg,* Justices Stewart, Powell, and Stevens wrote almost quizzically in the above-mentioned footnote: "If a jury refused to convict even though the evidence supported the charge, its verdict would have to be reversed and a verdict of guilty entered or a new trial ordered, since the discretionary act of jury nullification would not be permitted." They then added that "the suggestion that the jury's verdict of acquittal could be overturned and a defendant re-tried would run afoul of the Sixth Amendment jury-trial guarantee and the Double Jeopardy clause of the Fifth Amendment."[31]

These reservations against the defendant's argument turn the argument on its head. The appellant was not contending that such discretion was desirable, but that it was well-nigh inevitable. He was suggesting what some juries were liable to do; that they might seek such solutions to avoid having to confront the issue of the death penalty. If this argument is correct, then its implications undermine the arbitrary rule. And this is precisely what happened in the *Roberts* case. Here the law provided (in the words of the Court) that every jury in a first-degree murder case is instructed on the crimes of second-degree murder and manslaughter and permitted to consider those verdicts. . . . And, if a lesser verdict is returned, it is treated as an acquittal of all greater charges. . . . This responsive verdict procedure not only lacks standards to guide the jury in selecting among first-degree murders, but it plainly invites the jurors to disregard their oath and choose a verdict for a lesser offense whenever they feel the death penalty is inappropriate. There is an element of capriciousness in making the jurors' powers to avoid the death penalty dependent on their willingness to accept this invitation to disregard the trial judge's instructions.[32]

There are clear differences between the two situations. In the *Gregg* case, the lawyer was arguing as to a hypothetical situation in which a jury might convict on a lesser offense. On the other hand, in the *Roberts* case, the law itself provided for the jury to consider lesser offenses. This the Court held to be an invitation to arbitrary decision-making.

The Court, of course, had a much easier way of resolving the issue of what it terms jury nullification—by realizing that once the mandatory sentence was prohibited (as was decided in the *Woodson* and *Roberts* cases), there would clearly be less pressure for such jury deviations since the jury would, after its guilty verdict, no longer be obliged to impose a death penalty. At the time of the argument in the *Gregg* case, this issue had not yet been decided, and so the appellant in the *Gregg* case correctly pursued this perspective. But by the time the decision was handed down, the parallel decisions in *Woodson* and *Roberts* were known.

Several years later the Court dealt with a case involving the possibility of both instructions to the jury of a lesser offense and a quasi-compulsory death sentence. In *Beck* v. *Alabama*[33] the Court analyzed the law in Alabama, passed after *Furman* but before *Gregg* and *Roberts.* The appellant had been found guilty of a robbery–intentional killing; according to the law, the jury, in convicting the accused, was obliged to make a recommendation for a death sentence. Only after this formality, would a hearing be held to determine mitigating and aggravating factors, on the basis of which the judge would decide whether or not to accept the jury's automatic recommendation. Despite the obligatory capital sentence that flowed from a guilty verdict, the jurors were given no instructions as to the possibility of a guilty verdict for a lesser, noncapital offense. The court noted that evidence had indicated that the killing might have been unintentional, in which case the crime would be of felony murder for which there was no death penalty. It held that in such circumstances the jury must be permitted to consider a verdict of guilt for a lesser offense; in the absence of such instruction the death penalty was annulled.

Yet the Court ignored—and left untouched—the provision for an obligatory recommendation of death. The overall effect of the Court's decision was, of course, to create the very situation described by the appellant in the *Gregg* case. Faced with an automatic recommendation of death after a finding of guilt in a robbery–intentional killing case, the jurors are liable to seek means of avoiding such an outcome by opting for the lesser offense of felony murder. Or, to be more exact, some juries are liable to perform in such a manner—a ready-made formula for arbitrary decision-making in respect to the death penalty. The pressures of the jurors to seek such nullification of the death penalty are likely to be all the greater in the light of the fact, noted by the Court, that in the vast majority of cases, the judge accepted the jury's recommendation for the death sentence. It is difficult to reconcile the prohibition on mandatory capital sentencing, as decided in *Roberts* and *Woodson,* with the partial mandatory system of the Alabama law.

In any event there are other jurisdictions where jurors might seek a guilty finding on a lesser offense, where their role at sentencing is limited to an advisory capacity, and where there seems to be a marked tendency for the judge to ignore the recommendation, when it is less than death. This is precisely the situation that has developed in Florida, where the judge is empowered to impose the sentence based on the recommendation of the jury. It appears that there have been many instances in which judges have ignored jury recommendations and imposed the death penalty.

As this pattern becomes common knowledge, so there is a distinct possibility that some jury in Florida, or in another state where similar laws and similar conditions apply, may well resort to jury nullification in order to ensure that there will be no death penalty. This would lead to precisely that situation of arbitrariness and capriciousness raised in the *Gregg* case.

The manner in which a judge may ignore the expressed intent of the jury was brought out in the case of *Barclay* v. *Florida;* the jury recommended, by a vote of seven to five, a life sentence, but the judge had ignored the recommendation and imposed the death penalty.[34] On appeal, the accused argued that the judge, in sentencing him, had relied on irrelevant and inaccurate factors.

Although the Supreme Court did find errors in the judgment of the trial court, these were held (in a five-to-four decision) to be harmless, and the verdict was sustained. However, in a dissenting judgment, Justice Marshall noted that the particular trial judge had on three previous occasions rejected the jury's recommendation and opted instead for the death penalty; in each case he had adverted to irrelevant factors, such as his experience of death during World War II, this to accentuate, in the words of Justice Marshall, that "he was not easily shocked but that the offense involved shocked him."[35]

Justice Marshall went on to castigate the Florida Supreme Court, which had argued that the judge had been justified in imposing the death penalty since he had wished to avoid a disparity between this sentence and that imposed on another defendant: "The court's invocation of principles of equal justice is particularly inappropriate in this case in light of the treatment of two of petitioner's co-defendants . . . [who]

received prison sentences while Barclay was condemned to death."[36]

No less disturbing than these happenings in Florida was a recent incident in Georgia, when, at the sentencing stage, a juror was released from service after she had fainted during the jury's deliberation as to the penalty.[37] Her replacement by an alternate was challenged on appeal, but the court majority found nothing to render the verdict tainted, holding that the court was exercising its rightful discretion. However, a dissenting opinion by Judge Hill raises the distinct possibility that the juror had fainted because she was unwilling to be a party to a death penalty. The description of the developments given in the dissenting judgment are worth repeating in full, since they display the casual manner in which the trial judge dealt with a problem that arose as to the composition of the jury.

After deliberating a little over three hours, the jurors returned to the courtroom to ask: "Can a sentence be given, 'Life in prison without parole?'" The judge informed the jury that he was unable to answer the question. After asking if the jury could have a witness' answer to a question read if the jury decided it was needed, the jury retired. Twenty-five minutes later, the foreperson returned to the court to say that a juror, Dorothy Todd, had fainted in the corridor when leaving the courtroom earlier and was, in the foreperson's opinion, physically and emotionally unable to continue, and the juror had asked to be excused. The court excused juror Todd based on the foreperson's statement and replaced her with an alternate juror. On appeal the defendant alleges that after the court declined to answer the question about "life without parole," the juror, upon leaving the courtroom fell to the floor, shaking and waiving [sic] her arms and saying in a voice loud enough to be heard in the courtroom: "I can't do it, I can't do it, I can't do it." The state does not refute this assertion.

It appears highly probable that the reason the juror was unable to continue (and the reason she requested to be relieved) may well have been that she couldn't impose the death penalty. In my view, the trial court should have questioned the juror personally as to the reason for her being unable to continue. The juror was qualified during voir dire under *Witherspoon* v. *Illinois* . . . and from all that appears she was stricken by the court during deliberation because she was unable to vote for capital punishment under the facts of this case. This is a violation of Witherspoon just the same as if she had been stricken during voir dire.

For the foregoing reasons I dissent to the imposition of the penalty of death in this case.[38]

H O W E V E R   V U L N E R A B L E the Court's position seems to be in regard to the pretrial and trial stages, it is the third aspect of the defense argument in *Gregg*—the posttrial stage—that seems to pose the most serious threat to the very existence of capital punishment, at least so long as the Court considers itself bound by the rule against arbitrariness and capriciousness.

On this issue in *Gregg,* the plurality judgment curtly rejected the appellant's contention of arbitrariness in the posttrial stage: "Acts of executive clemency would have to be prohibited."[39] Once again the argument was being stood on its head. For it was not the issue of executive clemency that was in dispute and was being challenged, but the death penalty. The logical implication of any inconsistency between nonarbitrariness in administering the death penalty (the *Furman* rule) and the existence of a commuting mechanism is not to suggest that the commuting or pardoning power should be eliminated (since this is in any case not at issue), but to suggest (as the defense counsel did) that the death penalty should be eliminated (which *is* the question at issue).

In any discussion of the discrepancy between approaches to the death penalty and the pardoning process, it would be well to bear in mind that historically one of the major reasons for the development of the pardoning power was to provide a means of evading the harsh consequences of the death penalty. This power assumes added import in modern times, since today there are very few cases involving the death penalty in which a plea for pardon or commutation of sentence is not lodged. Even if the condemned person is not interested in contesting the decision, there are always family members, public organizations, and civil libertarians intent on challenging the penalty in as many cases as possible. However, though the Supreme Court has laid down standards to avoid arbitrary and capricious decisions in the trial stage, similar controls have not been specified, and indeed *cannot* be specified, for the final stages of the total process of sentencing.

Nevertheless, decision-making in the postsentencing stage is not an irrelevant issue, since, in practice, the overwhelming majority of condemned persons do not get executed. The implications of widespread use of pardoning power are extensive: such practice in effect turns the death penalty into no more than a marginal punishment, seldom used, and then only on a small minority of people who, often only through some quirk of fate (such as personal qualities, lack of influence, inefficient legal representation, or gubernatorial policy) have failed to receive commutation. This inconsistent use of the death penalty was the very situation which the *Furman* and *Gregg* decisions were trying to avoid.

The capriciousness of the commuting process may be noted by checking on the final outcome of those appellants whose cases were lost in the Supreme Court (such as Gregg and Jurek), and who were not subsequently executed. On the other hand, their cases became the basis for proceeding with the death penalty against other condemned persons, including Gilmore in Utah. In this case the specific provisions of the law in Utah were never placed before the scrutiny of the Supreme Court,

although doubts had been expressed as to the law's constitutionality, which those who were desirous of acting on Gilmore's
behalf were prepared to argue before the Court.[40]

Whereas Justices Marshall and Brennan did not discuss the
issue of pardoning in *Gregg*, it is ironic that the judge on the
other extreme of the spectrum and the one most strongly in
favor of retaining capital punishment, Justice White, did address this issue. Yet he failed to be impressed with the defense
argument. On the contrary, he claimed that it was possible to
have faith in clemency decisions to help offset any possibility
of unfair sentencing practices, thereby providing a further
safeguard against arbitrariness and capriciousness. Expressing
his opinion on this subject (not in the *Gregg* case, where he
concurred in upholding the law in Georgia, but in the *Roberts*
case, where he dissented against the majority overturning the
Louisiana statute), Justice White wrote:

> As for executive clemency, I cannot assume that this power,
> exercised by governors and vested in the President by Art.
> II, para. 2 of the Constitution, will be used in a standardless
> and arbitrary manner. It is more reasonable to expect the
> power to be exercised by the Executive Branch whenever
> it is concluded that the criminal justice system has unjustly
> convicted a defendant of first-degree murder and sentenced
> him to death. The country's experience with the commuta-
> tion power does not suggest that it is a senseless lottery,
> that it operates in an arbitrary or discriminatory manner,
> or that it will lead to reducing the death penalty to a merely
> theoretical threat that is imposed only on a luckless few.[41]

Although this was a lone dissenting opinion, inasmuch as it
is the most explicit statement as to why the contention of arbitrariness at the commutation level has been rejected, it
deserves closer scrutiny.

First, the clemency power is not used only to redress unjust convictions; indeed, whenever it is used for that purpose
it raises serious questions as to the capriciousness, not just of

the sentence, but of the conviction itself. In research by Marvin Wolfgang, Arlene Kelly and Hans Nolde on posttrial pardons, nearly half of the seventy-one commutations of the death sentences were for the purpose of affording redress against an unjust conviction.[42] It may well be asked whether a pardoning body can be fully trusted to rectify all the errors of a trial, which, according to the research, seem to be rather prevalent. Since the decision here is in regard to the irreversible death penalty, it seems there is a problem not only as to the lack of consistency in the sentencing, but also as to the lack of reliability in the verdict—and research has indicated positive proof of past mistakes.[43]

What is of particular interest in the research by Wolfgang and his colleagues is that their research was actually referred to in the *Furman* case (in the opinion of Justice Douglas) as evidence of racial discrimination in sentencing—one of the reasons for declaring the death penalty unconstitutional, even though the research itself dealt with pardoning. Yet, when the very issue of posttrial discrimination was raised by the appellant in the *Gregg* case, the earlier research was forgotten or ignored, even though its findings on discrimination at the commutation stage were far more relevant for the argument presented in *Gregg* than they had been in *Furman.*

As for the contention by Justice White that pardoning is not a senseless lottery, nor arbitrary and discriminatory, or that it is not merely a luckless few who suffer its actual imposition, it seems that today, a decade after *Gregg,* there is a vital need for empirical evidence on this matter—basically a replication of the original Wolfgang *et al.* study (which was of commutation in Pennsylvania between 1914 and 1962) and which would be able to show what has happened to the death penalty in practice in the decade since *Gregg.*

It seems, perhaps even more than before, that since the end of the moratorium on executions, it is still only the luckless few that are being executed, with the number of these few increasing as complacency sets in with the death penalty becoming again more of a norm—but this increase in numbers does nothing to diminish the chance nature of who is executed, given the even larger increase of those on death row.

The reluctance to examine the pardoning process for the death penalty is rendered once again inexplicable because of the fact that one of the judges in the *Gregg* plurality stressed its importance in a life-imprisonment case, once again adopting a position that he had rejected outright in the *Gregg* case. In a life-sentence case, Justice Stevens argued (with Justice Marshall concurring):

> This case involves the State of Connecticut's process for determining when a relatively small group of serious offenders will be released from custody. Routinely, the process includes three determinations: the judge imposes a life sentence; the Board of Pardons, in due course, commutes that sentence; and, finally, the Board of Parole discharges the prisoner from custody. Each of these three decisions is a regular and critical component of the decision-making process employed by the State of Connecticut to determine the magnitude of its deprivation of the prisoner's liberty. *In my opinion, the Due Process Clause applies to each step and denies the State power to act arbitrarily.*[44] (Italics mine.)

If this criterion were to be used in death penalty cases, serious questions could undoubtedly be raised as to whether due process had been observed. It is suggested that an examination of the evidence of the last few years would show clearly that the clemency process in death penalty cases is indeed standardless and arbitrary, though research here would be complicated by the fact that most people sentenced to death remain in a limbo state on death row for some years, with their sentences neither carried out nor commuted. In any event, it still seems that those who are executed are the luckless few for idiosyncratic reasons.

If this issue were to be raised in the future, the justices would have to decide whether they wished to confine their strictures only to what actually happens in court—as a procedural issue—or whether they are actually concerned with the moral issue of the fate of a human being. Judicial focus on the pardoning power of the executive undoubtedly raises very serious legal, constitutional, and political issues. For instance, it is not clear whether the pardoning power is an integral part of the sentencing process.[45] Furthermore, the exact manner in which this power is exercised differs among the states. In some instances the governor acts on his own; in others, on the advice and recommendation of a board of pardons (sometimes identical with the state parole board). Usually no execution can take place without a death warrant signed by the governor.

Where the use of clemency power is solely at the discretion of the governor, a particularly strong argument could be made for the inherent arbitrariness of the death penalty. In theory, the executive officer is accountable only to his own conscience. In practice, he is often subject to political or personal pressures which add to the capricious nature of his decision. Generally, there are no binding rules or guidelines for the executive office, not even practices or precedents set by his predecessors. A governor or even a candidate for this office may declare that under no circumstances will he grant pardon or, conversely, that he will never refuse a request for clemency. Thus, an individual's life may turn on the chance results of an election campaign. In this context it is interesting to note that Governor Winthrop Rockefeller commuted the sentences of all fifteen men under sentence of death in Arkansas near the end of his term of office, two months after he had been defeated in his bid for reelection,[46] an action repeated recently in November 1986, by the outgoing Governor of New Mexico, Governor Anaya, who signed five pardons for prisoners condemned to death. There have been reports that his action may be challenged in the courts.[47] Interviewed by the national media, he argued that the death penalty was inhumane, and then added, in defending his action, that life imprisonment was perhaps more severe.

An additional twist has also been given to the issue of clemency in the specific context of a differential approach to capital punishment and life imprisonment. According to the law in California, the penalty for murder is either capital punishment or life imprisonment without the chance for parole. The law further obligates the judge to explain to the jury that the governor has the power to commute a life sentence to a lesser sentence that includes the possibility of parole. Not only is there no similar statutory directive with regard to the death penalty, but there is, on the contrary, a judicial prohibition in California on providing such information to the jury (as decided in the case of *People* v. *Morse*).[48] This prohibition is intended to benefit the defendant, since a directive of this nature would be liable to make jury members more willing to impose a death penalty if they are specifically apprised of the fact that the governor has the power to commute the sentence—on the basis that it is his decision that is essentially the crucial one.

However, in certain contexts this prohibition might work to the disadvantage of the defendant, as was argued in the case of *California* v. *Ramos*.[49] The argument was put forward that a specific reference to the possibility of commutation of a life sentence without the prospect of parole, but silence as to the possibilities of commutation of a death penalty, might in some cases create an inevitable bias toward using the death penalty, as when the jury is deeply concerned about the potential dangerousness of the defendant in the future and most intent that he should not be released back into the community. If the desire to ensure future incapacity of a criminal is the cardinal factor in a jury's consideration, they are liable to be unduly—and unfairly—swayed by the possibility of the defendant's release if given "only" a life sentence. Under these circumstances, there is a greater likelihood of their opting for the death penalty.

By a majority of 5–4, the Supreme Court, overruling the Supreme Court of California, held that the legal obligation to inform the jury of the possibility of commutation for the life sentence was not unconstitutional, and that so informing the jury provided it with additional accurate information, which would help it reach a just decision. In particular, it was important for the jury to know that the description of the sentence as provided in the law—"life imprisonment *without possibility* of parole"—was inaccurate, given the governor's commutation powers.

The minority opinion in this case contains a scathing criticism of the majority decision. Justice Marshall suggests that the Court, by its decision, "authorizes the States to 'cross the line of neutrality' and encourages death sentences by deceiving the jury." Further, it encourages the death penalty to be imposed arbitrarily and capriciously on the basis of speculation as to possible parole. However,

> a jury simply has no basis for assessing the likelihood that a particular defendant will eventually be released if he is not sentenced to death. To invite the jury to indulge in such speculation is to ask it to foretell numerous imponderables: the policies that may be adopted by unnamed future Governors and parole officials, any change in the defendant's character, as well as any other factors that might be deemed relevant to the commutation and parole decision.[50]

Inasmuch as future dangerousness is the issue, this can possibly be curtailed without the death penalty, though not without creating new problems. According to Justice Marshall, "Life imprisonment and, if necessary, solitary confinement would fully accomplish the aim of incapacitation."[51] This is certainly so (short of a jail break, which is also an imponderable)—but it should be noted that solitary confinement (for life? for a fixed number of years? for as long as a psychiatrist would declare him dangerous? till he reached a certain advanced age?) would raise serious questions as to whether it would be compatible with the injunction of the Eighth Amendment against cruel and unusual punishment.

What emerges from this case, and with added pertinence, is the importance for the Court to directly confront the influence of the clemency power on jury decision-making. There are also further far-reaching implications that arise directly from the majority's argument that juries, on being apprised of a commutation procedure, are liable to be inclined "to approach their sentencing decision with less appreciation for the gravity of their choice and for the moral responsibility reposed in them as sentencers."[52]

For, truth to tell, the possibility of commutation by the governor is not an esoteric secret of the law requiring explanatory exposition by a judge in order for a jury to understand the full implications of their decision. It is a widely known aspect of the total criminal justice system since the mass media keep the average citizen informed of all its ramifications, including the extra-judicial battles of condemned persons, their lawyers or their families, or the concerns for the fate of those on death row. In recent years there has also been full exposure of those few (just over fifty since the end of the moratorium in 1977) who failed to receive a pardon or refused to request one, and the paucity of their numbers in relation to those sentenced can only confirm in the minds of the average person the high likelihood of an eventual commutation. It may thus well be that, in some cases at least, juries (especially in the course of secret deliberations in the jury room) are not just cognizant of the existence of some vague commutation power, but give due consideration to the incontrovertible fact that the vast majority of those sentenced to death will be finally reprieved.

Such knowledge is likely to increase a jury's willingness to impose a death penalty since, on the one hand, they may well feel satisfied that they are capable of expressing in a sufficiently stern manner the gravity of the crime and the public revulsion towards it, and yet, on the other hand, sensing that their own propensities to merciful understanding (and their own hesitations about the death penalty) will likely find expression in a later executive act of clemency. But what if their assumptions in this regard are not fulfilled?

There is at least one recorded instance of a person sentenced to death on the assumption, later shown to be mistaken, of a high probability that the sentence itself would not be carried out. Such a tragic fate befell the only American soldier to be executed for desertion during World War II, Private Slovik.[53] It appears that the judges who sentenced him to death were convinced that he would have his sentence commuted by the military authorities, as had been done almost automatically in every other similar case. Yet, in Slovik's case, despite the lack of any special facts warranting a deviation for that policy, by a fluke of circumstances clemency was not forthcoming, and he was executed by firing squad. It was only some three decades later that a presidential apology was given, after a determined struggle by his widow to clear his name.

Empirical examination of a state's commutation procedures seems to be required in order to avoid capriciousness, and could lead to a further complication in the whole odyssey of the death penalty. Identical legislation on capital punishment in various states, based, for instance, on the directives in the *Gregg* case, could lead to different decisions as to the constitutionality of the death penalty, based on each state's differing commutation procedures and practices. This would clearly be an anomalous situation, but it is inevitable if the courts are to give real meaning to the restrictions on arbitrariness and capriciousness.

This issue is related to one more problem that the Supreme Court has not yet addressed: whether it is at all possible for a federal system to control for arbitrariness and capriciousness if each state is free to pass different legislation as to the sentence for murder and to institute different procedures for pardoning and commutation. Are the concerns of the Court only with arbitrariness and capriciousness within a particular state, or do these concerns embrace the nation as an entity? Given the special nature of the death penalty, is it consistent to allow different states to follow different policies on capital punishment, and still claim that the standards constituting arbitrariness and capriciousness have been met? This seems to be a legitimate concern also in light of the worldwide concern over capital punishment seen in the perspective of universal human rights. If nations can show cross-national interest in the death penalty and if the Court is concerned about arbitrariness, then considerations of this nature become significant.

Hugo Bedau has pointed out the illogic of different laws in different states.

> Where is the rational difference in the crimes and criminals that justifies . . . upholding death sentences in Georgia but condemning the same sentence in North Carolina? Why should Gregg, a hitchhiker convicted of robbing and murdering the man who gave him a ride, have his death sentence upheld, when Woodson, convicted of robbing and killing a storekeeper, has his death sentence overturned? Why shouldn't both, or neither be spared? It is more ironic that if Woodson had robbed and killed in Georgia, and Gregg in North Carolina, it would be Gregg, not Woodson, who was spared and Woodson, not Gregg, whose death sentence was sustained. Is this evenhanded, rational justice where life and death are at issue?[54]

Bedau's questions take on even greater pertinence in the *Gregg* case since it dealt with hitchhikers, who, for all they knew, might well have crossed state lines during the car trip, moving in the course of the ride from an abolitionist state to one with the death penalty, or vice versa.

What emerges from the Supreme Court decision in *Furman, Gregg,* and related cases is a confusion as to the circumstances and manner in which the death penalty may be imposed. In some instances the Court has contributed to this situation, as in *Barefoot* v. *Estelle* when it has refused a stay of execution even though the petitioner was, at the time, attempting a new appeal of the verdict against him on constitutional grounds.[55] The essential thrust of the Court's opinion seemed to be that the needs of carrying out the penalty of death take precedence over habeas corpus rights (under which the petitioner had proceeded), sought in order to pursue constitutional rights.

Since it embarked on its confrontation with capital punishment as a constitutional issue, the Court has displayed much ambivalence. On one point, however, it originally spoke clearly and unambiguously—on the need to "minimize the risk of wholly arbitrary and capricious action," and for "objective standards to guide, regularize, and make rationally reviewable the process for imposing a sentence of death."[56]

As a result, the situation today is as follows. It is the Court that has stressed the unique nature of the death penalty and, accordingly, the need for stricter controls for this penalty. It is the Court that has laid down what the parameters of those controls are to be: the elimination of arbitrary and capricious action. How long can it continue to evade the logical completion of its equation? First, prosecutional discretion may affect who is subjected to the possiblity of the death penalty; second, at the trial stage, extraneous factors may intrude on decision-making, particularly by the jury; third, since executive officers have clemency power, there is an inherent and unavoidable arbitrariness in the administration of the death penalty; and, fourth, in a federal nation, for as long as there is no uniformity of legislation among the states, there is an inevitable arbitrariness in the imposition of the death penalty.

The Supreme Court decisions in *Furman, Gregg,* and related cases have perforce created uncertainty and dilemmas. Given the existing circumstances, it would seem that the only way to resolve the confusion and dilemmas is by total abolition of the death penalty (with the possible exception of special federal crimes). Any other approach allows an arbitrariness in the Court's own decisions, the very feature it is trying to eliminate in the directives it lays down for the lower courts.

However, such a solution would only resolve the problem of the constitutionality of the death penalty within the framework of the guiding rule of avoiding arbitrariness— it would not resolve the penological problem of the most suitable judicial response to the most serious crimes. On the contrary, it would probably raise a whole new area of concern. Put simply, if capital punishment were to be abolished, there is a great likelihood that the focus of concern would shift to the many ramifications of alternative punishments, notably that of life imprisonment. For instance, given the severity of this sentence, the questions would almost inevitably arise as to whether its implementation complied with the very standards the Court had laid down relating to "cruel and unusual," on the one hand, and "due process of law"— especially in terms of arbitrariness—on the other.

What would be the Court's position if it were to transpire that the imposition of life imprisonment suffered from the identical defects that had led to the death penalty being declared unconstitutional—for instance, that it was being imposed unfairly, mainly on certain population groupings, or capriciously, with no guiding principles.

Even more pertinent would be the more specific issue of *mandatory* life sentence—the total denial of discretion to a judge at the sentencing stage, and this for a punishment which, in lieu of the death sentence, would now become the most severe punishment available. Mandatory sentencing rules always raise serious questions as to sentencing policy, with its preference for uniformity of punishment over considerations of the convicted person's background, motivation, prospects for rehabilitation, and related issues.

Of course, even without the abolition of capital punishment, the issue of life imprisonment on a mandatory basis should be a major concern. These issues will be probed in the next chapter.

5

LIFE IMPRISONMENT AND HUMAN RIGHTS

W HEN LIFE SENTENCES are offered as an alternative to the death penalty, often the legislation provides for a mandatory punishment, and sometimes there is also a denial of possible parole in the future. Recently these factors have led to limited litigation, but there have been only rare challenges to life imprisonment as being cruel and unusual per se, none of these at the highest appeal levels, and none of them successful.[1]

As far as mandatory sentencing in general is concerned, judges tend to resent this as a usurpation of what should be one of the court's legitimate functions; and juries occasionally circumvent its provisions by convicting on a lesser offense, or even acquitting in order to avoid the inevitability of a sentence in conflict with their conscience. But these factors have had only a limited impact on life imprisonment cases, mainly because life imprisonment is perceived as being a lenient alternative to the harsher death sentence for serious crimes.

In the United States, the Supreme Court has expressed itself, as already noted, against any mandatory approach to the death sentence and has nullified all such laws passed in the wake of the *Furman* decision,[2] even though this would have been the best way to avoid arbitrariness. In the *Lockett* case it even stressed the need to allow for individualized consideration of factors personal to the accused—because, in the words of Chief Justice Burger, "The need for treating each individual in a capital case with that degree of respect due the uniqueness of the individual is far more important than in non-capital cases."[3] Yet, what of noncapital cases of the utmost severity? Surely it could be argued that a life sentence possesses sufficient severity and uniqueness to warrant the same need for minimal individualized considerations.

Indeed, the same court that rejects mandatory sentences in capital punishment but allows it in the case of a life sentence, may well do so because it has "judicial knowledge" that life sentences are not always fully implemented but are presumably reduced by an act of pardon. This fact, however, allows for ultimate arbitrariness, no less than that which characterizes the death penalty.

In fact, as presently constituted, *the life sentence often violates both of the main criteria of capital offense cases:* It is often mandatory at the trial stage, and then, in the posttrial stage, its duration is often totally arbitrary.

Although the Supreme Court has to date contemplated this situation with equanimity, since its strictures on capital offenses arise specifically out of the unique nature of the death penalty, a closer examination will reveal the inconsistencies of the distinction that it makes between the two penalties.

First, the Supreme Court has allowed mandatory sentencing in life cases even when the further criterion of disproportionality between offense and punishment is being violated; yet, this is an aspect of the interpretation of cruel and unusual punishment that has a long tradition in American precedents, dating back to the *Weems* case in 1910.[4]

Second, there is an inherent and unavoidable unfairness in the life sentence in that the age of the offender makes a crucial difference to the impact that it has upon him. The old have minimum prospects of receiving commutation before they die, whereas the young contemplate the long years ahead with no certainty of commutation and with the deprivation of freedom during a formative period of their life. Of course, it could be argued that for severe offenses this is the punishment that the criminals deserve. That may be so; all I am arguing is the inherently differential manner in which the sentence will be perceived by different people depending on their age at sentencing. On one occasion in fact, a life sentence was declared unconstitutional because of the young age of the accused— fourteen years old accused of rape.[5]

Third, countries that have abolished the death penalty have been confronted with general debate and specific arguments in respect to life imprisonment that are, in essence, very similar to those that have occupied the American courts in respect to the death penalty. Thus, it is not clear that any rules of sentencing policy laid down in resect to the death penalty can be limited only to this penalty. Whatever their value, they contain a certain inner logic that has some degree of relevance for other punishments too, particularly the more severe ones, and especially life imprisonment.

Fourth, life imprisonment has unique aspects of its own that would justify applying special rules, including super due process, to distinguish it from lesser punishments.

The time may be ripe, in terms of the "evolving standards of decency"[6]—the guiding rule for determining cruel and unusual punishment—to seek judicial rulings on the constitutional aspects of life sentences, both per se and when it is mandatory, with the courts denied any right to consider the circumstances of the case or the personal background of the accused. If a mandatory death sentence is no longer constitutional, not even for murder, surely similar reasoning could be used in the cases of mandatory life sentences, particularly for offenses less than murder. Likewise, there is a need to probe the issues of disproportionality, of discriminatory sentencing policies, and of denial of parole.

It is of particular interest to note the contrast between the United States and West Germany. The latter is one of the few countries in the world to have a total constitutional prohibition on capital punishment, but whose alternative of a mandatory life sentence has been subject to the scrutiny of the Constitutional Court. Here, although the court did hold the mandatory life sentence to be in accord with the constitution, one of the factors taken into account was the fact that in practically all cases, as a routine practice, the life sentence is later commuted to a fixed term, a practice followed in other countries as well.[7]

In the United States, some cases addressing life imprisonment have come before the courts and, occasionally, restrictions have been placed on the use of a mandatory life sentence. But the overriding thrust of the decisions is the lack of any connection between consideration of the use of the death penalty and the use of imprisonment. Most particularly, the Supreme Court has been less amendable to Eighth Amendment and Fourteenth Amendment arguments than the lower courts, which seem to be more sensitive to the meaning of life imprisonment.

In 1973, in the case of *Hart* v. *Coiner*,[8] the United States Court of Appeal, Fourth Circuit, heard an appeal on the constitutionality of a mandatory life sentence in terms of a habitual criminal statute. The accused had been convicted for a third time in just less than twenty years: the first conviction, in 1949, had been for writing a check for fifty dollars without sufficient funds; the second, in 1955, for interstate transportation of forged checks; and third, for committing perjury on behalf of his son in a murder trial.

Although it was accepted law, ratified by earlier court decisions, that there was nothing inherently unconstitutional in a recidivist statute with a mandatory life sentence, the court felt that the principle of disproportionality in sentencing entitled them to examine whether in the case under review, a life sentence might not be in violation of the Constitution. The court justified its distinction between the actual constitutionality of the statute and the constitutionality of applying it in any particular case.

[The accused] does not attack the statute itself. He does not urge that life imprisonment per se is either cruel or unusual. Nor does he urge that the statutory scheme has been discriminatorily applied. The issue he does raise is whether the recidivist mandatory life sentence *in this case* is so excessive and disproportionate to the underlying offenses as to constitute cruel and unusual punishment.[9]

The court held that, given the fact that "life imprisonment is the penultimate punishment [which] tradition, custom and common sense reserve . . . for those violent persons who are dangerous to others," there was no reasonable purpose to be served in imposing such a punishment on a petty thief who had been convicted for a third time in just less than twenty years; nor would there be enough prisons to hold all such petty thieves.[10]

The court cited four key factors to be considered in determining whether a sentence in a particular case was "constitutionally disporportionate":

1. The nature of the offense
2. The legislative purpose behind the punishment
3. A comparison of the punishment inflicted with what could have been expected in other state jurisdictions
4. A comparison of the punishment with other punishments for other offenders in the same jurisdiction.[11]

In applying these criteria to the case at issue, the court held that there had been a violation of the Eighth Amendment. A minority judgment also held that, on the facts of the case, the punishment was unconstitutional, but refused to apply the cruel and unusual provisions of the Eighth Amendment. The judge would have found for the defendant on the grounds of due process, namely, that on the occasion of the defendant's first conviction in 1949, he had not been provided with adequate legal representation. The judgment noted that his court-appointed lawyer had met with him for the first time on the day of the trial and had not sufficiently pursued all possibilities of seeking an acquittal.

Several years later, the Supreme Court had the opportunity to examine the doctrine of disproportionality in a case based on the Texas recidivist statute, *Rummel* v. *Estelle*.[12] The accused had been convicted over a period of a little less than ten years, on three different occasions, of forging or obtaining money by false pretenses, the amounts involved being $80.00, $28.30, and $120.75. On his third conviction, at the request of the prosecution, he was give a mandatory life sentence under the recidivist statute. The appeal was from a decision of the United States Court of Appeals, Fifth Circuit, sitting *en banc,* which, in an 8–6 vote, had held that the mandatory life sentence was not unconstitutional.[13] Two key factors in the majority decision of the Supreme Court were the practical consideration that the appellant would probably not serve out his full term but would be eligible for parole after twelve years or even earlier, and the theoretical argument that decisions in death penalty cases could not serve as a precedent in life imprisonment cases. The Court held that "because a sentence of death differs in kind from any sentence of imprisonment, no matter how long, our decisions applying the prohibition of cruel and unusual punishments to capital cases are of limited assistance in deciding the constitutionality of the punishment meted out to Rummel."[14] The Court also disapproved of the four-part test set out by the court of appeals in *Hart* v. *Coiner.*

A dissenting judgment held that since the appellant had no legal right of entitlement to parole, this fact should not have been considered by the Court; further, there was evidence to suggest that the governor of Texas rejected a large proportion of parole board recommendations (thirty-three percent over a six-month period). In the dissenting judgment, Justice Powell (joined by Justices Brennan, Marshall, and Stevens) argued that the basic philosophy laid down in the death penalty case of *Furman* was of prime importance in the case under review.

> The special relevance of *Furman* to this case lies in the general acceptance by Members of the Court of two basic principles. First, the Eighth Amendment prohibits grossly excessive punishment. Second, the scope of the Eighth Amendment is to be measured by "evolving standards of decency."[15]

Powell noted that only twelve states had ever passed mandatory life sentence laws for recidivism, and most had since rescinded them. In conclusion, he argued that

> it is . . . true that this Court has not heretofore invalidated a mandatory life sentence under the Eighth Amendment. Yet, our precedents establish that the duty to review the disproportionality of sentences extends to non-capital cases. . . . We are construing a living Constitution. The sentence imposed upon the petitioner would be viewed as grossly unjust by virtually every layman and laywer. In my view, objective criteria clearly establish that a mandatory life sentence for defrauding persons of about $230 crosses any rational drawn line separating punish- ment that lawfully may be imposed from that which is proscribed by the Eighth Amendment.[16]

Interestingly, whereas the opening statement of the dissenting judgment draws on the philosophical principles laid down in *Furman,* it did not measure the question of disproportionality against the fact that murder is in many states being punished by life imprisonment and that, given the seriousness of that offense and the irrevocability of the victim's situation, it may be necessary to reassess other punishments from the perspective of the maximum penalty provided for murder. That is, the unique seriousness of murder as determined by the Supreme Court in barring the use of the death penalty for all cases except where a life has been taken,[17] of necessity should lead by simple logic to sentences less than mandatory life when the crime is less than murder.

The following year the West Virginia Supreme Court of Appeals held in the case of *Wanstreet* v. *Bordenkircher,* on very similar facts, that the state constitution provided more protection than the Eighth Amendment offered, as interpreted by the Supreme Court in *Rummel.*[18] Article 3, Section 5 of the state constitution states that criminal sentences ''shall be proportioned to the character and degree of the offense.'' The court felt that the consideration of disproportionality was particularly applicable to the case of recidivist statutes, and that it was the court's duty to examine the nature of all the relevant offenses, particularly the final one. In the case under appeal, the third and final conviction was for the forgery of a forty-three-dollar check, which, under normal conditions, carries a maximum nonmandatory penalty of ten years. The court thus held for the appellant and ordered his discharge forthwith.

In this case the court did actually compare the fairness of a life sentence with that given for serious and violent crimes, such as murder and kidnapping involving bodily harm, for which the penalty was also mandatory life imprisonment—but even then only in the absence of a jury recommendation for mercy. In the case of the recidivist statute, there was not even any provision for a mercy recommendation. The court also stressed that the recidivist statute should be viewed in a restrictive fashion in order to mitigate its harshness.

Though the cases discussed heretofore revolve largely around the question of cruel and unusual punishment in the context of disproportionality, the Supreme Court has also considered, in *Bordenkircher* v. *Hayes,* whether the underlying circumstances leading to the use of the recidivist statute might not violate the due process clause of the Fourteenth Amendment.[19] At issue was the fact that during the plea bargaining the prosecutor had used the defendant's two previous convictions to suggest that, in return for a guilty plea, he would refrain from invoking the habitual criminal statute, and would recommend a five-year prison sentence; conversely, the prosecutor warned the accused that if the case went to trial, he would, in the event of a conviction, invoke the recidivist statute, with its mandatory life sentence.

The Court of Appeals for the Sixth Circuit had originally held that the prosecutor had acted unconstitutionally, especially in view of the fact that after an innocent plea had been entered, he went back to the grand jury to seek a new indictment under the Kentucky Habitual Criminal Act.[20] However, this appeal court decision was reversed by the Supreme Court in a 5–4 decision. After noting the conditions under which plea bargaining should normally take place, as set out in a series of earlier court decisions sanctioning the practice, the majority held (per Justice Stewart) that the prosecution had acted within legitimate constitutional limits, since it had "openly presented the defendant with the unpleasant alternatives of foregoing trial or facing charges on which he was plainly subject to prosecution."[21]

In separate dissenting judgments, Justice Blackman (joined by Brennan and Marshall) and Justice Powell acknowledged that the prosecutor could well have been within his rights to charge the defendant *ab initio* with the Habitual Offender Act, but noted (per the Powell judgment) that initially the

> prosecutor evidently made a reasonable, responsible judgment not to subject an individual to mandatory life sentence when his only new offense had societal implications as limited as those accompanying the uttering of a single $88 forged check and when the circumstances of his prior convictions confirmed the inappropriateness of applying the habitual criminal statute. I think it may be inferred that the prosecutor himself deemed it unreasonable and not in the public interest to put this defendant in jeopardy of a sentence of life imprisonment.[22]

The majority decision in the *Hayes* case is part of the Court's ongoing approach of construing the Fourteenth Amendment (and the Eighth Amendment) in such a way as to allow maximum flexibility for those entrusted with discretionary powers within the total criminal justice system outside of the trial itself. Here, in fact, it is less stringent in its control of the prosecution and other administrative decisions than of the lower courts. The net consequence, of course, is an arbitrariness that cannot always be remedied by stricter standards in the court system.

A later case exemplifies how the Court has applied its approach to the discretionary powers exercised in connection with parole. This case, *Connecticut Board of Pardons* v. *Dumschat,* is of particular interest since it deals with the issue of what actually happens to those sentenced to life imprisonment and the importance of such empirical evidence in deciding whether or not there has been a violation of constitutionally guaranteed rights.[23] As noted in the previous chapter, this is an aspect of postsentencing procedures that the Court has shunned in the death penalty cases.

The accused, sentenced to life imprisonment for murder, had claimed that the Fourteenth Amendment entitled him to be given written reasons why the board of pardons refused to commute his life sentence. (In Connecticut, power is solely in the hands of the board of pardons, without any need for affirmation of their decisions by the governor.) The district court and the court of appeal had found that the prisoner had at least a right to a written and reasoned statement, but the Supreme Court, in a 7–2 decision, held that a prisoner had no rights of entitlement, and certainly no right to commutation of a sentence. A significant part of the discussion revolved around the average prisoner's expectations of being granted a privileged benefit on the basis of standard practices of those possessed with the power to commute sentences. It appeared from the evidence submitted to the Court that once a life sentence had been commuted to a fixed term, there was also a strong likelihood of an earlier release on parole. In fact, it was specifically the denial of commutation that was preventing an early consideration of parole. Although the Court was reluctant to raise the expectations of prisoners to that of a right of entitlement, it was made clear that the vast majority of prisoners sentenced for life in Connecticut do not serve out their full term and do not, in normal circumstances, die while in confinement.

The fact that commuting and pardoning powers and procedures have meant that, in effect, a life sentence is not always served out in full seems to lie, at least partly, behind the reluctance of the Supreme Court to intervene in cases involving life sentences. This was clearly stated in *Rummel* v. *Estelle,* but it seems to be implicit in other cases as well.

However, in giving passing acknowledgement to standard commuting procedures for life prisoners, the Court has generally not been willing to confront the possibility of selective, arbitrary, and capricious practices. What of those, for instance, who, for whatever reason, have their requests for commutation, pardon, or early release denied? What of those who serve out the full sentence, including the inescapable final outcome of dying in confinement? Who are they; in what way do they differ from other prisoners who are released; on what basis are their fates determined? To what extent are arbitrary decisions being made in those cases without the possibility of judicial intervention, or without any recognized guidelines? Specifically, what is to become of Dumschat? Is he doomed to end his days in a prison cell? What is there about his case that makes him different from those others in Connecticut and elsewhere who have their life sentences, whether mandatory or not, reduced by the powers of clemency given to governors or boards of pardons?

In a more recent case, *Solem* v. *Helm,* the Supreme Court has finally moved closer to the more flexible approach of the lower courts.[24] By a narrow 5–4 majority, the Court held that the punishment imposed on a habitual offender of a mandatory life sentence *without the possibility of parole* was unconstitutional. Although the facts in this case were basically similar to the *Rummel* case, decided three years earlier, the majority felt that the absolute denial of parole created a qualitatively different situation, enabling them to distinguish the two cases, a result made possible by Justice Blackman joining the four dissenting justices from the *Rummel* minority. A vigorous dissenting opinion written by Chief Justice Burger claimed that the Court had violated the principle of *stare decisis* in blatantly overruling the recent decision of *Rummel* by purporting to distinguish between the two cases.

The majority held that there is a key distinction between parole proceedings and commutation decisions, and that therefore a life sentence without the possibility of parole was qualitatively different from a life sentence with no restrictions on parole. In addition to the penalty being disproportionate to the gravity of the crime, the Court stressed, in sharp contrast to *Rummel,* that the prisoner had no basis for believing he would receive a commutation of his sentence, one that would allow the possibility of parole. The Court in fact compared the liberal policy of allowing parole in Texas (where Rummel was sentenced) and the strict commutation policy in South Dakota, where Helm was imprisoned.

The Court stressed that whereas there could be some reasonable expectation that good behavior in prison would be rewarded by parole, when there was no chance of parole to start with, the prisoner would have to rely on a decision, based on unfettered discretion, to commute his sentence as an essential prior act to the later chances of gaining parole. The prospects for such an eventuality seemed remote, especially considering the fact that in the eight years since 1975, when the last request for commutation of life sentence had been granted, over a hundred subsequent requests for commutation had been denied.[25]

In this case the majority also took account of the fact that at the time that Helm was sentenced, South Dakota did not have any capital offenses, and thus Helm, convicted of his seventh nonviolent felony, was subject to the same penalty as someone convicted of murder. In fact, it appears that Helm was nonviolent in his criminality and apparently had far more problem with addiction to alcohol.[26]

These factors seem to have had little impact on the four justices in the minority. They held that Helm was indeed a felon; they rejected "the fiction that all Helm's crimes were innocuous or nonviolent. Among his felonies were three burglaries and a third conviction for drunken driving. By comparison Rummel was a relatively 'model citizen.'"[27] Indeed, much of the dissenting opinion dwells on the *Rummel* case, finding expression in the minority's insistence that the arguments advanced by Helm were "precisely the same arguments" heard in the *Rummel* case. "Will the Court," the dissenting minority queried, "now recall Rummel's case so five Justices will not be parties to 'disproportionate' criminal justice?"[28] The answer is indirectly provided in the majority decision, where, in a footnote, mention is made of the fact that "Rummel was . . . released within eight months of the Court's decision in his case"[29] (not because of parole, but by virtue of habeas corpus proceedings on the grounds of ineffective assistance of counsel).[30]

The minority found further justification for their stance in a more recent decision, *Hutto* v. *Davis,* not a case of life imprisonment, but of a forty-year sentence imposed for the possession of nine ounces of marijuana and the distribution of the drug.[31] In a *per curiam* decision, the Court had reversed an *en banc* decision of the Court of Appeals for the Fourth Circuit,[32] holding that it had "failed to heed our decision in *Rummel*" and had relied instead on the four-part test in *Hart* v. *Coiner,* which *Rummel* had specifically disapproved.[33]

Indeed, the determinative power of the *Rummel* decision in the *Davis* case is brought out even more clearly in a concurring judgment by Justice Powell, who categorically states: "I view the sentence as unjust and disproportionate to the offenses. Nevertheless . . . I reluctantly conclude that the Court's decision in *Rummel* v. *Estelle* . . . is controlling on the facts before us." He comes to the conclusion that, despite the "relatively minor degree of Davis' criminality," Rummel's offenses were "by comparison . . . far less serious"; yet his sentence "was *more* severe than Davis'." Most notably Justice Powell concludes "that *Rummel* requires reversal."[34]

Justices Brennan, Marshall, and Stevens refused to be bound by *Rummel* and criticized the Court's decision for disposing of the case *per curiam* with the "benefit of neither full briefing nor oral argument,"[35] for incorrectly expanding the *Rummel* decision to deny outright a disproportionality analysis, for ignoring both the fact that the prosecutor in the trial had himself declared that Davis' continued incarceration was unjust because of the grave disparity between his sentence and those of others convicted of marijuana offenses, and the fact that the legislature had recently greatly reduced the maximum penalty for the offense. Justice Brennan (speaking for the other two dissenting justices) concludes his dissent by stating: "Unfortunately, it is Roger Trenton Davis who must now suffer the pains of the Court's insensitivity, and serve out the balance of a 40-year sentence viewed as cruel and unusual by at least six judges below. I dissent from the patent abuse of our judicial power."[36]

There is manifestly a clear-cut rift between those members of the Court (Justices Brennan, Marshall, Powell, and Stevens) who wish to apply the Eighth Amendment within the context of proportionality between the nature of the crime and the severity of the sentence and those (Chief Justice Burger and Justices Renqhuist, White, and O'Connor) who wish to limit the Court's involvement in such issues. Limit, note, not reject completely; for the Court has clearly accepted the importance of proportionality in certain cases—from its original use at the beginning of the century in *Weems*,[37] to avoid the bizarre punishment in the colony of the Philippines of *cadena temporal* (twelve years of being chained day and night at the wrists and ankles), to its more recent use in declaring the death penalty unconstitutional (as in those cases in which there is no taking of life).

In what sense, then, is life imprisonment (or long-term imprisonment, say, forty years) different from these examples for the latter group of justices? Apparently because it possesses no unique qualities, being merely part of the accepted punishment of imprisonment. This is most clearly stated by Chief Justice Burger in the dissenting judgment in *Solem* v. *Helm* when he argues that "the Eighth Amendment reaches only the *mode* of punishment and not the length of a sentence of imprisonment,"[38] an approach accentuated by his contention that "only a fraction of 'lifers' are not released within a relatively few years."[39]

But this latter assertion is based on the flimsiest data, solely on the situation in Texas (which was, of course, a crucial factor for the *Rummel* decision) and South Dakota, for which, on the face of it, the data he uses seem to be incorrect. For Chief Justice Burger states that the "historical evidence shows that since 1964, 22 life sentences have been commuted to terms of years, while requests for commutation of 25 life sentences were denied."[40]—yet, in the majority opinion, the figure of 22 commutations refers specifically to the years between 1964 and *1975,* since which time no commutations had been granted (whereas the figure of 25 denials is given as 35 in the majority opinion, again only till the year 1975). He also completely ignores the more than one hundred commutations being denied in the eight years since 1975 with no commutations being granted at all.[41]

On this basis there seem to be no grounds for the conclusion of the dissenting opinion that "there is a significant probability that [the] respondent will experience what so many 'lifers' experience"[42]—an early release from prison. On the contrary, there would, it seems, have been every chance that had he lost his case, he too would have been denied commutation— and experienced what so many other lifers denied commutation experience, namely, interminable years incarcerated until their death in prison (as is clearly the case in California and Pennsylvania, as discussed in chapter 3). On this basis, it could be argued that if a person has no prospect whatsoever of being released, no scintilla of hope to sustain and encourage him that one day he may be free, then his punishment is tantamount to a delayed death penalty. Being so, it is thus qualitatively different from all other punishments of imprisonment, and therefore in need of consideration different from that accorded them, and akin to that given the death penalty or other unusual and extreme modes of punishment.

There are in fact historical antecedents for the myopic quality of the perceptions of the death penalty and life imprisonment. One of the leading criminologists of the modern age, Thorsten Sellin, has shown some of the fallacies in the abolitionist approach of Cesare Becarria,[43] namely, that the latter, in arguing against the death penalty, had offered an alternative of penal servitude that might be considered a much more severe punishment. Sellin points out that, in many instances, the condemned prisoner would spend a few years at torturous work till his early demise from the strain of hard labor within confinement.

Today there is no penal servitude, but a long-term prisoner denied the chance of early release might well consider himself—and be considered by others—to be in as bad a condition as someone condemned to execution. This is an issue that has forced itself into public consciousness in recent years as a result of the expressed desire of a few condemned persons, such as Gilmore and others, to choose death in preference to a life sentence.[44] The question of the relative severity of the death penalty vis-à-vis a life sentence—not just as objectively determined by legislators, judges, and academic experts, but as subjectively sensed by those convicted—is a delicate issue that, with only a few isolated exceptions, has not aroused the concern of criminologists and others involved in analyses of penal philosophy, policy, and practice.

For the moment, it is clear that the death penalty is commonly considered to be the most harsh and, indeed, unique both in its severity and in its irrevocability. Even so, at least in those countries that provide constitutional protection as to the type of penalty that may be imposed, there may well be a need for a probing investigation aimed at ascertaining the relative severities of these two punishments. In the United States specifically, there has never yet been a case in the Supreme Court that has discussed the issue of whether life imprisonment, in and of itself, should be considered cruel and unusual, and hence in violation of the Eighth Amendment. Yet it must not be forgotten that in its ultimate application, life sentence condemns a human being to die in prison, with his last years (and they may be many) in total deprivation of normal social intercourse with friends and family. Till now the attacks on life imprisonment within the purview of the Eighth Amendment have ignored this aspect and have concentrated mainly on the rubric of disproportionality between the nature of the crime and the excessiveness of the term of imprisonment; besides the habitual criminal statutes, this has been most noted in the cases of life imprisonment for drug trafficking, including one case with hard labor.[45]

No effort has yet been made to describe the human implications of confinement till death, nor has any research in this area been put before the Supreme Court, as was done in the case of capital punishment cases, to show the selective and biased procedures which determine who is given the life sentence or, alternatively, who has a life sentence commuted and then benefits from early release, compared with those denied commutation and parole.

This argument may sound irrelevant given what is perceived as the more urgent need of dealing with the problem of the increasing use of the death penalty. But it has a validity of its own, and may indeed appear urgent to those desperate to pursue means of avoiding the full consequences of life imprisonment.

I N   W E S T   G E R M A N Y the issue of the constitutionality of the life sentence *has* been raised. In a 1977 case, at the behest of a judge bound by law to impose a mandatory life sentence, the Federal Constitutional Court was requested to give a ruling as to whether such a penalty did not violate the First Article of the Basic Law, which stipulates: "The dignity of man shall be inviolable. To respect and protect it shall be the duty of all State authorities."[46] When this Basic Law was promulgated in 1949, West Germany, fully cognizant of the injustices and extremities in her recent past, also added a clause placing a constitutional ban on any use of the death penalty (making it one of the first countries in the world to do so). In its stead, the criminal code provides for a mandatory life sentence for murder, genocide, treason, and serious cases of manslaughter.

The judge, in raising the issue with the Constitutional Court, enumerated five reasons why mandatory life imprisonment might be considered unconstitutional.

1. The judges were denied all discretion in imposing sentences and were unable to take into account the surrounding circumstances of the case.
2. Lengthy prison sentences would cause a person to become a psychological and physical wreck, particularly when the imprisonment exceeds fifteen years.
3. There was no penological justification—neither general deterrence nor prevention—for a life sentence.
4. The prospect of a person's having a sentence commuted was hampered by the unsatisfactory manner in which the commuting procedures were organized.
5. There was very little recidivism by life prisoners who had subsequently been released.

In dealing with the question of commutation, the Constitutional Court spelled out in some detail the defects of the commutation system, noting that there was no precise legislation dealing with this topic and no guarantee that a prisoner would actually have his case presented for discussion. Powers of clemency were in the hands of different people and different bodies, and this militated against any consistency, since those having the power ranged from the federal president to local governments. The Court also noted that in practice, most life prisoners do receive a commutation of their sentence, and then an early release; most were presumed to serve from fifteen to twenty years.[47]

The Constitutional Court found that mandatory life sentences did fulfill the conditions of the constitution and, in fact, did contribute to deterrence, which was perfectly compatible with current ideas and values. Further, the Court held that there was no firm proof of irreparable psychological and physical damage occasioned by a life sentence; here the Court chose the path of judicial restraint since there was no undisputed evidence on this point.

However, in practical terms, the Court seems to have placed great weight on the fact that there was the real likelihood of a life sentence being reduced by commutation. Noting the lack of clear legal guidelines in these matters, the Court stressed that it is essential for a state founded on the rule of law to have a "legalization" of the existing system of pardons, if its penal system is to be humane.[48] K. C. Horton, in discussing this case, argues that the Court was here expressing its desire for a system of pardons to be clearly stipulated in legislation; in fact, the Court seems to have been hinting at the desirability of a system of entitlement which the American courts were so reluctant to adopt on the basis of customary practice. Indeed, the failure to set up such a system might well convince the German court to reconsider its position on the constitutionality of the mandatory life sentence. As Horton puts it,

> The Court thus gave the legislature a clear indication of its views on pardons; alongside the existing system which it assumed would continue, there should be a statutory system of pardons exercised by the courts.

He goes on to note that the Court's decision was well received, particularly its consideration of the "fact that even the most serious criminal is a human being and can remain so only if he has some hope for his life in the future."[49] According to Horton, the Constitutional Court has yet to make a final pronouncement on the mandatory life sentence. Any failure to legislate clearly or adequately on the issue of pardons in the future could well result in the existing legislation being regarded as unconstitutional.

What emerges from the present judicial attitude—and what must be strongly stressed—is the fact that the Court's willingness to regard mandatory life imprisonment as compatible with the "dignity" provisions of the constitution is, in effect, dependent on the existence of procedures allowing for legal circumvention of the life sentence. In other words, if the life sentences were indeed what they prima facie seem to be—imprisonment until death—then the Constitutional Court might very well declare the mandatory life sentence to be unconstitutional.

The German Constitutional Court has addressed issues that have never been brought before the United States Supreme Court. Although the terminological basis is different—"cruel and unusual" and "due process" in the United States, against the concept of "respect for the dignity of man" in the German constitution—there seems little reason why the American courts, too, should not be asked to address the issue of the constitutionality of a life sentence per se. In other words, to decide whether life imprisonment is not in violation of the cruel and unusual provision, not just because it is disproportional to the crime, nor because the due process provisions of the Fourteenth Amendment have been violated, but because, in and of itself, a life sentence constitutes cruelty, at least within "evolving standards of decency," as determined, for instance, by the evidence of the nature of confinement when there is no hope of release.

If such an issue were to be brought before the United States Supreme Court, it is possible that it would also find, as did the judges in Germany, that there can be no comprehensive decision on life imprisonment without examining the procedures and the consequences of the commuting and pardoning process.

In any event, the punishment of life imprisonment seems to be in a unique position; it has evaded the intense scrutiny that criminologists, jurists, civil rights activists, and others are giving to just about every other aspect of penal philosophy and practice. Thus, in addition to the far-reaching developments in the United States and other countries with regard to the death penalty, there is also a worldwide struggle, spearheaded by Amnesty International, for the total abolition of the death penalty.[50] In a parallel move, imprisonment in many countries is being challenged and various alternatives or adaptations and limitations to it sought.[51] Yet in almost all discussions on the prison system, little more than passing mention is given to the question of life imprisonment—and then it is often paradoxically in the context of acknowledging that different and more severe criteria might have to apply to some prisoners with long-term sentences, often because of their presumed dangerousness in the future. However, even when the very concept of dangerousness is challenged and the possibility of predicting violence in the future is denied, the problematics of what to do with those presently and undeniably violent is treated inadequately.

One of the most compelling arguments for total prohibition of prisons is the report of the Prison Research Education Action Project, which focuses on the inevitable evils of prison, the deficiencies of society as a contributory factor in crime, the search for alternative responses to crime in the form of restitution and conflict-of-resolution mediation, the need for community involvement for crime prevention, and the success of innovative self-help projects for delinquents and criminals. But the report fails to deal adequately with the troublesome issues of murder and torture. Most significantly, the report acknowledges that "there is little disagreement that for those very few people who exhibit continual violent and aggressive behavior in society, temporary restraint is not only indicated but demanded."[52] The report suggests that the restraint should be linked to community re-education centers, controlled by those who will be serving the sentences.

But beyond stressing the need for satisfactory monitoring and due process considerations, the report is wholly silent on such issues as the length of temporary restraint, the manner for determining it, the mutual protection to be provided in a confined group when membership is based largely on proneness to violence, and the assurances to be given to the public as to successful rehabilitation prior to release. The report also notes that much of the labeling of dangerousness is inherently political in nature, yet ignores the fact that there is also much violence that is politically motivated, including political assassinations and terrorist activities. It is doubtful whether people whose violence is politically motivated would be amenable to the presumed advantages of the report's program.

The report itself is an important document and deserves greater exposure and deeper consideration than it has hitherto been given, but it largely ignores the problem of extreme criminality and violence. For as long as it fails to address this problem in detail, its overall recommendations will be similarly ignored. Prison abolitionists must confront this issue no less than capital punishment abolitionists. Of course, the latter see long-term imprisonment as *the* solution to *their* problem, based on the perceived qualitative difference between capital punishment and any other sentence, no matter how severe.

What is it that makes for the singularity of the death penalty? It is irreversible, but so is mutilation; it is a severe punishment, but so is torture or a life sentence. It involves the denial of dignity, but so, for all intents and purposes, does a life sentence: a human life involves not just existence and survival, but the unique development of a personality, creativity, liberty, unfettered social intercourse. When these are denied, can those who, in the name of civil rights, are in the forefront of the struggle against the death penalty ignore the ultimate implications of a life sentence? And is the life sentence only acceptable because it is presumed that it is rarely implemented in full? There is little evidence on this—but, even if true, what of those who do live out their lives in prison? In fact, there are probably far more prisoners sentenced to life who die in prison than prisoners condemned to death who are executed.

I raise these points because, in the course of its confrontation with the death penalty, the United States Supreme Court has used as its starting point the uniquely severe nature of the death penalty, and has insisted that in imposing it, it is necessary to observe standards of care in judgment that are not required of any other penalty.

As Margaret Radin notes, "Irrevocability strongly calls for strict scrutiny."[53] In a thoughtful analysis, she tries to elucidate what it is about the death penalty that is so unique; yet, throughout the analysis runs a strain of ambiguity and ambivalence. The essence of the issue of irrevocability is set out in a footnote in which Radin acknowledges that "even one day in prison is irrevocable in the sense that all past events and their resultant effects on human beings are irrevocable." However, she goes on to argue that

> although it might be difficult to articulate, most people intuitively recognize a distinction between the irrevocability of everything and the irrevocability of death and mutilation. The latter is the strong sense of irrevocability referred to here. It encompasses irreversible deprivations of attributes or capacities essential to, or at least closely connected with, complete personhood. At a minimum, it encompasses irreversible deprivations of certain physical or mental functions included in our stereotype of a person. Someone who has had her hands cut off for stealing does not hereby cease to be a complete person; yet, when one thinks of what a person is, surely, the stereotype has hands.

Imprisonment will not be considered irrevocable in the strong sense, because a prisoner can think, write, talk, feel and may some day be released. Yet, if it were possible to give someone a pill that instantly induced in her the physical and mental effects of having spent a lifetime in a cell, an irrevocable deprivation in the strong sense would probably have taken place.[54]

She then enumerates several factors that make for the uniqueness of the death penalty, but some of them seem to include attributes of the life sentence. Further, Radin does not refer to death alone, but points out the parallels between death and mutilation. Perhaps the most significant part of her analysis is the attempt to probe the difference between the death penalty and life imprisonment, yet the examples that she gives seems, in essence, to stress also the irrevocability of a life sentence, of each wasted day.

What is the dividing line between the deprivation of life and the deprivation of liberty if the latter is decreed formally to be for all time? Radin herself defines *liberty* as "the freedom from governmental restraint on physical movement and choice of environment," and notes that it has "consistently been treated as a fundamental right."[55] However, it should be noted that Radin is dealing with imprisonment in general, and thus she notes that the prisoner may "some day be released." This would again make the life sentence without prospect of parole different from other terms of imprisonment.

Not only has the life sentence not been subjected to the kind of scrutiny that has been given the death penalty, but many civil right activists have often argued that a life sentence is an appropriate alternative to capital punishment; further, inasmuch as public opinion and legislation have opted for abolition of the death penalty, it is often the perceived severity of a life sentence (together with its presumed incapacitation for further crime) that has had much bearing on the decision.

However, even at the risk of undermining some support for the abolition of the death penalty, it seems to me that a direct confrontation with the total implications of the life sentence can no longer be avoided, and that it would be appropriate for judicial concern to be shown toward the life sentence, just as has been done in the case of the death penalty. It may be hoped that the ultimate guidelines that would emerge will be more clear and consistent. This may be a forlorn wish, with little prospect of satisfaction, since the issues surrounding life imprisonment are no less complicated than for the death penalty.

IT IS OF PARTICULAR INTEREST to note that one of the early pioneering articles on capital punishment (published a few years before *Furman*), by Arthur Goldberg, former justice of the Supreme Court, and Alan Dershowitz, clearly recognized that there were close interconnections between attitudes to the death penalty and attitudes to other severe penalties, and that rules laid down for the former might be relevant for the latter.[56] In fact, they felt that it was specifically this relevance and the implications that flow from it that might prevent the Supreme Court taking the far-reaching step of declaring the death penalty unconstitutional. After pointing out the importance of the *Trop* v. *Dulles* decision,[57] in which a court martial decision to deprive a native-born citizen of his citizenship for war-time desertion (basically, one day's AWOL) was declared to be cruel and unusual punishment, they add that

> The Court today might hesitate to extend *Trop* any further for fear that the extension would not stop. Life imprisonment, for example, destroys an individual's political existence nearly as much as does expatriation; indeed, an expatriate out of prison clearly has far more opportunity to enjoy the advantages of a free society than the inmate. Even if their levels of psychological distress could be reliably compared, it is not at all certain whose would be greater.[58]

Having posed the problem, they go on to solve it—not in terms of physical and psychological pain, in which they apparently see no real difference between expatriation, the death sentence, and life imprisoment, but in terms of "the sheer enormity of the punishment. 'An expatriate,' the Court said, 'is deprived of his "right to have rights." ' Similarly, an executed convict is deprived of his 'right to have rights.' " Among these rights is the right to have a decision reversed and vacated. They continue: "By contrast, one imprisoned even for life retains certain 'rights'; he is not deprived of all societal protection"[59] Yet, there is a whole host of rights of which a prisoner is deprived, such as the right to vote, to movement, to make autonomous decisions (for instance, he may not be allowed to volunteer for medical experimentation), to marry (if he is a long-term prisoner), to have ordinary social or sexual relations, to be with his family and friends, or even to avoid those with whom he does not wish to associate, some of whom may endanger his safety or his very life.[60] And, finally and most significantly, he may be deprived of the right to one day be free, if serving a life sentence without parole.

In their article, Goldberg and Dershowitz note that several articles, written in the 1960s, had expressed doubts as to the possibility that the Supreme Court would declare the death penalty unconstitutional. A leading criminal-law scholar, Herbert Packer, had declared in 1966 that the "Supreme Court is not about to declare that the death penalty *simpliciter* is so cruel and unusual as to be constitutionally intolerable."[61] But of course that is just about what the Court did several years later, even though it retreated afterwards. Packer's article was actually a criticism of a dissent that Goldberg had written when still a justice on the Supreme Court. In *Rudolph v. Alabama,*[62] Goldberg noted his dissent (together with Justices Douglas and Brennan) from a denial of certiorari in a rape case in which the death penalty had been imposed. They had questioned whether the death penalty could be imposed on "a convicted rapist who had neither taken nor endangered human life." This minority opinion, coming before *Furman,* had actually been prescient, for it was this very approach that was later accepted in the *Coker* case.[63]

Goldberg and Dershowitz also refer to a later note critical

of the *Rudolph* dissenting opinion which also stated that there was little prospect for significant judicial intervention in terms of deciding whether the death penalty was cruel and unusual, and expressed doubt whether a comparative basis between jurisdictions in the United States or even with other countries would be helpful.[64] Again it was the dissenting judgment that was proven correct. Even so, the note has significance for one further reservation that it expressed. It raised the question as to how to differentiate between the death penalty and life imprisonment, arguing that if the death penalty was to be considered too severe in terms of the interests the law was trying to protect through deterrence, a similar argument could be made against life imprisonment. "The Court conceivably could declare that even life imprisonment or any severe prison sentence would be unnecessary, and thus cruel and unusual if the defendant did not endanger life."[65] Admittedly the author did claim that such an argument would be an unlikely and drastic extension of Justice Goldberg's suggestion in *Rudolph,* but in any case, the author had not considered very great the possibility of Justice Goldberg's original suggestion being adopted. Now that it has been incorporated through *Coker* into the very foundation of the Court's approach to the death penalty, perhaps the "drastic" extension of applying similar reasoning (for example, "no life sentence where no life has been taken") to life imprisonment becomes a possibility.

Unlikely as it seemed in the 1960s that capital punishment would be declared unconstitutional, nonexistent as it was as a penological or constitutional issue prior to the 1960s, by the early 1970s the first breakthroughs in constitutional control and restrictions were being delineated.

A further possible harbinger may be noted in that the precedent-setting *Furman* decision was preceded by a California case. Less than a year before *Furman,* basing its decision on the more specific and restrictive wording of the California constitution, the California Supreme Court had declared capital punishment in California to be unconstitutional.[66]

Similar potential developments may be at hand for life imprisonment, for which the *Solem* v. *Helm* case may serve as
the basis for further litigation. More significantly, it has followed the reasoning in the little-noted *Wanstreet* case in West
Virginia, which, just as in the California capital punishment
case, relied on a state constitution and not the U.S. Constitution, since the former was couched in broader terms. On this
basis it did what the Supreme Court in *Rummel* v. *Estelle* had
not been prepared to do—declare a habitual sentence of life
imprisonment unconstitutional for disproportionality, thereby
providing a model of logical reasoning and practical applicability.[67]

However, any further progress in this field, not necessarily for abolition per se (which seems almost impossible at
this stage), but at least for clear-cut provisions of super due
process, including the issues of prosecutional discretion, mandatory sentencing, disproportionality, prison conditions, and
pardoning practices, will require intense organizational commitment, sensitive personal dedication, and accumulated professional expertise of the kind which has characterized the struggle against capital punishment, and which has been notably
absent in life imprisonment.

There are no easy answers to the issue of life imprisonment; since it is sometimes not carried out to the full, it might
seem that discretion dictates an evasion of the issue. However,
it is surely time to ask: Is society prepared to countenance the
sentence of life imprisonment implemented in such a way that
most of these prisoners would never be released? If so, then
why the reluctance to examine the implications, why the lack
of research? If not, then why the present procedures? Why the
mandatory life sentence that takes any effective decision-making
out of the purview of the judge and then transfers it to a parole
or pardoning board, where there will inevitably be discretionary
practices with far less judicial control or public concern?

At least in the United States the developing rules being laid
down for the death penalty seem to obligate the Supreme Court

to give similar attention to the issue of the life sentence. If there can be no mandatory death penalty, as the Court has declared, then surely, at the very least, there should be no mandatory life sentence (at least for offenses short of murder). Alternatively, if a mandatory life sentence is permissible, then surely it is the Court's obligation to probe the manner in which commutation is handled, to see if there is any arbitrariness or capriciousness in these procedures, not on the basis of guesses and presumptions, but of firm empirical evidence.

The overall position today is that whereas for the death penalty the Court has insisted that the decision to impose it be *neither* mandatory nor arbitrary, the decision in regard to life sentence is often *both* mandatory and arbitrary—mandatory in the initial stage, when the judge is obligated to give the only penalty available to him, and arbitrary in the second stage, when the authorities decide upon commutation.

In any event, what is becoming increasingly transparent is that serious civil rights and constitutional issues are raised by long-term imprisonment. Whether or not there is a difference between the two penalties, there still seems a need for a specially higher standard of due process. Recent decisions indicate the nature of the problem.

In *Mims* v. *Shapp*,[68] the legitimacy of prolonged solitary confinement was challenged. A prison inmate in Pennsylvania, while serving a life sentence for killing a police officer, killed the deputy warden of the prison. Immediately after the incident, he was placed in solitary confinement (known as the Behavioral Adjustment Unit), which is described as "undeniably severe. He . . . was permitted only two showers and one change of clothing per week. He ate all meals in his cell, slept on the floor because his mattress did not fit on the concrete slab bed, and, although permitted to exercise outside his cell for a minimal time each day, he was forced to undergo a thorough and degrading strip and body cavity search after each such temporary release." After five years in this isolated situation, he sued in civil court for release and damages, which he was awarded by the trial court, a decision confirmed by the Court of Appeals of the Third Circuit. However, the court, sitting *en banc,* later reversed the decision as to damages, holding itself bound by an intervening decision of the Supreme Court which had basically seen a prisoner in solitary confinement as being merely transferred from one restrictive confinement to another.[69]

Of course there can be no denying that the potential for violence in this instance is based on the proven facts of past personal history. But can the punishment, with its special conditions, really be considered less severe than a death penalty, less a denial of dignity, less dehumanizing for all involved in it?

It is interesting to note that the crime for which the prisoner was committed, a murder while serving a life sentence, is a crime that is often quoted as justifying a special exception to an abolitionist position. The Supreme Court, in rejecting mandatory sentencing for capital punishment, left open the possibility for an exception for murder committed by a person serving a life sentence.[70] A New York law to this effect had been declared unconstitutional, since there was a need, as the state court emphasized, to allow for the examination of any mitigating (as well as aggravating) circumstances.[71]

In contrast, an Arizona decision, handed down at about the same time, allowed a mandatory life sentence without possibility of commutation, pardon, or parole for a minimum period of twenty-five years for the lesser offense of dangerous assault in a prison by an offender, though a dissenting opinion did argue for the need for individualized consideration.[72]

But the key question that seems to transcend all these others and goes to the heart of the question raised in this chapter (and in the larger sense in this book) emerges from a recent case heard before the Supreme Court of New Hampshire, *in re Caulk,*[73] in which a thirty-six-year-old prisoner, condemned to long-term confinement for separate convictions of felonious sexual assault and burglary, and facing further charges that might have led to sentences "tantamount to a sentence of life without parole,'' sought the right to refuse solid food so as to allow himself to die slowly.[74] The motivation for these actions seems to have been a combination of a sense of failure, an expression of penance, and a desire to avoid the consequences of lengthy incarceration with little prospect of release. The prisoner, as described by the Court,

> has purposely selected this method of dying so that he can remain competent. He wants to think, to feel and to understand his death. He insists that he is not committing suicide but rather is allowing himself to die.
>
> The defendant never expects to be released from prison again. He says he is tired, unhappy, disappointed with the promise that life holds and that he does not "belong on the streets." He maintains that if he cannot live freely he does not want to live at all. While he is physically down, he claims that he is emotionally high.
>
> The defendant does not claim to be a religious person in the formal sense, but suggests there is a spiritual dimension to him and to his actions. . . . He testified that he has hurt a lot of people, and whenever he feels pain on his starvation diet, he believes he is paying another debt for his past misdeeds. In his words, he wants to leave the world as a man and to die with dignity, with his head up.
>
> The defendant's course of conduct is calculated to achieve only one purpose; namely, his death. He is not making any demands or asking for anything in return for his fast. There is no evidence that he poses a direct threat to the security of the institution or to anybody in the institution. He is prepared to execute a release absolving the state and its officials from any civil liability if he is allowed to starve himself to death.[75]

The Court held that the state's interests both in maintaining an effective criminal justice system (including the fact that there were further trials pending against him in need of resolution), and in preserving life (including avoiding the invidious position prison personnel would be placed in if he were to become comatose while in their custody) took precedence over any rights to privacy that he claimed. However, Judge Douglas, in a lone dissent, argued that

> the State has not demonstrated a compelling interest so as to override Mr. Caulk's fundamental liberty right to fast until his natural death without governmental intervention. Our State motto proudly proclaims the choice "to live free or die". If he can't do the former, I would permit the latter for Mr. Caulk.
>
> The majority and I agree that it is highly likely that Mr. Caulk will serve the remainder of his natural life in prison.[76]

As to the argument that pending cases against him necessitate his being kept alive so as to allow the criminal justice system to bring these cases to finality, Judge Douglas notes that "essentially, the State claims that it should be allowed to keep Mr. Caulk alive so that it may subject him to further prosecution and punishment."[77]

Seeing force-feeding as unwarranted intrusion into the individual's privacy, the dissenting opinion suggests that

> it would be difficult to imagine a greater intrusion upon one's right to bodily integrity and self-determination than force-feeding. Not only does it present significant health risks and subject the individual to a high degree of pain, if the individual refuses to eat voluntarily after force-feeding has been ordered, the painful daily ordeal may continue indefinitely.
>
> At trial . . . [a doctor] testified that the insertion of the tube has to be done very carefully because gagging often occurs. . . .
>
> Mr. Caulk . . . suffered a great deal of pain and discomfort . . . [until] the tube was removed due to the danger of

imminent ulceration of his throat and nasal passages. Given Mr. Caulk's position that despite the outcome of this appeal, he is not going to eat voluntarily, it is reasonable to conclude that painful government-controlled force-feeding in the manner set out above may continue indefinitely.[78]

Moving from the legal issue of individual privacy and governmental intrusion, and the medical issue of pain, the dissenting opinion deals with the larger philosophical issues of the petitioner's right to the dignity and autonomy embedded in his statement: "I am simply stating let me be," and the judge's personal dilemma: "This case is difficult for all of us to resolve. Under the Constitution of New Hampshire, I must respect Mr. Caulk's right to be free from governmental intrusion of his bodily integrity even though I might disagree with his position or the morality of it."[79]

Mindful of the delicateness of the issues and of the dangers of exploiting hunger strikes for ulterior ends, the dissenting opinion sets out the general conditions that should be applied when any prisoner on a hunger strike seeks to avoid force-feeding:

1. The prisoner makes no demands upon the correction personnel
2. He is competent and understands the consequences of his fast
3. He has been given an explanation by a physician of the physical changes his body will endure
4. He provides a release from any claims to those in whose custody he is
5. He waives the appointment of a guardian seeking to exercise "substituted judgment" for him should he deteriorate to the point of mental incompetence
6. He forgoes any assistance by the authorities in his dying process, so that he "must die truly unassisted by the government."[80]

I have dealt with this case at some length, for, although it encompasses unique issues rarely raised in penological debate and judicial dispute, it focuses indirectly on some of the key factors that form the essence of this book. In a nutshell, is the process of dying sought by the prisoner less compatible with his dignity as a human being than the procedures to sustain his life sought by the state? To what extent does the state's wish to force-feed him constitute not just an unwarranted invasion of his privacy, but a physical assault of a torturous nature? To what extent would his own planned dying process lead to unbearable pain, and unconsiousness, placing those responsible for him in an untenable position? To what extent does his own right to autonomous decision-making take precedence over these latter considerations? In pondering these and related questions, one cannot but become aware of how tenuous is the the line—in the context of prison conditions—between life, death, and torture, as punishments imposed by the state, as choices sought by the condemned, as dilemmas devoid of objective appraisal or of rational resolution by governmental and judicial authorities.

There are no easy answers to the penological questions I have raised, discussed, and alluded to. But if discretion does suggest a continuation of the practice of ignoring these questions because of their delicate and complex nature, the actions of prisoners themselves are denying this convenient option and obligating an earnest confrontation, requiring the need to draw on intellectual resources, humanistic principles, and empathetic identification with the plight and the problems of the long-term and life prisoner. Even before all the possibilities ensconced in the death penalty debate have been exhausted, empirical reality insists that thought, attention, and compassion be directed to the lifer, his needs, his rights, his wishes, and his actions. Certainly ideas and rulings that have been considered relevant for the death sentence should be considered analogous for the other ultimate penalty, that of life imprisonment.

6

GLOBAL SCALES OF JUSTICE

ANTHROPOLOGICAL STUDIES have shown how diverse are the forms of behavior that are considered to be socially unacceptable to a particular society, and how wide are the differences between societies as to the parameters of the forbidden and the permissible.[1] Students of deviant behavior argue endlessly as to what should be the limits of societal toleration of deviation, as to where the line should be drawn, and as to how the differences should be maintained.[2] The debate, for the most part, focuses on issues which are marginal, and on sanctions which are minimal.

However, even when dealing with the ultimate penalty of death, a surprisingly large degree of variety is encountered; certainly from a historical perspective, the list of activities for which death was the sanction is a potpourri of human conduct, ranging from the tens of offenses for which the Bible states the offender shall surely be put to death to the two-hundred plus capital crimes listed in the British criminal code until into the nineteenth century. In both these well-known examples, though, there is a division of opinion as to the degree to which the penalty was actually invoked. Although there is little doubt that it was used for what are generally considered today to be minor offenses, there are those who hold that the penalty was not mandatory but, being the maximum, was more a societal guideline as to the perceived seriousness of the prohibited activity than a declaration of intent as to the anticipated punishment.

Those responsible for implementing the law often used creative reasoning and compassionate feelings to avert the severe decree. Though the Bible itself, for instance, does give examples of people being put to death for what modern secular society would certainly consider minor offenses or, indeed, acceptable behavior of choice—collecting wood on the sabbath, and blasphemy—there is abundant research to indicate that the stringent tones of "thou shall surely be put to death" were rarely enforced. A. S. Diamond, a student of ancient and primitive law, suggests that the above two situations were described specifically because they were unique and no more than isolated acts.[3] There is certainly much data from postbiblical times that show the rabbinical authorities to have laid down strict conditions—of the type of evidence and procedure required for proof—the intent and the effect of which was to nullify, for all practical purposes, the use of the death penalty.[4]

In Britain, too, juxtaposed to the infamous instances of public execution of young children (including those who had not yet completed their first decade of life) for minor offenses, are the descriptions of the extensive use of the "benefit of clergy" (basically, diversion into the ecclesiastical courts in which there was no capital punishment) as a means of avoiding the harsh official penalty.[5]

Nevertheless, the use of the death penalty for minor offenses was a significant force in the abolition movement. The crowds at these public hangings seem to have reacted to the scene with a great deal of emotion, sometimes their passion for vengeance leading to abuse of the criminal, but at many other times their sense of justice leading to attempts to free him. In any event, it is clear that at the judicial stage the unduly severe penalties had a negative effect on the ability of the criminal justice system to adjudicate fairly, as jurors refused to convict or resorted to fictions in order to link the finding of guilt with a noncapital offense.

The forms of execution have also varied widely, from the stoning and burning outlined in the Bible, through the slicing in China, the drawing and quartering in England, to the utilization of sophisticated technology in modern times, ranging from the electric chair and gas chamber to the hypodermic needle and lethal drugs. Certain cultures seem to favor certain methods, the gallows being linked to Britain and many countries of its former far-flung empire, the guillotine with France, electrocution with the United States, with the method used in any one country often arousing distaste or disgust in others. The Inquisition favored burning for heretics and witches; most armies concede what is considered to be a more dignified death by firing squad. The range is shown through the manner in which some of the most famous executions in history were consummated—Socrates by hemlock, Jesus by crucifixion, Joan of Arc by burning, Raleigh by beheading. Whereas in the Middle Ages torture was considered an essential ingredient of the punishment, in modern times there is a growing acceptance that any extraneous physical discomfort should be avoided.

Where executions are not performed in public, the practice has developed of having select individuals present at the execution. In the United States today, this increasingly involves reporters for the mass media. In some other countries, the judge and the prosecutor are obliged to be present. The condemned person is generally allowed access to a clergyman in the time leading up to the execution. Some jurisdictions allow him to request his lawyer, family, and friends to be present; sometimes the family of the victim is invited to be present.

From time to time the suggestion has been put forward that the execution should be televised—this argument is even made, in a cynical way, by some abolitionists, who claim that if deterrence is the issue then this should surely be the best way to achieve it, but hope that the revulsion such a spectacle would evoke would turn the majority of viewers to their cause. Conversely, some retentionists oppose televised executions for fear of a negative public reation.[6] As it is, the written descriptions in newspapers serve a similar purpose—and description of the agony of the condemned person's final seconds, sometimes even minutes, have been used to contend that the death sentence in its implementation is cruel and unusual.

On occasion, a new method tried in the United States has been challenged on its first use.[7] Do the convulsions that often occur signify the pain the condemned person is undergoing or are they merely the muscular responses after all consciousness has ended? It is specifically when things do not go smoothly that the reaction is most intense. In England there are known instances in which the bungling of an executioner led to the intervention of the crowd to save the condemned person from further suffering, and often to the wrath of the crowd being focused on the executioner himself. The practice also developed of allowing a pardon when the attempt to put to death fails, the premise in such cases being of possible divine intervention to prevent a miscarriage of justice.[8]

In the United States, though, such or even other considerations were not recognized by the Supreme Court when an electrocution failed to kill, due to some technical malfunction. When the state made preparations for a further attempt, and when the governor failed to grant a pardon, the condemned person sought a reprieve through the courts, arguing that it would be cruel and unusual to subject him for a second time to the awesome ritual of an execution. The Supreme Court rejected these arguments, holding that the punishment originally imposed on him had to be carried out.[9]

In recent times, as the debate on capital punishment has intensified and the number of executions has increased, so the practice has arisen of the opposing protagonists of abolition and retentionist positions demonstrating or maintaining a vigil outside of the prison.[10] The full emotions bound up with the debate find expression in placards carried and in slogans chanted. I have indicated that a case may be made for the use of capital punishment, and that it may possibly be kept consonant with liberal and humane principles; but those retentionists who forego a good night's sleep to express their approval for the death penalty, at a moment when a life is being snuffed out, generally give vent to the most primitive of passions, and it is their wrath at the criminal that stands our far more than any sympathy for the victim or his family.

However, on occasion, members of the victim's family have also been present; this is part of a phenomenon of both abolitionist and retentionist camps using the responses of the families of victims to substantiate their stands. Sometimes they speak of the need for vengeance; sometimes they ask what purpose could be served by the further shedding of blood.

In these remarks may be noted once again a deeper philosophy running through them. People do not respond to the death penalty purely in terms of their own personal tragedy, but do so within the framework of their total world-outlook. This is true not only for individuals, but for total societies and the larger cultures of which they are a part. The specific issue of the death penalty provides also a glimpse of a larger value-system, of ideological background, and of cultural influences. Geographical entities often overlap with ideological divisions and with cultural antecedents. These differences often appear in the various policies adopted toward capital punishment. This is most noted in the contrasting approaches of Eastern and Western Europe to the death penalty. Similarly, most countries of South America tend to be abolitionist, even though their overall civil rights record is not a good one; yet in North America, where stress is so often placed on civil rights, human values, liberal principles, and constitutional protections, there has been continued resort to the death penalty as an acceptable and publicly supported punishment. In Africa there is widespread use of capital punishment, even though it tends to run counter to traditional practices and is mainly a relic from the more recent colonial past. The death penalty is used in most Arab countries, though the range and frequency of use differs often according to the degree to which fundamentalistic Islam has an impact. In most of Asia, too, there is a reliance on the death penalty, which in this case actually transcends the differences—cultural and ideological—among the countries.[11]

The range in the nature of the punishment is also apparent in the circumstances in which it is carried out—from the excesses of undue publicity on the one hand, to utmost secrecy on the other; from prior announcements of execution dates to *ex post facto* announcements of a completed execution; from immediate implementation of the court's verdict, sometimes seemingly in indecent haste, to a prolonged period of agonizing uncertainty in death row that may last for years.

In Asia, Africa, and Latin America, there are countries which still resort to public executions, some by statute, others by judicial discretion or administrative whim, sometimes in the case of political crime to impress on the populace the government's determination to enforce its view of a disputed norm. The scenes, as sometimes reported in the press, resemble the historical reports of such events in the Western world. There are several descriptions of the situation in England in the eighteenth and nineteenth centuries: of the ritualized procession from Tyburn Prison to Newgate Square, of the partisan crowds (generally hostile to the condemned person, occasionally supportive of him), of the prisoner's demeanor (sometimes brave and evoking respect, other times cringing and evoking pity or contempt), of the executioner's ability (generally competent, occasionally bungling).[12] In the United States, judicial support for the constitutionality of public executions (in the case of public shooting in Utah) was given by the Supreme Court in 1879,[13] and the last public execution (in Kentucky) was as recent as 1936.[14]

Though public executions have received much criticism and—in worldwide perspective—are on the wane, no less disturbing are instances of executions carried out in secret without prior warning, occasionally even without subsequent announcement. Knowledge of the date of the planned execution has some significance, for it enables the condemned and those acting on his behalf to make last minute pleas for clemency. Although this sometimes leads to frantic efforts to find a judge who will agree to a stay of execution (the pattern often noted in the

United States), it does at least assure the possibility of exploring all possible avenues to save the condemned person before the irreversible action takes place.

The length of time between the verdict of death and its being carried out is also a significant factor in any consideration of capital punishment. Sufficient time should be allowed to enable the condemned person and those acting on his behalf to make the necessary representations, if they so desire, of appealing the sentence or of submitting a plea for clemency. Yet, some countries specify that there should be no appeal and others that there be an immediate disposition of the sentence, within forty-eight hours, for instance, in Cuba, Guatemala, and El Salvador. In Peru a 1974 law providing for the death penalty for political terrorism states that the sanction must be "rapid, intimidating and exemplary," and that the sentence should be "graphic, the procedure summary and the execution of the sentence immediate."[15]

On the other hand, there are countries where procrastination may become the rule, especially when the overall desires for using capital punishment clash with the complications of its implementation in any specific case. Often the route followed is to make no decision or to defer a final decision. This process has contributed to what is known as the pile-up on death row, most noted in the United States, where in the last ten years closest to two thousand death penalties have been imposed, but only a small number, less than five percent have been carried out. In some instances clemency has been granted, in others appeals are pending; but in yet others the final formal act of a governor's signature on a death warrant is lacking, with officials caught in the dilemma of being unwilling to grant clemency because of political pressures and public demands, but unwilling also to allow the irreversible step of the execution to take place because of the possibility of error or personal distaste for involvement in the execution process.

Within the judicial framework it may, in many respects, be much easier to pronounce a sentence of death on an accused than it is to deny a condemned person his last opportunity to be saved; and so judges give last-minute stays of execution or governors refrain from signing the death warrant.

As David Brick argues: "No judge wants to discover after it is too late that he permitted someone to be executed on the basis of factual or legal error, and for that reason alone the backlog of death row prisoners can be expected to persist."[16] There has indeed been a considerable increase in the number of death-row inmates since Brick wrote. In fact the pile-up on death row has possibly done much to undermine support for capital punishment and to justify an abolitionist stand.

However, the problem is almost insoluble since the converse situation is also true—a democratic society will not easily accept concerted actions to do away with the existing pile-up by a sudden spate of wholesale executions. The limbo situation—of increasing numbers of death sentences but limited numbers of actual executions—provides a sort of unsatisfactory compromise: retentionists are satisfied at the original sentence, and abolitionists have ample time to try to prevent its implementation.

The period that a condemned person spends in death row is important not only in terms of time alone, but also the conditions, which are often differentially strict. There may be long hours in a solitary cell, minimum contact with other inmates, restricted access to medical, psychological, and legal personnel, limited visitation and other privileges. These conditions are sometimes of such a nature as to raise serious constitutional issues as to their being cruel and unusual—and this has indeed been argued in United States courts, thus far unsuccessfully.[17] Some commentators, as already noted, believe that these conditions are deliberately made so in order to encourage the inmates to forego their legal battles—to the state costly, time-consuming, and unsettling—but the truth is that it is not just inmate perseverance but, no less, governmental procrastination that leads to deferment.[18]

Those condemned persons who have unavailingly asked

to be executed indicate the ambivalence over the issue. Recently, in a joint move, a group of death-row inmates requested to withdraw their legal battles because, so they claimed, the suspense of uncertainty was unbearable. In any event, strict surveillance of the condemned is constantly maintained, for society does not easily accept the idea of a condemned person cheating the executioner by committing suicide. It is clearly not merely the demise and removal of the condemned that concerns society, but the need for there to be a vivid expression of state power. In the wake of the sudden increase in death-row inmates there has been an upsurge of research attempting to probe the personal and psychological impact on the inmates.[19]

With the revival of the widespread use of the death penalty in the United States in the early eighties, a national organization, the National Coalition for the Abolition of Capital Punishment, was set up.[20] It serves many purposes, from a clearinghouse for information and monitoring the fate of condemned persons to lobbying and education. Recently the organization has given its support to a chain hunger strike, started by an ex-inmate and maintained by volunteers in and out of prison, each committing himself to a period of set days during which he will refrain from taking all but fluids to protest the continuance of the death penalty. Many arguments are brought forward by the organization and those linked to it, but the role of human rights concerns is often manifest. It is this aspect that gives any debate over capital punishment its international dimensions. This is, in many respects, similar to other social struggles, the most notable parallel being perhaps the struggle against slavery, which also used the nomenclature of abolition, and which also evoked transnational concern.

In the modern world, the work of Amnesty International is perhaps the most pertinent, interesting, and effective. This is an independent, nonaligned, grass-roots international body, with observer status at the United Nations. Originally formed as a spontaneous reaction to an article, published in the early sixties by a London newspaper, dealing with the tragedy of political prisoners,[21] today it has a professional staff, an organizational structure, and a vast network of members, all acting on the basis of carefully articulated principles and clearly delineated guidelines for action. It has a respected name and a record of achievement, including the award of the Nobel Prize for Peace. From a political and ideological perspective, it professes and tries to maintain a neutral stance; this is perhaps best indicated by the criticism it has been subjected to by governmental authorities of vastly different ideological and political hues. Most of the cirticism emanates from totalitarian governments, of both right and left. As I argued in chapter 2, there is a great deal of overlap between right and left, a fact borne out in part by attitudes and policies in regard to punishment, including capital punishment.

Although initial concerns of Amensty International were with political prisoners only, and though this remains its major area of activity, involvement in this field led, inevitably perhaps, to concern for some of the additional aspects of political imprisonment—at first torture, then extra-judicial executions, and subsequently capital punishment. In these areas Amnesty International has declared its unreserved opposition, not only insofar as political prisoners are concerned, but for all prisoners—with no exceptions.

Amensty International sponsors research and conferences on these issues, monitors ongoing developments all over the world, and makes representations directly to relevant government authorities through mass write-ins by its members and direct approaches by its leadership, together with attempts to put together a worldwide consensus for the abolition of capital punishment. It argues, in the words of its 1977 declaration, that the "death penalty is the ultimate cruel, inhuman and degrading punishment and violates the right to life,"[22] and calls upon the world community to put an end to it and to declare it illegal by international law.

The international concern for the issue of capital punishment was first given tangible expression in Article 6 of the Covenant on Civil and Political Rights.[23] As it was clear that no international consensus was possible on capital punishment, an attempt was made to restrict its use. Thus, after the first subsection declares that "every human being has an inherent right to life" and that "no one shall be arbitrarily deprived of his life," subsection two tries to come to grips with the reality of the death penalty. It states: "In countries which have not abolished the death penalty, sentence of death may be imposed only for the most serious crimes in accordance with the law in force at the time of the commission of the crime." The article goes on to address issues relating to genocide, pardon, and the special position of the young (urging no executions for persons under the age of eighteen) and of women (who ought not to be executed while pregnant).

Since then the United Nations has returned to the topic of capital punishment. It has sponsored a number of surveys on the position of capital punishment throughout the world, and some of its constituent bodies have dealt with the topic on numerous occasions. In 1975, at the fifth U.N. Congress on the Prevention of Crime and the Treatment of Offenders, a statement submitted by twenty-six international nongovernmental organizations—humanitarian, religious, and professional—called on governments to abolish capital punishment and the United Nations to issue a declaration urging its worldwide abolition.[24]

IN RECENT YEARS some of the most significant developments have been at the regional level, particularly in Western Europe and in South America, where regional declarations have taken a stronger stand than the more general wording of the U.N. document; these regional declarations also seem to have a stronger impact than the universal ones.

In 1983 the members of the Council of Europe incorporated an additional protocol (No. 6) into the European Convention on Human Rights.[25] It affirms the principle of the abolition of the death penalty; all states wishing to become a party to the protocol will first have to abolish the death penalty. However, there is an important rider to the abolitionist stance—it applies only in peace time. It is recognized that for certain crimes the circumstances might be different in time of war or when there is an imminent threat of war. The protocol reflects a situation that exists among the member states in that the original signatories (Austria, Belgium, Denmark, France, Federal Republic of Germany, Greece, Luxembourg, Netherlands, Norway, Portugal, Spain, Sweden, and Switzerland) have almost all abolished the death penalty, at least in peace time.

Linking the question of capital punishment to the issue of human rights certainly provides an added dimension and places it in a worldwide context. From this perspective the death penalty is not just a penological issue or a question of response to crime, nor even merely of a political or ideological nature. For human rights issues are presumed to transcend such consideration and to deal with universal values and undisputed norms.

However, in fact, the position is not so clear-cut, for human rights are in many respects an expression of ideology. Although states may readily acknowledge the amorphous value of human rights, there is a great deal of disagreement as to the content with which they are clothed. The problems in enforcing the Helsinki Accords are an example of such dilemmas. International debate often revolves around the differing interpretation and meaning assigned to human rights, depending on underlying ideological factors. Whereas for most of the countries of Western Europe and North America human rights issues mean the traditional liberal and ideational issues of freedom of speech, of the press, of movement, of belief and religion, etc., for many of the countries of Eastern Europe as well as of Africa and Asia (for a mixture of ideological and practical reasons) human rights are closely bound to economic factors such as the right to food, shelter, clothes, medical aid, etc. And so, paradoxically, in some of these countries the death penalty is used for economic crimes, seen as being not a violation of human rights but a means of ensuring and enforcing them. Worldwide consensus, in principle let alone in practice, is therefore not easily attainable, neither for human rights nor for the specific issue of capital punishment.

The Western European nations that signed the Sixth Protocol have similar ideological and indeed cultural backgrounds, and the agreement between them is far more a confirmation of existing trends than an affirmation of desired aspirations. Their agreement flowed easily from their separate prior practices. Other geographical entities tend to have similar overlapping ideological and cultural frameworks. Certain patterns have emerged, though they are not decisive and clear-cut; but it does indeed seem that penological policies do reflect an interchange of ideas and common ideological overtones.

If Western Europe reflects a basically liberal ethos, then Eastern Europe is an example of prevailing communist approaches to punishment. Here, a further factor is the overriding influence of the Soviet Union in this region. Its experience and its geo-political position has naturally had an impact on the criminal law structure of the other communist countries of Eastern Europe.

In the Soviet Union a mixture of factors—a traditional authoritarian approach to government and the needs of the communist economic system—have led to the death penalty being used for economic crimes, those which undermine the very essence of the communist planned and centralized economy. This penalty was used extensively in the early sixties, but although many commentators believe that there has been a significant reduction since, others claim that it is still in regular use.[26] Though the ideological and cultural influence seems to be clear, there are nevertheless a number of factors that should be noted.

The theoretical basis of communism does not lead ineluctably to a death penalty. On the contrary, there is the concept of the withering away of the state, there are hopes for the erection of a new society and the rise of a new citizen, there are expectations of the success of education and of rehabilitation of the criminal. It was in this context that in the early years of the revolution the death penalty was abolished. Since its reintroduction, the death penalty has been acknowledged to be an exceptional penalty, and the intention of its eventual abolition has been expressed. A further noteworthy factor is that even Czarist Russia attempted to be abolitionist—indeed, was one of the first countries to try abolition, as early as the eighteenth century. Helping to consolidate this approach was the impact of Becarria's book; he was invited to Russia to help draft a new criminal code. Although he declined the invitation, his ideas had a great impact.[27] Alexander Solzhenitsyn's critique of the system of justice in the Soviet Union points out the paradox of Russia's having been progressive in this area at an early stage, and of a regression since then.[28] Recently the death penalty has been used less against political dissenters (for whom internal exile, labor camps, or even psychiatric hospitals are preferred), yet there are few examples which so bring out the ideological basis of attitudes toward, and policies on, the death penalty as its use by the Soviet Union and other East European countries for economic crimes. For the overwhelming theoretical importance attached to the economic substructure of society, and the corresponding significance of state ownership of property and control of the market forces leads them to choose the ultimate penalty of death for violations of economic laws.

The position in Poland is probably representative of most communist countries and is well described by Alicja Grzeskowiak and Georges Sliwowski.

The criminal activity involved must do great damage to the national economy. The perpetrator of this crime, in collaboration with other parties, makes personal use of important funds to the detriment of a branch of the socialized economy, exploiting consumers or retailers by distorting or abusing the regular activity of the economic branch. A grave disturbance is thus created in the functioning of the national economy. One of the legal signs of this offense is significant economic damage. . . . This death penalty can only be applied to a perpetrator who organized or directed such criminal activity. This offense thus consists of violation of the State's basis for economic order.

The authors go on to argue that the death penalty is rarely imposed; nevertheless, it is necessary because

it plays a deterrent role and aims to reinforce the notion of integrity of property within the society. . . . The death penalty as a penal sanction emphasizes the great value attached to the legal good destroyed or endangered by criminal acts; at the same time, the penalty indicates that the law regards the particular crimes as extremely dangerous.[29]

Even in the relatively liberal clime of Yugoslavia, the death penalty is an acceptable punishment, sometimes in questionable circumstances. As Zvonimir Separovic writes, "In Yugoslavia, the death penalty may be imposed for forty-five different offenses. Much of classical socialist doctrine rejects the death penalty, but it has been used throughout the history of Yugoslavia and Eastern European countries." He adds, though, that there has been some publicly expressed academic opposition to the death penalty, especially because some research indicates that some of the condemned may be mentally ill. Separovic concludes that "in many cases, the death sentence is imposed when the courts are not in a proper position to decide whether or not the defendant is sane."[30]

The dangers of political overtones to capital punishment may be seen in the practice in Hungary, where a particularly macabre twist has been given to the death penalty in some cases—the family of the executed person are denied all subsequent rights relating to the rites of death. They are neither given the body for burial nor informed of the site of the grave, so that they are deprived of fulfilling the normal rituals of paying respect to the dead.[31]

Of all the regions and cultural areas of the world, Latin America's policies are in many respects the most perplexing. Many of these countries have been abolitionist for a long time, and despite the vicissitudes of fragile democracies alternating with powerful military dictatorships, the overall official pattern of punishment has undergone little change. Unfortunately, this broadly abolitionist stance has not prevented—and may sadly even have fueled—greater violations of human rights, including extra-judicial executions, ranging from death squads to wholesale disappearances.

Ignacio Gomez de la Torre points out that "the anachronistic status of many of the laws, which, totally removed from the reality they regulate, patiently await reform."[32] He refers to "a sad reality in many states; the illegal executions that are frequently reported," and stresses that "the application of 'La Ley de Fuga' [Law of Escape] in guerilla warfare or simply the physical elimination of a political enemy by those who hold power or who systematically violate the law for their own personal gain, is much more reprehensible than maintaining capital punishment in the catalog of sanctions."[33]

The trend in South America is fairly clear. In the nineteenth and early twentieth century, many countries abolished the death penalty; despite radical changes in government, including military take-overs, there was little regression; once abolished, few countries subsequently reinstituted it. Gomez claims that "there is a great abolitionist tradition in Latin America. . . . Even though some of the military governments have tried to implement the death penalty, they have failed because the countries consider that life imprisonment is sufficient punishment and they are afraid that the death penalty could be used for political purposes."[34] Some countries have incorporated a prohibition on the death penalty into their constitutions; included among them are Venezuela, Costa Rica, Ecuador, Uruguay, Columbia, and the Dominican Republic. As in Europe, there is a split between those countries that are unreservedly abolitionist and those that have exceptions to a basically abolitionist approach.

The trend in South America is reflected in the American Convention on Human Rights.[35] Article 4 addresses the death penalty and states that it should be limited to exceptional cases only and that where in force it should be eased out of use. Subsection 2 states: "In countries that have not abolished the death penalty, it may be imposed only for the most serious crimes and pursuant to a final judgment rendered by a competent court." Further, "the application of such punishment shall not be extended to crimes to which it does not presently apply." Subsection 3 reaffirms this tendency in abolitionist states: "The death penalty shall not be re-established in states that have abolished it." Subsection 4 bars capital punishment for political offenses or related common crimes.

Even more than the legal formulas of the Convention, the essential spirit and thrust of the Latin American approach is expressed in a special declaration submitted by fourteen of the nineteen states who participated in the conference that adopted the convention. They affirm their "unwavering goal of making all possible efforts" so that in the near future they may "consecrate the final abolition of the death penalty and place America once again in the vanguard of the defense of the fundamental rights of man."[36]

The compelling power of the convention and the accompanying authority of the Inter-American Court of Human Rights may be gauged from an advisory opinion given in 1983 in which Guatemala sought to evade the prohibition on capital punishment for common crimes relating to political offenses.[37] In signing the convention, Guatemala had specified a reservation to

Clause 4.4, accepting the prohibition only for political offenses, but not for common crimes related to political offenses.[38]

At the time of ratification, Guatemala did not have legislation of this type. When it subsequently passed such legislation, the court held that it was subject to Article 4.2, which excluded the possibility of adding capital punishment to other crimes. Since Guatemala had not made any reservations to this subsection, it was debarred from enacting any new death penalty crimes. The court held that Article 4.2 must be read in conjunction with Article 4.3, with the latter's clear implication that

> it is no longer a question of imposing strict conditions on the exceptional application or execution of the death penalty, but rather of establishing a cut off as far as the penalty is concerned and doing so by means of a progressive and irreversible process applicable to countries which have not decided to abolish the death penalty altogether as well as to those countries which have done so. Although in the one case the Convention does not abolish the death penalty, it does forbid extending its application and imposition to crimes for which it did not previously apply. In this manner any expansion of the list of offenses subject to the death penalty has been prevented. In the second case, the re-establishment of the death penalty for any type of offense whatsoever is absolutely prohibited, with the result that a decision by a State Party to the Convention to abolish the death penalty, whenever made, becomes, *ipso jure,* a final and irrevocable decision.[39]

In any event, the abolitionist status of many of these countries is often only formally so; the reality is often vastly different. The situation is briefly summed up by Amnesty International.

> The death penalty in Latin America cannot be seen only in terms of sentences which are judicially imposed. Para-

military groups, the existence of which are condoned or actively supported by the authorities, as well as units of official security forces, carry out murders and illegal detention in a number of Latin American countries, particularly Argentina and Guatemala. Detention, not officially acknowledged, known as disappearances, as well as killings, are also grave matters in Chile, Nicaragua, Uruguay, Paraguay, Brazil, El Salvador, and the Dominican Republic.[40]

These problems reached a peak in Argentina in the late seventies and early eighties, when tens of thousands of people were apprehended and never heard from subsequently. For the most part, mystery surrounded the circumstances of the apprehension and their fate while in custody, an uncertainty compounded by silence or denials on the part of the authorities, and by the fact that the people apprehending were often without uniforms or any other identifying insignia.

In the course of time, mounting public pressure—both within the country by families of the victims and local human rights activists, and by international organizations—led to limited acknowledgment of official wrong-doing, at first explained in terms of personal or localized deviation. With the return of civilian rule, more knowledge has become available, and several of Argentina's leading political and military figures have been tried, convicted, and sentenced, including three ex-presidents of the military regime, two of whom received life sentences.[41]

The situation in the neighboring Carribean states, predominantly English-speaking and linked, in one form or another, to the British Commonwealth, is different. Most of these states do have a death penalty, used only rarely, an accepted relic of the preindependence period when, directly under Britain's rule, they incorporated the British approach, which at that stage was retentionist.

In sub-Saharan Africa, despite a greater diversity than in Latin America of language (both tribal and colonial), religion

(Christian, Muslim, and traditional), and ethnicity (mainly of a tribal nature), there is a great degree of homogeneity with regard to capital punishment; it is widely used throughout the continent.

Tibamanya Mwene Mushanga, a leading East African criminologist, has noted that capital punishment is supported both by public opinion and the leadership.[42] Adopting an abolitionist position, he argues that the populace, being largely illiterate, is unable to relate in a sophisticated manner to this issue, and much of the common attitude is susceptible to facile indoctrination. "In Africa," he writes,

> public opinion is nowhere nearer to influencing the trend of events whether these are political, economic or of a universal nature; but with the right kind of education which will put a higher value on human life and dignity, positive public opinion could be expected to emerge and also to be respected. Public opinion is now being used as a rubber stamp to legitimize brutality, inhumanity and general nastiness by military regimes all over the continent for political or economic exigencies.[43]

Mushanga believes that there is a need for the press, the church, and the universities to speak out on the issue and to help educate the leaders and the public to a more humane understanding of the issue. He notes that there is no organized movement to abolish capital punishment in Africa, and that, almost by default, the punishments originally systemized by the colonial powers are maintained. He contrasts the lack of a progressive influence in this area with other areas of volunteer activity, from women's groups to trade unions, and wonders why nothing has been done to stimulate African sentiments in regard to the death penalty. Adding his voice to those who have based their arguments partly on the discriminatory manner in which the death penalty is imposed, Mushanga argues that it will inevitably be inflicted on the less fortunate members of society. He feels that the world "will never know the number of Blacks that have been executed in countries where racism has been practiced."[44]

The major trend in the black African countries seems to be a broad use of capital punishment for most major crimes, such as murder, rape, and armed robbery, and for political crimes. In the former instances, public support for the harsh penalties may be noted from the phenomenon in some countries of bystander attacks on criminals, especially thieves caught in the act being beaten to death, a trend that has caused much concern.[45] In the case of political crimes, the Amnesty International report describes many deviations from strict standards of justice and from the rule of law through the use of special courts, often military tribunals, designed for rapid, summary justice, occasionally offset by a willingness to grant clemency in some countries.[46] As in South America, those African countries confronted with chronic social unrest and economic crisis have moved increasingly to military government, and in those circumstances there is a tendency for an increase in the use of capital punishment against political rivals—those recently removed by a coup or those unsuccessfully challenging for change.

There have also been a few African countries that, similar to the communist approach yet without their ideological commitment, have imposed severe sanctions for economic crimes. One of the best-known examples is the strict law imposed in Nigeria for contraventions of its commerical regulations in regard to oil transactions. Particular attention was aroused by a year-long trial in which an American businesswoman was charged with a violation of the law, the sentence for which could have been death.[47] Civil liberty and human rights groups in the United States evinced an interest in this case not only for the sanction to which she was subject, but also because the legislation was retroactive. She was finally acquitted.

A few months later, much controversy was aroused in Nigeria when the death penalty was imposed on three drug traffickers.

Interestingly enough, and in contrast to Mushanga's critical comments as to the lack of public opinion, the *New African* notes
that pleas to pardon them "came from the clergy, the bar and
bench, women's organizations and . . . the press. Yet the
government did not change its mind. And promptly on the
morning of April 10 the three men were tied to the stake and
publicly shot."[48] Similarly, public executions for robbery take
place, as Oluyoni Kayode describes: "Armed Robbery Tribunals
headed by high court judges were set up in each state capital
to cope with the volume of cases arising from the enforcement
of the decree. The public execution of condemned armed rob-
bers has become a routine event attracting huge crowds of spec-
tators. Whether the government's rather harsh punitive reaction has reduced the spate of violent robbery incidents has not
yet been empirically ascertained."[49]

The bulk of human rights interests in Africa focuses on
Southern Africa. South Africa has one of the highest rates of
capital punishment in the world, both in absolute terms and
certainly proportionate to size, some seventy to one hundred
people being executed each year for nonpolitical crimes, nearly
all of them black.[50] Further concern has been aroused in the
South African situation because of the number of political detainees who have died in confinement. In many instances the
official announcement is of a suicide or an accident, but the
well-known case of Steve Biko, a black political leader, and
the subsequent official investigation indicating that he had been
the victim of police brutality and medical connivance, has suggested that there may be extra-judicial executions through contrived situations.[51] More recently, international concern has increasingly been expressed for the welfare of Nelson Mandela,
one of several black leaders serving a life sentence after being
convicted of treason. According to persistent press reports, offers have been made to release him (he has been over twenty
years in prison) conditional to his renouncing the use of force
and refraining from involvement in political affairs—but he has
refused to accept any restrictions on his freedom.[52]

In what was Rhodesia there was a rather unique issue relating to the death penalty imposed during the period of the unilateral declaration of independence (considered by the British as an illegal act), namely, the legal culpability of all those, including the prime minister, judges, and executioners, directly and officially responsible for death penalties carried out by what was considered to be an illegal regime. Warnings had been issued that if executions were performed, those responsible would, in the event of British rule being restored, be held criminally liable. A number of executions of blacks fighting the illegal regime did take place, but subsequent to the restoration of British rule, and shortly thereafter, to the creation of the state of Zimbabwe, no action was taken against the Rhodesian officials. In fact, the former prime minister of Rhodesia was subsequently elected to the Zimbabwe parliament as an opposition member.

On one occasion an attempt was made to avert an execution by seeking the intervention of the British courts.[53] The Rhodesian courts were asked for a verdict that would bar the execution for four months so as to allow time for an appeal to be made to the Privy Council in London. This plea was rejected by the Rhodesian court on the grounds that the Privy Council was unlikely to accede to the request for an appeal. To this the court added the rider that if it should hear and decide in the appellant's favor, the Rhodesian government would be unlikely to be bound by such a decision—both issues were speculative on the court's part, and capable of being decided by each of the bodies, which the court was paternalistically trying to protect.

In fact, this decision did not prevent the British authorities from publicly announcing the commutation of the death sentence. As the court had foreseen, the Rhodesian government refused to consider itself bound by any decision of British authority, and despite the royal pardon, announced their intention of carrying out the death penalty. Once again the Rhodesian court was asked for an interdict against the execution and once again the plea was rejected, though not without pro-fuse professions of respect for the Crown and a concomitant reprimand for those, the defendants, who had asked for the Crown's intervention. In his judgment, the Rhodesian chief justice stressed that the refusal to carry out the will of the British Crown should not be seen as detracting "from the high regard and great respect which this court has, and will continue to have, for the person of her Majesty the Queen." He went on to state: "I think it is a matter much to be deplored that the name of her Majesty the Queen should have been brought into this dispute"[54]—as though there was something offensive in condemned persons pursuing every possible avenue to save their lives. In any event, the executions were carried out shortly after the court rejected the plea for a stay of execution.

As in black Africa, so in the Moslem countries of the Middle East—both North Africa and West Asia—the death sentence is widely used, particularly in those countries that adopt a fun-damentalist approach to religion, where the use of the death penalty evokes the Koran and attempts to replicate the prac-tices of earlier periods. Strict interpretation of the Koran af-fects all aspects of the criminal justice system, including capital punishment, sometimes through public executions, for serious offenses and for violation of the sexual moral code, and, for lesser offences, bodily mutilation, such as chopping off the hand of a thief.[55]

This approach has often led to bitter political polemics, particularly in those countries where the strict approach follows earlier years of a more flexible and modern penal policy, or where a substantial non-Moslem minority rejects the imposi-tion of a religious law to which they do not subscribe. In the Sudan these were among the factors that led to the overthrow of Numeiri in 1985.[56]

In Iran a combination of extreme religious fundamentalism and a totalitarian political philosophy has led to a pattern of executions, some of them in public, some of them of leaders of religious minorities such as the Bahai and the Jews. However, it should be noted that capital punishment had been extensively used also during the rule of the Shah. The Amnesty International report on capital punishment (which was published about the time of the change in regime and contains no information about Khomeini's regime) states that on average twenty percent of murderers were executed, that in a period of two-and-a-half years prior to the report 239 drug smugglers and peddlers were also put to death, and that twenty-three political prisoners were executed in 1976.[57]

Both regimes seem to have been equally consistent in their violation of human rights, including extensive use of the death penalty; but international criticism of these acts—both from political leaders and from political activist groups—seems too often to have followed far more the biased perspective of ideological affiliation than genuine concern for the victims.

A similar extensive use of the death penalty for religious and political offenses (as well as for ordinary crimes) occurs in other countries, most notably in Libya, although the former monarchial regime had refrained from using the death penalty. In fact, this position was actually maintained in the early years of the Khadafi regime, whose coup had been bloodless. It was only in the course of time that increasing resort was had to capital punishment, including expansion of the number of offenses, the institution of people's courts, and, more recently and most notably, the systematic pursuit in other countries of expatriates known or suspected to oppose the regime, by death squads sent out with the support of the government, and acting, according to the government, in the name of the people.[58]

This is, of course, a more brash and unabashed manifestation of a phenomenon that is more widely, yet covertly, practiced by other countries. The open espousal of these actions by the Libya government is in keeping with its own deliberate disregard for the niceties of international law and diplomatic norms, as, for instance, in it use of nondiplomatic terminology to define its embassies as "peoples' bureaus." These are the very precincts widely regarded as providing support for international terrorist groups, such as by transferring weapons by diplomatic pouch. The peak was perhaps reached in the violent confrontation in London in 1983, when a policewoman was shot from inside the embassy while helping control protesters outside in the streets. The suspect responsible was subsequently allowed to leave the building by the British authorities and to fly back to Libya.[59]

Two other interesting and rather unique aspects of the death penalty in the Middle East are worth noting. First, in some countries, in cases of murder the court authorities may consult with the family of the victim, or at least request them to present their own views on the question of punishment, including whether the death penalty should be imposed. The court's decision is generally based on whether there has been prior reconciliation reached between the members of the victim's and criminal's families, most often the product of mediation efforts carried out by third parties and focused on payment of compensation to the victim's family.

In a 1980 decision in Pakistan, one of the judges argued that the death penalty would be unconstitutional if no effort was made to seek reconciliation.

> The great Imans and the jurists who followed them to date are unanimous on the point that an offense affecting the human body can be disposed of on the basis of a pardon or a payment of "Diyat" [blood money] by the person offended, if he is alive and in case he be dead, by his heirs. . . . The heirs of the deceased have got a right to pardon the murderer, and in that case it is not appropriate for the court that it should insist on taking the life of the murderer.[60]

It should be added that these protective provisions apply to crimes against the person but not to crimes against the state.

Second, in Turkey, a country that straddles Europe and the Middle East, the approach to capital punishment is more akin to the latter. There is a special provision that all death sentences have to be ratified by the parliament before the execution can take place; because of this situation, the commuting powers of the president are strictly limited, confined only to reasons of age and ill-health.[61]

Even more blatant expression of political power in the adjudication of the death penalty is the situation in Thailand, in which the constitution allows the courts to be completely bypassed in national security cases and invests in the prime minister the power to impose the death penalty.[62]

In general, in Asia there is widespread use of the death penalty although ideologically and culturally there is a far greater diversity among the countries than in other geographical areas, and so the rationale for its use may differ. Thus, as in the Caribbean and in Africa, some countries formerly under British rule maintain the death penalty because of practices instituted by the British. In fact, the situation now exists that although Britain itself has abolished the death penalty, its highest court of law, the Privy Council, continues to handle appeals from some of these countries. In recent times the Privy Council rejected an appeal from an accused sentenced to death in Singapore for drug trafficking.[63] The Singapore Misuse of Drugs Act imposed a mandatory death penalty for trafficking in more than fifteen grams of heroin. The Privy Council accepted the punishment as reasonable since "the social object of the Drugs Act is to prevent the growth of drug addiction in Singapore by stomping out the illicit drug trade." As David Pannick points out,[64] the court forewent the possibility of pursuing a series of civil rights and due process of law issues, from the possibility that a lesser penalty might achieve the same result, through the arbitrary distinction between those dealing in more than or less than fifteen grams, to the awesome implications of an obligatory death penalty.

The crime of drug trafficking is a capital offense in many other countries of Asia, though the existence and implementation of this severe penalty does not seem to have deterred those involved in this illegal activity, since the trafficking has continued unabated over the years; it might, however, have served to warn and deter others. The traffickers themselves might well have more to fear from hostile acts by rival groups.

In terms of ideological approaches to the death penalty, it is interesting to note that one of the only countries to abolish the penalty, Sri Lanka, did so on the basis of a recommendation by a commission chaired by a Western jurist, Norval Morris, an articulate abolitionist from the United States. It is a quirk of historical fate that shortly after abolition the prime minister, Solomon Bandaranaike, who had been a strong supporter of abolition, was assassinated; and subsequently the legislation was repealed.[65]

As in South America, there have been instances of the abuse of political power to eliminate opponents of a regime. In at least two cases, the executions reached genocidal proportions— in Indonesia in 1965, about half a million communist supporters and sympathizers were killed in the wake of the overthrow of Sukarno, its first president, and a million or more people were killed in Cambodia (Kampuchea) in the course of the struggles in that country, both between internal groups and the invasion from Vietnam.[66]

In India, an intersting development is an amendment to the law that has led to a subtle change in the emphasis when dealing with ultimate penalties. Formerly, when an offense was punishable by death, the court was obliged to state its reasons for imposing a lesser penalty, whereas when the death sentence was imposed, there was no need for any reason to be given. Since 1974 the obligation to provide a reason has devolved on the court when it sentences the accused to death, and not when a lesser penalty is given, suggesting that, for extreme crimes such as murder, life or long-term imprisonment is now the norm and the death penalty the exception.[67]

In Japan there are two significant facts relating to the death penalty: one, the extraordinary degree of secrecy that surrounds the execution; the other, the inordinate length of time that sometimes elapses between the imposition of the sentence and the carrying out. There is very little detailed information in the English-language literature on this topic, but it is clear that both factors raise serious questions in terms of human rights, for example, the ability of the condemned person, and those acting on his behalf, to pursue all the possibilities of commutation of sentence.

No announcements are made of the time of the execution, neither before nor after; both the condemned man and his family remain in a state of constant uncertainty as to when his fate will be finally sealed. This applies not only to specific cases, but even to the overall figures, since, as the Amnesty International report points out, the Japanese Ministry of Justice "declines to give information either on the number of people executed . . . or on the numbers sentenced to death. . . . The only way to find out whether or not a death sentence has been carried out is to check the family register in the condemned person's home town. When the name of the condemned is struck out, the execution has apparently taken place."[68]

This situation becomes all the more intolerable in the light of the other aforementioned factor, namely, the length of time that a condemned person may have to wait for his sentence to be carried out. According to a United Nations report on capital punishment from the 1960s, the average period of incarceration—from the passing of sentence to the execution—was, for the period surveyed, the longest in the world, more than four years. Occasionally, reports of specific instances reach the mass media, as in the recent instance of a man, ninety-three years old, who sued unsuccessfully to have his sentence commuted after he had been kept in a death row cell for thirty years.[69] His lawyer had argued that since the statute of limitations applied automatically after thirty years, he should be released, since it was no longer legally possible to execute him, nor was it possible to maintain him in prison for any other purpose, as he had not been given a prison sentence. The court refused to apply the statute of limitations. The case itself had been a *cause célèbre,* as it involved a well-known artist in a particularly gruesome crime, in which twelve bank employees were poisoned to death at work so as to facilitate a robbery. However, there have been many doubts expressed as to the guilt of the accused, and it would seem that this fact has had some influence on the refusal to carry out the death penalty, whereas, conversely, the heinous nature of the act has prevented any overt commutation.

It is of interest to note the critical attitude adopted to this case in a recent abolitionist argument; Eugene Block indicates clearly that there is room to commute his sentence to life imprisonment.[70] But, of course, at this stage it is almost certain that he will never be executed—*de facto* he is serving a life sentence and will probably die in prison—since all attempts in thirty years to prove his innocence have failed.

In the People's Republic of China, in contrast, a unique policy has been adopted of providing a legally sanctioned and utilitarian-oriented waiting period of two years before execution, the purpose being to allow sufficient time for the condemned person to repent of his past crimes and to undergo a process of rehabilitation. This is applied mainly in the case of political prisoners, one of the most noted instances being the case of the "gang of four," including the widow of the late leader Mao; the executions were deferred, and the sentence subsequently changed to life imprisonment.[71]

This approach of the commutation of sentence represents a faint echo of the traditional use in China of regular amnesties—not individual rehabilitation in personal terms, but public reconciliation in human terms.[72] This practice was based on a larger penological approach that involved the regular use of general amnesty, at times on an annual basis. The system, reflecting the philosophical concept of harmony with nature, was linked to the changing of the seasons, autumn and winter being the times for vigorous enforcement of punishment, spring and summer, with its growth and reinvigoration of nature, for reintegration of the deviants into society. In addition, there were large number of other days in the year when executions could not be performed—some linked to the seasons, such as the winter solstice and the equinoxes, some to fast days and sacrifice days, some to specific events, such as the accession of a new ruler. Thus, according to Derk Bodde and Clarence Morris, there were probably less than sixty days in the year in which executions could actually take place.[73]

If a condemned person had survived into the spring, he would be entitled to a stay of execution until the next season of executions, and meanwhile he could hope also for a commutation of sentence. In some cases a full pardon might be given, in others a lesser penalty, which could be exile for life, or even military exile for life (that is, incorporation into the armed forces serving in an outlying area of the empire), these being the next most serious gradations of punishment.

Today, China's policy on the death penalty is generally similar to that of the communist countries in Eastern Europe, namely, a professed reluctance to use the death penalty and an expressed hope for its eventual abolition. An official explanation of the criminal law and procedure was presented in June 1979 at the fifth National Peoples Congress.

> At present the death penalty cannot and should not be abolished in our country, but it should be as rare as possible. Back in 1951, the Central committee of the Communist Party of China and Comrade Mao Zedung repeatedly advocated minimum use of death penalties. Now that almost thirty years have passed since the founding of the Peoples Republic, and particularly with the increase in stability and unity in our domestic situation since the smashing of the gang of four, the draft Criminal Law therefore includes fewer articles relating to the death penalty.[74]

Yet however much Mao might have favored minimum use of death penalties, according to some authorities on China's modern history, there seems to have been a maximum use to further the goals of the revolution. A writer extremely critical of the Chinese revolution, Simon Leys, claims that in the years 1949–52, five million counterrevolutionaries were executed in furtherance of the policy of land reform.[75]

Two recent visitors to China, Judith Shapiro and Liang Heng, also paint a disturbing picture of current practices. Executions peaked in 1983, not of political dissidents, but chiefly of "those charged with ordinary crimes. Many are executed without appeal, even for petty crimes such as stealing watches."[76] They also claim that draconic measures are sometimes taken to instill fear in the populace: "In the apparent belief that the people will have a safer holiday if they are sharply reminded of the penalties for crime, numbers of prisoners are shot before major festivals each year. Mass rallies are held before the executions, with tickets distributed to the main local work units. Posters describing the offenders and their crimes are distributed all over the cities. Large red check marks show that they have been shot."[77] These posters often provide the only reliable information as to executions, since no official overall figures are provided. In fact, the report of Amnesty International relies mainly on accounts by visitors or items in newspapers.[78]

Thus, although there is often strong verbal support for abolition, in practice there seems to be recurrent use of the death penalty, both for political criminals and common criminals.

IN BRITAIN, in contrast, there has always been strong support for capital punishment, both from the highest echelons of government and from expressed public opinion.[79] Yet, in 1983, comprehensive and controversial debate in Parliament led to a historic decision for total abolition. This was the culmination of a struggle against the death penalty that had begun over a hundred years earlier,[80] had aroused intense passions on both sides of the debate, had involved a combination of partisan party politics mixed with recurrent free votes based on conscience, and a final denouement in which the will of the populace at large, as expressed through public opinion polls, had been largely disregarded.

In the past the British code had been notorious for its extensive list of capital crimes. Some writers have attributed this to the reaction to social chaos, including a rising rate of crime caused by the Industrial Revolution (which developed sooner, quicker, and further in Britain than on the Continent); others have suggested that the end result is intimately bound up with the antecedent position, namely, that since extensive procedural protections were provided for the accused, there was a greater sense of certainty in the justness of the final result and, accordingly, a greater sense of confidence in imposing and implementing an immutable punishment. Further, since the procedural protections led to a lower rate of conviction, there was also a greater need for a stronger deterrent penalty to compensate, as it were, for all those who were acquitted mainly because they were, despite strong suspicions of their guilt, the recipients of a lenient procedural system. The smaller number of cases ending in a conviction created pressures for stricter penalties in order to ensure sufficient deterrence. However, there was a contrary trend, namely, that it was the very severity of the penalties themselves that often induced the jury to give the defendant the benefit of the doubt, and sometimes even flatly to acquit in the face of contrary evidence. It was an awareness of this factor that contributed to a significant diminution in the number of capital offenses in the nineteenth century.[81]

In the twentieth century, the battle for abolition was led by organizations such as the Howard League for Penal Reform and the National Council for the Abolition of the Death Penalty, as well as by a small number of dedicated parliamentarians, of whom the most noted was a Labor party member of Parliament, Sidney Silverman.[82]

Despite the extensive changes made in capital punishment policy, the death penalty was retained as a mandatory punishment for murder. In fact, the real decisions as to the use of the death penalty were made not in court, but by the home secretary who, basing his decision on the recommendations of experts in his office, would decide whether or not to recommend that the royal pardon be extended to the condemned person. Over the years certain patterns developed; for instance, any recommendation for mercy made by the jury has become a major factor in the decisions.[83]

After several unsuccessful parliamentary attempts to abolish capital punishment, a positive decision was finally made in the 1950s to have a trial abolition period of five years—with a few exceptions, such as the killing of police officers or a murder committed by a prisoner serving a life sentence. As had become customary over the years, the vote was by a free vote of the Parliament, that is, the members voted according to their consciences and were not bound by official party policy. In fact, despite the free vote, a fairly persistent pattern was maintained over the years with the vast majority of Labor and Liberal party members voting for abolition.[84] In any event, it is clear that policy on the death penalty constitutes an important aspect of a government's work in the realm of home affairs and criminal law policy.

In the final analysis, what affected the vote were three *causes célèbres* that captured the public's attention—the Craig-Bentley case in which a felony murder committed by two teenagers led to the younger, who had done the shooting, being given a long prison sentence because he was still a minor, whereas his accomplice, already an adult, (though only a few months older) was sentenced to death; the Evans-Christie affair in which Evans was convicted and executed for murder largely on the basis of the evidence of Christie, who, some three years later, was charged with murder under circumstances that caused suspicion that he had also been responsible for the murder for which Evans had been executed; and the Ruth Ellis affair, in which a woman was executed for killing her lover despite the many pleas for clemency made on her behalf by the public.[85]

Later, in 1983, six separate situations for use of the death penalty, ranging from murder to acts of terror, were put to the vote in Parliament, and in each case the abolitionist stance won out. It had been assumed by most observers that the results would be extremely close, but the abolitionist majority ranged from 98 to 175, the smallest majority being for the murder of policemen and the largest for murder in the course of theft.[86] These decisions were especially significant since they came in the wake of a landslide victory for the Conservative party, the traditional supporter of a retentionist stance, fortified in this particular instance by the firm support of the prime minister and intensified by the heightened activity of political violence in Northern Ireland.

There was widespread feeling after the vote that the issue of capital punishment—often a volatile issue among the British public—had, with this vote, perhaps been settled for all time. Yet it would be well to recall the comment of some of the leading abolitionists in America, who after the *Furman* decision had confidently and triumphantly declared that there would never be another execution in the United States in this century.[87]

So it may be assumed that the struggle for capital punishment in Britain is not yet over. In its analysis of the vote, the respected London *Times,* in an editorial called for a special committee to investigate all aspects of capital punishment, and warned that the representatives of the people in the House of Commons could not risk being so out of step with public opinion.[88] Other proponents of capital punishment, citing public opinion polls showing a large majority in favor of capital punishment, called for a national referendum on the topic. Yet other voices were raised insisting on a stricter application of life imprisonment, including the denial of any prospects of release.

The large and convincing parliamentary majority provides no guarantee that the issue has been resolved for all time, given the conflict with prevailing public opinion. The vote itself can best be understood in light of some of the particular circumstances that might well have affected the considerations of many members of Parliament. Most significant and noteworthy is the fact that among those who were opposed to the death penalty was the minister for Northern Ireland, who bears responsibility for order in that territory and for coping with the problems of civil unrest, sectarian strife, and bilateral terrorism. In presenting his abolitionist stand the minister relied on the chief constable for Northern Ireland, who, in contrast to the vast majority of his fellow officers throughout Britain, also opposed the use of the death penalty specifically because of its ineffectiveness as a method of combatting the violence in the region.

These arguments against the death penalty were likely a key factor in the whole tenor of the debate and the outcome of the vote, for at least superficially it would seem that acts of terror were perhaps the prime and the most logical area in which to use the most extreme penalty, both as a means of deterrence and as a means of retribution. Yet the paradox was that it was specially in this area that some of the most compelling arguments were put forward against its use, including the danger of making martyrs of those executed, an assertion given further pertinence by the fact that the execution in 1916 of one of the leaders of the Irish Rebellion, Roger Casement, is widely considered to have been one of the major stepping-stones on the way to the independence of Eire in the south in 1922.[89] It was further pointed out that there are many indications that the IRA would actually welcome the existence of the death penalty, since they perceive that this would further their cause. Those in charge of security arrangements were also acutely conscious of the fact that the existence of a death penalty was liable to exacerbate the tensions in Northern Ireland and increase the level of violence—both in possible warning actions before execution and reprisals in their wake, and in the intensity of encounters between security forces and the IRA.

Finally, the disregard of the prospect of death evinced on many occasions by the members of the IRA was dramatically demonstrated during the hunger strike in prison in 1981 by Bobby Sands and nine other members of the IRA. They were not deterred by their weakening physical condition and the inevitability of their death in their protest against the conditions of their imprisonment.[90]

As if to accentuate the validity of these arguments, there were a number of terrorist attacks in the days leading up to the debate, culminating in a major incident in which four policemen were killed on the very day of the vote. There were those who felt that so strong were the pragmatic arguments against the death penalty for crimes of terrorism that these latter acts, intended as direct provocations and challenges, served only to reinforce the arguments against the death penalty. They were seen as proof of how little the death penalty would deter. To vote in favor of the death penalty in these circumstances would be seen as playing into the hands of the IRA, acceding to their wishes and allowing for a situation which would act to their advantage politically.

If it is true that such pragmatic considerations determined the issue at the expense of ideological factors, then it becomes easier to understand the surprisingly large majority against reintroducing capital punishment. Simply put, if the ultimate penalty was not to be used against those who used the most ruthless methods in pursuing a political aim, how was it possible, in good conscience, to impose it in other instances of relatively lesser gravity? If terrorists, disrupting the very fiber of society, threatening the very make-up of the political comity, willing to shed innocent blood in promoting their aims, were not to be subjected to the most severe penalty, what justification could be given for imposing it on others who could, for the most part, be seen to be less ruthless, less dangerous, less despicable?

Underlying all this was the open secret that, despite support for the death penalty, some government officials were thought to harbor the hope that the resolution would not pass, thereby being spared the difficult decision that would have to be made by the authorities in those many cases in which public battles, perhaps involving international pressures, would be mounted to use the executive authority of clemency to avert judicial decisions imposing the death penalty.

Thus, after over a century of debate in Britain, it was paradoxically a predominantly Conservative Parliament that provided the votes that confirmed an abolitionist stance with no exceptions, not even in special cases which are often recognized as acceptable exceptions—for instance, for political crimes, for fatal violence used against the police, or for acts of murder committed by those already serving life sentences.

In any event, for as long as Britain is faced with political violence, the resort to the death penalty again is surely a possibility. The acts of the IRA in killing policemen on the day of the vote did not prevent the abolitionist vote, but another subsequent act by the IRA might indeed have had an influence in favor of the death penalty, for it undermined the effectiveness of life imprisonment and stressed, in contrast, the need for irreversibility. Some three months after the vote, thirty-eight prisoners escaped from prison.[91] Almost half of them succeeded in evading immediate recapture, including some who were notorious for violence prior to their imprisonment, including murder. One cannot but wonder whether their escape would not have had an impact on the British legislature had it come before the vote. No doubt some members of Parliament would have felt that the only means of ensuring that there would be no repetition, with its concomitant dangers for the public, would be a death penalty.

It would thus seem that the issue of capital punishment in Britain has not been resolved for all time. However, any change in policy would raise certain serious legal complications. One is related to the fact that political trials in Northern Ireland take place without a jury, the Diplock formula, in order to avoid the pressures and threats to which the jurors might be subjected as well as the prejudices and biases that their membership in one or other of the warring communities would probably entail. However, it is traditional in Britain for juries and not judges to determine guilt in capital cases.

Another is related to a factor that was not applicable when the death penalty was last in force in Britain, namely, its membership in the European community and its agreement to subject its administrative and judicial procedures to the scrutiny of the European Court of Human Rights. In the twenty-odd years of its existence, this court has not been faced with a question involving the death penalty, partly because most of the countries of the community have abolished it, and most of the others have used it only sparingly. However, the court and its component institution, the Commission of Human Rights, have been confronted with many other issues relating to penological practices and in many cases have not hesitated to intervene and to override the practices of the individual states. If Britain were to reintroduce the death penalty, there is every likelihood that, at some stage, its legislation and specific applications of it (for instance, a death penalty for a political prisoner in Northern Ireland without the jury trial that is vouchsafed to people tried elsewhere in Britain) would be challenged. A decision of the court in this area would serve to emphasize the manner in which penological issues touch upon human rights, an area that almost inevitably has international implications.

In such a circumstance, the court would no doubt make a wide-ranging survey in its deliberations of attitudes and policies toward punishment. From the abolitionist point of view the court would examine such factors as the fact that most other countries of the community have abolished the death penalty, the slow development of an international norm through international declarations calling for an end to the death penalty, and the norm that no country that has once abolished capital punishment should revert to a retentionist position.

Indeed, whatever the position in any particular country,

in the long run the death penalty—an extreme example of the supreme power of the sovereign state—is liable to become increasingly subject to the surveillance and scrutiny of the world community—a prospect that will be probed more explicitly in the final chapter.

III

ULTIMATE CRIMES

■

7

GENOCIDE

A N I N T E R E S T I N G and significant development in relation to capital punishment has been its recent use in the
realm of international law, arising mainly out of World War
II. The excesses of Nazi atrocities before and during the war—
both in the conduct of military operations and, even more
so, in actions taken against noncombatants—led to widespread
demands that those responsible be subjected to criminal
sanctions.

The exact nature and the parameters of international law
were still highly debatable, and there was a great deal of uncertainty and controversy as to both the substantive and procedural
aspects of the law; it was not clear what sort of legal tribunal
could try the vanquished Nazi leaders, or what charges could
be laid against them. Although the Moscow Declaration of
November 1943 had indicated that action would be taken against
those responsible for excesses in the course of the war,[1] and
though the postwar London Agreement of 1945 provided the
formal instrument for a trial,[2] there were many who doubted
the validity of international law and the legitimacy of any international tribunal. In Allied-government circles the suggestion was even made that the best outcome would be to forego
official judicial proceedings, and to opt instead for immediate
summary justice;[3] that is, a kangaroo court which would ignore the niceties of a formalized hearing, the complications
of a precise formulation of a recognized delinquency, and
possible passionate pleas for mercy, but would mete out a rough
and ready justice outside of the court system, thereby giving
vent to the widespread desire for a speedy and severe punishment for Nazi crimes.

Wiser counsels prevailed, however. In fact, some leading legal and other scholars had devoted much thought, while the war was yet on, to what would be the appropriate response to the atrocities committed by the Nazis. A feeling for the sentiment of that time and the nature of the debate may be gained from Sheldon Glueck's thoughtful discussion of the prosecution and punishment of war crimes.

On the one hand, Glueck warned against the danger of "those who cry for indiscriminate vengeance" against all Germans and Japanese, and who would allow the survivors of atrocities and their relatives to take the law into their own hands. He noted that "so embittered have millions of victims of Nazi-Japanese hatred and blood-lust become that a major problem of the United Nations will be to police lands freed from Axis domination until such time as the thirst for indiscriminate mass-vengeance will have died down."[4] On the other hand, he rejects the approach of those "who insist that the offenders should be magnanimously forgiven and told to go and sin no more." Though rejecting vengeance as a motivation, he argues that it "ought not to be confused with the legitimate, commendable and morally virtuous desire of the survivors of Axis brutality to see that mankind's law and justice speak out, at long last, on their behalf."[5]

These latter considerations were ultimately to prevail, and the stage was finally set for the historic Nuremberg trial at which the leaders of the defeated German people were put on trial before a bench of judges from the four major Allied powers. The issues involved in the trial were varied and complex, including philosophical issues as to universal norms of human behavior; jurisprudential issues as to the validity of international law; legal issues of many types, ranging from immunity for acts of state to *tu quoque* arguments that the Allies were also at fault; and moral issues as to the right and the duty of an individual to retain his integrity in the face of superior commands. The International Military Tribunal at Nuremberg served as the model for further judicial actions, including a similar international tribunal in Tokyo to try the leaders of the Japanese people, a series of lesser military tribunals throughout Europe, Asia, and the Pacific, and the trial of Adolf Eichmann in the national courts of the state of Israel.[6]

The original Nuremberg trial spawned intense legal and political controversy, touching in detail on all the points at issue.[7] Conspicuous by its absence was any real discussion of the penological implications arising out of criminal guilt for war crimes, the new crime of genocide, and other crimes against humanity. What punishment would be apt for the crime and for the criminal in these instances?

The first Nuremberg trial, in which the death penalty was imposed on twelve of the accused (including one, Martin Bormann, *in absentia)*, heard almost no argument on this last issue, and, in announcing the punishments, the court gave no reasons for its decisions. Indeed, the Nuremberg trials consisted of only one stage, with no opportunity for either side to argue as to the factors that should be considered after the verdict of guilty had been pronounced. There was also no appeal to a higher court, only a plea for clemency to the nonjudicial Allied Control Council, which had a rule that there had to be unanimity amoung the four Allied powers in order to allow for commutation.

Similarly, the bulk of commentary on this trial deals with issues of the substantive law and the procedures followed with no more than passing allusions to the punishments imposed. In contrast, the Tokyo trial does contain a certain amount of consideration of the penological issues, but then mainly because the court was generally divided as to what penalty to impose on the convicted, including whether or not the death penalty should be invoked, with the dissenting judges elaborating on the rationale for their decision.

The court of the Eichmann trial in Israel did hear full argument on this score in the course of a two-stage trial, as well as at the hearing of the appeal. Whatever the problematics associated with the Eichmann trial (including his capture in

Argentina and the right of a state that was not in existence at the time of the commission of the crimes to try a person for crimes committed outside of its territory), it did at least relate directly to what was one of the most important and difficult questions that arose: How is an enlightened people to treat those of their fellow-beings whose bestiality and cruelty, persistently practiced and loudly proclaimed, seem to put them beyond the pale of civilized behavior?

This is, indeed, an issue not for judges alone, but for all humankind; in a sense it is the ultimate issue of capital punishment. It certainly should have been seen as a major, independent issue by both the courts themselves and by those who wrote analyses of the war trials. Yet, although there are learned discourses addressing a host of substantive and procedural issues that arose, the judgments at Nuremberg contain no reasoned presentations of the factors that led to the imposition of the death penalty, for example, whether the court was swayed by deterrent or retributive factors, and if so, to what extent; whether any weight had been given to personal factors, and if so, how much; and what was the key factor in differentiating between the death sentence for some and life imprisonment or a shorter term for others. Of the writers dealing with the trial, Bradley Smith is almost alone in dealing with this issue; but his use of archival material to describe the internal debates among the judges, important and revealing as it is, is of course no substitute for a reasoned summation by the judges themselves.[8]

The issue of what to do with those convicted of international crimes is surely one of the most delicate and difficult issues confronting humanity today: May the most extreme penalty be used against those who have committed the most extreme abominations? The issue is all the more acute for abolitionists, especially for those whose opposition to the death penalty is based on broad humanitarian concepts of respect for the sanctity of life, and whose arguments stress that inhumanity cannot be requited by equivalent acts on the part of the state. But is there real equivalence in these instances? Indeed, there were those who, paradoxically, argued against the death penalty for the war criminals precisely because there was no equivalence, claiming that there was no human punishment that could equal the enormity of the original crime.

What, then, is to be done with people who have committed the most extreme violations against humanity? Are they to be branded with a humiliating mark of Cain, set free to roam the earth with no social comity prepared to accept them? If so, where are they to wander: in uninhabited places, the wastes of the Arctic areas, the burning equatorial desert, a deserted pacific atoll, an uninviting South American jungle (where, indeed, some of them apparently did seek refuge in an attempt to evade detection and capture)? Or are they to be given a life sentence in prison as an expression of more moderate principles, as was done to Rudolph Hess, who, now in his nineties, is still being kept prisoner in isolation in Spandau Prison, guarded by representatives of the four major Allied powers whose judges sentenced him some forty years ago? One of these countries, the Soviet Union, (whose judge had originally opted for a death sentence) has refused to acquiesce in the willingness of the three other countries to release Hess in his old age. In a sense, he remains a symbol of the larger futility of attempting to find adequate expression, within the bounds of enlightened norms, for punishment of the worst depravities that the human mind can conceive and human hands execute. Hess himself was not convicted of all the crimes that some of the other accused were, and this, together with his flight to England near the start of the war to try to bring about a peace, might have been important factors leading to the lesser sentence awarded him. On the other hand, his efforts at rapprochement with the West might have led the Russian judge in an opposite direction and the Soviet authorities now to deny release. But, in retrospect, can it be considered a lesser penalty? Is his fate, today and during the last forty-odd years since his capture in England, alone and secluded, cut off from almost all ordinary human contact, an easier and more desirable one than that of those who were condemned to death almost two generations ago? Recently there were reports of attempts being made to free him by a group known as the Rudolph Hess Liberation Commando Unit.[9]

The Nuremberg trial raises some very pertinent penological issues both for liberal abolitionists and for those jurists and others intent on setting up a recognized basis for international criminal law, issues which they have, for the most part, chosen to evade. The very idea of a crime which is an affront to the world community hints at the seriousness of the act; yet it does not, in and of itself, indicate that an exceptional penalty is called for, nor what form it should take. Historically, one of the few recognized international crimes was piracy, mainly because the crimes were committed on the high seas, outside the jurisdiction of any one country.[10] A pirate was considered to be *hostis humani generis*—an enemy of the human race. For piracy the maximum penalty was death, but it should be noted this was at a time when most countries still used the death penalty for many other crimes.

What is the situation today, when the national laws of many individual states show an increasing tendency to abolition? Does this obligate international law to limit itself, or does the unique and extreme nature of some of the acts prohibited under international law suggest that, for that very reason, there sould be an exception to the general rule?

A perusal of international conventions passed in recent times, defining the nature of some international crimes, shows that generally the penalty to be imposed is left open.[11] The formula normally adopted is that the offender should be punished, but with no specifications as to the nature or severity of the sentence. Commentators discussing these conventions have also generally not addressed the question of how the international community should punish those who contravene the conventions, which are being enacted in the attempt to slowly build up a recognized body of international criminal law.

Granted, so as long as there is no international court of criminal justice, the actual implementation of these conventions will be left to the individual states, and it is clearly difficult for the convention to lay down what penalty should be adopted by each nation state; yet the difficulties do not preclude the possibility or the obligation of trying to achieve some consensus. Certainly what can be expected is a directive as to the maximum penalty, and whether or not the death penalty is to be allowed. Thus, for instance, many countries have the death penalty for traffic in drugs, while there is also an international convention on drug trade.[12] Should the convention recognize this tendency among some states and specify the death penalty as maximum punishment; should it ignore the trend, not spelling out a penalty at all; or should it declare a maximum penalty less than death in order to ensure that an international convention will not be used as a pretext or justification for a death penalty at the national level?

The opposite situation existed after World War II, when a number of countries that had abolished the death penalty before the war reinstated it in the course of trying some of those accused of crimes committed during the Nazi occupation. Given the exceptional conditions of that time—the excesses committed by the Nazis and their collaborators, the lengthy duration of the occupation, and the hostile resentment of the local polulation—there were demands for immediate punishment of those responsible.

Whereas in Britain government circles had seriously considered, but finally rejected, a policy of summary execution of Nazi leaders, in other parts of Europe that had been under occupation, the personal involvement and rage led to many cases of public lynching, particularly of those who had collaborated with the German occupying power and been most vicious in their action against the local populace.

Perhaps the best known instance of a public lynching is the fate that befell the leader of one of the vanquished nations, Benito Mussolini. Had Mussolini lived, it is not clear whether he would have been tried in a national court by his fellow citizens or whether the Allied authorities would have attempted, as in the case of the Japanese leaders, to try him in an international tribunal for war crimes.[13]

The problematics of the death penalty in the Nuremberg trial actually relate to both substantive and procedural questions. The basis of the death penalty in this trial is to be found in the London Agreement of 8 August 1945. Article 27 lays down that "the Tribunal shall have the right to impose upon a defendant on conviction death or such other punishment as shall be determined by it to be just." There are two other directives as to punishment. In Article 8 there is a passing, marginal reference to the issue of punishment in the context of a nonpenological aspect of the law. This article specifically disallows the legal defense of obedience to superior orders, adding that this defense "may be considered in mitigation of punishment if the Tribunal determines that justice so requires." In contrast, Article 7 nullifies any penological consideration of acts of state by declaring that the official position of the defendant shall not free him from responsibility, and then adds that no argument on this score shall be used as a mitigating factor in punishment.[14]

The Nuremberg trial itself was conducted, as already noted, in one stage, and there was no appeal. What is of particular interest is that the defense counsel summed up first, then the prosecution, and finally each defendant was provided with the chance to address the court. The defense attorneys thus could not have known whether the prosecution was going to ask the court for any specific penalty, and, if so, which—a fact which obviously would have inhibited them from addressing the question of punishment. Thus, most defense counsels ignored this aspect, focusing instead on arguments for acquittal. Curiously enough, the prosecutors also avoided any attempt to indicate to the judges what kind of punishment would be suitable in the event of a conviction. No philosophical arguments were quoted, no references to the relevance of deterrent or retributive factors were made, no precedents cited. Moreover, although the defendants themselves had the opportunity of the last word in addressing the court, they, too, no less than the lawyers, were handicapped in referring to mitigating factors which the court might consider; first, since the prosecution had not discussed this question, and second, because they could not know whether they would be convicted or not.

The sentences were pronounced shortly after the verdict of guilty had been handed down. Twelve of the defendants were sentenced to death: Goering, von Ribbentrop, Keitel, Kaltenbrunner, Frank, Frick, Rosenberg, Stricher, Saurbel, Jodl, Seys-Inquart, and Bormann, the last *in absentia;* three other defendants were sentenced to life imprisonment: Hess, Funk, and Raeder; two others, von Schirach and Speer, received twenty years each; von Nemch, fifteen years; and Doenitz, ten years. Three others were acquitted. Raeder immediately asked for his sentence of life imprisonment to be changed to a death penalty, but the request was rejected. The judgments were handed down on 30 September and 1 October 1946, and the sentences of death were carried out two weeks later. Of those sentenced to life imprisonment, Raeder was released less than ten years later, and Funk, in 1957.

After the completion of this first major trial, a further series of trials were held. The basic procedures of these subsequent trials were similar to those of the original Nuremberg Tribunal, except that the judges were of the nationality of the occupying power in the zone. In the American zone, of the total of 123 defendants who were convicted, the death penalty was imposed on 23; 20 others received a life sentence; and several others received long prison terms, the longest being for 25 years. In the British zone, 240 persons were sentenced to death, 24 to life imprisonment, and almost 500 others to shorter prison terms; in the French zone, there were 104 death sentences, 44 life sentences, and over 1,000 shorter terms of imprisonment. Subsequent clemency proceedings in all the zones led to several of the death sentences being changed to imprisonment for life.[15]

During these trials, little attention was paid to the question of the penalty to be imposed. In some of the cases in which the death penalty was imposed, a key factor in the judge's decision seems to have been the personal involvement of the defendants in acts that constituted torture. One particular case, in which most of the defendants were doctors, focused on torture commited in the course of medical experimentation, such as the testing of the resilience of a person's body to exposure to the extremes of icy water or freezing weather conditions.

A case that has particular pertinence is one dealing with the killing of hostages as a means of collective punishment against communities in which German soldiers had been attacked and killed. Here the court held that "an examination of the available evidence on the subject convinced us that hostages may be taken in order to guarantee that peaceful conduct of the population of occupied territories and, when certain conditions exist and the necessary preliminaries have been taken they may, as a last resort, be shot."[16] However, the tribunal indicated that in putting hostages to death, there had to be a reasonable relationship between the intended impact of the act and the number of hostages actually shot. Since the defendants had failed to comply with this condition, they were found guilty and given the maximum penalty.

Elsewhere in Europe, those who had collaborated with the Germans were tried for treason, sedition, and sabotage. The most famous of these trials were those of Vidkun Quisling in Norway and Marshall Petain in France.[17] Both were sentenced to death, but the latter received a commutation to a life sentence out of consideration for his advanced age and the great service that he had rendered his country in the past, particularly as a general in World War I. In all, there were over 700 executions in France, 25 in Norway, 23 in Denmark, 36 in Holland, and 230 in Belgium.[18]

In many cases actual court trials were preempted or the formal implementation of a judicial decision was frustrated by the prior action of masses of people intent on wreaking communal revenge on those who had betrayed their country and participated in violations of the basic rights of its people. These acts, too, no less than formal adjudication of capital punishment, warrant serious consideration and will be dealt with separately in the context of extra-judicial execution. In the unique circumstances of the time, in the social and political polarities that existed then, in the darkness and anguish which had been Europe's lot, these actions were somehow understood and forgiven.

In the estimation of Peter Novick, there were at least 4,500 summary executions in the purge of collaborators after the liberation of France. Novick writes: "The arrogation of state authority by the resistance was seen—and most tragic in its consequences—with respect of the purge. There were understandable reasons for this . . . the habit learned in the underground days of personally settling accounts with collaborators and *miliciens* was not readily set aside after the Liberation."

He goes on to say: "Sometimes the executions followed drum head trials which were held discreetly . . . but whose results were posted publicly afterwards to show that . . . justice is implacable and fair. . . . Sometimes a *milicien* was simply shot out of hand when his identity was discovered. There were unquestionably executions that were carried out 'in good faith' but in error—on the basis of insufficient or inaccurate information."[19] Novick points out some of the more negative aspects of these extra-judicial executions, when personal revenge was a factor or when there was infiltration of criminal elements. He also notes that occasionally orders for commutation of a death sentence would so anger the public that they would resort to lynching the accused person.

I know of no instance in which those responsible for such actions were put on trial for what were, for all intents and purposes, acts of murder. Such a trial would certainly have raised intriguing legal and moral issues as to the responsibility of partisans for killings in the furtherance of their cause. Did acts that might have been considered as legitimate during the occupation become illegal after the liberation? No doubt there would have been several legal approaches that could have been adopted in defense; and there were certainly some precedents, including, in the 1920s, verdicts of not guilty in the case of a Jew who, in Paris, had killed a Ukrainian whom he recognized as being responsible for a violent pogrom committed against his people in the Ukraine, and an Armenian who, in Germany, had assassinated one of the former leaders of Turkey whom, he argued, bore responsibility for the genocide of the Armenians.[20]

SECOND IN IMPORTANCE to the Nuremberg trial is the Tokyo trial, in which the leaders of the vanquished Japanese people were put on trial. Although based on the principles and practices of the Nuremberg trial, there were many differences between these trials, notably in their composition (eleven judges, one from each of the victorious nations) and in that the court was often split and presented dissenting judgments. In particular, the court was divided on the key issue of the death penalty: All of the seven death sentences that were passed were based on a majority vote, in one case by the narrow margin of six votes to five.

Richard Minear, in his book *Victors' Justice,*[21] is extremely critical of the trial in all its aspects, and quotes from some of the minority judgments to substantiate his claim that the trial represented mainly a vindictive pursuit of the leaders of a defeated people. Some of the most pertinent points he makes relate to the differences between the Nuremberg and Tokyo trials, and an important aspect of his thesis relates directly to the penalties imposed. Thus, whereas the Nuremberg Tribunal required a three-quarters majority for its decisions, the Tokyo trial allowed for a simple majority, and even a one-vote difference was considered sufficient to allow a death penalty.

As in Nuremberg, the majority judgment contained no reasoned explanation of the considerations that influenced the judges in their decision, nor of the factors that led to a differentiation among the sentences given to the various defendants.

The nature of the decisions is, in fact, best brought out in the appeal made by the defense lawyers to General MacArthur, the supreme commander for the Allied forces, and in whom was invested, according to the charter setting up the tribunal, the power to ratify or alter the verdict and to confirm or reduce the penalty. Their defense appeal against the verdict states:

> It is known that death sentences were imposed by vote of six to five in some cases, of seven to four in others, but in no case by vote of more than seven judges. The law of most of the civilized world requires unanimity for imposing a sentence of death, and usually for conviction of a crime; we Americans would consider it an outrage that six or seven men out of eleven should convict and sentence to death, and the community of civilized nations must consider it an outrage here.[22]

The defendant for whom there had been the closest vote for the death penalty was Hirota Koki, who had held the posts of foreign minister and then prime minister in the years 1933 to 1937, but had not held any top official post subsequently. He was even acquitted on all counts by two of the judges. Several of the dissenting judges used their minority opinion to spell out specifically their opposition to the death sentences in some or all of the cases, apparently in the hope that their views might be more persuasive in the eyes of the supreme commander when he would be faced with the task of ratifying or modifying the sentences.

Of particular interest is the opinion of Justice Webb, an Australian, who had been the president of the tribunal. Suggesting that the main purpose of punishment was deterrence, he argued that "imprisonment for life under sustained conditions of hardship in an isolated place or places outside Japan . . .

would be a greater deterrent to men like the accused than the speedy termination of existence on the scaffold or before a firing squad." Webb also felt that "it may prove revolting to hang or shoot old men."[23]

One further argument used by Webb addresses the delicate issue of allocation of responsibility and related differentiation among the punishments of the various leading figures in Japan. Of particular importance is Webb's reference to the fact that the emperor had not been put on trial at all because of political considerations of the likely reverberations his trial would cause in Japan and the implications it would have for later relationships between Japan and the United States. After noting that the evidence brought forward in the trial indicated the emperor's complicity in many of the crimes that had been proven, Webb argued that though it was the legitimate function of the prosecution to decide who would be indicted, nevertheless, "a British Court in passing sentence would, I believe, take into account, if it could, that the leader in the crime, though available for trial, had been granted immunity." He therefore concluded, in rejecting the death penalty, that "justice requires me to take into consideration the Emperor's immunity when determining the punishment of the accused found guilty."[24]

MacArthur, after due consultation with the relevant authorities representative of the various Allied nations, decided to ratify the verdicts as given. He stated in his public announcement,

I pray that an Ominpotent Providence may use this tragic expiation as a symbol to summon all persons of good will to the realization of the utter futility of war—the most malignant source and greatest sin of mankind—and eventually to its renunciation by all nations. To this end, on the day of execution, I request the members of all the congregations throughout Japan of whatever creed or faith in the privacy of their homes or at their altars of public worship to seek help and guidance that the world will keep the peace, lest the human race perish.[25]

An appeal against the trial, under writ of habeas corpus, was lodged in the U.S. Supreme Court, but the Court held that it had no power to intervene.[26]

Three days after the Supreme Court decision, the seven death sentences were carried out. The mode of execution was hanging: this, too, on a split six to five vote, the minority being in favor of firing squad, traditionally considered to be a more dignified means of death and more suited to political figures who were not petty criminals. A further sixteen defendants received life sentences, and two other defendants lesser prison terms. One of the latter, after his release from prison, reentered political life; several years later, in 1954, while serving as foreign minister, he negotiated the release of all the remaining prisoners. In the intervening years, six of them had died in prison.

Among the six justices in the majority, it is of particular interest to note the concurring opinion of Justice Douglas, for it forms a strong indictment of the Tokyo Tribunal. He held that the Court could not intervene because the tribunal was not a judicial body at all, but that its actions had been purely political! "The conclusion is therefore plain," he argued,

that the Tokyo Tribunal acted as an instrument of military power of the Executive Branch of government. . . . It was solely an instrument of political power. Insofar as American participation is concerned, there is no constitutional objection to that action. For the capture and control of those who were responsible for the Pearl Harbor incident was a political question on which the President as Commander-in-Chief, and as spokesman for the nation in foreign affairs, had the final say.[27]

Justice Douglas's decision to side with the majority seems to be seriously at fault, given his strictures on the nature of the tribunal. For at stake were the lives of people. Justice Douglas himself, in referring to the power invested in the political authorities, referred only to their power to "capture and control," and not to punish, still less to execute, on the basis of what he himself considered a political decision. The decision was not made, as he suggests, by the president, but by the supreme commander. Most significantly, the Supreme Court was not required to sit in appellate review of the tribunal's decision (which might, on the basis of Justice Douglas's argument, have been beyond their capacity), but to allow a writ of habeas corpus—which was certainly within their power. I would argue that Douglas's reasoning logically led to allowing the writ of habeas corpus. However, a different vote on his part would still have left a majority of five justices rejecting the writ.

No dissenting opinion was written. It seems that there was a presumption that Justice Rutledge intended to join the minority and had apparently been designated to write the opinion, but he died before the completion of his task. On an earlier occasion he had forcefully presented his views as to the danger or using judicial proceedings in order to give vent to vengeful sentiments. At the war's end the leader of the Japanese forces in the Philippines, General Yamashita, had been put on trial and charged with responsibility for atrocities committed by his troops in the final stages of the war.[28] Although the prosecution had failed to show that General Yamashita had personally participated in any such atrocities, nor that he had given any orders for such acts to be committed, the military commission that judged him held that his responsibility arose out of his lack of control of his troops. His defense lawyers (six American soldiers serving with the advocate general's office) argued that it was specifically the success of the American invasion force that had led to Yamashita's incapacity to keep his army in check, and that he neither knew of what was happening nor had the capacity to prevent it. The military commission found him guilty, and then concluded its judgment: "Accordingly upon secret ballot, two-thirds or more of the members concurring, the Commission finds you guilty as charged and sentences you to death by hanging."

This trial has been subjected to probing and effective criticism by one of the defense counsel, Frank Reel.[29] Though Reel's views are undoubtedly subjective, based on his tireless endeavors on behalf of a man, a defeated foe whom he came to respect, they form a vivid factual account of the fight to save his life, a passionate brief for the need to preserve the highest standards of justice in dealing with a vanquished enemy, and a severe critique of the role of the army in setting up an ad hoc military tribunal to try him.

Moreover, Reel's account and his contentions cannot be dismissed out of hand as the biased response of an involved participant at the losing end of a legal battle. For the two Supreme Court justices who were in the minority were no less scathing in their criticism of the trial. The majority justices did not address the nature and fairness of the proceedings at all, but limited themselves to declaring that the military authorities did have the prerogative to try an enemy soldier for war crimes, while simultaneously holding that the actual manner in which the proceedings were conducted could best be examined by the appropriate government authorities.

In contrast, the minority opinions did consider the proceedings. Justice Rutledge negated them *in toto,* enumerating the defects: The terms of its constitution were invalid, especially as they specifically allowed serious deviations from accepted rules of procedure, leading to a situation where the commission became, in his words, "a law unto itself"; the judgment itself contains no clear findings and is characterized by "vagueness, if not vacuity"; most of the evidence against the accused was in the form of "untrustworthy, unverified, unauthenticated evidence which could not be probed by cross-examination or other means of testing credibility, probative value or authenticity"; the defense was not given sufficient time to prepare for the trial, especially with regard to the fifty-nine items added to the indictment on the opening day of the trial.

Justice Rutledge's attitude is based on a firm conviction that in dealing with the conquered foes the same high standards of justice are required as any citizen is entitled to, for, in his words, "More is at stake than General Yamshita's fate." He notes that "this trial is unprecedented in our history. Never before have we tried and convicted an enemy general for action taken during hostilities or otherwise in the course of military operations or duty." Pointing out that legal aspects of the case were novel (the case was decided before the Nuremberg trials were held), yet recognizing the need to allow the law to develop in response to changing needs, Justice Rutledge attempted to provide an overall outline for such progress.

> If, as may be hoped, we are now to enter upon a new era of law in the world, it becomes more important than ever before for the nations creating that system to observe their greatest traditions of administering justice, including this one, both in their own judging and in their new creation. The proceedings in this case veer so far from some of our time-tested road signs that I cannot take the large strides validating them would demand."[30]

Justice Murphy concurred in the dissenting opinion and added an opinion of his own, stating that the "trial was unworthy of the tradition of our people or the immense sacrifice that they have made to advance the common ideals of mankind. The high feelings of the moment doubtless will be satisfied. But in the sober afterglow will come the realization of the boundless and dangerous implications of the procedure sanctioned today." Noting that "war breeds atrocities," Justice Murphy argues that

> If we are ever to develop an orderly international community based upon a recognition of human dignity it is

of the utmost importance that the necessary punishment of those guilty of atrocities be as free as possible from ugly stigma of revenge and vindictiveness. Justice must be tempered by compassion rather than by vengeance. In this, the first case involving this momentous problem ever to reach this court, our responsibility is both lofty and difficult. We must insist, within the confines of our proper jurisdiction, that the highest standards of justice be applied in this trial of an enemy commander conducted under the authority of the United States. Otherwise stark retribution will be free to masquerade in a cloak of false legalism.[31]

Reel is critical not only of the proceedings of the trial, but of the internal review proceedings of the army. According to him, General MacArthur, who, as in the later Tokyo trial, had the power to review and amend the verdict, carried out this function with unseemly haste and without any probing investigation. His final decision to ratify the tribunal's verdict was announced immediately after the Supreme Court had handed down its decision, manifestly before he had time to read the opinions, including those of the dissenters, or consult adequately with the army's legal authorities.

Subsequent appeals to President Truman were also to no avail; he refused to intervene, leaving the final decision to the military authorities. In Japan itself, 86,000 Japanese signed a petition, which was presented to General MacArthur, requesting Yamashita's "sentence be commuted to life sentence or that he be given an opportunity to take his own life."[32] However, MacArthur rejected all these appeals and Yamashita was hanged. In the case of another Japanese general, General Homma, who had also been sentenced to death, MacArthur did intervene to change the mode of execution from hanging to a firing squad, apparently out of deference to Homma's wife, with whom he met briefly after the conclusion the trial.[33]

SEVERAL YEARS LATER, in the early sixties, Adolf Eichmann was captured by Israeli agents in Argentina and put on trial in Israel. He was charged before a district court on several charges of crimes of genocide, against the Jewish people and against humanity. Although the trial was partly based on, and followed, the precedents of the Nuremberg trial, it contained many novel aspects, which evoked much reaction, both critical and supportive.

The trial took place in a national court according to the legislation of that country.[34] The 1951 Israeli Law on Nazis and Nazi Collaborators was based on recognized principles of international law, and was passed in the early years of the state, as a direct response to the tragedy of the Holocaust of the Jews of Europe. In the course of the trial, legal arguments were raised by the defense as to the lack of jurisdiction of the state of Israel: the legislation was *ex post facto,* the alleged crimes had been committed outside of Israel itself, and Eichmann had been captured by Israeli agents and brought to Israel without extradition proceedings.

Apart from this, calls from many quarters went out to Israel to forego trying Eichmann and to hand him over to an international tribunal. Since such a court did not exist, it is not clear how or whether at this stage, some fifteen years after the end of the war, it could have been possible to reconstitute an ad hoc international tribunal, especially considering the strained relationship between the former allies, which became apparent in the fifties during the period of the cold war.

When Eichmann was put on trial, the death penalty in Israel had been abolished for crimes in the criminal code but had been retained for the legislation dealing with crimes against humanity and related delinquencies. Indeed, because of the exceptional nature of the penalty and of the circumstances, the law had a number of special procedural provisions. For instance, the law provides that when the accused is not an Israeli citizen, he is permitted to appoint a foreign defense counsel who is not a member of the Israeli Bar. (Eichmann appointed a

German lawyer, Dr. Servatius, who had also seerved as defense
counsel in the Nuremberg trial.) The court is also obliged to
hear evidence even if the accused pleads guilty, before returning any verdict. Similarly, when the death penalty is imposed,
there is an automatic appeal, even if the accused himself does
not wish to appeal.

After a trial lasting over a year, Eichmann was convicted
and sentenced to death. On appeal the court upheld all of the
lower court's verdicts, including the death penalty. Of the latter
it said:

> We know only too well how utterly inadequate this
> death sentence is as compared to the millions of dreadful
> deaths he inflicted on his victims. Even as there is no word
> in the human speech to designate deeds such as the deeds
> of the appellant, so there is no punishment in human laws
> that would fit in its gravity the guilt of the appellant. But
> our knowledge that any treatment meted out to the ap-
> pellant would be inadequate, that no penalty or retribu-
> tion inflicted on him would be sufficient, dare not move
> us to mitigate the punishment. Indeed, there can be no
> sense in sentencing to death he who killed a hundred
> people while setting free or merely keeping in custody and
> in security he who killed millions. When the Israeli
> legislature provided the maximum penalty laid down in
> the law, it could not have envisaged a criminal greater than
> Adolf Eichmann; and, if we are not to invalidate the will
> of the legislature we must impose on Eichmann the max-
> imum penalty . . . that is: the death penalty.

Public opinion in Israel seemed to have been overwhelm-
ingly in support of the verdict, yet pleas were made from both
within and outside of Israel for commutation of the sentence.
The most notable of the pleas was that raised by the distinguised
Israeli philospher Martin Buber, who argued that opposition
in principle to the death penalty, and the denial of the right

of the state to claim life, were applicable in this case. In particular, he claimed that no penalty, not even that of death, was commensurate with the horrendous nature of Eichmann's crimes.[35]

Buber had no easy solution as to what alternative punishment should be imposed, but suggested that Israel should try to temper justice with imagination. He raised the possibility of a sentence of hard labor, in which Eichmann would be obligated to spend the rest of his life working on the soil of the country whose people he had attempted to destroy. Finally, he claimed that the death penalty for Eichmann would provide expiation for the German people and would assuage the guilt feelings of their youth. Buber, however, saw these guilt feelings as providing a positive solid base on which a new system of humanistic values could be built for the German nation. To provide an escape for these guilt feelings could possibly destroy the prospects for such a healthy humanism developing.

The pleas on behalf of Eichmann were all rejected by the president of Israel, and shortly afterwards Eichmann was hanged, his body cremated, and the ashes scattered into the sea.

The novel aspects of the Eichmann trial gave rise to a spate of comment. One of the best-known and most critical is that of Hannah Arendt,[36] who had attended the trial as a reporter for the magazine the *New Yorker*. Her criticism of the trial are far-ranging, including not only legal and procedural issues relating to the trial itself, but also a negative appraisal of how the Jewish leadership in Europe had conducted itself. Yet, despite her many reservations, Arendt concedes, in the final analysis, that justice may be considered to have been done and that there was indeed no alternative penalty that would have been appropriate for what she termed as the "banal" acts of evil committed by Eichmann.

Arendt claims that the "supreme justification for the death penalty" was that "Eichmann had been implicated and had played a central role in an enterprise whose open purpose was to eliminate forever certain 'races' from the surface of the earth.'' The crime was against mankind, not just the Jewish people. She goes on to suggest that the judges should have directly addressed this aspect and should have spelled out their use of the death penalty as follows:

> Just as you supported and carried out a policy of not wanting to share the earth with the Jewish people and the people of a number of other nations—as though you and your neighbors had any right to determine who would not inhabit the world—we find that no one, that is, no member of the human race, can be expected to want to share the earth with you. This is the reason, and the only reason, you must hang.[37]

A more balanced view of the trial may be found in the book written by Peter Papadatos, a Greek lawyer who attended the trial as an official observer for the International Commission of Jurists. In six chapters he discusses what he calls the "main problems of the Eichmann trial," and then goes on to consider three "other questions concerning the judgment and the sentence of Eichmann"—one of these questions being that of the death penalty.[38] Papadatos discusses the possibility of using the death penalty in terms of general penological arguments. He argues that its use is not justified by "special prevention," what is normally called individual deterrence. Potential criminals charged with crimes against humanity are usually only brought to trial after their fall from power, at which stage "once removed from power . . . it is impossible for them—usually forever—to continue their criminal activity."[39]

Papadatos goes on to note that "general prevention" is also "only partially achieved in international penal law." He suggests that although international law can hardly be said to intimidate, it may be seen to contibute "greatly to the formulation and the reinforcement in the conscience of people of their feeling that international society is controlled by rules of law and that acts disturbing peace or violating the fundamental rights of men are odious crimes which require a punishment to be meted out by international society in its entirety."[40]

Papadatos declares unequivocally that "vengeance has and can have no place in international criminal law."[41] He controverts the argument of some that there might be room for vengeance in the present primitive state of international criminal law, just as characterized early national criminal law. However, he does not consider a recognized aim of modern criminal law that is close to, but essentially different from, vengeance; namely, the aim of retribution, which is undergoing at present a strong revival in penological theory.

Papadatos further sets out the specific factors relative to the state of Israel in dealing with the death penalty. The country had by then, he notes, adopted an "enlightened scientific conception" and expressed an "elevated spirit" by abolishing the death penalty for other crimes.[42] Yet in Israel itself, "public sentiment was almost unanimous . . . in its firm conviction that death was the only punishment for Eichmann."[43] (It should be mentioned that the president of Israel, Yitzchak Ben-Zvi, had expressed his reluctance to act against the strong feelings of the majority of his people, in his reply to Buber and others who had asked for clemency.) In allowing the death penalty, the Israeli legislature and the people of Israel had, in Papadatos's opinion, made "a move backward in this field, in which they had made a considerable achievement"—yet he adds that there might be an understanding for their approach, given the "horror and revulsion" the Nazi activity aroused, and the "atrocious and odious method of perpetrating it."[44]

The ultimate lesson to be learned from the Eichmann trial and the punishment was, according to Papadatos, not of vengeance but rather of education, deterrence, and prevention of such acts in the future.

From a philosophical point of view the issues go even deeper; for abolitionists they even take on added pertinence. The question is whether there are not certain acts committed against humanity that are so beyond the pale of normal social intercourse that even considerations of mercy, justice, or forgiveness cannot serve to mitigate the ultimate penalty of death. The question arises even as to what are the obligations owed the the memory of the victims. Those opposed to the death penalty are here confronted by a stern test of the sincerity and depth of their beliefs, the logic and consistency of their arguments, and the relevance and applicability of their approach in extreme cases. Does a committed opposition of the death penalty allow for exceptions in exceptional cases? More to the point, does a willingness to concede the need for the death penalty in such cases undermine the overall case against capital punishment? Specifically, is it possible to retain one's opposition to the death penalty and yet justify its use against a Himmler or an Eichmann? What relevant alternative punishments are there?[45]

Alternatively, could it not be claimed that there may be a purpose in limiting the use of the death penalty only to such extreme instances—to ensure both that the full enormity of the crimes will be appreciated, and, conversely, that the death penalty will not be used for any other offenses, since they all pale in comparison.

The use of the death penalty in such limited and extreme cases does not necessarily undermine the overall argument for abolition, but may, on the contrary, give it added emphasis.[46]

8

BEFORE NUREMBERG AND AFTER EICHMANN

IT WAS THE SHEER ENORMITY of the Nazi crimes that led inexorably to the subsequent Nuremberg trials, for whatever criticism may be made of the specifics of the trials, the need for some form of official and judicial reaction was inescapable. In fact, inasmuch as there were problematics in connection with the trials, they related largely to the lack of precedent and of prior recognized norms for the legal liability of political leaders; yet this fact was in itself a product of the nature of the acts committed by the Nazis, for rarely had a war effort been accompanied by so many excessive violations of the basic norms of human behavior and of the rules of international law pertaining to the conduct of war (even if some were still disputed).

What distinguished the violations was not just their extensiveness and extremity, but the fact that they were methodically planned and systematically and meticulously performed, as an integral part of an ideological commitment. Here were not chance deviations carried out in the heat of battle and the furor of armed hostilities, but a carefully conceived plan of action. The Nuremberg trials were then not to be regarded as a vengeful exploitation of a military victory, but a determined, almost desperate, attempt to lay down norms that would place beyond doubt or dispute the protection which the civilized world community provides for defenseless groups of people, be they religious or ethnic communities, captured soldiers, innocent citizens, vanquished enemies, or political foes. The trial was to be a norm-creating precedent that would prevent a future repetition of the tragedies of the war.

Yet unique as the Nazi acts were, there were before and there have been since, on a smaller scale and less intensive, acts of a similar nature; and occasionally similar demands for judicial response to these acts have been raised. Just thirty years before, the First World War had evoked many calls for punishing and trying the leaders of the defeated nations, particularly the German kaiser, largely for responsibility for the outbreak of war and for the brutal manner in which neutral Belgium had been overrun in the early days of the war, including the killing of civilian hostages. There was also the intention to try individual soldiers for atrocities committed in the course of the war. The former trials never took place; of the latter there were a few selective examples.

Even though there was no background of Nazi ideology to the German war effort, and no planned, comprehensive excesses of the type that characterized the Second World War, the issue of the trial of the kaiser erupted into a major controversy. In Britain the prime minister, David Lloyd George, was strongly in favor of a trial, and pressed his view on the cabinet and on the British public. The prime minister's stance seems to have evoked a strong responsive chord in the British public. Many of those eager for a trial were of the opinion that the punishment to be imposed, on conviction, would be death. Indeed, as James Willis notes, the slogan "hanging the kaiser" was one of the most popular slogans in the 1918 election, and candidates opposed to the idea often encountered hostile receptions.[1]

Legal opinion in Britain as to a trial was divided. The attorney-general and the majority of the members of a special committee of legal experts supported the idea of a trial, but others felt that there was no chance of proving in a court of law any criminal culpability. It is interesting to note the attitude expressed by Lord Bryce, one of Britain's leading academic lawyers, who tried to make a distinction between the acts of inhumanity committed by the Turkish people against the Armenians and the lesser acts of war crimes committed by the Germans. Bryce argued that whereas there was no room for a trial against the kaiser, the Turkish leaders, Enver Pasha and Talaat Bey, "the two chief villains, ought to be hanged if they can be caught."[2]

However, the determination of Lloyd George backed by the public support that he received, including winning the election, did not resolve the issue. In addition to some opposition within England itself (including from the king, who was a cousin of the kaiser), the other Allied countries were not as eager for a trial; and the Netherlands, where the kaiser had taken refuge, was adamant in maintaining its tradition of granting asylum to political refugees, the status which the kaiser had requested and been granted. Some of those who were opposed to a trial argued that it would be sufficient if the Dutch were to transport the kaiser to one of their distant colonies or possessions, as had been done in the case of Napoleon's exile to St. Helena. Even though this would be tantamount to transportation for life without the benefit of a trial, it was considered a moderate response in which it was not so much punishment that was sought as removal of the kaiser from proximity to the scene of his former power.

Lord Curzon, the British foreign minister, was reluctant to pursue the matter of a trial too insistently and was apparently opposed to the idea of a possible death penalty. He argued that the shame of worldwide opprobrium expressed through an official court would be sufficient, and could even be considered a more severe response. He conceived of the idea of a trial *in absentia* if the Dutch stood fast on their refusal to extradite the kaiser. If the kaiser were to be convicted in such a trial, to continue his life "under the weight of such a sentence as has never before been given in the history of mankind, would be a penance worse than death."[3] Here is a pertinent assessment of the meaning of life after a conviction for a major offense; but, of course, the moral impact of such a decision would have been seriously blunted by virtue of the absence of the defendant, this in a trial with such strong political overtones.

Although Britain provided most of the thrust for the trial and punishment of the enemy leader, support, particularly among the public, was also forthcoming from other countries. This seems to have been more prevalent and insistent in countries that were not under direct German occupation than in those that were, and may be a result of the impact of a few atrocity stories, widely repeated. Although President Woodrow Wilson was a voice of moderation in the United States, concerned more about consolidating the peace and building a new world, "many Americans came to believe in a punitive peace and personal punishment for the kaiser."[4] Included in the demands were calls for the death penalty for the kaiser and others guilty of war crimes.

The desire to have a trial was finally expressed in the peace treaties that were signed in 1919, in which were incorporated references to the possibility of future trials, though not without much resistance by the Germans, who almost repudiated the whole peace treaty because of these clauses. Article 227 of the Treaty of Versailles states:

> The Allied and Associated Powers publicly arraign William II of Hohenzollern, formerly German Emperor, for a supreme offense against international morality and the sanctity of treaties. A special tribunal will be constituted to try the accused, thereby assuring him the guaranties essential to the right of defence. . . . In its decision the tribunal will be guided by the highest motives of the international policy, with a view to vindicating the solemn obligations of international undertakings and the validity of international morality. It will be its duty to fix the penalty which it considers should be imposed.[5]

Unlike the London Agreement, but similar to most recent international treaties, no specification of the possible punishment is made, this at a time when many in the public and among the leaders were demanding a death penalty. There is no indication of what was to be the maximum penalty. If the kaiser was found guilty, would any tribunal have dared to proclaim a death sentence if no specific reference to this ultimate penalty had been made in the treaty that constituted the legal basis for the court? In any event, this became a moot point as the Netherlands refused to surrender the kaiser, and he spent his remaining years in Holland, living into the second year of the Second World War.

Similar clauses were inserted into the treaties with all of the other defeated countries. In the light of the subsequent Nuremberg and Eichmann trials, it is particularly significant that the treaty with Turkey contained an additional unique clause, relating to the allegations of the genocide committed against the Armenian people during—and some would say under the cover of—the war. Article 230 of the Treaty of Sevres obligates the Turkish government to "hand over to the Allied Powers the persons whose surrender may be required by the latter as being responsible for the massacres committed during the continuance of the state of war on territory which formed part of the Turkish Empire." The treaty also recognized the right of the Allied countries to set up a special tribunal and acknowledged the possibility that, if an international court were to be constituted, for the massacres to be adjudicated by it.

However, the fluid state of Turkish politics at that time, the lack of consensus among the Allies, and uncertainty as to the legal position in regard to war criminals, all led to procrastination, hesitant policies, and to final capitulation by the Allies on the issue of the trial.

Several leading Turkish officials were held for two years in detention without trial in Malta; others, including the leaders Talaat and Enver, fled to Germany, which refused to consider extradition. In Turkey itself, a local military tribunal tried some of those responsible for massacres;[6] in the first trial, one of the accused was sentenced to death and hanged forthwith, an action which aroused protests among his fellow countrymen and made of him "a national martyr and turned his funeral into a patriotic protest against abject submission to the allies."[7]

In later trials a few further death sentences were handed down, including *in absentia* decisions against Talaat and Enver, but only one further execution took place, this of a minor official. Internal developments in Turkey, including a change in government, not only put an end to the trials, but led to the arrest of several members of the military tribunal.

Attempts made by the Allies, during the peace negotiations, to reach agreement on the judicial reaction to the massacres of the Armenians broke down because there were still many who were of the opinion that no international crime had been committed since the victims were citizens of Turkey and the actions taken were only incidental to the prosecution of the war. Willis sums up the failure of these efforts to have international judicial action taken against the Turkish leaders and other civilians and soldiers responsible for the Armenian tragedy.

> The first tentative step toward defining and punishing genocide failed because of Turkish nationalism and Allied indifference. The Armenians, victims and survivors, had been virtually unrepresented in Allied Councils. They were too easily ignored and forgotten. The League of Nations might have established an international tribunal to bring to justice men whose policies and actions had led to the deaths of hundreds of thousands of Armenians, an act of genocidal magnitude. But the League ignored the effort, and the British mishandled and then abandoned it. Of all failures to punish the war criminals of the First World War, this was perhaps the most regrettable, and it would have terrible consequences.[8]

One of the consequences was that the Armenian massacres served as a precedent for later action by the Nazi regime. When challenged once as to his genocidal policies in Poland, Hitler is reported to have replied "Who after all is today speaking about the destruction of the Armenians?"[9]

The failure of action by the world community led unfortunately to the pursuit of offenders by their victims. According to Willis, "Private vengeance now took over. Several young Armenian families decided to inflict the retribution that the allies had not exacted. They assassinated former Turkish leaders one after another in 1921–1922. . . . Such action was, of course, no proper substitute for impartial judgment, but the Armenians had no other recourse. The Allies had abandoned war crimes trials."[10]

Willis's statement shows his understanding of these extrajudicial executions, done not, as is generally the case, to further a political struggle or to intimidate opponents, but as an act of retribution in pursuit of what was perceived by the assassins as rightful justice, in response for the wrongs done their people. At least one court of justice, in Germany, thought likewise when it found the assassin of Talaat, not guilty, basing its verdict on the defense presented in the case, that the act was justified in the light of the historical circumstances and motivations.[11]

This was not the only decision of that time to find in favor of a defendant accused of committing a politically motivated killing in the name of a powerless, victimized nation. A French court also acquitted a Jew, Shalom Schwarzbard, for killing a Ukranian leader, Simon Petlura, living in exile, who had been responsible for the deaths of thousands of Jews during pogroms committed by soldiers under his command several years before.[12]

Although judicial recognition was thus given to the justification for what were essentially acts of revenge in lieu of the political power to adjudicate, the properly constituted trials of those considered responsible for war crimes and atrocities for the most part never took place. In Bulgaria, several members of the war-time government were tried by their successors, but the motives here were mostly internally political, not universally humanistic.

Though the declarations to have trials were for the most part ignored, the deliberations did have an impact. In the years between the two world wars the debate continued, with many renowned international lawyers arguing for, and working toward, the creation of an international norm outlawing war, or at least some of its more excessive manifestations, and the establishment of an international court, which would avoid the problem of a biased victor's justice. But although a Permanent Court of Justice was set up, it did not deal with criminal issues, and in any case had no procedures or personnel for law enforcement.

Open violations of international norms, all in a sense being a prelude to the Second World War, went unpunished— the Italian invasion of Ethiopia, the Japanese invasion of Manchuria, and the German invasions of Austria and Czechozlovakia. Although the Kellogg-Briand Pact, which renounced war as an instrument of national policy, was signed in 1929, it was not sufficient to restrain any of these invasions. It has been argued that had stricter action been taken against the German leaders and others after the First World War, and had an international criminal law come into existence, it is possible that the lessons learned and the message enunciated would have helped avoid the horrors of the Second World War. This is, of course, mere speculation, and perhaps doubtful given the failure of the Nuremberg and other trials to achieve that effect in the years since—whether in terms of outbreaks of war or atrocities committed during the course of the wars, or, for that matter, during periods of peace.[13]

It is even possible that the special nature of the Nuremberg trials has paradoxically hindered the development of international law norms. On the one hand, the major Nuremberg trials dealt with an extreme Nazi ideology so evil and pervasive that however perverse other similar modern-day doctrines sometimes are, they pale by comparison. On the other hand, the vindictive aspects of the Tokyo trial has doubtless tended to serve as much as a warning of the dangers of the injustice of such trials as a beacon of the positive results and the clarity of norms to be gained from them.[14]

WHATEVER THE POSITION of the trials, and however unique the Nazi ideology and policies, the fact is that political and military leaders have continued to perpetrate genocidal acts in furtherance of their interests. Eugene Davidson has written of what he calls the "Nuremberg fallacy," and has shown convincingly that the norms laid down there and the punishments handed out have had minimal, and perhaps negligible, impact on the manner in which political, diplomatic, and military decisions are made.[15] The needs of national, political, ideological, and even personal interests seem always to be of superior persuasive impact than the norms of internationa law or the values of human decency. The fear of punishment in the event of defeat seems to be an irrelevant consideration given the fact that the major factor weighing on decision-makers is the prospect of victory.

Davidson's legal analysis is matched by a comprehensive historical and sociological exposition by Leo Kuper, who describes genocide as a new word but an ancient crime.[16] Modern examples, many of them since the Second World War, appear together with reminders of past aberrations. Further examples of the extensive nature of genocide in the modern world may be found in Irving Louis Horowitz's book on genocide, in which he focuses on the nature of state power vis-à-vis the rights of the individual.[17]

The psychological aspects of the problem have been probed by Israel Charny, who claims that the fact of genocide is one of the great issues confronting humankind today, and insists that no study of human nature or of social behavior can be considered truly meaningful or really comprehensive without understanding the factors making for genocidal practices and exploring the means to avoid them.[18] He intersperses his probing psychological analysis with references to the genocidal practices happening today.

But for all the excellent and important data in these books, their groping toward a theoretical perspective, their contribution to an awareness of the extant evils around us, their search for preventive measures, they deal minimally with the issue of what to do, at the personal level, with those who bear responsibility for such acts. Should they be regarded as criminals and tried in a court of law to determine their legal culpability; and if so, if found guilty, what should be their punishment?

At first glance it seems almost impossible to separate the partisan political background from the objective judicial role. For if ever a concerted effort to end genocide and related crimes is made, it will have to ensure that the power and success of the perpetrators will not serve as a bar to action against them, if necessary, any more than the mere fact of defeat and failure will serve as a pretext for the vindictive justice of the victors.

Charny's book is of particular import because it emerges out of the concerns of a psychologist for the fact that psychology has for too long engrossed itself in a host of aspects of human behavior, but has largely ignored what is perhaps the most important, and most puzzling aspect—the capacity of ordinary human beings to be so easily drawn into the vortex of evil actions, and to contribute to their consummation by eager enrollment or by active, if reluctant, participation, by embarrassed passivity or by callous indifference.

By the same token, those who ponder over the problems of social control of criminals and the appropriate punishment due them must surely at some stage face the issue of how to control the most evil and harmful of acts. What psychologists are called upon by Charny to explain and, if possible, to prevent, penologists—in the event of the failure to prevent—are called upon to seek an appropriate punitive response.

The mass or serial murderer—the prototype of the candidate for execution—is often only a pale reflection of the bigger massacres carried out by those with political power. Conflict theorists and radical criminologists have long argued that crime is to be understood not so much within the obvious framework of failures in home, community, peer relations, etc., but as a consequence of the overall societal structure in which the laws are first enacted and then enforced in terms of the needs and interests of the dominant group in society.[19]

George Vold, preceding, perhaps presaging, the radical theorists of today, had early on raised this as a major issue of concern for theoretical criminology.[20] He succinctly defines crime as the behavior of people in groups responding to conflict situations that they confront. Vold's examples are drawn largely from the political arena, where the losers later become the accused in the judicial arena. However, no less pertinent are the deviations of the "winners," those who use the instruments of political power to further their own interests and ideologies and to harm those they fear or hate.

This is an issue not just for theoretical criminology, in order to understand crime in all its fullness, variety, and complexity, but also for the practical penologist, trying, in particular, to determine what to do with the most evil of society's deviants. In terms of the scale of human tragedy, the import of, let us say, a serial murderer is of less consequence than, for example, political massacres that have taken place with the open encouragement or tacit consent of powerful politicians, those who by their legislation determine the framework of the punitive mechanism or, in some cases, whether society's grace, in the form of a pardon, shall be granted.

All too often politicians do stand trial, but not so much for harm that they have caused to the innocent, as by virtue of their being deposed, their trial intended more to throttle opposition than to seek a judicial resolution of the charges brought against them. All too often other foreign dignitaries pay such politicians, while yet in power, obsequious respect, way beyond that which the diplomatic niceties require, and, in the process, cause untold distress to those who have been victimized by these politicians—for instance, the elevation of the Ugandan President Edi Amin (against whom there was substantive authenticated evidence of massacres committed at his order) to the presidency of the African Organization of Unity.[21] The norms of international law, as laid down in the Nuremberg trial and confirmed in subsequent trials, seem to have had little impact on the political behavior of Amin. In the end his removal was brought about with the active intervention of a neighboring state, Tanzania, who helped the first president of Uganda, Milton Obote, who had been overthrown by Amin, to return to the presidency. Unfortunately, the excesses did not cease, though changing in their focus and admittedly diminishing in their scope, till Obote himself was deposed for a second time.

Just as at the national level, justice can only be meted out in accordance with international norms and rules if there is power to investigate, adjudicate, and punish the culprits. In the case of Nuremberg, the aftermath of the war created the most convenient conditions for so doing. In the normal course of events, such close collaboration among states does not exist, but it certainly characterized the period immediately after the Second World War.

On the contrary, ideological rivalry, diplomatic suspicion, covert hostilities, and national interests make it extremely difficult for any concerted action. This is true even when applied to weak states; all the more in respect to strong states, especially the superpowers. Yet, on the international level, they, too, have been accused of genocidal actions, most persistently and vociferously in regard to their recent military actions in Asia, the United States in Vietnam, the Soviet Union in Afghanistan.[22] Now it is clear that the historical debate as to these two wars is involved and complicated, and not easily to be resolved within the framework of a judicial hearing—but so were the issues, at least, in the Tokyo trial.

Occasionally, however, the evidence is almost incontrovertible, and so it was presumed to be in the Nuremberg trial. Thus a useful starting point for an investigation of governmental culpability for the most serious of crimes might be the unprecedented and epoch-making speech made by Nikita Kruschev at the Twentieth Conference of the Communist Party of the Soviet Union in 1952.[23] Here is a history of atrocities committed by, or at the order of, Stalin as ruler of the Soviet Union for about a quarter century. Here is a litany of evil that repeats many of the accusations made against the Soviet Union by its most implacable ideological rivals.

On this basis, what sort of indictment would have been drawn up against Stalin, if he had been overthrown—or, more pertinently, if the Soviet Union had lost the last war? How many parallels are there in this list of crimes (which is probably only partial; for instance, it contains no reference to the exile and execution of returning Soviet prisoners of war) to the acts for which the Germans were indicted? At the Nuremberg trial, the defendants had tried—with only minimum success—to use the *tu quoque* argument, but mainly in respect to military activities, such as an aerial bombing of civilian areas (Dresden vis-à-vis Coventry) or submarine warfare. Yet in hindsight it might be that the real *tu quoque* situation was not of the manner in which the war was conducted, but the excesses committed in the Soviet Union against citizens without any relevance to the war, and much of it in peace time.

Would an international judicial organ have been able to deal with this issue or would it have been beyond their jurisdiction since (as had been argued in connection with the Armenian massacres) the victims were mostly citizens of the Soviet Union, and thus the international community was barred from intervening?

Paradoxically, the consequences of Kruschev's revelations were to impose upon Stalin—after his death—the kind of "penalty" that Lord Curzon had suggested for the kaiser in his life time, through an *in abstentia* trial: the opprobium of world opinion. The fame and power that Stalin once possessed are today as of naught; his name and memory have all but been erased from the annals of the country which he ruled as a colossus for so long.[24]

How judge such acts? Can they only be judged in the final court of history—or can there be personal attachment of culpability? How judge other actions of the Soviet Union in the years since, its invasions of Hungary in 1956, of Czechoslovakia in 1968, and of Afghanistan in 1980? In each case, of course, the claim was made that the authorized government authorities had invited the Russian soldiers in. How prove or disprove this contention—how apportion blame if culpability be proved?

Most significant are the problematics related to the ongoing fighting in Afghanistan, because scattered newspaper reports have persistently described acts that prima facie constitute crimes of war and crimes against humanity—deportations, deliberate bombing of civilians, use of illegal weapons, and other assorted atrocities. [25]

Many people have drawn attention to the parallels between the Russian actions in Afghanistan and the American in Vietnam, with most of the examples relating to the real-politik of a situation in which a major power is thwarted in its military aims by the effective guerilla tactics of the local population. But there seem to be other parallels also, relating to the dubious manner in which the war was conducted relative to international norms. On one occasion, the atrocity of My Lai, some of the soldiers involved were tried, found guilty, and sentenced in a court martial; but many believed that the accused were really the victims of a policy that led almost inevitably to what transpired in My Lai, and that the superior officers, responsible for overall planning and policy, as well as the overall political echelons really bore the responsibility for what had happened. [26]

In fact, so intense were the feelings in North America and Western Europe, that an unofficial trial against the United States was held under the aegis of the Bernard Russell War Crimes Tribunal. After hearing evidence for several days (though not from the American government), it came to the conclusion that crimes of war were being committed in Vietnam. [27] It is quite likely that the decision of the tribunal was a biased one—which does not necessarily mean that their conclusions were wrong, only that they were probably foreordained given the known political beliefs of those who organized the trial and sat in judgment. However, two factors should be borne in mind. First, similar charges were leveled against the Nuremberg, Tokyo, and Jerusalem trials—that they were foregone conclusions in which the accused had no chance of proving their innocence.

Second, some of the factual data presented raises some very serious issues as to the gross violations of the rules laid down at Nuremberg.

These examples of the aberration of the Soviet Union and the United States are just two of many that could be described for other countries as well; but they are of particular pertinence because they deal with the two strongest military powers in the world, both of them allies in the Second World War, both responsible for helping organize the Nuremberg and Tokyo trials and providing the judges and the prosecutors for them, each committed to a different way of life, each searching for influence in the rest of the world. Certainly, similar examples of violations of norms could be given for the other two Allied powers involved in both of these trials—such as the executions and tortures committed by the French in Algeria, and British actions in various parts of its former far-flung empire.[28]

Any attempt to apply objective legal standards in the realm of gross violations of international law would be dependent on the active and joint support of these countries (as happened after the Second World War)—but any such application would be meaningless unless the ambit of the law, where necessary, could embrace the strongest as well. The problems of so doing are immense—but unless such a possibility arises, the impact of the Nuremberg and related trials, the values that underlie them, and the norms that they enunciated, will become no more than a passing episode, a historical oddity, a fading memory.

9

HUMANICIDE

T HE CRIME OF GENOCIDE, once recognized, posed very difficult penological issues as to what punishment could be considered suitable for a crime of such a nature—satanic in its conception, precise in its implementation, massive in its compass, ruthless in its consistency. The norms laid down in the post–World War II trials indicated, not always with any reasoned opinion, that the death penalty would in some cases be appropriate. Even some with abolitionist principles have conceded that an exception may have to be made for these kinds of crimes—if only for the lack of any other penalty that might, though retaining the commitment to humanity which is part of the essence of an abolitionist position, give expression to the horrendous enormity of the crime.

The sheer numbers involved were a major factor in the attitudes formed toward the crime, indeed, for the very need of defining it as the destruction of a people. But numbers alone were only one aspect of the aversion and horror which it aroused. Beyond this was the evil intent and the ruthless implementation; and, above all, the very denial of the victims' humanity, the unbearable suffering inflicted upon them, together with the lack of any culpability on their part, and their inability, for lack of political power, to defend themselves.

It is possible that similar acts on a smaller scale might be committed—including similar special degrees of criminality on the part of the perpetrator and similar callous disregard for the humanity of the victim. Awareness of the existence of these kinds of crimes has grown in recent years, mainly because of the concerted effort by a number of international organizations to provide information and to arouse awareness. Foremost among them has been Amnesty International, which has suggested the concept of *extra-judicial executions* for those phenomena in which people, generally innocent of all crime, guilty only of their undesirable social status or their political opposition to those in power, have been executed without the benefit of a trial, or if tried, without the benefit of those processes that allow for a fair defense.[1] Often they are subject to severe torture, while being kept *incommunicado;* if killed, they may be denied formal funeral rites, and information of their fate may be withheld from their family and friends.

The use of the term 'extra-judicial executions' makes a major contribution to our understanding of an important phenomenon of social life, but it also contains many problematics, some relating to the substantive nature of the definition, some relating to the awkwardness of the term. Objections have been raised by some people to the convoluted use of a hyphenated three-word concept, and by others to the fact that the conjunction of 'extra' and 'judicial' creates confusion as to the nature of certain processes that might be considered at least quasi-judicial but are really no more than kangaroo-style courts under the appellation of revolutionary courts or in the guise of military tribunals—and there could be uncertainty as to whether to include them in the ambit of the new concept.

To overcome the latter objection, there has been occasional reference to 'political murder' as conjuring up a clearer picture of what is entailed in the scope of the definition.[2] This, too, has its limitations because some extra-judicial executions do not have a political background, and they might represent a hostility to the victim stemming from some other source. Further, the term 'political murder' is too close terminologically to 'political assassination,' which is often directly the opposite of what is intended by the term 'political murder.'

Given the nature of Amnesty International's work, its focus was also clearly on governmental actions of those in power—and voices have been raised claiming that nongovernmental groups, too, commit similar acts—the acts of those with power but lacking political sovereignty and international recognition, for instance, when a rebel group has control of territory. Further examples might encompass those having recognized absolute legal power in a limited situation, for example, the captain of a ship who has it in his power to determine the fate of others—to rescue or to ignore boat people on the high seas claiming to be refugees fleeing oppression, or to reject a stowaway, as in a few known cases of ships putting stowaways off the boat in mid-ocean and leaving them with little hope of being saved.[3]

All of these acts seem to be characterized and distinguished by their total disregard for the humanity of the victim, not just for political reasons or for the kind of blanket hatred that leads to genocide, but for a denial of the victim's rights at the very personal and direct level. It is not just that one's political beliefs or ethnic affiliation is being singled out for punishment, but that one's humanity per se is being denied, and this denial used as a release from any normal inhibitions. Under these conditions killing and torture become acceptable sources of action. Whereas genocide conjures up a total plan of campaign, these kinds of acts are more directly focused on a particular individual, even when it is the person's group identity that initially arouses the hostility; sometimes there is even chance in the choice of the victim and in the nature of his predicament.

In the above examples there is a wide range of activities, but what unites them and distinguishes them from other criminal activities is the killing or attempted killing of a human being, or wilful disregard of possible fatal consequences to a human being, by persons possessed of power in the process of denying the victim the basic human right to fairly defend himself in any proceedings or decision-making process, particularly when his life is at stake. Often these actions are accompanied by torture, but this is not of the essence of the definition, although its presence might well give an indication of the background for the death, for instance, when callous disregard for a person's human dignity and rights might end in death, as when people die suddenly while incarcerated, after undergoing ruthless interrogation.

I suggest that this is a self-contained and comprehensive form of social action and criminal activity, sufficient to distinguish it from other social actions and crimes, and to warrant special consideration and nomenclature. Resembling many of the facets of genocide, there are also many unique aspects that justify differentiation and necessitate a separate definition.

There is a special importance to be attached also to the broad range of activities covered, on the one hand, and the unique, shared aspects that overlay the apparent diversity, on the other hand. Thus they clarify the fact that violations of human rights are not within the sole province of a corrupt regime or of officials abusing the power that state appointment gives them, nor, alternatively, the typical acts only of those, correctly or incorrectly, known as terrorists. In the realm of human rights nothing is easier, or more typical, than outright condemnation of one's opponents for acts that would be either heartily lauded or at least vigorously defended, or even embarrassingly explained away, when carried out by those with whom one shares a common basis. What needs to be stressed is that beyond the politics, ideology, and social nexus, there is a violations of rights, an infringement of dignity, a victim's suffering, a diminution of the sense of the unity of humanity, and a denial of the sanctity of human life.

The ultimate definition of 'humanity' is the ability to empathize with another human being qua human being, across the borders of sociological differentiation and political opposition. It was the inability or unwillingness to do so that triggered the genocidal acts of the Nazis and of other groups responsible for similar genocidal crimes—and it is the inability or unwillingness to do so that is the cause of the killings committed in the course of human rights violations.

I accordingly suggest that a special concept be used to describe the nature of this phenomenon—and that it be called the crime of *humanicide,* the destruction of a life by those with power, while depriving the victim of his human rights. Both of these two distinguishing characteristics are conjured up in the term itself.[4]

The crime basically deals with the rejection of the restrictions that accompany power and that, in a sense, alone give power true legitimacy. The key factor is not state sovereignty, but power in its widest generic sense, whether exercised by state authority or by rebels in possession of territory, kidnappers in control of their captives, captains of ships in defined, if limited, positions of decision-making; power made all the more excessive by the vulnerability of the victim, because of their legal subservience (as for prisoners), their physical powerlessness (as in kidnapping), or their geographical isolation (as for boat people).

In many instances the situation of the victim is liable to be exacerbated by the infliction of torture. Such actions, where they existed, would form part of the description of the specific crime, but they are not integrated into the definition itself. There are plenty of circumstances in which rapid commission of the killing takes precedence over torturous activity, such as in a summary trial and execution. In fact, it is specifically under circumstances of summary proceedings that the authorities are likely to forego torture in their haste to carry out the execution.

Once the crime is so distinguished and so defined as humanicide, the key problem becomes determining the manner of adjudication and the range of punishment for such a crime. As in the case of genocide, we are dealing with some of the most extreme examples of human depravity.

In the past, acts of this nature have led to severe responses, but not always within the framework of due process. Often, in the wake of a coup the deposed leaders, formerly responsible for human rights violations, have been submitted to summary trials, which in many senses become a reenactment of the crime for which they were charged. For the most part, these trials, carried out by vindictive successor regimes, are aimed not at the elucidation of human rights, but at the furtherance of political interests, seeking not so much the meting out of justice as the exaction of revenge.

Since so often these crimes have strong political overtones, it may be that a concerted effort to define the crime and to control it can only be successful if an impartial and objective judicial body can be assured; otherwise the framework of a court could be used to commit what might well constitute a further act of humanicide. Ideally, the crime of humanicide should be an international crime, which would be adjudicated in a supranational framework—of a regular international or regional court, or a specially constituted one.

A major feature of such a court would be to guarantee to the accused the very rights he had denied to others. He would have full access to legal counsel, and when detained prior to and during the trial, the conditions would answer to the minimum standards of decency and dignity compatible with restrictions on a person's liberty.

At trial, in order to ensure the highest standards of fairness, particularly in regard to the issue of sentence, *tu quoque* arguments would be allowed in mitigation of sentence—focused on the actions of any group involved in a complaint or victim role in the proceedings. Any conviction and penalty would only be possible if the judges could ensure a fair-handed allocation of criminal responsibility between the various sides involved in the proceedings—either that only one side had resorted to humanicidal actions or had done so in an utterly dispropor- tionate manner, or that both sides, similarly culpable, were equally being made subject to the possibility of the same penalties.

The range of sentencing would in any case have to be a broad one because of the diversity of actions contained in it. Certainly the court should have the flexibility to differentiate clearly between a systematic campaign against human rights and a fortuitous aberration, for instance, the captain of a ship casting a stowaway into the sea to his nigh certain death. Such an act would constitute humanicide or attempted humanicide, but would entail a lesser sentence than for more wholesale and systematic violations, just as there are degrees of complicity and culpability in genocide, and accordingly a range of penalties less than the ultimate ones imposed on the leaders and chief culprits after the Second World War.

The suggestion of a special international crime involves a fundamental change in present-day thinking. In the light of the numerous violations at present being recorded (many in protected situations, in which people are state functionaires almost exempt from control and almost immune from challenge), it is clear that the recognition of a crime of humanicide is not an easy one: even less so is the possibility of it being properly and fairly enforced. The mere number of persons who are potentially liable is staggering. In practice, of course, it is highly unlikely that most would be tried. But this is common enough in criminal proceedings. In order to try those accused of Nazi activity, there was a necessity to be selective. This is true also in the realm of ordinary criminal processes; authorities constantly exercise a discretion to indict and prosecute, in terms of resources, priorities, possibilities, etc.[5]

THE ISSUE OF HUMAN RIGHTS in general is a controversial one, but there have certainly been interesting and important developments in recent decades. Certainly the information available is vastly in excess of what was the situation several decades, or even years, ago, much of it the result of the existence of the mass media, particularly electronic media, and of the formation of international organizations. An insight as to how extensive human rights issues can extend is shown by the attempts, often faltering and often aborted, to make them a basic facet of foreign policy and ongoing diplomacy. The increasing work of some of the regional human rights institutions, commissions, and courts has also been instructive, and the future developments in this area, particularly in the judicial area are difficult to foresee but basically promising.[6]

One should not forget that there was a stage when it was strenuously argued that there could be no judicial control over the actions of soldiers in military situations. One could not expect, so it was said, for an ordinary soldier to challenge commands of his superiors. This would introduce an intolerable strain on the basic hierarchical structure of the army and would unfairly and unnecessarily compromise soldiers, demanding of them a knowledge and understanding of complicated international and criminal law, and a display of ethics in situations dangerous in themselves and liable to become even more so as a result of individual objections, challenges, and argumentation. The fact though is that today soldiers may be and have been charged and convicted for acts that are violations of human rights. This was perhaps unthinkable in former times, and the development of the law in this regard is indicative of how progress may be made in difficult, sensitive, and ethical issues. A soldier today is presumed to realize that a blatantly immoral act is also manifestly illegal.[7] Similar presumptions should, and generally do, apply to citizens.

Historically, the parallel to the prevention of humanicide would be the international actions taken against piracy in earlier times, when pirates were declared to be enemies of humanity, *hostes humani generis,* and were subject to the judicial jurisdiction of any nation able to capture them. The accepted penalty for what was basically the first recognized international crime was death.[8] To what extent this international norm contributed to the lessening of piratical activity is a historical question of no small significance but which has not yet been adequately probed. Some information exists as to activities in certain notorious geographic areas, such as the Barbary Coast in North Africa and the Pacific. In this latter area of so much sea and so many islands, piracy continues to plague shipping—and it is of some significance for my thesis to note that there have been many reported incidents of "boat people" being attacked by these pirates.[9]

Both at the official level and through nongovernmental organizations, much previously unavailable evidence has been collected in the past few years. There has been increasing recognition that international protection is needed in order to guarantee the right to human life. The abuses of power at the national level have been too prevalent and variegated to allow for the comfortable assumption that the rights of the individual to life can be fully protected within the framwork of national sovereignty.

B. G. Ramcharan has presented a strong argument for international surveillance of human rights violations since so often it is the sovereign power of nation-states that provides the cover for arbitrary deprivation.[10] The International Convention on Civil and Political Rights states categorically that "no one shall be arbitrarily deprived of life," and regional statements have used similar or identical language. The exact parameters of such protection has been the subject of much dispute, a reflection of different perceptions of human rights that people have in terms of their ideological beliefs; but there is little doubt that deliberate killings without due process of law are commonly assumed to fall within this category of protection. In this context Ramcharan claims that

more and more, deprivations of the right to life are carried out by governmental authorities or by their cohorts, in such a manner as to circumvent the safeguards provided for in national laws. The practice of disappearances is a classic example of this. Faced with such situations, in which national control is deliberately circumvented, is it not incumbent upon international law to offer a response and to interject international control where national control has been by-passed? . . . It would . . . seem necessary to develop the principle of universal jurisdiction for the trials of persons guilty of gross violations of the right to life so that, even if such persons are pardoned by their national governments, for the atrocious crimes which they have committed, they may, if caught outside their countries, be amenable to international proceedings. Can the international community afford to continue permitting persons who engage in serious violations of the right to life go by unpunished?[11]

Basically there seems to be a long-term, slow-moving process underway—whereas one of the original factors, which led historically to the emergence of organized society and eventually a global network of nation-states jealously and zealously guarding their sovereignty, was the desire and need to provide protection for the individual against the ravages of predatory actions by his fellow beings, so today there is an increasing awareness that it is specifically that sovereignty which may threaten the well-being of the citizen, whose security can only be vouchsafed by the concern and protective activities of those outside of that sovereignty in the international community.

In another article from the same book of essays, David Weissbrodt has documented some of the work by international and regional groupings such as the Human Rights Committee, the United Nations Commission of Human Rights (with its Special Rapporteur), the Inter-American Commission on Human Rights, and the European Commission and Court on Human Rights.[12] He gives several examples of documented evidence of arbitrary killings in different parts of the world. However, extreme as these aberrations are, their description is often couched in the moderate language of diplomatic discourse. Especially at the United Nations, the capacity to be definitive in these matters is often circumscribed by the need to be deferential to member states. Weissbrodt concludes that "the principal remedy for international rights violations has been and probably for some time will be embarrassment and the threat of embarrassment."[13] He claims that at the present stage the major means of controlling human rights abuses is thus not punitive sanctions for past delinquencies but publicity or even the threat of publicity to prevent their continuation or recurrence. C. K. Boyle also notes the importance of deterrence in these cases and bemoans the fact that the prospect of deterrence is often "frustrated by the phenomenon of state amnesties awarded by governments to security forces personnel after a period of killings or torture."[14]

The Amnesty International report on political killings by governments provides a concise summary of the problem, with practical suggestions and specific recommendations, including educational programs for law enforcement personnel.[15] Israel Charny has put forward a suggestion for an early warning system to monitor gross violations of human rights.[16] At the United Nations, resolutions have been passed condemning such acts and some machinery set up for dealing with complaints. The legal fraternity is becoming more involved with international and regional organizations, such as the International Commission of Jurists, ready to provide observers to monitor trials. If anything, there may be a need to focus more attention at this stage of human rights concerns on nongovernmental bodies, such as rebel groupings holding territory. But whatever steps are taken, the ultimate decision will be of what punishment would be the most suitable. And linked to this is whether those sitting in judgment on persons accused of human rights violations, including humanicide, will afford them a fair judicial hearing with the full protections of due process.

Some of the dilemmas here may be noted from the Amnesty report. Though on the one hand, a recommendation is made that "asylum should not be extended to perpetrators of extra-judicial executions," on the other hand, a footnote comment adds that "Amnesty International opposes anyone being forcibly sent from one country to another where they can reasonably expect to become a prisoner of conscience, or be subjected to torture or extra-judicial or judicial execution."[17] For as long as crimes of this nature remain solely within the purview of national jurisdiction, the unfortunate consequence may be a choice between giving asylum to a known violator of human rights or his own subjection to human rights violations in the event of extradition.

The case of ex-Emperor Bokassa of the Central African Empire is particularly instructive, for it seems to involve almost every feasible aspect of response to humanicidal acts (short of an international penal tribunal)—a death sentence, a reluctant grant of political asylum, a subsequent trial, with the likelihood of a life or long-term prison sentence, and the rumored prospect of a pardon. In 1979 he was sentenced to death in absentia for a series of crimes committed by his authority or with his direct personal involvement, including one widely reported notorious instance when he was allegedly responsible for the deaths of over a hundred school children after they had expressed dissatisfaction with a school dress code.[18] He found asylum in France, where he lived under restrictive conditions, until finally deciding to return to his homeland, where he was immediately arrested and put on trial. During the course of the trial there were reported rumors that the present government had no intention of exacting the full measure of punishment from him, but seemed inclined to offer him an early pardon.[19] The atrocity incident itself was originally given extensive publicity by Amnesty International and later their basic findings were corroborated by a specially constituted panel of jurists from five African countries, a further example of the trans-national nature of human rights violations, and the possibilities of at least regional cooperation in such matters. In the case of the killings of the schoolchildren, it seems clear that the crime itself was not of genocide; on the other hand, it manifestly seems to be more than murder. At the original trial of Bokassa, six other people were also tried; they were found guilty, sentenced to death, and executed.

In the same year as Bokassa's first trial in absentia, a second deposed leader was put on trial. Ex-President Masie Nguema of Equatorial Africa was tried, together with ten others, for a series of crimes including genocide and human rights violations, and after conviction, they were all sentenced to death and executed.[20] There has been some criticism of the trial because of complicated legal issues, including the lack of ratification of the Genocide Convention by Equatorial Africa; but the fact of mass killing, basically humanicide, seems to have been proven beyond reasonable doubt.[21] Both these cases, attempts to respond judicially to extreme criminality, seem to suggest the need for a separate recognized international delinquency of humanicide.

The attempt of adjudicate human rights violations is certainly commendable, but it is by no means clear that the basic human rights of the accused were safeguarded in the judicial proceedings, for instance, the right of appeal. It is interesting to note the manner in which Amnesty International reports the event. For instance, in recording the death sentence imposed originally on Bokassa, they add in a footnote the organization's opposition to the death penalty but do not suggest what alternative penalty might have been considered.

In terms of the safeguarding of the basic human rights of the accused, would the position of the accused have been better had he been given an alternative punishment, let us say of life? Is it conceivable that the conditions of such imprisonment would have answered to the minimum standards of international conventions on prison conditions or of overall human rights norms? It is possible but rather unlikely, especially given the extensive documentation by Amnesty International of human rights abuses of political prisoners.[22] Even so, the reports of possible moderation toward Bokassa in his second trial may suggest respect for such norms—although, of course, an overly early pardon may also cause problems, including hurt to the sentiments of the families of his victims, a factor that cannot be disregarded in such matters.

In any event, one of the most significant recent developments in Africa has been the forthright attitude adopted by the new leader of Uganda, President Museveni, in terms of demanding that human rights violations on that continent be openly divulged and vigorously prosecuted. In the light of recent history in his own country, his comments take on an added and poignant significance. At the OAU summit in Addis Ababa in June 1986, Museveni said that "while Ugandans perished on such a scale, the rest of the world kept largely silent; others colluded with the tyrants."

I must state that Ugandans were unhappy and felt a deep sense of betrayal that most of Africa kept silent while tyrants killed them. The reason for not condemning such massive crimes has supposedly been a desire not to interfere with the internal affairs of a member state, in accordance with the charters of the OAU and the UN.

We do not accept this reasoning because in the same organs there are explicit laws that enunciate the sanctity and inviolability of human life.[23]

In South America there have been similar developments of judicial response to human rights violations. Life sentences were imposed on two of the ex-leaders of the military regime in Argentina, with long prison terms being imposed on other leading figures in that government. Given the liberal and democratic nature of the present government, it might be assumed that their conditions are reasonable; it is further possible that at some time in the future they might be allowed out of prison. In any event, the verdicts (including some acquittals) and the sentences have aroused conflicting reactions, some desiring heavier sentences, others lighter. An article in *Africa-Asia,* a monthly magazine that covers Latin America as well as Africa and Asia, claims that families of the victims and human rights activists "were outraged" by the leniency of the court.[24]

A large part of the problem lies in the fact that so many lower ranking officials and officers have not even been tried; "lesser members of the military establishment who were deeply involved in the torture and extermination of their fellow citizens—including infants—will never be called to account."[25]

Yet many observers are no less concerned that too severe reaction to army personnel in a prolonged series of trials may run the alternative risk of alienating the army. As noted critically by Emilio Mignone, Cynthia Ertland, and Samuel Issacharoff, "many argue that, if the members of the armed forces face the punishment that justice would demand, the survival of civilian rule could be jeopardized." To this kind of argument the authors reply,

> On the contrary, the future of Argentinian society requires a subordination of the military to civilian justice. . . . If the hundreds of junior officers who committed acts of repression are shielded from criminal responsibility, they will emerge as the new leadership of the armed forces. . . . In both Argentina and the rest of the world, those concerned with human rights await with hope and anxiety the outcome of the bold project launched by the government of the people of Argentina.[26]

THE PROBLEMS that Germany and Japan faced at war's end in trying those who had led their nations into a disastrous war are replicated. Whereas West Germany opted for prison sentences (the death sentence was banned by constitution), Japan executed over nine hundred soldiers and officials.

Meanwhile, today, deposed leaders seek their own physical safety, often living off the proceeds of their corrupt practices. Yet were they to return for trial in their own countries, they might face dire consequences of a vengeful people—from Somoza of Nicaragua and the Shah of Iran in the late seventies, to Duvalier of Haiti and Marcos of the Philippines in the last year.

And for as long as the leaders are beyond the reaches of the law, it clearly becomes problematical to arrest, indict, and punish those lesser officials who were, as they are wont to exclaim, "only" carrying out orders. And going beyond that, from a global perspective, there are others guilty of gross human rights violations in regimes never overthrown, who are provided with protection because their political stance is acceptable, or their political power places them beyond the reaches of the law.

Much thought must still be devoted to this problem— academically and practically; at the local, regional, and international levels; by official and government bodies as by voluntary nongovernmental organizations. Many fruitful ideas have been explored and partially implemented—ranging from habeus corpus writs to regional and international courts, through compensation for victims and their families, including an international compensation fund, to monitoring procedures and observer teams, similar to those that are essential for any form of international control, for instance, arms control.[27] Means must be found of encouraging people to report instances of human rights violations, including pleas beyond the national boundaries of state sovereignty and of protecting them when they do so.[28]

One particular aspect that provides intriguing and practical possibilities is in the realm of tort law, where the victims of human rights violations may sue their tormentors in a third country, with the tort action based on the fact that such violations are an international delinquency. In the United States the Alien Tort Claims Act provides an excellent model for legislation of this type, and has already been successfully used in litigation.[29] The message of such legal and judicial approaches is that torturous acts under the protective secrecy of official power may lead to tortious actions in the arena of public scrutiny. Whereas any monetary awards, if enforced, would be of great significance, the symbolic message may be of no less consequence.

The most important precedent was set in the case of *Filartiga* v. *Pena-Irala,* in which former Paraguayans living in the United States sued a high-ranking Paraguayan police official who had tortured their son and brother to death in Paraguay.[30] The suit, for $10 million, was filed when the family learned that the official was living in the United States, apparently illegally after his visa had expired. The trial court ruled that it had no jurisdiction in the matter, but on appeal, a higher court held that international humanitarian norms allowed for the jurisdiction of a United States court. However, by this time the respondent had left the country because of a deportation order.

The opinion of Judge Kaufman concludes with a strong statement on the importance of international norms when dealing with human rights violations.

In the 20th Century the international community has come to recognize the common danger posed by the flagrant disregard of basic human rights and particularly the right to be free of torture.

Civilized nations have bonded together to prescribe acceptable norms of international behavior. . . . In the modern age, humanitarian and practical considerations have combined to lead the nations of the world to recognize that respect for fundamental human rights is in their individual and collective interest. Among the rights universally proclaimed by all nations . . . is the right to be free of physical torture. Indeed, for purposes of civil liability, the torturer has become—like the pirate and the slave trader before him—*hostis humani generis,* an enemy of all mankind. Our holding today, giving effect to a jurisdictional provision . . . is a small but important step in the fulfillment of the ageless dream to free all people from brutal violence.[31]

Recently the Chilean government was also sued in a United States court for responsibility in the death of one victim and the serious injury of another arising out of alleged police brutality when they were arrested at a demonstration, doused with gasoline and set on fire. The potentialities of the law are also exemplified in another case brought by a journalist for injuries suffered in a bomb explosion in Costa Rica. Those being sued are a group of United States citizens alleged to be involved in a series of clandestine activities in Central America, possibly acting in collusion with governmental agencies.[32]

The use of tort law is commendably innovative. It allows the victims themselves and human rights organizations acting on their behalf to initiate judicial action when official authorities of state and international bodies are reluctant or unable to act. It represents an example of a victimological perspective, focusing on the needs of the victim vis-à-vis the criminal as being of the essence of judicial concern. It allows for documentation of the crime and denunciation of the criminal. These are developments that may be welcomed, even if they skirt the problematics of punishment as such.

They also represent an awarenesss of catering to the special needs of the victims and their families. For instance, at the United Nations a Voluntary Fund for Victims of Torture has been established; this could easily be used also to help the families of victims of humanicide. Similarly their emotional needs could be aided, as is being done in a number of therapeutic centers for the victims of torture.

In some cases tort actions may avoid some of the complications that are traditionally associated with the higher standards of the criminal law. For instance, during the war between Great Britain and Argentina, an Argentinian soldier, notorious for his use of torture, was captured by the British forces. Apparently the possibility of instituting proceedings against him was examined, but in the end no action was taken, largely out of consideration for his protected status as a prisoner of war. Yet a civil action may have resolved these complications. Even so, victims and their families alone cannot be expected always to undertake such actions. Their resources are limited, their emotional strength spent. Others, organizations and individuals, must be prepared for an ever increasing role in combating human rights violations and responding to them when they occur.

Certain professions must be made aware of the extra responsibilities that devolve upon them—law enforcement personnel not to abuse their power even in the face of superior commands and peer pressures; journalists to courageously divulge the truth, particularly for the outside world; lawyers to be relentless in their pursuit of all legal and other legitimate means of serving the needs of those deprived of their basic rights; judges to be strict in laying down the limits of state power and sensitive to the vulnerability of those in custody; doctors to be available to help the abused, not least by confronting the abusers.[33]

But after the legal rights and the human needs of the victims have been attended to, the inescapable question remains of what to do with the victimizers. As already noted in other areas, this key question goes by default; no overall principles are laid down, and ad hoc and ad hominem solutions have to be improvised by those in power—unfortunately, too often opponents of the abusers and perhaps even their former victims. In the aftermath of the Second World War, abolitionist countries restored the death penalty, and the populace often resorted to its own more immediate retribution. How to avoid such a response is clearly a major issue for human rights activists and organizations. Amnesty International fails to confront the issue directly, noting only its opposition to the death penalty as a possible punishment. And if life imprisonment, too, is to be considered an ultimate penalty, what other alternatives are there?

Amnesty International is well aware of how many abuses are practiced within the prison system, especially when there is a political background to the punishment. How will it be possible to guarantee the basic rights of a former victimizer now serving a long prison sentence? And if there can be no guarantees for the maintenance of minimum standards, then Amnesty would rightly prefer to forego extradition; but with what other consequences for the victimizers is not stated.

Perhaps all such issues can only be resolved through international bodies—which might have to include a policing, prosecutorial, and correctional personnel in addition to judicial. The latter would then have to determine the penalty—specifically, can an ultimate penalty be imposed for an ultimate crime?

10

TREASON AND TERROR

ACTS OF TREASON and acts of terror share a common
base in that the manner in which they are defined is often
a consequence of the political perspective from which they
are perceived. What is treason for some, is patriotism for others;
what is terrorism for some, is heroism for others. The legality
of the act may depend on the legitimacy of the cause for which
it was committed; the judicial disposition of the act may reflect
retroactively the result of an armed struggle.

Both treason and terror constitute extreme challenges to
the political authority of a state, and as such evoke extreme
penal responses. Even in states which are otherwise abolitionist,
exceptions may be made for treason or terrorism. In fact, international documents and conventions aimed at abolition sometimes recognize that exceptions may be made in times of war
for acts that threaten the integrity of the state. The very uncertainty associated with such acts creates the twin dangers that,
on the one hand, the power of the state will be exploited for
political aggrandizement, and, on the other hand, that acts of
extreme violence may go completely unrequited and may
even be rewarded. Terrorism itself can evoke the most am-
bivalent of responses, even in the most unambiguous of situations, since the essential extremity of the means is sometimes
excused because of what is considered to be the worthiness
of the ends.

Yet it should be possible, as I shall try to show, to draw
a clear and unequivocal distinction between acts that are permissible by a universalistic, humanistic standard and those that
are not; between acts that even a political opponent can
recognize as part of a legitimate struggle for a defined, if denied,

cause, and acts that even a supporter of a particular cause may be able to condemn; between acts that, by their nature, enhance the particular cause in whose name they are made and illuminate its essential justness, and those that are either a distortion of the political message, bringing the cause into disrepute, or else perhaps expose essential weaknesses in that cause, as well as perhaps portending future dire consequences should the struggle actually succeed.

Theoretically, at least, it should be possible to support a particular struggle for freedom, independence, social justice, or whatever, yet be able to condemn specific acts that are committed on its behalf or overall strategies that are adopted for its furtherance. Indeed, it *must* become possible to do so if any progress is to be made in effective elimination of terrorism, while not denying deprived groups the possibility of effective and legitimate pursuit of justifiable aims.

Some acts of terrorism are akin to treason and may even constitute overt treasonable activity, as in the case of a political assassination by a citizen who owes fealty to the state. Some acts of terrorism are akin to, or constitute, humanicide, as when innocent people are indicriminately taken hostage, tortured, and killed. Some acts are of a much more moderate nature, as when property damage is inflicted with care being taken to avoid any harm to life or limb.

Even given the strong overtones of political involvement and inevitably biased assessment in dealing with such actions, it should nevertheless be possible to have outright condemnation of humanicidal acts—certainly by the world community at large, but also even by those in whose name the acts were committed. It should, for instance, be possible to draw a clear distinction, when necessary, between the legitimacy of a political aim and the unacceptability of the means by which that end is sought. Unfortunately, the reality is often of an opposite nature. Sometimes acts of extreme and indiscriminate terror arouse interest and then evoke support, whereas, in contrast, acts of a more moderate nature fail to arouse interest and, by default, lead to ignorance about, or indifference toward, claims that may be legitimate.

Difficult as it is to determine when legitimacy may be accorded to violent acts done in the name of a political cause, similar problems have been encountered in the past—and still exist today—in the manner of determining the boundaries of treason. For often there are only fine nuances between legitimate political opposition and treacherous violations of oaths of allegiance. These issues, naturally, become even more acute when recognized parliamentary opposition is lacking or peaceful transferences of power are unknown.

But even democracies are not immune to the obfuscation of the boundaries between legitimate criticism and illegal treachery. The McCarthy era in the United States showed how tenuous can be the line between respectable political opposition and total de-legitimization—for what, in the final analysis, is the meaning of *un-American* (as in the un-American Activities Committee, now defunct, of the House of Representatives), if not something closely akin to treasonable activities.

In the course of the bitter debate in the sixties over the Vietnam War and the invasion of Cambodia, the then vice-president, Spiro Agnew, accused opponents of the war of giving aid and comfort to the enemy, the very phrasing so carefully chosen to define one of the meanings of treason.

Earlier, opposition to the Korean War had been declared by the administration to be a treasonable act when a veteran of an earlier war had forfeited his benefits because of a clause that allowed such forfeiture for acts of treason. This ruling was upheld by the district court but was eventually ruled illegal by a court of appeal; however, the administrative decision and original judicial approval for it shows how easily the parameters of treason may be manipulatively expanded.[1]

Further, although the definition of treason may itself be narrow, the range of forbidden activity may be extended by incorporating the additional concepts of espionage, sedition, etc. Julius and Ethel Rosenberg, considered by many to have been executed for acts of treason, were not charged with treason as defined in the Constitution, but with espionage as defined legislatively.[2] The death penalty imposed on them was, in any event, probably more a reflection of the political climate of the time—the cold war—than an objective appraisal of the judicial implications.

More than for any other crimes, the political overtones of treason and terrorism have a direct impact on the penalty that is imposed and that is carried out. Although there is widespread legislative use of capital punishment, including in states otherwise abolitionist, the actual implementation of the punishment—at the prosecutorial level of pleadings in court, at the judicial level of sentencing, and at the executive level of pardoning—is a product often of the perceived political implications and consequences of an execution. For more is at stake than the life of the accused or convicted person; a message is also being transmitted—of moderation or of ruthlessness, of a desire to seek reconciliation or of a determination to utilize to the hilt political and judicial power, of an intention to exploit the potential advantages of using prisoners for bargaining (in exchange deals or in larger contexts of peaceful settlements) or of deliberately foregoing such eventualities, with the implication that no early reconciliation is contemplated.

Otto Kirchheimer has described the manner in which the judicial apparatus of the state may be manipulated for political purposes. He has shown how, depending on the circumstances of the case, political prisoners may be given either special favorable consideration (for instance, in the conditions of their confinement) or, on the other hand, may be subjected to the most painful of tortures and the most humiliating of experiences.[3]

Yet the connection between the kind of punishment meted out and the ultimate consequences is not always readily discernible. Certainly those groups that wished to use the death penalty for general deterrence, in a supposed show of strength, have not always been successful. The list of countries whose struggle for independence is marked by its martyrs who were executed for treason or terrorism is legion. But then, conversely, moderation does not always achieve its goal of thwarting support for, and denying success from, the groups defined as traitors or terrorists.

Often the attitudes and policies adopted toward such people reflect not merely overall strategic and political considerations, but more limited tactical assessments, as in the manner in which some degree of mutuality can be ensured, for instance, the possibility of safeguarding the welfare of prisoners who fall into the hands of a rebel or terrorist group. Thus the fate of such prisoners—captured soldiers or kidnapped citizens—held by such groups may depend on the prior manner in which members of that group taken prisoner are dealt with by the courts of the state that they are fighting. Extreme punishments, particularly the death penalty, may lead to extreme responses, an escalation of violence, the taking of hostages, the torture of prisoners. The use or non-use of the death penalty is certainly a factor that must be considered in dealing with treason and terrorism, but often its role in political offenses is determined more by the reality of the political situation than by the considerations of criminal justice. In any event, these factors are often better understood with the wisdom of hindsight and the advantage of retroactive analysis than in the uncertainty of prediction and the vagaries of prospective assessment. Neither the moderate stance adopted by the English toward the American rebels and their reluctance to try them for treason, nor the harsh measures including the use of the death penalty taken nearly two hundred years later against some of their colonies fighting for independence, prevented the success of the rebellions against British rule.

Within the historic tradition of the common law there seems to be some degree of overlap between acts defined formerly as treason and presently as terrorism, especially when seen in terms of the threat to the social order that was posed. In fact, the concept of treason has undergone gradual, often subtle, change. In earlier times it was directly linked to the person of the king and the personal fealty owed him. Treason consisted if a breach of trust between the king and his subjects. Only later was the idea of injury to the body politic incorporated into the definition of treason; it became, in the course of time, the dominant factor.

John Bellamy, a leading British historian of treason, notes: "Concepts of treason never flourish in a vacuum. They depend greatly on the prevailing thesis of government."[4] Indeed, the list that Bellamy provides for the Middle Ages includes highway robbery, destruction of judicial documents, speaking badly about the king, and imagining and compassing of the king's death (that is conceiving that he was dead).[5]

From a penological point of view, the crime of treason was differentiated from other crimes not just by the nature of the act or its substantive definition but also by the punishments which were inflicted. At a time when most executions were generally preceded by some form of torture, the traitor was subjected to additional and more extreme physical suffering. Quoting from contemporary treaties, Bellamy writes that the guilty person "was to suffer physically the extreme penalty 'cum poenae aggravatione corporalis' . . . judgment for lese-majesty should be executed by torment . . . and by death . . . the traitor was dragged at the horse's tail to the place of execution,"[6] where he would also be disembowelled and quartered. Additional secondary punishments were confiscation of goods and the disinheritance of heirs.

The very breadth of the meaning of treason led to a distinction being drawn between high treason and petty treason, with the latter applying primarily to breaches of faith to one's lord, the former to the king; often there was "considerable uncertainty" about which crimes were treason and which mere felony.[7]

It was this broad and loose approach that led the framers of the United States Constitution to carefully define the crime of treason and specifically limit its nature: "Treason against the United States shall consist only in levying War against them, or in adhering to their Enemies, giving them Aid and Comfort."[8] The word "only" has a powerful impact on the meaning of treason, preventing any subsequent casual or systematic extension of the definition (though not preventing other laws dealing with related issues).

Specifically excluded from this definition was any reference analogous to the "compassing of the king," the rationale being not just that there was no such person in a republic, but that there was no need for such a provision in a democracy. For, as James Hurst notes, "charges of compassing the king's death had been the principal instrument by which 'treason' had been employed in England for the most drastic, 'lawful' suppression of political opposition or the expression of ideas or beliefs distasteful to those in power."[9] At the time of the adoption of the Constitution, the limited nature of the treason clause was highly praised as a means for preventing the use of treason trials as an instrument of political policy.

Hurst sums up the use of the treason clause: "There have been less than two score treason prosecutions pressed to trial by the Federal government; there has been no execution on a federal treason conviction; and the Executive has commonly intervened to pardon, or at least mitigage the sentence of those convicted."[10] He quotes from a Supreme Court decision (in the *Cramer* case): "We have managed to do without treason prosecutions to a degree that probably would be impossible except while a people was singularly confident of external security and internal stability."[11]

Indeed, even America's greatest act of internal violence, the Civil War, did not lead to any major treason trials. Jefferson Davis, though originally indicted, was never brought to trial; and subsequently, in speeches and writings, he defended the right, and the actual attempt, to secede.[12] On the other hand, there have been instances of the use of the death penalty in related contexts and for related offenses—treason against one of the states and the lesser offense of espionage, the best-known case being that of Julius and Ethel Rosenberg. It is paradoxical that this latter crime allowed the same maximum penalty of death that Congress laid down for treason but lacked the protection—of the need for two witnesses to an overt act.[13]

Most recently, when a spy ring in the Navy was divulged—the Walker case—in which monetary considerations served as the motivating force, calls went out for the reintroduction of the death penalty. Secretary of Defense Caspar Weinberger clearly stated his approval. In an interview he argued that if guilty, the accused persons "should be shot, though I suppose hanging is the preferred method."[14] He suggested specifically a change in the law that would allow for the death penalty for peacetime espionage. Shortly thereafter, such a draft bill was passed in the House of Representatives—by voice vote, with little discussion, tacked on to a larger defense bill. Some legislators even suggested that executions be shown on television.

In contrast, the moderate reaction to the Civil War reflected, in many respects, the earlier moderation of the War of Independence, in which the British, after some hesitation, decided to refrain from invoking treason clauses against insurgent Americans captured during the course of the fighting. Bradley Chapin describes the deliberations over the fate of a group of thirty-four American prisoners (chief of whom was Ethan Allen), who were brought to England with the intention of putting them on trial.[15] They were finally returned to America and released. According to Chapin: "The real reason for the release of Allen was the certain knowledge that Americans would execute British prisoners if he suffered a traitor's death. . . . Information that the British treated prisoners as criminals caused Washington to write to Gage [the British general] to expect retaliation if he departed from the practices observed by nations at war."[16] In fact, for some time, the British held their American prisoners in an uncertain limbo state, their final status—traitors to be tried and hanged or prisoners of war to be eventually released—would be determined by the outcome of the war.

In most of the colonies, too, there was a reluctance to try on a charge of treason those accused of collaborating with the British. As Chapin notes: "Only a small percentage of those arrested and committed on suspicion of treasonable action were ever indicted." Further, juries "showed a real reticence to expose men to trial for treason."[17] Chapin goes on to state that when there was a trial, "though a verdict of guilty in a trial of treason traditionally required the death penalty, the states used several alternatives—fines, imprisonment, and other punishments."[18] Further, when the death penalty was actually imposed,

> executive and legislative authorities used their pardoning powers generously. . . . Often pardons were withheld until the accused was in the shadow of the gallows. Officials thought that mercy shown when punishment was imminent would not lessen the force of the example. Frequently, states offered general pardons or 'acts of grace'. . . . This liberal use of the pardoning power established a precedent basic to American policy. Those in power have shown a real reticence to execute persons for political crimes, however heinous.[19]

Nevertheless, there were a few exceptions; individual states did actually implement a death sentence. In Pennsylvania over one hundred people were detained for refusing to take the oath of allegiance, twenty-two were indicted, three of whom were convicted, two of them being sentenced to death. James Wilson writes that "despite numerous requests for pardons, they were both hanged. After the hangings virtually everyone took the oath of allegiance."[20]

However, Wilson stresses that Thomas Jefferson had been strongly opposed to using treason as a basis for indictment in what was essentially a political struggle. He writes that "Thomas Jefferson was particulary concerned about improper use of treason law. Jefferson bitterly remembered when British General Gage proclaimed in 1774 that citizens in Massachusetts committed treason if they assembled to consider grievances and formed associations for such purposes."[21]

The essential thrust of Wilson's work is not so much the debatable parameters and disputable uses of treason (though he does examine in some detail more recent cases, including those that emerged from the Second World War),[22] but to attempt to extrapolate from the essence of recent Supreme Court decisions on capital punishment to argue that, in terms of the present guidelines pertaining to capital punishment, its use in the case of treason would probably be unconstitutional. Since the Supreme Court has basically limited the constitutionality of capital punishment to crimes that take a life, Wilson examines the crime of treason vis-à-vis murder in terms of these standards and the accompanying factor of aggravating circumstances, such as the severity of the offense and the depravity of the criminal.

The correct standard to lay down would consider the consequences for the victim—by the proportionality rule, when there was no death, there should be no death penalty; though, of course, treasonable activities may result in untold and unforeseen consequences, including loss of life.

But the chief argument that Wilson puts forward is the ever-present danger of using the ultimate penalty of death (irreversible even if political circumstances were to change) when political considerations might be the key factors. Referring to the need to enumerate mitigating and aggravating factors in death penalty statutes, Wilson argues that such standards would be almost impossible to incorporate into the law of treason. He states that it is not clear "why John Brown had to be shot for his treason but Jefferson Davis, who led the Civil War for the South, could live."[23]

Finally, Wilson focuses directly on the politics that invariably becloud treason trials. "Killing political criminals," he writes, unleashes many undesirable side effects. Controversy pervades political trials, polarizes the community and creates martyrs. Debates continue for years about the government's motives, the defendant's guilt, and the propriety of the punishment. Supporters of the executed traitor frequently seek vengeance, escalating domestic violence (while proponents of the death penalty would reply that killing the traitor eliminates the possibility that supporters would engage in terrorism to secure the traitor's release). Assuming that the treasonous faction eventually succeeds, leaders may be far more vengeful if many of their members were killed when they were not in power. A positive effect of refusing to kill traitors is that a form of solidarity and pride may be created in the country.[24]

This is a strong plea for moderation in a very sensitive area. It could be argued that in the United States, the wounds of the Civil War healed that much easier because there were no vindictive reactions after the war. Alternatively, it could be suggested that the moderation practiced by the British did not save them their American colony—but neither, some two centuries later, did harsh criminal penalties do so. And in some instances, as in the struggles in Palestine and Cyprus, executions did lead to reprisal executions of captured British servicemen, without achieving British political aims.[25]

GEORG SIMMEL cites Kant, and describes how important it is to realize that the manner in which a struggle is conducted may effect the possibility of a reconciliation.[26] This may well be applicable to the specific issue of capital punishment. Yet, as a universal norm, widespread recognition, in regional and international conventions and in national legislation, is accorded what is considered the special situation of wartime. Thus, for instance, though the Council of Europe's Protocol is aimed at the abolition of the death penalty, it has a built-in reservation allowing for the use of the death penalty in wartime. In a clarifying statement, it is stated: "The obligation to abolish the death penalty is, however, limited to peace-time. Thus, a State can in fact become a Party to the Protocol if its law makes provision for the death penalty in respect of acts committed in time of war or of imminent threat of war."[27]

Indeed, treason per se was considered by Beccaria to be such a serious offense that he suggested that it might be the one offense for which an exception could be made to an abolitionist stance.[28] Basically, he saw the person accused of treason as being an internal enemy who might be killed just as enemies were in a war.

In the aftermath of the Second World War, some countries reintroduced the death penalty—for instance, Denmark, Norway, and the Netherlands.[29] The most celebrated treason trial after the war—that of Vidkun Quisling in Norway—was, for this reason also, based on debatable grounds. As Paul Hayes notes in his biography of Quisling,[30] the criminal code in existence at the outbreak of the war contained no death penalty, but, as there was a death penalty in the military code, Quisling was tried under these provisions. However, "Section 14 of that act required execution of the penalty before the close of hostilities. By an enactment of 3 October 1941 the government-in-exile had waived the provisions of Section 14, and this had been confirmed by the Storting [the parliament] after liberation. There remained only the question of retrospective imposition."[31] Although retroactive legislation was barred by Section 97 of the constitution, both the trial court and the Supreme Court, on appeal, held that there was no bar to a death penalty, and since in Quisling's case there were no mitigating circumstances, the death penalty was held to be appropriate.

In contrast to the treason trials in formerly occupied countries, in Germany those who had fought against the Nazi regime—in effect in some cases committing treason—were in the postwar era accorded honor for the stand that they had taken. Their treason was indeed to salvage some degree of honor for their people. Not all survived the war, some paying the price by being sentenced to death or sent to death camps. One of the outstanding examples of treasonable activities during the Nazi period was that of Willy Brandt, later to become chancellor of West Germany, who fled the country of his birth whose citizenship he bore and then worked against it, including a clandestine visit to link up with anti-Nazi groups.[32]

In chapter 7 we discussed the kinds of punishment that could legitimately be imposed on the perpetrators of genocide. What actions, however, can legitimately be taken against them while yet in power? On the one hand, their ruthless power normally involves extreme penalties, to which opponents of the regime are liable to be subject even for minimal acts of opposition. On the other hand, minimal acts themselves may be utterly futile, whereas only concerted acts of violence may provide some prospects for the demise of the regime. The cruelties of the dictators sometimes cease only with their violent overthrow. Thus there has to be a basic acknowledgment as to the right, under special circumstances, to resort to violence. International law does indeed recognize a *ius resistandi*—the right of resistance, including violent means— a right traditionally applied when governmental authorities have apparently forfeited the support of their people.[33] Theoretically, then, violent actions may be used to overthrow an unjust regime. It is not violence per se that is forbidden; the test is the reason for the violence and the manner in which it is used.

What, for instance, would have been the fate of the conspirators against Hitler in the bomb plot if their assassination attempt had succeeded, if Hitler had been killed and his regime had fallen? Presumably no judicial action would have been taken against them—in any case, theoretically, they may well have had a defense for their action in terms of the defense of necessity; they could have argued that their action was the lesser evil to the continuation of the Nazi regime and the war. However, for such an argument to succeed they would have to be able to show that their action was the lesser evil, that, for instance, only the minimum amount of violence necessary to achieve the aim of frustrating the regime's evil had been employed.[34] This was part of the argument used in the cases of judicial tolerance of assassinations.[35]

In many respects the terrorism of today resembles treason of earlier times. For many of the acts defined as treason then involved acts of violence which undermined the sovereignty of the king by exposing his inability to maintain control over his subjects, many of whom showed only minimum loyalty to him. By the end of the Middle Ages, included in the crime of high treason (apart from direct acts against the king) were the offenses of highway robbery, abduction of women, saying that the king needed his subjects' consent to their taxation, selling a fortress or refusing the king entry to it. At a later stage, during the Tudor regime, there was an extension of the offenses considered to be treason. Certain crimes were "classified as treason so as better to maintain public order";[36] between 1485 and 1603, according to one calculation, there were no fewer than sixty-eight treason statutes enacted.

Bellamy utters a word of caution that the proliferation of acts defined as treason was more an indication of royal concern for the king's power and his ability to ensure his own rule and that of his successors, than of the actual power in his hands or his ability to enforce the law in these areas.

T E R R O R I S M   D I F F E R S from these earlier acts of treason in the tactics and the techniques used—largely a consequence of the weaponry available and the exposure to the public via mass media coverage. In democractic countries, at least, since opposition to the regime is not a treasonable activity, it is the violence associated with terrorism that becomes the key differentiating factor; in addition, much of terrorist activity takes place trans-nationally, partly a consequence of political partnerships entered into by different terrorist groups. What adds immeasurably to the gravity of the act is the often indiscriminate victimization of innocent people. Indeed, the strategy of terror is often based specifically on harm to the innocent—for it is the fear of such harm that undermines the sense of well-being and security that is provided by the modern state. Yet, of course, it is specifically the focus on the innocent that denies—or should deny—any legitimacy to the act, no matter what credentials of justice the cause itself embodies.

Under these circumstances, what penological approaches are acceptable? Those similar to conceptions of genocide that tend to see terrorism as such a violation of the minimum level of universal norms as to warrant the use of the death penalty?—or those that claim that the overriding value of the sanctity of human life applies here too, and denies resort to the death penalty? Or are there, as in treason, more prosaic and utilitarian factors at work, such as the possible advantages to be derived from a more moderate penal policy—from mutuality as to treatment of prisoners, including potential exchange, to larger political factors of conflict resolution and peace terms?

These are issues considered more by political scientists, but they impinge also on those concerned with penal policy and its logical consistency, its humanitarian implementation, and its political implications. In one of the few articles to address specifically the penological aspect of terrorist activities, Thomas Thornton notes that terrorism is "along with treason and murder committed by persons serving life terms, one of the prime tests of arguments against the death penalty."[37] Conceding that "terrorism is outrageous in the public view," Thornton nevertheless argues that "the death penalty is a gravely serious measure to invoke in any circumstance, and in this case there are weighty legal and logical counterarguments in addition to the unavoidable moral considerations that weigh against any taking of life."[38]

In adopting a strong abolitionist stance against the death penalty, Thornton notes that many terrorist acts are similar to ordinary criminal acts, such as hostage-taking and kidnapping, bank robberies and arson, indiscriminate bombing and selective elimination of enemies. The difference between political terrorism and ordinary criminality stems, then, not from the overt action, but from the state of mind. Since, in the United States at least, acts, however serious, that are short of killing do not allow for the death penalty, Thornton suggests that it would be unjust to single out terrorists for such a penalty when there is no loss of life.

In 1937, in the wake of the political assassination in France of King Alexander of Yugoslavia and French Foreign Minister Louis Barthou, the first international convention to deal with terrorism was signed, though never put into effect. Its list of crimes includes several that are reminiscent of earlier definitions of treason, such as illegal trade in arms and ammunition, the murder of heads of state, members of his family, or other leading officers of government, and willful destruction and damage of property which endangers the lives of the public.[39]

The convention does not lay down any penalties, but another related convention signed on the same day (16 November 1937), provided for the creation of an international criminal court and notes the possibility of a death penalty.[40] The reference to the death penalty is an indirect one; Article 41 states that "if sentence of death has been pronounced, the state designated by the court to execute the sentence shall be entitled to substitute therefor the most severe penalty provided by its national law which involves loss of liberty," this latter being presumably a reference to life imprisonment.[41]

The later Draft Convention for the Prevention and Punishment of Certain Acts of International Terrorism, submitted to the U.N. General Assembly in September 1972 but never ratified, deals with the issue of punishment by obligating the states that are parties to the convention "to make the offenses set

forth . . . punishable by severe penalties,"[42] but without speci-
fying which severe penalties should be used. The definition
of an international act of terrorism is set out in Article 1, and
includes killing, kidnapping, and causing bodily harm outside
of one's own national territory with the intention of damaging
the interests of a state or an international intergovernmental
organization, or of obtaining concessions from them.

In their introduction to the collection of documents on
terrorism, Yonah Alexander and his co-editors note that
although terror has been used by both governmental and opposition groupings from time immemorial, its "present-day prac-
titioners have introduced into contemporary life a new breed
of violence in terms of technology, victimization, threat, and
response," leading to "formidable problems and frightening
ramifications."[43] They envisage the possibility of catastrophic
casualties from terrorist activities arising from the potential that
terrorist groups "will have access to biological, chemical and
nuclear instruments of massive death potential"—an "entire
city's water supply can be poisoned with lethal chemicals,"
nerve agents "can cause hundreds of thousands of fatalities,"
or "single incident involving biological agents . . . or nuclear
bombs, would obviously produce far more casualties."[44]

It is considerations of this nature that create a problem
so immense that it might even justify a unique exception, by
the defense of necessity, to the banning of torture. The torture
of one person to elicit vital and urgent information designed
to prevent a terrorist attack of this type might be permissible.[45]

Indeed, the problems that terrorists pose for states are accentuated for those states that are committed to standards of
justice, liberty, and decency. Thus Alexander et al. note that
democracy "is seriously threatened by terrorists. Unlike dictatorships that are both physically and emotionally condi-
tioned to deal with opposition forces, democratic societies generally make it possible for terrorist groups to organize, although
not necessarily to achieve popular public support. When the

challenge of terrorism is met with repression, democracy is considerably weakened."[46]

These factors are of critical relevance when dealing with the punishment that should be meted out to terrorists, and especially the issue of the use of the death penalty. Thornton suggests that

> there would be a spectacular irony . . . if terrorism were among the crimes that urge our society to restore the death penalty. The ultimate aim of the true terrorist is to undermine the values of the society that he detests. . . . Both individuals and societies at times take on the attributes of their tormentors as a means of self-protection. If we abandon our respect for life in order to cope with the terrorist, we will become an unwitting but sadly willing accomplice in his attempt to destroy us.[47]

Worse than this is the danger that although terrorism may conceivably be eradicated by ruthless methods, the consequences are often the erection of a social structure and state apparatus that is even more repressive since the "terrorism of government is vastly more destructive, both physically and morally, than the actions of a few dozen, or even hundreds, of bomb-throwers, hijackers and assassins."[48]

His conclusion is that the dangers posed by terrorism are not sufficient to justify a deviation from the basic values of a democratic society, one in which, as he sees it, capital punishment should be banned. But his argument is based on the lack of a "clear and present danger," which, in the context of free speech, has been used as the test of when to allow a violation of basic values for the sake of self-preservation.[49] The examples provided by Alexander et al. of chemical or nuclear weapons are certainly of such a nature. The question is, would their examples allow for the death penalty as a punishment or torture as a preventive measure?

I have used throughout this chapter the word *terror,* even though I acknowledged, at the outset, that the nature of the act may be perceived differently depending on one's political perspective. A more neutral word would perhaps be *guerrilla,* as used by Edward Kossoy in his book, *Living with Guerrilla.*[50] Nevertheless, there is a difference between terrorism and guerrilla activity, the former being illegal, however noble the cause, the latter being recognized in international law, although the cause may be challenged politically.

Till now I have addressed mainly the response to terrorism—what sort of punishment should be imposed; and punishment is, of course, an issue only when the act is illegal, as is terrorism. If an act is a legitimate guerrilla activity, then there should be no need for penological consideration of punitive measures—for there are rules of international law setting out the rights and duties of guerrilla movements, and both they and states fighting them are bound by such rules.

The key issue then becomes whether it is possible to draw a distinction between terrorist and guerrilla activities.[51] This is often done, but mainly in terms of positive definitions of "guerrillas" with whom one identifies and sympathizes, and negative definitions for "terrorists," whom one opposes. However, I would argue that a distinction can be made based not on political propensities, but on conduct (the *actus reus* of criminal law), and one that is logically consistent, morally valid, and legally pertinent.

In international law clear and obligatory rules have been laid down as to how to conduct wars.[52] The combatants have rights and obligations, protections are provided for prisoners of war and for innocent citizens in conquered territory, certain forms of warfare are outlawed, limits are placed on the extent of military power. All this is supposed to be applicable irrespective of the particular ideology that the warring nations uphold. The Nazi leaders tried after the war were convicted not for their ideology—pernicious as it was—but for the specific acts committed in the name of the ideology. It is true that the ideology spawned and fostered these acts; but without the acts there would have been no crime (except inasmuch as member-

ship in what was declared at Nuremberg to be an illegal organization was considered a crime, but that, too, on the basis
of the acts committed by the organization). Further, there is
a personal responsibility attached to soldiers, officials, and
citizens that the guiding norms of manifest morality are superior to any presumed obligation to obey blatantly illegal
superior orders.[53] Similarly, lines of distinction can surely be
drawn between legitimate guerrilla activity and illegitimate
terrorism.

The guerrilla, acting according to the rules of international
law, is entitled, if captured, to all the protection that his com-
batant status assures him.[54] The captured terrorist, on the other
hand, is guilty of a major crime and must be tried—and, if found
guilty, sentenced to punishment in accordance with the law.
There can be little doubt that actions that involve kidnapping,
torture, and killing, often combined, are among the most serious
aberrations from the demands of civilized behavior and deserving of the most severe penalties that a society can impose. The
fact that these acts are committed in the name of a cause is
often seen as being a mitigating factor; on the contrary,
however, this may make it a much more serious offense. Not
only does the validity of the cause not purify the evil of the
means, but the illegitimate means should challenge and undermine the validity of the ends. And for none more so than those
on whose behalf the means were adopted.

In his play *The Just Assassins,* Albert Camus poses
dramatically the manner in which a person's conscience and
regard for humanity may determine the limits of permissible
struggle.[55] A group of anarchists bent on assassinating a grand-
duke fail in their mission when, at the last moment, they realize
that their target is accompanied by two children, who, if the
anarchists proceed with their plan, will become innocent victims. The play then addresses their attempts to justify their
last-minute hesitation and change of heart. The drama has an
added poignancy and pertinence by virtue of it being based
on an actual happening in Czarist Russia.[56]

Kossoy argues that it is "grossly inaccurate" to couple terrorism with guerrilla even though some basically guerrilla movements do resort to terror on occasions. Yet, as he points out, "a number of important guerrilla movements steadily refused to resort to terrorism. To name only two: The partisans of Mao Tse-Tung and the Peshmergas of the Kurd leader, Barzani."[57]

IN THE AREA OF EXTRADITION, the law is often confronted with similar dilemmas of differentiating between protected guerrilla activity and outlawed terrorism. Most extradition treaties draw a distinction between ordinary criminal acts and politically motivated crimes. For the former, extradition is enforced; for the latter, asylum may be allowed.[58] In two recent extradition cases, the courts in the United States, in two different jurisdictions, decided on extradition in one case, in which the request was based on an act of indiscriminate violence against innocent victims, when there was no connection or proportionality between the killing and the political goals;[59] but in the other, extradition to Britain was denied, as the violence was not indiscriminate, but was part of an armed struggle in which the victim was a member of the armed forces.[60]

Extradition is usually linked to a limitation on the severity of the penalty that may be imposed, and invariably the extraditing state conditions its positive response to an agreement by the receiving state that it will not resort to the death penalty. These limitations were imposed in the case of the extradition to Israel. In Israel there is theoretically the possibility of the death penalty for acts of terror, but in practice it has never been used. The law itself is the same basic emergency legislation promulgated by the British mandatory authorities in 1945 and used against various members of the Zionist underground movements, ten of whom were executed for violations of its provisions. Nominally, the death penalty is retained, but a series of administrative decrees by the cabinet obligates the prosecutorial authorities, both in the civilian and military courts, not to request a death penalty. On a number of occasions, when the judges, on their own initiative, have imposed such a sentence, the authorities have intervened, either to immediately commute the sentence in the process of ratifying the conviction (in the case of military courts on the West Bank), or by refusing to support the verdict in an appeal.[61]

Legally, then, Israel, basically an abolitionist state since its inception (by pardoning practices in its early years—when the British Criminal Code with the death penalty was still in force—and by legislation since 1954), still retains the death penalty in the exceptional cases of genocide and related crimes (used once in the case of Eichmann), and for terrorism (for which it has never been used). But this basic abolitionist stance does not solve all the problems of punishment in such cases. Israel's experience is instructive of some of the delicate and adjacent issues that are closely intertwined with any direct decision on the death penalty. Three different responses have been noted and given publicity. They are certainly not unique to Israel.

First, retaliatory raids are sometimes carried out; in some specific cases, as in the Munich Olympic games massacre, it has been claimed that hit teams systematically killed off those known to be directly responsible in planning, organizing, and participating in the action.[62]

Second, on a number of occasions actions have been taken by individual Israelis, acting zealously in lieu of what they perceive to be weaknesses of the authorities. For example, a member of the Home Guard on reservist duty shot and killed an Arab inhabitant of Jerusalem shortly after one of the worst terrorists attacks, in which over thirty Israelis were killed—his reason being that the judicial system could not be trusted to exact the revenge he considered necessary.[63]

Third, on at least one occasion there has been an instance of overreaction. Terrorists, originally captured alive, were announced to be dead shortly after their capture—raising the possibility of an overzealous response to a judicial situation perceived to be ineffective and overly tolerant.[64]

It is possible that when there is no death penalty, there is a greater likelihood of these negative manifestations—which end in death without due process of law.[65]

In any event, given the prevalence of international terrorism, there is a need for carefully formulated rules as to the manner of response, similar to rules of war, which will bind the sides. The problem of course in doing so is the inability to incorporate the terrorist group in such rules—for their choice of terrorism (in contrast to guerrilla activities) reflects their contempt for international norms, or the mutual rejection by the opposing combatants of each other's very legitimacy.

As an Israeli I have struggled with the moral and political implications of such situations; in polemical articles and debates arguing against the use of the death penalty, as well as in an academic article, written jointly with David Libai, in which ethical, political, and pragmatic arguments were expounded against the death penalty for terrorism.[66] Among the points put forward was to ensure mutuality of security for Israelis—innocent citizens and captured soldiers—who might be held in the future. Indeed, Israeli soldiers captured in the course of both the 1978 and 1982 wars in Lebanon were held captive—for periods up to three years—before being released in a prisoner exchange which was lopsided in the extreme, and which aroused the ire of many in Israel, both because of the numbers released, a total in 1984 and 1985 of several thousand for less than ten Israelis, and because of the crimes which some of them had committed, the brutal killing of innocent victims.

Until these exchanges, it had been declared Israeli policy not to bargain over hostages. In effect, of course, the Israeli soldiers were not hostages but captured prisoners of war; it is acceptable, at the cessation of hostilities, to exchange prisoners. The problem in Israel was that the war in Lebanon had been fought between two sides (the state of Israel and the Palestine Liberation Organization) each of which refused to recognize the claims to independence and nationhood of the other. Under these circumstances, normal end-of-war negotiations were inoperable.

However, as a result of these prisoner exchanges, some of the arguments used in Israel against capital punishment for terrorism have now been clearly undermined, particularly those based on the severity and the efficacy of life imprisonment. It is now clear that Israeli concern for its citizens and soldiers makes it vulnerable to further pressures for release, through the taking of more hostages in further terrorist acts. It should, of course, be noted that Israel's present vulnerability is now far more apparent and more exposed as a result of this unforeseen consequence of its military intervention in Lebanon in 1982 than it had been previously when dealing with a straight terrorist hostage situation (*vide* its successful release of the hostages in Entebbe in 1976). Further, it means that a severe sentence (life or long-term imprisonment) is potentially meaningless, because contrary to past policy of no negotiations over hostages, the Israeli government, on these two occasions, has clearly indicated its agreement to release those convicted of humanicidal murders.

However, not all of the former pragmatic arguments are completely irrelevant, such as the inability to carry out a judicial execution given the possibilities of preemptive terrorist action, made more likely by the urgency of an approaching execution date or, after an execution does take place, the possibilities of retaliatory action.

Basically, Israel faces—but has not yet fully succeeded in confronting—the awesome and agonizing dilemma of the restrictions which a commitment to democratic and humanistic values inevitably imposes on responses to a terrorist situation. Further, the very fact of sovereignty places demands and limitations that groups lacking sovereignty can far easier ignore or evade.

Some Israelis have resolved this dilemma by rejecting outright any such demands and limitations and have done so—

either explicitly or implicitly—partly by denying the very validity of the democratic and humanistic values which are, according to others, enshrined in its Declaration of Independence, articulated in its traditional political debates, and expounded in its judicial precedents.[67]

Some have even used the political atmosphere evoked by the debate to exploit the thrust of the former position (a denial of democratic and humanitarian values), together with a perceived inability on the part of the governmental authorities to act effectively—both militarily and judicially—against perceived dangers—both terrorist activities and general unrest on the West Bank—as a justification for vigilante action, including killing and maiming. The members of a Jewish terrorist group have been tried by Israeli courts and given varying sentences, including life imprisonment, according to the degree of their involvement; but now their supporters are arguing for their release in the wake of the decision to release the Arab terrorists.

The debate over these matters goes way beyond the political issue of the rights of the Palestinians or the penological issue of the punishment of terrorists. It strikes at the very root of the kind of society which the Israeli people wish to create and maintain, a debate of the kind which must inevitably occur in all societies at various times, but which is certainly much easier to conduct in the tranquil conditions of peace, and all the more difficult, if all the more urgent and important, in conditions of violence, war, and terror.

I would argue that those who perform acts of terror on behalf of a cause to which one subscribes should be the most harshly punished—their acts are not only terrorist acts by universalistic humanistic standards, but sully the cause on whose behalf they are ostensibly acting, as well as making so much more difficult the prospects of rapprochement between the warring parties in the future. Indeed, an approach of this kind on the part of all protagonists to all violent political disputes would hopefully do much to minimize the raging prevalence of terror. It is easy to condemn terror by one's opponents. But it is only by withdrawing legitimacy from terror associated with one's own cause, and by punishing those who nevertheless persist in such activity, that real inroads may be made against the use of terror.[68]

The world community also has a role to play in such an approach by making its support for nongovernmental groups contingent not just on the assessed legitimacy of the cause, but also on an examination of the means used to achieve that cause. One of the ways of giving tangible expression to such sentiments would be to have a court of international jurisdiction which could determine whether acts of violence were guerrilla activity (and therefore legitimate), terrorism (to be punished), or humanicide (for which an ultimate sentence might be imposed).[69]

The Israeli debate over values, which I can do no more than allude to, is, of course, an internal one, but it is by no means a unique one. It is the kind of debate, open or muted, which arises often in times of social distress and political unrest. I have already made ample reference to similar kinds of actions, from the killings of collaborators by the underground during and after the Second World War, through the extrajudicial executions ordered by some political leaders, to the covert practices of the KGB in the Soviet Union and the CIA in the United States.[70]

Almost every country, then, has perforce to examine the manner in which its sovereignty is utilized to create the conditions for a civilized and just society. It is when its sovereignty is challenged that its highest aspirations may be jettisoned for quick, popular, and so-called strong actions. It is at such times that leadership—intellectual, moral, political, judicial, and religious—is needed to assure a climate of opinion that will make sober and reasoned debate possible and that will prevent the creation of a framework supportive of rash and extreme actions—be they within or outside of the judicial system.

Never were the crowds so large or so vocal in medieval Britain as when traitors were dragged through the streets to be publicly degraded, then hanged, and finally drawn and quartered.[71] Not all of those condemned were traitors—but, whether correctly defined as such or not, *none* deserved, by the wisdom of hindsight, the compassion of time, and the modern standards of humanity, the kind of punishment meted out to them.

In another context, never were the crowds so full of self-righteous indignation as when black suspects, accused of crimes of murder and rape, were lynched in the southern states of the United States.[72] Not all of them were guilty of the crimes attributed to them, but *none* of them deserved the vicious treatment to which they were subjected.

One of the factors making for overly severe reaction against terrorism is the totality of the battle, the nullification of the terrorist's cause, the denial of his humanity consequent on his own inhumane acts.

At the outset I argued for the need to draw a distinction between the fact of a political struggle and the manner in which it is fought. As an Israeli I subscribe to what is a minority political position in Israel, namely, recognition of the national aspirations of the Palestinian people and acceptance of a territorial compromise that would allow, if so desired by free vote, a Palestinian state; but I reject *in toto* the means of terror against innocent victims almost exclusively used by the PLO. I do not believe that the use of terror has brought them nearer their goal; other movements have sought other means such as civil disobedience, as in India, or restraint and limits on violence, as in the Zionist struggle against the British, with far greater success than indiscriminate terror.

I accordingly accept that in any political struggle those caught and convicted of terrorist activity should be severely punished, not because they struggle for a particular aim nor even because they resort to violence, but because of the unacceptable nature of their violence, which often borders on or is equivalent to humanicide. In many cases they should be given a severe sentence—but the only ultimate penalty that seems feasible is that of life imprisonment. First, since choice is at the basis of my willingness to have capital punishment, I do not believe that in a political struggle it is possible to afford such a choice to one's foe, since some would choose just such a punishment for its political value in terms of creating martyrs.

Second, it seems to me that beyond the morality there is a host of additional pragmatic arguments against the use of the death penalty. It would escalate the violence and make a final resolution of the conflict less likely; it is liable to lead to reprisals specifically focusing on the execution—prior to it in an effort to stop it, and subsequent to it as an expression of revenge, making extra-judicial executions all the more likely; prisoners, tried and imprisoned for proven crimes, might one day have their release linked to truce or peace talks; there would be a greater assurance as to the welfare of prisoners and even hostages taken by the terrorist groups; it is impossible to draw a distinction between those deserving of death and those not, and any such distinction would be invidious in terms of the demands and the anguish of the families of the victims. The one possible exception might be when an act of terror was more than terror and constituted in essence the crime of genocide (for example, in the use of chemical or nuclear weapons) or extreme humanicide (for instance, systematic torture preceding a killing). But here I doubt whether a state court would be capable of the dispassionate and objective analysis of an act so fraught with emotion, so as to allow for a fair and reasoned decision. An international court might conceivably provide the necessary objectivity in such cases.[73]

Third, my own reservations as to life imprisonment would not be entirely applicable in this situation, for it would be a reasonable assumption that, in the event of a peace settlement, the release of prisoners would conceivably be part of the terms agreed on. In other words, life imprisonment would be superseded by a political agreement between the sides. This could mean that a terrorist would, in the event of an early settlement, serve only a short sentence for what is a major international crime—but the resolution of the struggle would, one feels, provide sufficient justification for leniency and release.

There are no easy solutions for terrorism—just as there are often no easy solutions to the political and historical antecedents which give rise to such activity. The options within the judicial system are also by no means easy ones—in many respects they are a great deal more complicated than some military responses.

Indeed, the simplest solution may be to deny the very humanity of one's protagonist. But it is just such a denial by the terrorist that makes his terrorism possible. To adopt a similar approach could be to render the terrorist movement its greatest victory. Terror cannot really be fought with terror or its equivalent—at least not without paying the price of terror, which is an erosion and perhaps destruction of one's own values and ideals.

Just as the freedom fighter is theoretically required to exercise restraint in his struggle in order to justify his status as a guerrilla, together with all that is entailed in such status, from justified support for his struggle to protection offered by the norms of international law, so must his opponent exercise restraint in order to justify its status as a sovereign state and a respected member of the community of nations. Even when the freedom fighter rejects the role of guerrilla and chooses to become a terrorist, the ultimate responsibility still rests with his opponent in terms of the responsibility a state has to the world community and to international law to maintain strict adherence to the norms of civilized struggle. His enemy may no longer be a guerrilla, but he remains a human being; he may no longer be entitled to the protective rules of international law and if captured he will not be considered a prisoner of war, but he is still entitled to the procedures of due process of law and to limitation on the punishment to which he is liable, for instance, no torture, and no extra-judicial executions.

The courts in democratic societies are in many senses the respository of the principles and values of those societies. They need to show the independence of spirit and the impartiality of judgment that will enable them to remain above the passions that underly the political and military struggle, with all its violence.

It is these very passions that are liable to spawn demands for the death penalty. Although I have argued that the death penalty is not necessarily the most severe punishment, it may be that, in this one instance at least, the conventional wisdom as to its uniqueness should be conceded—for the dangers of exploiting judicial authority for political ends are too great. The death penalty must be avoided for terror in order to deny the terrorist his politically motivated wish for martyrdom, and the zealous patriot his politically motivated urge for revenge.

IV

WRONGS AND RIGHTS

■

11

WORSE THAN DEATH

TORTURE IS A PHENOMENON which is universally disapproved yet widely practiced. Once forming an integral part of most punishment, indeed almost the essence of punishment, it is now prohibited by international conventions and by the constitutions of many countries. Considered to be mainly physically induced pain, it may also be used in a far more subtle manner by sophisticated psychological techniques. Its parameters are difficult to determine, its definition varies in different periods and different societies. Although generally acknowledged as the most reprehensible of acts, torture is often given legitimation when performed in pursuit of an ideological cause or on behalf of a political movement.

Torture is inextricably bound up with the whole nature of the criminal process—ranging from its definition as a criminal act, which often calls forth the most extreme penalties, through methods, illicit or of dubious legality, used by investigative authorities to extract confessions or other information from suspects or witnesses, to the various aspects of punishment that manifestly constitute, or controversially border on, torture, such as solitary confinement, corporal punishment, physical mutilation, sexual abuse, sensory deprivation, and emotional terror.

Nothing is easier to condemn—or more difficult to eradicate. Too often pious public denunciations are a convenient verbal cover for the physical reality of secret torture; legal prohibitions do not always prevent the ongoing *sub rosa* activities. Often the consensus of condemnation lulls the critical sensitivities, and the focus on the undoubted horrors of past practices allows for present-day complacency. Once again criminologists and penologists have been remiss in their treatment of this topic, largely ignoring it; and it has been mainly human rights and prison reform organizations that, in the last decade or so, have heightened the awareness of the public to the prevalance of torture in modern police and prison settings.[1]

Torture indeed continues to exist; whatever the legal situation in any particular country, there is a possibility that, in certain circumstances, torture will be used at some stage of the criminal process. Information as to its use is inevitably difficult to obtain—there are no official records, and complaints of detainees and inmates are almost always met by official denials. The factual knowledge available may be even in inverse ratio to the actual extent and intensity of the practice, for it is often in totalitarian societies where the worst excesses take place, but where the least information is available. In contrast, in open and democratic societies there is often documented evidence—in personal affidavits, in official commissions of enquiry, in judicial pronouncements, in investigative journalism.

It is mainly through the painstaking efforts of international organizations and nongovernmental bodies, such as Amnesty International, the Red Cross, and the International Commission of Jurists, that a partial picture has slowly emerged of abuses committed against those held in custody.[2] But though these organizations can ensure that their credentials as objective fact-finding bodies are unimpeachable, and their credibility as to the accuracy of the information provided beyond reproach, they are unable to guarantee that their reports are exhaustive and comprehensive.

In such reports it sometimes happens that countries which are lesser transgressors are the most severely dealt with, specifically because the democratic nature of the regime allows for easier access to information and less fear of subsequent reprisals. It is in the more totalitarian states that the very extremity of the excesses (where torture may lead to death or is accompanied by banishment) makes for a conspiratorial silence of officialdom which is well-nigh impenetrable.

Amnesty International, which has produced estensive country-by-country reports on the existence of torture, spells out the problematics of work in this area. The aim of its report, it states, "has been to summarize the information available in each country mentioned but there are other countries where the organization does not have sufficient information to include; this cannot be taken to indicate that torture or other ill-treatment have not taken place." The report adds that "secrecy and censorship often prevent the free flow of information about such abuses."[3]

It is, in my opinion, not possible to conduct a full-scale enquiry into the question of the death penalty or life imprisonment without giving due consideration to the policies and the practices of states as to torture. There are several factors which obligate such an analysis.

First, torture is an extreme penalty, containing parallels with the death penalty, and may be considered, as I have already suggested, more serious in some respects. In some cases torture may lead, whether intentionally or unintentionally, to the death of the victim, by the failure of his life-support systems while undergoing the torture, by suicide in order to escape further suffering, or by an early death brought on by the consequences of what he has undergone. In all these instances, just as in the case of a full life imprisonment, the consequences of the torture are similar to a death sentence; indeed, it may be considered all the worse by virtue of the pain and suffering which precedes the death.

However, when death does not result, torture may still be a more extreme penalty; certainly when it is prolonged—over months or years—or when the sheer cruelty used is of such a nature that irreparable harm—physical, emotional, mental—is done to the victim.

The irreversibility of death as a penalty is often matched by the fact that the victim of torture undergoes an experience that marks him and scars him for all time and that possibly induces deep-seated psychological changes which cannot always be remedied. When there is actual physical mutilation, as in the excising of a limb, the damage is for all time—but the really serious results are perhaps in the emotional crisis engendered by physical torture, sometimes causing a total transformation in the personality of the victim.[4]

Second, an examination of torture is necessary for any analysis of extreme penalties, since often it is varying acts of torture that stimulate the most concerted and compelling arguments for the death penalty.

The public demands for capital punishment often become most insistent after incidents in which the victim of a major crime such as murder was subjected to physical, psychological, or sexual abuse in the hours or days, or even longer, that preceded death. The kidnapping of hostages or the abduction of a rape victim linked to torture and death typically arouse strong societal reactions, leading to calls that the only penalty for such sadistic acts is death. A mixture of emotions and motivations underlie these demands, and it is often difficult to maintain a level of objective discourse as to the appropriate response. Retribution, and even stark desires for revenge, are generally of major import, but so is a desire for a strong sentence that will deter similar acts in the future. The reaction is also fueled by strong feelings of compassion for the victims and the agony of what they had to endure, and empathetic sentiments for the family and friends, who, particularly in the event of death, are ceaselessly haunted by the tragedy that befell someone so close to them.

Abolitionist reponse to such demands is to reiterate the need at such times for society to display the resilience and fortitude that will avoid allowing passing anger and temporary anguish to affect the norms and values that must be the basic bedrock of a society. If the death penalty is considered to be an unacceptable punishment, then there can be no exceptions. Indeed, when most provoked by perversion, it is the duty of society to reaffirm its commitment to the values of human dignity that form the framework for its penal philosophy and policy. Society cannot degenerate to the level of the criminal— the more heinous the crime and the more hardened the criminal, all the more must a society adhere to the standards of justice and the levels of punishment that it applies in all other cases. Society can best express its repugnance for the crime by the measured moderation of its response. Since a severe penalty is clearly in order, the abolitionist would probably argue that a life imprisonment, perhaps even with extra conditions, is apt.

But there is a contrary reason why the death penalty might be acceptable in such exceptional cases. If torture is indeed the reason for the killing to be considered a more serious act, then the real retributive act would be not the death penalty but torture. Since torture is indubitably unacceptable, the death penalty becomes a possibility almost by default.

Retentionist arguments for the death penalty are often imprecise. When retentionists argue that a death penalty is required so that deserved retribution is forthcoming, that measure for measure is a necessity in such cases, the truth of the matter is that civilized society when confronted by crimes of special enormity or viciousness is *unable* to respond in like manner. It is the revulsion that society senses toward an act that prevents it from responding in like manner. The very value system that it is concerned to uphold places limitations on its reactions. The physical cruelty that gives the crime its horrendous nature is of a kind that civilized society rejects as a legitimate form of punishment. The penalty that sheer revenge dictates is one that responsible response denies. The horror that the crime evokes stems from the same source that creates the decency underling the social control of the penal system.

Conversely, then, the death sentence may arguably be a suitable punishment for the most cruel of crimes—but not because it expresses parity. It may in fact become a permissible penalty in such instances specifically because it does *not* represent parity. For in the examples of a torturous death, it is not the death as such, tragic as it is, but the surrounding circumstances that evokes the particularly strong societal concern. In such cases the penalty that raw human emotions might call for is that of a *quid pro quo*, torture; in contrast, the death penalty becomes no more than the most severe penalty that a society may conceivably impose while yet remaining true to those values which shun the use of physical torture in its penal system.

There are many people who might be willing to be abolitionists but who sense the need to preserve a special penalty for the extreme cases of utter depravity—indeed, there may even be those who define themselves as abolitionists but who are prepared to allow for exceptions to this rule in these limited and well-nigh unique cases.

A death penalty might become a viable possibility because of the need for a specially severe societal response. Here is perhaps the ultimate test for the ultimate penalties—Which penalty can in all decency be imposed when dealing with an "ultimate" crime? The question becomes which of the presently accepted ultimate penalties is the most appropriate in these cases. As torture itself is clearly not feasible, the choice focuses then on a death penalty or life imprisonment.

For pure abolitionists there can be only one answer—that of life imprisonment. But it must be realized that in these instances the conditions attached to life imprisonment are liable to render it uniquely severe—including special confinement and an absolute bar to commutation and parole. It was specifically these implications of a sentence of life imprisonment that were for John Stuart Mill the compelling factors that persuaded him to draw a line on the limits of penal reform and argue for the death penalty in these cases; he felt that a life imprisonment which inevitably would be linked to additional conditions was more severe than a death penalty. Humanistic concepts of mercy would thus permit capital punishment.[5]

Indeed, a paradoxical possibility presents itself. Those persuaded by the logic of Mill's contention might yet opt for life sentence in these cases, as being, precisely by virtue of its potential severity (including the additional conditions) a more appropriate sentence. This was, after all, also part of Beccaria's argument. By this reasoning, a person guilty of the most depraved of crimes should be forced to live out a life of deprivation, shorn of all those factors that make a "life" or any other long-term imprisonment bearable. This would be a punishment that might cause suffering and pain commensurate with the suffering of the victim, and be far in excess of an earlier death penalty. Thus, a leading American abolitionist of the nineteenth century, Edward Livingston, suggested that the prisoner be placed in "solitary confinement in cells painted black, with no visitors and no reading material except the Bible and religious tracts." Basically the prisoner is "dead to the world and his cell is his grave."[6]

But under these circumstances the question would then certainly arise as to whether minimum international standards or constitutional protections were being preserved—and the issue would then be whether an immediate death sentence would not be more desirable as providing a penalty severe enough for the crime yet not in violation of minimum penal standards. In terms of the earlier argument as to choice, these very doubts as to severity of sentence would raise again the possibility of allowing the condemned person himself to choose.

However, although the need for an ultimate—or *the* ultimate—penalty seems to be almost self-evident in cases of sadistic murders (and the argument till now has been largely based on this assumption), the actual implementation of an ultimate penalty might pose several serious problems because of the special standards that should be a prerequisite. For though society might be entitled to impose its ultimate penalty on those considered the most despicable of criminals, guilty of the most dastardly of crimes, it could surely resort to such special punitive responses only if it maintained the strictest integrity and fairness in carrying them out. Quite clearly no patterns of discrimination should be allowed, nor any haphazard approach involving arbitrary or capricious decision-making, whether by judicial fiat or executive injunction. The deviation from the normal framework of punishment would obligate the strictest adherence to equitable standards in judging and carrying out the judgment. There would have to be guarantees that the sentence was being applied only to those unquestioningly deserving of the punishment on the one hand, and, on the other hand, that others guilty of similar actions were not eluding the full force of the law and its extreme punitive mechanisms. In a sense, an insistence on this double guarantee would be a reaffirmation of the trend of the United States Supreme Court, which made the death penalty, in its decisions in the 1970s, dependent on the full measure of checks and comparative analysis to ensure that the death penalty was being applied in a fair and equitable manner, not arbitrarily and capriciously, nor deliberately discriminatory. It is at this point that the problem of the application of an apt ultimate penalty becomes problematical.

The real tragedy of torture is that it is far more widespread than is indicated by the criminal acts of isolated individuals committing major crimes of kidnapping, rape, and murder aggravated by physical or mental torture. This is one category of torturous behavior, but it is not the only one. It is certainly the category that engenders most societal anger and public calls for stern reaction. Yet it may be only a small aspect of the totality of torture.

THE OTHER FORMS OF TORTURE are far more difficult to divulge, and when divulged are far more difficult to control because of their sensitive and secretive nature, and because of the partial legitimacy which they are accorded. A significant amount of torture still takes place within the framework of law enforcement, whether as part of the investigative process or the punitive response; and a further amount of torture takes place within the intimate confines of the home.

As for the latter, it is only in the past two decades that information about violence within the family has become widely available—child abuse and spouse abuse are syndromes that are far more prevalent than was generally known or than any official figures would even hint at. Some of this abuse may be limited to sporadic fits of anger or one-time spontaneous reactions to a tense situation. Much of it, however, consists of premeditated and systematic physical abuse that in its essence, certainly in its cumulative effect, constitutes a pattern of torture, in many respects far worse than any other pattern of torture, specifically because of the close relationship between the culprit and the victim, and because of the ongoing and nigh inescapable framework within which it takes place.

Here are some of the most inhumane patterns of behavior, yet society lacks an adequate response. Richard Gelles has estimated that as much as half the total violence in a society occurs within the home, and it may be suggested that a certain amount of that violence involves acts of torture as serious as any of those committed outside the home.[7] He writes that "people are more likely to be hit, beat up, physically injured, or even killed in their own homes by another family member than anywhere else, or by anyone else in our society."[8]

The last twenty years have given rise to a copious literature on battered children and battered women, while researchers and social workers, doctors, nurses, and others in the field have pieced together a reality of what they call abuse (but which is often tantamount to torture) in the family setting. Most of the research and field work has focused on the victim—in many cases the best solution is to remove the victim from the clutches of his tormentor. In the case of a spouse, divorce or at least separation may be sought, and this is the solution increasingly advocated by women's groups active on behalf of battered women. In the case of children, temporary transference to a foster home or institution, or even permanent forced adoption (sanctioned by court order) is sometimes sought.

But what is to be done with the culprit? Is he to be treated as an ordinary criminal? Here it should be remembered that there are real legal and ideological problems still to be resolved—for instance, in many cases the abuse of women consists of forced sex, what amounts in essence to rape, but which was, till recently, never recognized as such (since a husband could not rape his wife according to the legal definition); and there are still jurisdictions that maintain the old rule.[9] For children, hitting is widely considered acceptable and educational.

Nevertheless, in any scale of human depravity (if such be at all possible), it is perhaps this violence and torture that is the most reprehensible, being forced on one's chosen beloved, on one's own kith and kin, on the vulnerable and helpless, on those for whom there is almost no escape, partly because the bonds of love persist ambivalently, partly because the norms of society decree respect, and for some even obedience. Here is abuse of prior professions of love; here is exploitation of the sanctity and privacy of the home. Yet, however stark and cruel these acts may be depicted, few have called for an ultimate punishment for the guilty. For the most part, the focus is on the possibility of rehabilitation, and often even reconciliation. All this is well and good, and in line with the most progressive trends of penology in society. But, the question may be asked, if no penal sanction, or no severe penal sanction, is to be imposed on family members for monstrous acts, how justify then the extreme penalty—of death or life imprisonment—in other cases of cruelty between strangers or acquaintances?

This reference to violence in the family in order to understand the totality of torture should not be seen as a peripheral issue. For there is a very close connection between violence in the family and violence in society in general, not only in the sense that criminal patterns of behavior learned in the home (violence as a solution to problems) are repeated outside the home, but also in the sense that *punitive* patterns of behavior learned in the home (corporal punishment as a response to misbehavior) are also repeated in society.[10]

Similar considerations may be applied in the case of torture used in the course of law enforcement. Here, too, the last two decades have seen an enormous increase in the amount of information available. The data gleaned by human rights organizations from all over the world indicates the widespread use of torture, sometimes ending in death.[11] In some cases these acts are connected with political struggles, in others used against ordinary criminals.

There is little doubt that torture persists, both in the course of investigative proceedings and in the subsequent punitive stage. Evidence of at least some of the excesses committed in the name of justice may be gleaned from journalistic accounts, but, more authoritatively, from a number of judicial decisions in which various practices of the authorities have been carefully scrutinized and severely criticized.[12] Particularly noteworthy in this regard are some of the decisions of the European Court of Human Rights, which has drawn on some of the most fundamental and deepest values of human rights in order to lay down overall norms and specific rulings as to the policies and practices of individual countries sued for violations.[13] Similarly, in the United States, a series of decisions have given concrete meaning to the various pertinent protections of the Constitution.[14]

Some of the most significant advances have taken place in an area of the world most noted for its human rights violations, Latin America, where the Commission on Human Rights has often been innovative and displayed initiative in imposing universalistic standards on nation-states.[15]

Generally, however, the sanctions in these cases, are generally not criminal, let alone ultimate penalties. In most instances the nature of adjudication is civil, involving writs to desist, or of habeas corpus or compensation or similar directives.[16] Given the pioneering nature of much of this adjudication (including the willingness of the participating nations in regional associations to voluntarily accept a certain limitation on their absolute sovereignty), it is difficult to conceive that more stringent action could be taken or that severe criminal sanctions could be imposed.

The fact is that many of these abusive violations of human rights involve the use of physical torture (including unto death) that is no less cruel and vile than that committed by criminals, and, given the protective framework of state apparatus and the utter helplessness and powerlessness of the victim, often far more so. For as long as these culprits do not get their "due" deserts, the focus on criminals alone, from a universalistic humanitarian perspective, becomes a selective process of the worst kind.

If anything, it is those who commit torture in an official capacity who are most deserving of society's retributive anger; for they have abused the trust invested in them and, in so doing, undermined the values they were pledged to safeguard. More than that, they are also presumed to possess those personal qualities that would enable them to satisfy testing mechanisms that enable a society to distinguish those who are capable of fulfilling its trust from those who are liable to abuse the power given them. The presumption is that the former are not manifestly sociopathic; on the contrary, they should be upright and law-abiding citizens as a condition of their recruitment into law enforcement positions. Their deviant acts seems to be a deliberate exploitation of their power, often with the collusion or the connivance of their superiors and their peers. I raise this issue of official torture as a warning against the self-righteous anger that selectively focuses on the outcasts of society and complacently ignores the similar evils perpetrated by officialdom on behalf of the society and in the name of so-called justice. Indeed, the justification for such torture is often clothed in the sanctimonious garb of devoted patriotism.[17]

Let me clarify this line of thinking. For the ordinary criminal accused and convicted of a major crime accompanied by the aggravating circumstances of torture, there is no doubt that a severe penalty should be imposed; the question is whether that severe penalty should be a unique one and include one of the two possible ultimate penalties. If, under normal circumstances, the ultimate penalties of life or death should not be used, can they be used in exceptional cases? What attitude should abolitionists and civil rights activists adopt?

The key question now is whether in extraordinary cases exceptions should be made, just as was done at the end of the Second World War when extreme penalties were sought for those reponsible for acts of genocide, crimes against humanity, crimes of war, etc. Are individual acts of torture to be placed on a par with the larger collective evil dealt with in some of the Nuremberg trials? If so, if a parallel is to be drawn, then again it would seem that the official perpetrators of torture bear a greater responsibility than that of ordinary criminals; and additionally, in the light of the Nuremberg decisions, they can not even claim the defense of acts of state or superior orders.

There is one more factor that must be taken into account in analyzing the desired response to the vicious criminal. Too often there are compelling mitigating factors that must be taken into account, too often the horror of the act for which he stands trial is a mirror image of the horrors to which, in his childhood, in his home, or in his community or society, he was subjected. A criminal's act of sheer inhumanity is the outcome of the lack of warm human feelings in his own life; the hatred that he vents on his victim reflects the hatred that he once absorbed. The backgrounds of some of the worst criminals are certainly of this type.

To raise this issue is not to make a melodramatic plea for leniency. It is rather to put the whole problem in its proper perspective. For, after all, those who cry out for the just deserts of retribution are often only echoing the criminal's own life experience—of hurt and reaction to hurt. Research in criminology has shown how much antisocial activity stems from prior feelings of victimization.[18] Unfortunately, it is also sometimes the most extreme form of victimization that leads to the most extreme form of criminality.

The fact that a criminal must pay for his crime, irrespective of his motivations and as long as he is sane, does not tell us the nature of the punishment to be demanded of him and, in particular, whether an ultimate penalty is to be used. This—the question of the ultimate penalty—is the issue. And because of its extreme and exceptional nature it can surely only be used when the aggravating circumstances of cruelty and torture inflicted are not offset by the mitigating circumstances of cruelty and torture previously suffered. This background may not hold for all the criminals involved—but for those for whom it does hold (and they may well be the vast majority), special moderating considerations must be brought to bear. In many instances these should be sufficient to cancel out the possibility of an ultimate penalty, even when, theoretically, such a penalty may be considered an acceptable response. In any event, the torturer with no or few mitigating circumstances is liable to be one whose torture is expressed in an official capacity—and thus all the less likely to be tried and punished.

A DISCUSSION OF TORTURE cannot be limited to the punitive stage of the criminal process, but must take also some minimum cognizance of the other stages at which, and other reasons for which, resort is had to torture. In fact, torture differs from the other two ultimate penalties not only in being potentially the most severe, but also in the fact that it can be used for utilitarian and nonpunitive purposes. Unlike the death penalty with its finality and life imprisonment with its interminability, torture carries the temptation of being used in a rapid and effective manner to help with the investigation of a crime or the prevention of one.

The international convention dealing with torture draws no distinction and declares an absolute ban on torture.[19] Article 1 of the convention refers to three possible situations—the obtaining of information or a confession, the punishment for an act committed, and its use for intimidation. Although the act is still the same, its meaning differs; and though the pragmatics of a total ban are compelling, a fuller understanding requires separate reference.

Torture has a long history; it has perhaps most often been used in the investigative stage. In earlier societies it was often legally sanctioned; today it is generally illegal. But where practiced, legally or illegally, a similar rationale is used, namely, that the ends justifies the means, that the needs of security necessitate drastic action, that the forces of law and order cannot be too hidebound by the niceties of civilized practices in their ongoing struggle against the antisocial elements in society. These arguments, however, break down not only in the framework of the humanitarian values that characterize modern society, but also in terms of its technological capabilities. For torture in earlier times was often resorted to not because—or rather *not just* because—of the ruthless and cruel minions who abused their power, but also because of the limited capacities of law enforcement.

In a fascinating historial analysis, John Langbein has stressed how closely intertwined the uses of torture was with the need for proof, and how its use diminished parallel to changes in the law of proof.[20] When allowed, the rules for the use of torture were generally precisely spelled out and practically enforced, just as the general rules of procedure and evidence are today. Langbein notes that torture could be used for investigative purposes only in the case of capital crimes, and only as a last resort. "Torture was not to be used," he writes, "unless other means of gathering evidence were lacking. This rule was a natural corollary of the subsidiary role of the law of torture in the system of statutory proofs. If there were two eyewitnesses of voluntary confession, investigation under torture was unnecessary."[21]

Most important was the need for there to be probable cause before torture could be used. The society imposed a rule in some ways similar to that applicable today as to the circumstances under which arrest can be made or people kept in pretrial detention.

> The critical chapter of the law of torture was the set of rules designed to determine whether there was sufficient suspicion against the accused to warrant examining him under torture. This was the point at which items of circumstantial evidence, called indicia, were permitted to bear on guilt by becoming the basis for a decree authorizing examination under torture.

Further,

> Consistent with the principle that torture could be used only in the last resort, the Roman canon-law of proof that required full proof for conviction required half proof for torture. The testimony of two eyewitnesses constituted full proof; half proof was the testimony of one such witness, or, more often, circumstantial evidence of sufficient quality.[22]

The administration of torture would be undertaken in an organized manner by an investigating magistrate with a full recording of the proceedings, including whether a confession was forthcoming and if so what it was. Before the torture was imposed, the accused had to be given due warning in the hope that the threat itself would be sufficient to induce him to confess. Finally, "the accused who withstood all examination under torture without confessing was said to have purged the indicia against him, and was entitled to be acquitted and released."[23] The presumption here was, of course, not that the accused was heroic enough to withstand the torture, but that he had no information to give and was thus clearly innocent.

Although there can be no justification for torture to extract a confession, fairness demands a recognition of the fact that it was linked far more to the exigencies of law enforcement with limited resources than any predilections for cruelty that are thought to have characterized the period. Societies that lacked a professionally trained police force, the sophisticated and scientific technology for accurate detection, and the communication network for rapid transfer of information and the deployment of forces, would seek the most practical means at their disposal to compensate for these deficiencies. Indeed, as Langbein points out, torture as a means of eliciting information and confessions came into extensive use only when ordeals—which involved just as much physical pain, and no more certainty as to veracity—fell into disuse.

In any event, because of the requirement of probable cause, a rationale, admittedly disputable, existed for the use of torture. Since the protective device of the rules of evidence made conviction dependent on a minimum standard of proof, the lack of sufficient eyewitnesses necessitated a confession in order to gain a conviction. If the suspect was indeed guilty, he could avoid the torture by confessing. (Although the subsequent punishment itself might also involve torture.) Clearly, psychological pressure was brought to bear on the suspect to confess before being subject to torture, just as there is a subtle (and sometimes not so subtle) intimidation in the pretrial detention of a suspect, which often leads to confessions, some of them later retracted in court.

Of course, the wrongfully suspected person would inevitably be subjected to torture with no recourse, since he would not have anything to confess. His only hope might be that if he withstood the torture successfully, he might be released.

As described by Langbein and others, it would seem that torture was seen as a necessary evil, as essential to the functioning of a criminal law system in its earlier stages, when it was without the means to independently prove the allegations against the suspect. Torture was in a way the unfortunate other side of a development that was basically positive, providing for clear proof of guilt in place of the idiosyncratic decisions of the various ordeals. The torture itself took place under the strictest of conditions; and during certain periods almost fell into desuetude. As soon as changes that rendered the confession of less importance were introduced into the law of evidence, the laws as to judicial torture were changed.

In an earlier period, then, since torture served some important utilitarian purpose, it was given legal status, which led to control by strict rules. In the absence of its recognition, there is no means of direct, ongoing control of the investigating officials, and thus, in reality, far less protection for the accused. When states flatly deny that torture is practiced and ritualistically append their signature to conventions banning it, then there is presumably no need for a controlling mechanism.

The one saving grace of judicial recognition in the past was that it might have assured at least more judicious use than in the present. The solution is clearly not to revert to official torture, but to reiterate its incompatibility, not just with humanitarian principles of respect for human dignity and integrity, but with scientific possibilities of more precise proof. Even a cruel act might have a logical rationale that provides if not justification, then at least mitigation. A historical perspective suggests that this might have been applicable in the past, but is not so today.

Indeed, it has been suggested that reliance by the police on illicit methods of investigation is often self-defeating—not only does it raise the possibility of the confession elicited being declared invalid in court, but often deflects the investigators themselves from persevering in pursuit of the best evidence and of additional independent evidence.

Be that as it may, a ban on torture leads to other inevitable consequences, which the international convention has tried to spell out. First and foremost, the concluding article states that "any statement which is established to have been made as a result of torture or other cruel, inhuman or degrading treatment may not be invoked as evidence against the person concerned or against any other person in any other proceedings."[24] Such a provision provides important protection for the defendant, though obviously he is still faced with the enormous difficulty of proving his allegations as to the illegality of the confession—often it is only his word against the combined denials of those who interrogated him. Even then, some jurisdictions, such as in Britain, will allow looking beyond the event and the circumstances to the substance, and if they believe that despite the police misbehavior, the truth was told, the confession may still be admissible.[25]

An alternative approach relates to what is known in the United States as "the fruit of the poisoned tree" doctrine, concerning the acceptability of any independent evidence procured as a result of the blemished and rejected confession. The convention makes no mention of this aspect of a disqualified confession. In the United States, this "fruit" is considered marred and the evidence tainted—and so it is also rejected.[26] Elsewhere the ruthlessness of logic (if the evidence was found then the accused was telling the truth) and legal need to convict the accused take precedence over humanitarian considerations and the evidence will be acceptable, with the societal sanction against infractions being, at least theoretically, punishment of those responsible.

Punishment is indeed provided for in Article 10 of the international convention, which states that "criminal, disciplinary and other appropriate proceedings" shall be instituted. Depending on the nature of the torture, the penalties here could be heavy; in fact, if extreme torture was used, an extreme concomitant punishment could be considered—but only rarely do such possibilities emerge, for, because of the official role of the perpetrator, a full probe and a subsequent adequate punishment are generally unlikely.

Given the perceived needs of the state to solve crimes and to convict the guilty, given the temptations which flow from the power the police possess, and given the pressures on them to be successful, it is not through a reactive punishment that torture will be abolished, but by a stricter and more efficient control of the investigative proceedings. There is an urgent need to utilize more fully the advantages to be derived from the latest technology—for instance, a video recording should be used instead of a signed statement; a neutral official should be present at key stages of the interrogation; regular and frequent medical check-ups should be made during the interrogation, with the results to be presented to the court as a prerequisite for a confession to be accepted. Judicial involvement has characterized the official *use* of torture in the past—surely it could be evoked again now to ensure the *prevention* of torture.

THERE IS A FURTHER ASPECT of torture that the convention refers to; having laid down the ban, the convention disallows any exception, neither in the case of war, internal political instability, nor "any other public emergency." This last prohibition denies the possibility of dire need creating its own special norms, even though the law generally does recognize the need to retroactively sanction certain violations of the law because of emergency circumstances, such as for self-defense or necessity. If society recognizes the need to approve retroactively past illegal acts, even when the consequences are disastrous (self-defense being used to excuse an act of killing, necessity to justify one), then it should perhaps also be able to recognize prospectively the need for a normally illegal action.

Under normal rules, an emergency would allow for a defendant to claim that he acted out of necessity—but it is specifically "public emergency" that is excluded by the convention. This may require reassessment, on the grounds that it is wiser to provide rules for a deviant act that is liable to occur, rather than give it a blanket denunciation that implies a denial of the act's possible existence.

The need to gain information and the temptation to use torture to do so applies not just to a past crime but also to a future one. It is this latter situation that creates special problems. Sometimes vague information is available as to the potential commission of a criminal act, or, more acutely, of a terrorist act; in such circumstances the authorities might wish to resort to torture, especially when the presumed future danger is imminent, massive, and irreversible. Robert Gerstein argues that torture, even though a violation of a person's rights, might be justified "if the stakes were sufficiently high and the facts sufficiently clear."[27]

A member of a terrorist group held in custody and presumed to have reliable information as to a planned crime or attack in the near future poses a real problem for those anxious to ensure that the needs of societal protection are made compatible with the values of human decency. If time is of the essence and if the safety of innocent lives is at stake, an argument might be made that an exception be allowed when simple utilitarian stock-taking indicates the undeniable advantages that would accrue to the potential victims at the expense of the pain and suffering inflicted on an accomplice before the fact of the crime. If the crime is committed, such an accomplice will in any case be liable to severe sanctions (including perhaps a death penalty or life imprisonment). Further, he can avoid the torture by helping to avoid the crime—under such circumstances, would it be possible to allow it subject to a high degree of probable cause, including prior permission from a duly-constituted authority, as well as proof of extremity of the anticipated act—perhaps limited only to genocide and humanicide? It should also be noted that in sharp contrast to the situation when torture is used as a punishment, its infliction for the purpose of eliciting information would be of limited duration, in fact, probably for far less than the period—and perhaps even the intensity—of pain that is sometimes allowed in hospitals for some terminal patients (an aspect of pain and suffering that will be discussed in the following chapter).

None of these possibilities as to torture is pleasant to contemplate—neither the actual infliction nor the legitimacy accorded it—but it must be remembered that the circumstances conceived of are rare, and the potential harm at once immense, immediate, and irreparable. In reality, it may almost be presumed that in such circumstances the exigencies of the situation are liable to take precedence over the sanctions of an international convention; the police are not going to stand idly by waiting for a hidden bomb to explode. It might thus be best to acknowledge the possibility of such a situation arising, and by honestly and openly confronting it, to ensure the existence of conditions that would provide for the necessary societal control of normally impermissible actions done in the name of, and on behalf of, the society, perhaps even for its very survival.

Jeremy Bentham came to a similar conclusion as to the need to allow for the practice of torture as a preventive measure—based on a utilitarian assessment reflective of his overall philosophical stance.[28] However, an example that he gives—namely, of an anticipated crime of arson—would not answer to the minimum requirements, for surely strict utilitarian standards would not justify physical torture to save a house. Yet if there were people who might become victims, the need to save life might take precedence over society's revulsion at using physical torture. In contrast, Beccaria, who convincingly exposed the illogic of using torture to divulge the truth about past crimes, never considered the possibility of its use for preventive purposes.

W. Twining and P. Twining, drawing on Bentham's ideas, examine the conditions under which torture may be used to elicit information:

1. There is evidence of a type sufficient to guarantee a conviction in a court of law that the person has the relevant information.
2. It is reasonable to assume that he will tell the truth if torture is threatened or actually applied.
3. It is unlikely that there are other means of compelling him to tell the truth.
4. There is a good prospect that prompt knowledge will help to avert the danger.
5. The presumed harm that it is sought to forestall will

be of much greater magnitude than the harm of inflicting torture.

6. The torture will not lead to worse consequences (such as a later severely punitive retaliation) than the harm to be averted.[29]

In the case of both Bentham and the Twinings, the issue is not just the substantive question of whether in certain circumstances torture may be allowed, but the meaning to be attached to torture. Because of the vagueness of the term, an action defined as torture may actually have less adverse consequences than an action not so defined. Often the real question is as to the choice of a lesser evil. In this context the comparison is made specifically with imprisonment; there is a temptation "to assume uncritically that all examples of torture are worse, from the victim's point of view, than other analogous kinds of painful experience, such as imprisonment."[30]

In any event, the strictest controls must be maintained. While there is always a danger of abuse, this applies no less to the dangers that might emanate from imprisonment. Where abuse is proven, compensation must be made. Bentham is aware that the abuses are most likely in a political context, when governmental interests are at stake, and so he specifically rules out torture for offenses against the government, including in times of war or danger.[31]

The Twinings sum up their discussion by noting that "it is not easy to be rigorous in dealing with the problem of torture; nor is it easy to be intellectually honest."[32] And they end their own thoughtful deliberations about Bentham's provocative ideas by arguing:

In the modern world there is a real danger that public debate will be bedevilled by a mixture of sentimentality, self-deception and taboo. If the current epidemic is to be tackled realistically and effectively an important first step is to free ourselves from the "delusive power of words" and to face the difficulties with relative detachment, honestly and rationally.[33]

One of the insightful beauties of the criminal law is its recognition that special circumstances may obligate special considerations—thus the defenses of self-defense and duress, or the partial defenses of provocation and diminished responsibility. Most pertinent is the defense of necessity, which recognizes that in unique situations of emergency there may be a need to make a utilitarian accounting of evil against evil—and of allowing proven criminal acts to be excused or justified and the accused absolved of all culpability. The pertinence of this defense has to do with the fact that it is specially designed to cater for those rare and extreme situations that are difficult for the law to encompass specifically since they are, by their rarity, so unforseeable. People adrift on a raft in a stormy sea, exposed to the elements, may decide to cast some people overboard in order to save the others; or lacking food and water, may decide to kill one of their number in order to give the others a chance to survive by eating his flesh and blood; a persecuted group in an attic hiding from Nazi storm-troopers may kill a crying baby to prevent their presence being revealed. Of the latter case, there were a few examples, acts committed *in extremis* which may leave strong feelings of guilt and remorse, may lead to a strong desire to make expiation by charitable and good deeds, but which would hardly be considered in need of criminal adjudication, and, to my knowledge, never were tried after the war. On the other hand, the first two examples have been the subject of judicial examination—and in both instances those responsible were found guilty (though given light sentences and later commutation of sentence).[34] But in both cases there were factors hindering the acceptance of a necessity defense. In the first case, the sailors in charge of the raft decided that all the male passengers who were not sailors would be thrown overboard; the judges in the case hinted that a more arbitrary decision-making process for deciding who would live (for example, a lottery) might have constituted an acceptable manner of choosing. In the second case, the victim was the youngest and weakest on the boat, his victimized situation being exploited by the others. The logic of these two unique cases suggests that, with slightly different facts, the verdict could have been not guilty—and at least in the first case probably should have been on the facts.

Lon Fuller describes a hypothetical situation that contains some interesting similarities to the above cases.[35] Five cave explorers trapped by a fall-in have communication with the outside world and are apprised of the fact that the chances of surviving until rescue crews arrive are negligible given their lack of food and liquids. As a group they then seek advice from the outside world whether it would be permissible—morally and legally—to conduct a lottery to determine who would be killed so as to facilitate the survival of the others. After representatives of the church, medicine, and the law refuse to respond, the men in the cave break off communication. On being rescued many days later, it transpires that they have survived after conducting a lottery and eating the flesh and blood of the sacrificed member. They are put on trial and convicted. Fuller's article is based on the judgment on appeal with five separate opinions, each representing a different philosophy—two opinions sustaining the conviction, two overturning it, and one judge refusing to give an opinion on the case because of its uniqueness, the consequence of his "abstention" being, of course, to allow the conviction to stand.

It seems that an outright annulment of any special emergency provisions in respect to torture is similar to the attitude of the religious, medical, and legal officials who refused to respond and of the judge who abstained. It is to opt out of a difficult and delicate situation.

Torture clearly has to be stopped, and its unacceptability to the world community has to be expressed in the most uncertain terms. All attempts should be made to avoid any loopholes or ambiguity. But to deny outright the possibility of any exception is to block the potential wisdom of the law in an unforseeable situation. It is to deprive a person who may have acted under great duress, in a great emergency, for a greater good, of a defense that is legitimate and acceptable to every other violation of the law, including what would have been murder, in the case of self-defense.

If the convention on torture is no more than a mere exercise in goodwill, then the actual formula chosen is unimportant—and the fine language and extreme position may be accepted. But if there is a genuine desire to implement these guidelines, then an exception, just as for any other law, becomes necessary. Indeed, if a special approach is required, it should deal with the possibility of recognizing not just retrospective excuse, but prospective permission—the latter, in fact, to be the desired situation, with the former—retrospective excuse—being permitted only if proof is provided that the exigencies of time did not allow for such procedures, similar to accepted procedures for search and arrest.

Given the sophisticated weaponry in the hands of criminals and political terrorists, and given the future (and present?) possibilities of the nuclear age and the computer society, wisdom decrees that foresight and forthrightness determine policy directives. It is these kinds of considerations that, for instance, allow for exceptions from laws relating to privacy, in the form of wire-tapping, etc., the exceptions being of a limited and defined nature, the societal need being proven, and permission from a duly-constituted authority being required.[36] There is undoubtedly a clear danger that such an exception could easily be exploited, but if the law is really to be respected and enforced and not remain a hollow and disregarded norm, then surely it requires the same exception for possible unforeseen eventualities that are applicable for any other criminal act by virtue of exceptional and emergency circumstances. Not to do so in fact probably reveals a cynical acknowledgment that many states do not intend abiding by the provisions of the convention in any case—or at the least, have not adequately considered all the possible eventualities. It is clearer easier to condemn torture outright in all circumstances than to confront the agonizing question of the possible dire circumstances that might justify its use. The failure—or the refusal—to face this challenge in the sedate forum of calm and measured deliberation might conceivably cause a serious lacuna when the urgent exigencies of immediate decision-making would require action devoid of any guidelines.

In any event, there are situations in which, specifically for security reasons, states are prepared to contemplate the possibility that their citizens, especially in the military, might have to be prepared to suffer torture. A captured prisoner of war is expected to submit to torture rather than divulge information to his captors or even to be too cooperative with their demands, even though the security factor may be often specious. A United States court-martial from the time of the Korean War, bears out the nature of official thinking.[37] The accused was found guilty of collaborating, communicating and holding intercourse with the enemy through various actions of his while a prisoner of war during the Korean War. The court specifically rejected the defenses of necessity, duress, and coercion. Of particular interest is the casual manner in which the court describes the horrifying conditions to which he was subject: "Living conditions were not good, the diet was poor," when the reality was of starvation and exposure to cold and filth. Or that, before succumbing to his captors, he was threatened with sanctions likely to have fatal consequences. The court felt that he should have first ascertained whether they intended to carry out these threats. Simply put, it is a standard norm of military law that a captive soldier must prefer to suffer torture rather than to evade it by cooperating too closely with his captors. Why then, at the least, not allow torture to save a society or community from immediate, life-threatening terrorist actions. And, given these norms, why the simplistic consensus of diplomats as to their universal condemnation of torture with no recognized legal exceptions, this despite the fact that international conventions generally allow for suspension of human rights in emergency situations.[38]

THE FINAL PROBLEM of torture has to do with its definition. This seems almost insurmountable, with cultural concepts affecting perception, both as to what is deemed to be permissible by humanitarian standards and as to how pain is physically felt by the recipient, which in turn may be affected by such factors as social status, ethnic background, age, gender, or personal characteristics.[39]

In one case the European Court of Human Rights found that the five kinds of interrogation practiced by the British in Northern Ireland were not torture, but constituted "only" inhuman and degrading treatment (which is likewise banned by most of the international and regional conventions but is considered of lesser severity).[40] Matthew Lippman notes that the "difficulty of distinguishing between torture and inhuman and degrading treatment is illustrated by the fact that, in contrast to the [Court], the European Commission of Human Rights [which is a lower instance] unanimously found that the 'five techniques' used . . . constituted torture."[41] The commission noted a clear resemblance to the systematic torture of earlier times.

The easiest solution is to outlaw all forms of physical punishment, but that seems to be an impossibility given the differing approaches of cultures and religions to physical pain and the attribution by some of physical pain to ostensibly non-physical situations, such as confinement in a limited space.

In some parts of the world mutilation as punishment is practiced, with what are claimed as efficient results—particularly deterrence, both individual (and which may also constitute incapacitation), and general. In a number of fundamentalist Moslem countries, Saudi Arabia, Libya, Sudan, Pakistan, Mauritania, and Iran, authority for such penalties is sought in religious sources.[42]

Western-oriented humanitarian organizations have declared their outright condemnation of such practices. And certainly chopping off the hand of a pickpocket seems only slightly removed from the excesses of execution as provided for by the law of some Western countries as late as the nineteenth century. It is clear that the basis for such physical punishments is not just the recommendation of experts (who may be easily ignored) or the policies of politicians (who may be eventually replaced), but the authority of divine revelation, linked to a tradition nearly fifteen hundred years old. It is clear that any confrontation on this issue between international human rights organizations and government goes much deeper than that normally between the commendable watchdog surveillance by the former and the insistence on noninterference in the sovereign rights of a nation-state by the latter, but touches at the heart of deep-seated ideological conflict. Indeed, the very capacity of international organizations such as Amnesty International and the various United Nations human rights bodies to function effectively—in this and other human rights activities—may be dependent on the capacity to fully comprehend the depth of commitment that the fundamentalist leaders of these Moslem states have to a traditional religious penal system. Ways must be sought of developing a meaningful discourse on the issue. It is possible that the inflexible attitudes of some of the fundamentalist leaders brook no further debate; in fact, if inroads are to be made into the present penal practices of these states, then the debate may have to revolve not around presumed consensus as to the humanistic principles of modern civilization, but the intricate debates as to the interpretation of the religious commands and ethical values of the Koran. The direct influence of Egypt on Sudan, of Morocco on Mauritania, of Tunisia on Libya, is liable to have far more effect in moderating the forms of official punishment than the reproaches of Western liberals and international humanitarian organizations.

At the same time it should also be realized that the Western consensus against physical punishment is based on an inverse widespread support of prison. When prison itself is challenged as being harsh and inefficient, then different perspectives are brought to bear and other punitive alternatives may be canvassed. Few things can arouse the ire as much as descriptions or pictures of instruments of torture, or of physical pain being inflicted—much more difficult to convey is the suffering associated with confinement. I have already argued that the physical punishment of death may, in some circumstances or for some people, be considered preferable to the presumed nonphysical punishment of prison. But similar arguments are applicable at other levels, even when not dealing with ultimate penalties (except and inasmuch as physical punishment is always, and by definition, equated with torture, which would in any case, then, always make it an example of an ultimate penalty). The reality, however, is that there are degrees of physical punishment; just as the sheer length of imprisonment may, as I have argued, transform what could be considered an acceptable punishment into an unacceptable one, so, conversely, a form of punishment—physical punishment, which in its most intense manifestations, is clearly unacceptable—may, in more moderate form, be considered acceptable. Quantitative differences may make for qualitative differences both in respect to imprisonment and in respect to physical punishment or "torture."

In a recent provocative book, Graeme Newman has argued that earlier forms of punishment may contain a wisdom, a relevance, and an efficacy that has been lost over the years due to the reliance on prison as the normal form of punishment.[43] Using a medical model, he draws a distinction between acute pain and chronic pain, the former being exemplified, in the penological context, by corporal punishment, the latter, by prison. Working on the assumption that the purpose of punishment (logically and semantically) is to cause pain, Newman suggests that acute pain—quickly administered and soon over—may well be preferable to the chronic pain of prison, even when efforts are made to make the prison environment more palatable. "Our purposes could be served much better," he writes, "by substituting the application of acute pain for the drawn out prison terms of mild painfulness—provided that the punishment were appropriate to the crime. . . . It is important to understand that the question is not, which is 'better' punishment—chronic or acute—but rather to which crime are chronic pains more applicable, and to which ones are acute pains more fitting."[44]

Newman argues that if all factors are taken into consideration, including the impact on the convicted person's family, then a rapid acute penalty might make more sense than a lengthy chronic punishment. Pain itself is not torture, since the aim of punishment is to cause pain. But what may be considered as torture is time (mainly psychologically) and the prison itself. "The necessity to control time makes abundantly clear that the expert use of torture requires as its base a prison system. Prison not only provides the possibility of manipulating time, but also the necessary secrecy for the administation of torture."[45]

This statement focuses on the heart of the problem. For it is specifically within the confines of a prison that there is the greatest possibility that forms of torture will be practiced—ranging from brutality by the prison guards to physical and sexual abuse by fellow prisoners. Newman suggests that an officially-recognized acute physical punishment is preferable to the uncertainty of a prisoner's fate within a prison system. In addition to the chronic pain of time, prison exposes him also in many instances to the vagaries of physical violence that flourishes in a prison environment. Again, it is the withdrawal of public scrutiny from the prison (which itself allows for the physical violence) that makes for the complacency as to prison (despite the known propensity to violence there) as contrasted with the horror evoked as to any sanctioned physical punishment.

It must be emphasized that Newman is not dealing with physical punishment as an ultimate penalty. On the contrary, he stresses that his suggestion of the use of acute physical pain "be introduced to fill the gap between the severe punishment of prison and the non-punishment of probation."[46] For him, then, the administration of corporal punishment does not constitute torture, and should not be considered as cruel or severe. In fact, it is prison that "is a form of torture."[47] What he considers the severe punishment of lengthy prison sentences should be reserved for the most serious crimes, and here he suggests a simple two-tier system: fifteen years for first-timers, life for recidivists. The latter, according to his assumption, would be really for life, the conditions would be extremely harsh, and the inmates themselves would be few in number. Interestingly, Newman ignores completely the role of the extreme physical penalty of death in his analysis, although it is clear that he has no use for it in his system.

Newman has made a significant contribution to our understanding of the nature of punishment by drawing a distinction between two types of punishment—acute and chronic. It may be that the public is more shocked by the idea of acute punishment, but the recipients may be more adversely affected by chronic punishment. The medical model is particularly apt since, on occasion, acute violation is made of the body (in an operation or an amputation) in order to allay chronic suffering.

Newman shows how people are drawn into a pattern of thinking determined and dominated by the conventional wisdom of the time. Prison is the norm by which punishments are judged—and it is interesting to note that in those few jurisdictions in which corporal punishment has been used in more recent times, it was generally not as an alternative to prison, but an addition, and sometimes more specifically as a disciplinary measure against prisoners without safeguards.[48]

Newman, on the contrary, is insistent that the corporal punishment that he suggests be given as an alternative to the prison system. He stipulates that "acute corporal punishment should never be used in conjunction with prisons, because it is their special combination with prison that makes real torture possible."[49]

In sum, Newman is not suggesting that torture should be allowed in the penal system, but rather that certain forms of corporal punishment should not be deemed to be torture. If corporal punishment, in various controlled forms, is administered to adolescent students at educational institutions, it is difficult to believe that those educators and jurists who allow it regard it as being torture.[50] If it is permissible for nondelinquent youths, why should it be considered torture when inflicted on criminal adults? Indeed, the desirable situation seems to be just the opposite. The young should be protected from the pain of corporal punishment, often imposed on them without adequate safeguards, for instance, of due process, whereas the adult criminal should perhaps be subject to it, since he at least can be assured of due process protections.

Newman devotes part of his argument to practical questions such as the comparative costs of prison and corporal punishment, but ignores what I would consider to be a major issue, namely, the acquiescence in the punishment of the convicted person. Just as in the case of the choice between a life sentence and the death penalty, there seems to be a real need for the determination of the preferable penalty by the accused himself between an acute corporal punishment or a chronic prison sentence. Once again, the experts can suggest the range of acceptable alternatives; they cannot decisively determine which is preferable.

An approach to this type opens up many more possibilities of different types of punishments, particularly those in which a form of acute pain is substituted for a more regular form of chronic pain. Newman's arguments are solid and convincing—in the nice academic niche of academia; but the key question to determine is whether they bear any relevance in the less refined atmosphere of the penal system.

THAT SOME CONVICTED PERSONS would prefer physical punishment to long-term imprisonment may be gathered from the decisions of at least some to choose in this manner when confronted with the alternatives. On one occasion a group of French prisoners cut off the joints of their fingers to protest unbearable prison conditions. In the Scandinavian countries and in Holland, the law had provided that people convicted of sexual crimes may choose to undergo castration as an alternative to a prison sentence or as part of a shorter sentence. The punishment may be imposed only with the consent of the accused, sometimes even at his initiative. Giles Playfair and Derrick Sington describe implementation of the rule as follows:

> The pros and cons are fairly presented to [the offender]; he is fully forewarned of the consequences, including the possibly harmful ones to his physical health, and he is helped therapeutically to make up his own mind about accepting or rejecting those hazards. . . .
>
> But, of course, there is no denying that indirect pressure inevitably arises out of the very fact of his having been sentenced to indefinite preventive detention. His apparently free choice cannot be genuinely free under such circumstance. When a man expresses a "wish" to be castrated, realizing that otherwise he is likely to be kept looked up for the rest of his life, this, one suspects, may be nothing more than a cry of desperation. The point would be of less consequence if castration were generally accepted as a sound and beneficial treatment method in suitable cases.[51]

The writers note that castration is clearly illegal in Britain and has evoked critical response as being a punishment that involves mutilation, "a kind of half-killing." Yet they argue that "before castration or any similarly violent means of treatment can be rationally rejected, certain considerations ought to be taken into account."[52] For example, such punishment might be "an extraordinarily effective method of crime prevention"; in Denmark as high as 97 percent never repeat the offense.

Playfair and Sington conclude that it is not possible to ignore that

> violent sex offenders, who might otherwise have been incarcerated indefinitely, have been restored to freedom and have continued to live in freedom as a result of being asexualized by surgery. They are neither a threat to the community, nor a charge on it. . . .
>
> Under these circumstances it seems to us that a country such as Britain is in no position to condemn castration on humane grounds so long as it tolerates practices that are palpably less humane.

Would castration and early release of a sexual offender "be less humane than simply letting him rot in prison for the rest of his life or until such time as authority may feel satisfied that his deviant sexual drive has burned itself out?"[53]

Recently a choice between castration and a thirty-year sentence was presented in the United States to three rapists; after initial hesitation, all agreed to the former.[54] The law does not provide for punishment of this nature, and such cases clearly raise issues of its being cruel and unusual. However, this innovative approach to punishment was introduced in a novel way by a judge who made it a condition of probation, with the alternative for those who refused to agree, a heavy thirty-year sentence. Initially only one of the convicted gave his consent, whereas his co-accused took the case on appeal, together with the appeal of the prosecutor. While the appeal was pending, the other accused was kept in prison, and his request to have the terms of the sentence carried out was denied because of understandable doubts on the part of the authorities as to the legality of the proposed punishment. By the time the case came to appeal, the two appellants had changed their mind and decided to accept the offer, leaving the prosecutor as the sole party interested in hearing the appeal. At the appeal hearing, one of the judges gave expression to his surprise at the unusual form of punishment, but this idea was greeted by others with support, including some women's liberation groups. It should be remembered, however, that the crime is basically one of violence, not sex.[55] The final decision on appeal was to declare the punishment unconstitutional on a narrow 3–2 vote.[56]

There is no doubt that sexual mutilation, no less than corporal punishment, raises the issue of a torturous form of punishment. Yet it is not clear why this should be so. Inasmuch as the negative reaction would focus on the consequences, they are surely not much more severe than enforced abstinence from all normal sexual relations as a result of a lengthy prison sentence. Worse than this, the very denial of such sexual relations leads directly to one of the most difficult problems of prison, that of homosexual relations often based on coercion and abuse. A prisoner either succumbs to the temptation triggered by enforced heterosexual abstinence or becomes the victim of sexual violence, itself one of the cruelest and most deplorable aspects of prison life.[57]

One solution to the problem of sexual relations is to allow conjugal relationships. This has been tried with a fair degree of success in a number of prisons in South America, Scandinavia, and some states in the United States, but this possibility is denied in most jurisdictions. Those who object to the possibility of castration in lieu of part of a long prison sentence for a violent sexual crime should consider whether a lengthy prison sentence creates a better situation. James Jacobs and Eric Steele argue that the policy of sexual deprivation is "unjustly severe and destructive" and bemoan the fact that silence on this issue "gives the practice . . . the facade of principled policy."[58] Those who are concerned about the chosen alternative of castration in order to be free, might ponder the enforced imposition of sexual deprivation in prison.

Like other physical punishments, the idea of castration is not pleasant to contemplate—yet for years a similar act in a medical situation has been a widely accepted practice, namely, hysterectomy for women. There are many differences between the two in terms of function, consequences, sexual satisfaction, self-esteem; but there are also underlying similarities, for instance, the denial of procreative capacity, which should not be ignored. Recently, criticism has been voiced of the often casual manner in which gynecologists have suggested operations of this nature and on occasion carried them out without prior permission during the course of another operation.

Robert Mendelsohn,[59] himself a gynecologist, has noted that American surgeons performed almost 700,000 hysterectomies in 1979, of which only about a fifth could be considered to be justified and necessary "on the basis of life-threatening medical needs. That means that more than a half a million endured the operation for reasons that were frivolous at worst and dubious at best."[60] He quotes a leading official of the American Medical Association who argued that the general reasons for such an operation are either as a prophylactic against cancer in the future or as a convenient form of sterilization. Yet, the operation may be more dangerous than the purported cure—for, in 1975, more than 1,100 died from the procedure. On this basis Mendelsohn asks if women would "deliberately choose hysterectomy as a means of sterilization if they were told that the procedure is twenty times more likely to kill them than is a tubal ligation?"[61]

As to the sexual aspect, Mendelsohn quotes a study that found "reduced sexual drive in 60 percent of the women who have had their uterus and both ovaries removed. Others have reported that after hysterectomy from 20 to 42 percent of the women studied abstained from sexual intercourse." He goes on to argue that "much of the sexual dysfunction that propels women to psychiatrists and marriage clinics is a direct result of hysterectomy."[62]

The fact that women may have needlessly undergone hysterectomy—for exploitative reasons and under potentially dangerous circumstances—is no reason, in and of itself, to argue for castration of male sexual criminals. But it certainly puts the problem in a different perspective and raises serious questions as to the legitimacy of outright rejection of surgical procedures being carried out on convicted sexual criminals—on a voluntary basis and in lieu of a long prison sentence—when similar procedures with similar sexual consequences (and with far greater potential dangers) are being carried out regularly on women. Indeed, the male criminal may, under conditions of consent, be in a much better position than many of the women, who are not even fully apprised of the dangers of hysterectomy or of the advantages of alternative procedures for achieving prophylactic ends.

The possibility of castration as an alternative to prison, or at least part of the anticipated prison sentence, may not appear to be a particularly enlightened punishment; but, within the context that I have outlined, I doubt whether it could be considered to be torturous. It might even be chosen as preferable to a long sentence, which is what happened in the recent American case and happens in Scandinavia. As long as choice is provided, no matter how limited that choice, the question of the cruelty associated with a particular punishment takes on a new dimension. If the accused themselves prefer this alternative to prison, and assuming they are not masochists, then either castration is not cruel or a thirty-year sentence is. In either event, or when both apply, there is a need for a reassessment of penological policy in this matter.

A partial reassessment is already under way in the use of a drug, Depo-Provera, to control the sexual behavior of repeat sexual offenders. The use of the drug poses key issues that are the essence of the consideration in this chapter. Thus, although the drug is being used for therapeutic purposes, there are those who see its use as being punitive and, indeed, as constituting cruel and unusual punishment.

A recent article by Dennis Rainear brings out in all its fullness the ambiguity of meaning and the ambivalence of attitudes that revolve around the areas that touch on treatment and punishment, on medicine and penology.[63] He notes that the use of the drug decreases libidinal feelings and sexual capacities. As such, it has consequences similar to sterilization but without the permanence.

Under punitive conditions, the willingness to undergo treatment with the drug is sometimes made a condition of probation or parole. Discussing Fourth Amendment rights to privacy, and noting that some researchers have claimed that the drug may have adverse side effects, Rainear argues that "for repeat sex offenders where a propensity for unacceptable and uncontrollable sexual behavior is exhibited, it is not more violative of an individual's rights to be treated by the state with Depo-Provera than it is for the state to incarcerate him in an attempt to modify his behavior."[64] However, strong objection has been lodged as to the use of a drug in this fashion, since, it is claimed, the offenders are basically being coerced into agreeing to accept it. Thus he quotes Sidney Wolfe, who argues that the treatment "makes a mockery of the whole concept of informed consent when your option is to go to jail or get injected with a carcinogen that can increase the risk of heart attack."[65] As for the negative side effects, Rainear indicates that the most serious effects have not been proven, and notes that most medicinal drugs in any case tend to have some side effects.[66] As for the lack of informed consent, this is part of a much larger problem—it seems that the only way to resolve the issue would be to deny the offender any choice at all, and leave him with the imposed alternative of a long-term prison sentence. It is difficult to see what compelling advantages this denial of options has over the admitted problematics of ensuring informed consent within the framework of imposing a sentence.

Rainear also discusses the specific penological issue of whether the administration of the drug to a prisoner, a probationer, or a parolee, could be considered cruel and unusual.

Examining the precedents in point, he argues that the use of the drug seems to be clearly within the accepted guidelines, and adds: "As public opinion, scientific knowledge and technological capabilities change a court must be permitted to continually fashion humane justice, such as Depo-Provera treatments."[67]

Further, whereas some raise questions of cruel and unusual punishment, of due process, and of informed consent, others argue, conversely, that the drug's therapeutic qualities create a right to its use. Just such an argument was raised in an appeal against a prison sentence of twenty-five years to life imposed on a repeat sexual offender.[68] On the occasion of his first offense, he had been placed on probation after medical evidence had been submitted to court that he was liable to be helped by behavior modification, including the possibility of drug therapy. However, the doctor treating him chose an alternative therapy (insight therapy) that was apparently not successful; the offender subsequently committed further offenses for which he was given the aforementioned severe prison sentence. His plea that he had been denied the most effective therapy that was available (shades of informed consent!) was dismissed. However, the nature of his argument shows how one person's treatment may be another person's punishment.

In this context Rainear notes that divergence "may arise in the rights of sex offenders to receive Depo-Provera treatment depending on whether the individual is involuntarily incarcerated and committed to a Depo-Provera program or is offered the treatment as a condition of probation. While in prison the individual may have a right to treatment adequate to meet his personal medical needs, if any, but while on probation . . . he would not be constitutionally entitled to the most effective treatment."[69] Thus, the individual may have to reject offers of probation or parole in order to receive the drug treatment in prison—clearly an issue of coercion. All of which goes to show how tenuous is the distinction between punishment and treatment, between coercive penology and therapeutic medicine, between imposed sentence and informed consent.

Fundamental to our discussion is the issue of pain. There is a need to understand it in all its manifestations. At what stage does pain become cruel, at what stage does it constitute torture? The infliction of physical pain alone cannot provide an answer. It is the nature, the intensity, the prolongation that are of crucial importance. Chronic pain may be worse than acute pain. One of the ways of measuring would be to use a medical model—for it is a major part of medicine's task to prevent pain and to prolong life. An understanding of the aims and the functioning of medicine may prove enlightening for a study of penology. What penology aims to inflict, medicine aims to prevent. Therein lies a paradox, but also a clue to the permissible and the humane as well as to the limits of human endurance on the one hand, and of authoritative power on the other. We shall explore these factors in the next chapter.

12

THE MEDICAL MODEL

A T FIRST GLANCE it would seem that the medical model is almost the antithesis of the penological model; the former is oriented to healing, diminishing pain, and saving life; the latter to hurting, inflicting pain, and (occasionally) the taking of life. Yet, opposites are often also complementary to each other, serving as mirror images, reflecting parallel, if inverse, processes.

Beyond the obvious polarity, there are also important subtle similarities. Erving Goffman drew attention to one aspect of this similarity by discussing both correctional and medical institutions as two examples of total institutions. He showed how similar they were in their underlying rationale and in their everyday operations, with their control of all aspects of life.[1] But the similarities are more numerous than this—and more complex. Medical and legal authorities are confronted sometimes with similar dilemmas in extreme situations. Doctors not only save lives but also allow lives to be "taken"; judges or pardoning authorities may act to "save" lives that were condemned. Further, the legal and constitutional concepts of cruel, unusual, or inhumane punishments are often determined in terms of medical proof as to the pain and suffering sensed.

Whereas medical personnel have traditionally been present at legal executions mainly to determine the successful completion of the execution, medical means are now being used to implement executions. Conversely, medical decisions as to heroic efforts to save a patient or to "pull the plug" are often dependent upon prior—or subsequent—judicial approval.

Some medical procedures are declared at certain times to be illegal, for instance, abortion. The major argument against abortion is, of course, that it constitutes murder—and this against the most innocent and helpless of human creatures. If this argument is correct, then an ultimate penalty is perhaps called for. Yet despite the passion with which anti-abortionists argue this point, they have not, to my knowledge, demanded that the death penalty or life imprisonment be instituted for abortion.

Traditionally prisoners have been seen as being one of the most accessible and willing groups for medical research. Often participation in such programs serves as a means of earning credits for early release or confers benefits of better conditions (food, earnings, leisure), or is seen as a means of expiation. Yet, because of the coercive conditions of prison, arguments have been put forward that the willingness to be a human guinea pig cannot be considered as emanating from informed consent or altruistic volunteerism, and that the dependent position of the prisoner is exploited.[2] There have been those who have argued for a total ban. Though there are examples of abuses (as there are in many other aspects of prison life), the civil rights issue seems much more complex, involving the right of the prisoner to make decisions for himself, even when constrained by the conditions of prison.

In any case, a larger issue of medicine and law is looming, with the offer of a condemned person (the first woman to be executed after the end of the moratorium) for the parts of her body to be donated for organ transplant and for scientific research; and the suggestion (made contemporaneously, but independently) by a doctor in a medical journal that the organs of executed people should be made available for research and medical purposes in the light of the present shortage and the anticipated future needs.[3]

The prison environment causes, directly or indirectly, certain medical consequences—of deteriorating health, of geriatric problems for lifers, of mental illness, of suicide and attempted suicide—to the extent that the availability of medical treatment is an important factor in the daily running of the prison, and has, on occasion, become an issue when the conditions were challenged as being inhumane and therefore unconstitutional.[4]

Involuntary hospitalization, as in the case of mental patients, may bear some resemblance to imprisonment, requiring a judicial decision, involving interchange of ideas and interdependence of mutual responsibility between legal and medical experts, and resulting in similar consequences of long-term confinement, with occasional or even systematic mistakes and injustices. More specifically, Nicholas Kittrie has shown how therapeutic treatment may be used in the social control of deviants.[5]

Certain forms of medical treatment are also adaptable for the purpose of punishment. Thus, where practiced, the removal of a limb may be carried out as punishment, but amputation itself is a recognized medical procedure used in dire circumstance. The suggestion of castration for sexual offenders involves a procedure that bears some similarities to hysterectomies carried out on women. Some forms of torture are based on a certain understanding of physiological functioning. The question thus inevitably arises as to the implications of the differing meanings that may be assigned to a similar act.

These polarities and parallels in the areas of medicine and penology require further study, because deeper meanings may be ensconced in the attitudes adopted. Recently references have been made to the apparently paradoxical situation that some people who are most active in pro-life groups fighting abortion are in favor of the death penalty; yet, conversely, many abolitionists are supporters of, or at least tolerant of, abortion. Inasmuch as this is factually so, is there an inconsistency here or not? Does it tell us anything about the meaning to be attached to the concept of sanctity of life? Or does it tell us more about their overall ideological stance? In these issues, is life so important that abolitionists, by the very compelling logic of their argument, must also be pro-life on abortion, and pro-lifers must be concerned about the existence of a death

penalty—or are the situations so different (the fetus is innocent, the criminal is guilty; or, alternatively, the criminal has
foreknowledge of his fate, the fetus has no known consciousness) as to allow for different approaches to these problems without violating the canons of simple logic? At least one
group, Witness for Peace, has argued for consistency in these
matters, and their concern for sanctity of life is expressed equally
in their opposition to abortion and capital punishment as well
as war. It may well be that only a pacifist may, in all consistency and sincerity, be a total abolitionist.

In his work on penology, Gabriel Tarde drew parallels between attitudes to war and to capital punishment, calling on
the need for the finer feelings of "intellectual and moral culture"
to prevail over the "indignation" felt by the crowd. There is
a need to resist "the cries of honest rage which demand the
death of a guilty man as well as the attacks of blind patriotism
which drive a nation into war." He adds:

> The question whether in fact the death penalty can be en-
> tirely done away with and the question as to whether war
> between civilized nations can entirely disappear are almost
> of the same order and ought to be solved by means of
> analogous considerations. So true is this that the interrup-
> tion and then the retrogression of the abolitionist current
> have coincided in our century with the objectionable return
> to militarism in 1870.[6]

Recently, Margaret Radin has similarly drawn parallels between the life-and-death question of capital punishment and
life-and-death questions relating to general social welfare, seeing even that the involvement in the capital punishment debate
may serve to help distract "from the real tragedy of widespread
suffering." She suggests that racism and poverty may be worse
than capital punishment. "Think of the suffering and death,"
she challenges, "because of inadequate prenatal care, inadequate

nutrition for children, inadequate shelter, etc. Think of the suicides as well as the homicides. The magnitude of social evil in our tolerance of these conditions our society could alleviate if it chose is far greater than the evils assumed by those on either side of the execution debate if the other side should prevail.''[7]

Arising out of these and related questions, are there reasons to compare the medical and the penological situations, and what are the implications for so doing? Specifically, it is possible to appreciate some of the finer and more subtle aspects of the penological debate, particularly inasmuch as they pertain to civil rights, by using the medical model as a touchstone—of knowledge, of sensitivity, of insight? Inasmuch as there are parallels, are the conclusions to be drawn of an identical nature; if there are differences; are there lessons to be learned?

I believe that penologists have much to gain by testing their theses and their practices against the experiences of the medical model. Therein lie perhaps hidden truths and sober realities that can affect and influence our ideas in penology. The doctor, stethoscope in hand, informing the executioner that the execution has been successful, is symbolic of the overlap between these penological and medical models. Alternatively, the revulsion with which humanity reacts to torture is matched by the commitment with which it responds to the alleviation of suffering.

In his utopian novel, *Erehwon,* Samuel Butler did indeed reverse the roles of criminality and illness, of punishment and treatment.[8] It was the ill who were considered deviant and in need of punishment; it was the criminal who aroused pity and was given treatment. In some totalitarian societies, political criminals are declared to be mentally ill, this being an easier way to undermine their ideas than prison. Persons suffering from leprosy (known as Hansen's disease so as to avoid the stigma attached to its traditional name) are still the ultimate deviants, shunned and shunted off as few criminals are.[9]

Restrictions on the right to certain privileges, such as the acquisition of citizenship, are often based on both prior criminal record and prior medical illnesses.

Whatever parallels there may have been in the past, the advances in medical technology in recent years have created a vastly changed set of circumstances for any discussion of life and death—of the determination of death and the sanctity of life, or the dignity of death and the quality of life.

When abolitionists do speak in terms of the sanctity of life, they are obliged to enquire whether similar criteria are applicable to what some consider a living creature, such as a fetus, even if not yet fully formed as a person and even if not independently viable. Further, if abolitionists speak in the name of the dignity of the individual as an argument against the death penalty, they are obliged to enquire as to the dignity accorded a person in other circumstances, not just in prison for example, but in other total institutions, and not just in terms of the lack of dignity attendant upon an execution, but the manner in which society in general attempts to ensure a dignified death, for instance, in a hospital setting for terminal patients.

And, conversely, diametrically opposite postulates must be applied when working from the medical model back to penology. If abortion is allowed in society, then already a serious reservation may have been made to the doctrine of the sanctity of life. The fact that the legality of abortion may be logically justified does not diminish the fact that there is the termination of a potential being. If society is willing to do so in the case of an innocent being yet in utero, it may be able also to do so in the case of a convicted criminal, or else show, which may be possible, the reasons that would justify the distinction between the two. But at the least, the issue must be addressed.

If society, in its determination to keep terminal and comatose patients alive, affects also the dignity of their death and the manner in which they and those close to them prepare for and accept the inevitable, then we may have to revise our concepts as to the lack of dignity in the death sentence. For the problem of the dignity of death is not a problem unique to penology and should be resolved on a far larger scale.

The medical model may, in any case, have a contrary message—that the importance of forestalling death and prolonging life is of such paramount importance that these factors take precedence over safeguarding the dignity of the individual. If that is so, if life itself, as physical existence, is so central to our concerns, then there must surely be some relevance in that stance for the death penalty, specifically, that such a stance should deny also the right to take a life.

Even so, the real answer as to the circumstances and the conditions of life and death—whether in a medical or penological framework—may be neither the sanctity of life nor the dignity of death alone but more defined areas of concern, which may affect both the penological and the medical model. I would suggest the ideas of *pain* and *meaning*. These ideas, particularly the former, are of no small relevance already, but there is a need to focus on them more clearly and precisely. Simply put, the aim of society, in terms of questions of life and death, should be, *inter alia,* to ensure for its members a life free from pain and full of meaning.

These are obviously optimal conditions. When a person is punished, a certain amount of pain is caused, but it must be kept within reasonable limits, for instance, not to be cruel. But when pain becomes intense and not avoidable in the foreseeable future, or when meaninglessness becomes too prevalent and all-encompassing, then serious questions are posed, which cannot always be encompassed by the standard phraseology of the sanctity of life. The key to most of the issues of life and death is neither the sanctity of life per se nor the irreversibility and tragedy of death, but the quality of life (free of pain and full of meaning) and the process of dying (when possible, a meaningful farewell and a painless parting).

Looking at the problem from another perspective, if medicine (or society's directive to medicine) refuses to allow the suffering terminal patient or the incapacitated comatose patient whose wishes are known the chance to choose whether to end his life, then it is not surprising that criminals are not granted a similar kind of choice. If doctors fight by heroic means to save lives, even against the patient's wish, then it is not surprising that civil rights activists should ignore the criminal's wish to be put to death if so be his wish. This was recently expressed by Judge Warriner in rejecting a petition by a condemned person's lawyer a few days before the execution: "We are performing the legal equivalent of inserting tubes . . . into him so that we can satisfy the quite appropriate urge to save his life, not so much for the good it does the client, but for the good it does us."[10]

YET THE TRUTH OF THE MATTER is that although some of the above approaches reflect the practice of several years ago and the major trend of today, other considerations are being increasingly activated. The great advances in medical technology have perforce created new problems for doctors and fostered a new awareness of the issues among the public. The members of the medical profession are increasingly realizing that the prolongation of life cannot be seen outside the context of pain and meaning, even if the problem has not been articulated exactly in such a fashion.

Interestingly enough, some rights of patients have been established not by developing medical understanding, but by activist judicial injunction. This is particularly the case in the United States, where both the high rate of medical progress and the known propensity for litigation have led to a number of key changes in recent years. From the perspective of my thesis, what is most interesting is the evidence of pain and suffering, sometimes physical, sometimes mental, sometimes both.

Perhaps the most significant case is the recent attempt by a quadriplegic patient, Elizabeth Bouvia, to embark on a course of action to end her life.[11] In this case, the issue is the right to die of a person neither comatose nor terminally ill, vis-à-vis the right of society and the medical authorities to preserve life even against the person's wish. On several occasions, she has sought judicial help to achieve this end and to evade the medical procedures of her doctors aimed at thwarting her openly expressed and clearly articulated desires. On the first occasion, she asked for the hospital to stop feeding her, so that she might be allowed to die. The court rejected her plea, holding that there was a need to preserve life, and to assure the best medical treatment. Later, she went on a hunger strike, refusing to eat the food given her, at which hospital authorities began to force-feed her. She once again sought help in the court to have force-feeding (which is a painful procedure) stopped. This time, the court held in her favor, though not directly recognizing her right to end her life. However, her problems were not resolved, for when she asked to be given sufficiently large doses of morphine to ease her hunger pains, the doctors refused on the grounds that such drugs in large doses were meant for terminal patients, which she was not.

Sometimes the evidence of medical ambivalence in the face of the suffering of patients emerges from cases never challenged in the courts but reported in the press. One of the most poignant reports was of a patient in a state of extreme ill-health because of the culmination of five different illnesses. He was in control of his faculties and capable of articulating his desires. According to a *New York Times* report, he pleaded with his medical personnel to desist from all efforts on his behalf and to allow his death, which alone could end his sufferings.[12] His lawyer claimed that "the hospital is inflicting a living hell on this man. They have sentenced him to death prolonged as long as medically possible." At times they even tied his hands to prevent him committing suicide by pulling out the tubes. His intended legal battle became moot when he died before his legal rights vis-à-vis those treating him could be adjudicated.

A further moving account is given by the daughter of a patient. She describes her desperate efforts to convince the doctors that there was no point in their attempts to keep her father alive in a state in which he had almost no awareness of what was happening, and of how she attempted to communicate to him the fact that she was not neglecting his needs but doing her best to release him from the agony of the medical struggle to ward off the death that alone could bring him succour.[13] She writes that a medical bill received after her father's death for twenty thousand dollars seems to indicate that the need to recoup the investment in sophisticated technology might well have played some part in the consideration of the medical personnel. In this case, too, her efforts to have the issue decided in the courts were preempted by her father's death.

It seems to me that such "heroic" efforts by the medical profession, even against the wishes of the patient and those closest to him, reflect similar efforts by civil rights activists to avert the judicial decrees of death when the condemned person accepts the death penalty. Of course, in this case the client, unlike the patient, is not physically in a terminal state, but his psychological suffering, specifically because it is potentially so prolonged, may also be severe. In both cases the right of the affected person to determine his fate is being denied.

Within a liberal context, this right of autonomous decision as to one's very life seems to go to the heart of the matter. Liberal thought clearly recognizes, for the most part, the right to suicide (and most modern states affirm such an approach in their legislation). Liberal thought, in theory, tends also to support arguments for euthanasia, at least the passive kind, though here there is little legislative recognition nor, for that matter, a firm and principled stand on this issue by academicians or politicians.

Indeed, euthanasia raises very serious issues for liberal philosophy, for often its illegality involves denying to the most helpless of human beings—such as persons paralyzed, who may be in pain and for whom life in this restricted form has become meaningless—the simple right to decide to end their agony, a right which, ever since suicide was made legal, is recognized for all able-bodied people. Inasmuch as the essence of the liberal philosophy is to allow the citizen freedom of action and control over this destiny consonant with allowing others similar rights, it would seem that the right to euthanasia, to what the Greeks called a "painless death," to choose the moment and the form of one's death, may be considered an emerging human right, one which has been hitherto denied in modern Western civilization.[14]

The impact of religion provides much of the understanding for the traditional approach of Western civilization—briefly, that one's life on earth is a gift of God, that one's soul is derived from Him and will return to Him, and that we accordingly lack the freedom to make conscious decisions as to the moment of departure from this world. Secular liberal thought (as well as some modern liberal theology) is not bound by such a framework of thought, yet it has, as an overall thesis, failed to formulate a comprehensive approach to the topic. The great modern liberal thinkers have largely ignored it—among philosophers it is mainly those of Greek and Roman times, Socrates and Seneca, for example, who dealt seriously with the problem and favored such a right.[15]

The full meaning of a denial of this right to euthanasia— particularly pertinent for the thesis of pain and meaningfulness—is that in those instances (and they are becoming increasingly prevalent, though full statistics are not available) when doctors evince a willingness to allow nature to take its own course—or a court gives prior approval for such an approach—the most that is allowed is a passive withdrawal of aid or perhaps "double effect" treatment, when pain-killer drugs also have the secondary effect of hastening death. Yet positive steps taken specifically and primarily to hasten the death that is considered inevitable are not allowed. How insistent society is on this distinction between act and omission may be learned from the strong reaction, including indictment for murder, against those few medical personnel who, generally out of deep human compassion, have taken actual steps (sometimes no more than a deliberate over-dose of a drug) to bring about a speedy death.[16]

As long as death is the major concern, then attempts to prevent it will be the main aim. But if the focus were shifted to the problem of pain and meaningfulness, other options become feasible and reasonable.

Indeed, perhaps there is nothing worse than the compromise solution that seems to be emerging—in which doctors cease their active efforts to maintain life, but refuse to hasten death. By allowing nature to take its course and no more, they may be prolonging and even accentuating the pain. Once the decision is made to end the active aid, society should have the courage and the consistency to allow the positive pursuit of a rapid and peaceful death, for, after all, the active aid efforts were stopped specifically to allow death to take place. Why then, by default, prolong the dying process and the accompanying agony?

As some medical doctors and many specialists in bioethics are arguing, there is a need to recognize a right to die. In many respects the present situation may be the worst of all possible solutions; the law sanctions acts of omission to allow for an early death, but prohibits any direct acts of deliberate intent to hasten the desired and anticipated death.

Doctors are being increasingly put in precarious positions when the validity of their treatment depends not only on their medical expertise and their personal and professional perceptions of what empathetic humanity demands, but on judicial determination of whether the treatment constitutes an act, in the legal sense, or an omission, in which the former may constitute an act of murder, and the latter have no criminal consequences whatsoever. Peter MacKinnon, for instance, discusses what he terms "true omission," which "typically are bystander cases: an observer watches and does nothing as a respirator malfunctions and the patient dies. Though the philosophers remind us that his inaction may be no less reprehensible than disconnecting the respirator or causing it to malfunction, in general he is not liable." He concludes that in most situations killing is worse than "permitting death to occur."[17]

I would argue that this narrow distinction between an act and an omission is in these kinds of cases often irrelevant; that as a general rule it is undesirable; and that for the specific purposes of our debate, any distinction that is drawn may actually make the omission the more reprehensible. The distinction is irrelevant because in most medical situations the observer has, or should have, a legal duty to act, the patient being totally dependent on the capacity of the medical personnel to keep him alive (and it could, of course, be that the malfunction may be of a machine when the patient wishes to live). It is undesirable because it may be an unfortunate lacuna of the Anglo-American law that it fails to recognize a duty to rescue or offer aid on the part of observers when the danger to a potential or actual victim is great, and the inconvenience to the bystander insignificant, this being generally the legal situation in other jurisdictions such as in Europe and Asia.[18]

I make these two points merely to clarify an overall situation. For the specific examples given are not necessarily applicable to my intention in regard to the problem of the terminal or comatose patient dependent on life-support systems. I would argue that there should, firstly, be no distinction between the two situations—of act or omission—and that, secondly, there should be no culpability for either in certain clearly and carefully defined situations, namely, when there is the agreement of the patient or those acting on his behalf and the intent is to hasten death. In such circumstances, it might be the omission which is the least satisfactory, for though allowing death to be hastened, it would not do so in the most rapid and desirable manner.

One obvious argument for what is in essence active euthanasia is that the patient ought to be allowed final respite from his pain and suffering. Of a different order would be an approach based on the second criterion of a meaningful life, to which might be added the prospect of a meaningful death.

As the work of Elisabeth Kubler-Ross and others has indicated,[19] there is a dying process, which can, and should, be made beautiful and meaningful, but which cannot become so as long as death is seen as an evil to be warded off for as long as possible, including the use of new sophisticated instruments and the heroic efforts of medical personnel. What is needed is the possibility of allowing people a pleasant and meaningful farewell from this earth, whenever possible.

Instead of seeing death as a threat to be thwarted as long as possible, we need to forego the essentially Sisyphus-like strivings of heroic medical measures for a means of allowing those, terminally ill or in constant pain, a graceful exit from this world if they so desire. In many respects it is strange that the norms of society provide for all sorts of meaningful and memorable rites of passage, yet for death only after the demise, for the mourners but not the deceased; and that society decrees that people partake of a farewell from each other at significant times—leaving home, going off to college, to war, on journeys—yet in the fear of death, our taboo on it, our fight against it, we often deny the opportunity for this final farewell in a meaningful, compassionate way. This is indeed the real meaning of euthanasia, a pleasant death, and it goes beyond the alternative term of mercy-killing. Parenthetically, it may be noted that one of the advantages of life-supporting systems is to enable a person to be kept alive until such time as all the necessary farewells have been said, something of particular importance in the modern mobile society, when family and friends may be far away.

Instead of the anguish of waiting for the moment when the dying person finally expires, it should be possible by direct action and through deliberate intent for a time to be set aside for a final and meaningful farewell. In this sense, then, the act of commission becomes not a crime, but a desirable aim, whereas the omission of merely allowing the death to take place is the less desirable situation.

At present the only legal way of achieving such an end is through the act of suicide. In reality, of course, most suicides are not carried out under such circumstances, but emanate from a life of torment, of loneliness, of meaninglessness, or of passing crisis. In any event, if others are participants in any way at such an act, they may even find themselves criminally liable as aiders or abettors to an act which in itself is not criminal.

What has all of this to do with capital punishment? MacKinnon has pointed out, in the context of differentiating between euthanasia and suicide, that

> our attitudes to euthanasia are necessarily affected by our feelings about suicide. Indeed the morality of the latter is a threshold question in the morality of the former. If it is concluded that any suicide is morally intolerable, it is impossible to make a case for voluntary euthanasia or as it may be called, "agent suicide." If on the other hand it is morally acceptable for one to bring an end to his life in some circumstances, *a fortiori* there can be no moral fault in his refusal of life-saving aid so that he may die, and we can then enquire whether it should make any difference that he seeks his end at the hand of another.[20]

If this be so, and I would endorse this position, then recognition of a person's right to be put to death on request suggests similar possibilities for those accused of extreme crimes and subject to ultimate penalties.

Should a right granted to a patient be denied a condemned prisoner, who under the conditions of constant surveillance and limited access may not be able to perform an act of suicide, and certainly not under conditions of meaningful leave-taking? Those who argue in the name of the sanctity of life and the

dignity of the human being for total abolition of the death penalty are, in essence, arguing for a position which would by
the same logic deny the right to suicide and the right to
euthanasia. The first right has been conceded by most modern
liberal societies (thereby undermining one of Beccaria's strongest
arguments against the death penalty).[21] The latter is still forbidden, yet is being practiced in a *sub rosa* manner, which, though
perhaps alleviating the pain, denies the meaningful death. Since
the arguments for euthanasia are based on consensual acts, there
seems to be no reason why a similar argument could not be
applied in the case of those convicted of capital crimes, allowing the convicted person the choice to determine whether he
wishes the pain of prolonging his life under conditions of incarceration or the alternative of an early death.

Once suicide is allowed, the issue of the sanctity of life
takes on a different perspective—as MacKinnon argues,
euthanasia then becomes morally permissible—and I would
argue, so does capital punishment, *as long as the conditions
of a consensual act are maintained.* For passive euthanasia,
certainly consent is essential—by request of the patient through
a prior living will, by a guardian acting on behalf of a comatose
patient—all subject to possible judicial review.

Beyond that, I believe that in the course of time active
euthanasia will become both morally possible and legally acceptable. For as family members, medical personnel, and
bioethicists battle over the present alternatives—maintaining
a person on life-support systems (which may include support
as basic as food and fluids) in a meaningless, vegetative state,
perhaps for years or even decades, or withdrawing them (which
may involve consequences as disturbing as starving the patient
to death and waiting for days or perhaps even weeks or longer
for him to die)—sooner or later, some lawyer will argue and
some court accept, the proposition that the most humane and
decent solution may be to peacefully, but actively, bring about
his death after allowing those close to him a meaningful and
dignified farewell.[22] In fact, the present emerging position seems

to be the worst of all alternatives—namely, to allow the removal of sophisticated life-sustaining equipment or the denial of simple sustenance such as food, with the sole intention of letting death take place, but then refusing to help deliberately and actively hasten that death, even though the prolongation of life may be painful and torturous, and even though the special last farewell may thereby be denied. These issues have till now been a debate carried on by doctors, jurists, philosophers, bioethicists, and other medical personnel, but they may well become a larger political issue. Efforts are now being made to have a right-to-die initiative put on the California ballot in the 1988 elections by a group known as Americans Against Human Suffering.[23]

If and when a dignified death becomes a moral and legal option, it will affect our whole conception of the sanctity of life—not undermine it, but provide it with new contextual considerations. If full compassion leads us to permit the comatose or terminal patient to be released—by dying—from the imprisonment that his physical situation imposes on him, then similar considerations may apply when a prisoner would wish to exercise his option—as some do—of terminating their lives rather than suffer interminably the constraints of prison and perhaps lengthy solitary confinement.

We are moving slowly but ineluctably—precipitated inevitably by the advances of medical technology—to a position in which the dignity of death will be juxtaposed to the sanctity of life. Under these circumstances, if death is to be imposed on prisoners, then certainly the means sought must be, not those that attempt only to minimize the pain, but those that also maximize the dignity. It is at that stage that medical executions may well be preferable. In any event, the condemned person should be allowed to choose. The doctor—in a hospital or prison—will have to accept that he may no longer take shelter behind a Hippocratic oath that forces him to seek to evade death, but may have to take courage and inspiration from the same oath that commits him to avoid pain and suffering.

Within the prison system itself this may involve a host of new problems. First and foremost, assuming, on the one hand, a right to active euthanasia and, on the other hand, a willingness to allow capital punishment based on autonomous choice, would doctors be entitled to take part in such a process in order to ensure the most painless and most dignified death process, that through drugs and injection? A new trend of this nature has recently developed, and several states in the United States now use lethal injections as their form of execution. The medical profession has reacted sharply to this trend and rejected outright active participation of medical personnel in these procedures.

Official pronouncements on behalf of medical bodies have been made, claiming that such involvement is a gross violation of medical ethics, and calls have gone out to doctors to refrain from participation.[24] Yet to the best of my knowledge no similar statements have been made as to the presence and indirect participation of doctors during executions of a violent type—hanging, electrocution, gassing, shooting, etc.—when doctors are required to confirm the fact of death. Their position as passive bystanders to a coercive killing (unless the condemned person is desirous of ending his life) can become acutely invidious when the execution process itself is marred by fault. In such circumstances, the doctor is required to check whether death has finally taken place, whether a further ''dose'' of whatever means was being employed will complete the process, or whether medical considerations dictate that the process be halted, the condemned person be tended to and revived to face the same process at another date. On at least one occasion, pain-killing drugs were administered to the condemned person to ease his pain as the execution was held up and the necessary rectifications made.[25]

It seems to me that an active medical role in hastening and easing the death process is perfectly compatible with basic humanistic considerations—certainly in the case of euthanasia and, as an extension thereof, in the case of consensual capital punishment. There are those who refer to this as state-aided suicide, in a negative sense. Yet, it may be seen in different terms; certainly, if desired, it is preferable to state-imposed confinement until ultimate death. In fact, what does seems to be untenable is the situation just described—of a doctor's passive presence at the site of an execution, when a person against his volition is brought to the death chamber. There is, of course, legal basis for the execution, but that does not automatically obligate the doctor to be present and the medical profession to be silent. In any event, lethal injections also take place based on law. Why then, one may ask, object to the procedure only because it is the doctor who is called upon to do the "dirty" work, especially when by so doing he makes it a bit "cleaner," that is, easier for the condemned person?

If the doctor is indeed present at the execution, is he entitled to intervene in order to help the condemned person cope with his ordeal—by giving him drugs or an injection to calm him, and to numb any anticipated pain at the moment of execution? Descriptions of the last minutes in the cell and of the procession to the place of execution indicate a very active role for the clergy, but no such provisions are made for active participation of medical personnel to help through drugs or verbal therapy.

Some condemned people go proudly and surely to their death, but some cringe or resist, collapse or scream. Few descriptions are as disturbing and horrendous as that of Aaron Mitchell, the last person to be executed before the moratorium in 1967. According to Burton Wolfe's account,[26] Mitchell had been a model prisoner and had been presciently perceptive (in terms of later research and court decisions) as to the death penalty being cruel and unusual, and in violation of due process, not least because it was being imposed on him, a black man, in a discriminatory manner. Be that as it may, from being a model prisoner, Mitchell became desperate, violently resisted the guards when they came to dress him on the day prior to the execution, and had to be strapped into a wheelchair. The following day when the guards came to take him to the gas chamber, the was delirious, shouted out that he was Jesus, and stood like a crucifix.

What was, or should have been the role of a medical doctor in such circumstances; was he obliged to intervene? Was Mitchell fully in control of his senses; was he even legally sane? In conditions of war there are situations in which medical personnel may override the commanding officer. Should a similar possibility not be available for medical personnel as against the commands of a prison warden carrying out the order of a court?

It seems to me that objections by the medical profession to an active role in a legal, painless death but allowing a passive role in a legal, violent death are part of the same approach that characterizes their attitude toward euthanasia. Further, it seems to me that civil activists should at least accept the execution by lethal injection—so that if all their efforts to save a life fail, they can at least ensure that the act of execution will be a minimum violation of the dignity of the condemned person, and should actively work to make sure that it is so. It is true that by making an execution ostensibly more palatable the abolitionist argument is possibly weakened, but if an execution cannot be avoided, humanistic considerations dictate that the least offensive form of execution be used. As already noted, even Albert Camus, in his eloquent statement against the death penalty, took cognizance of a requested lethal drug, suggesting even that it be self-administered.[27]

SIMILAR PROBLEMATICS apply in the case of torture. Here, too, the medical personnel in a prison system are placed in an invidious position, where they may be torn between their humanitarian and professional obligation to alleviate suffering and their involvement in the aiding and abetting of torture.

Amnesty International has been in the forefront of the struggle to raise awareness of the existence of torture and the means of coping with it, including providing special therapeutic facilities for the treatment of victims of torture and sponsoring research in this area. Under their auspices, Alfred Heider and Herman van Geins have formulated a professional code of ethics.[28] In a preamble, they describe the various methods in which medical personnel participate in the administration of torture—performing examinations on suspects prior to an interrogation which might include torture, attending torture sessions to check on the victim's health and to intervene to halt the torture when the victim's life seems endangered, treating the victim for the harm suffered (often mainly for the purpose of enabling him to be exposed, after recovery, to further torture), and even themselves using medical techniques, including psychiatric persuasion, to help in the interrogation.

In 1975 the medical profession issued the Declaration of Tokyo, which states, *inter alia,* that "the doctor shall not provide any premises, instruments, substances or knowledge to facilitate the practice of torture or other forms of cruel, inhuman or degrading treatment or to diminish the ability of the victim to resist such treatment. . . . The doctor shall not be present during any procedure during which torture or other forms of cruel, inhuman or degrading treatment is used or threatened."[29]

Matthew Lippman examines the inevitable conflict of interests that arises in such cases.[30] For though the prohibition on any sort of role—primary or secondary—must obviously be clearly articulated, the dilemma still exists as to a doctor's response when, without his collusion, torture takes place and he is then asked to alleviate the suffering, especially when he knows that such therapeutic treatment may be only a prelude to a hastened renewal of the torture. "A conflict may arise . . . where a doctor is asked to care for a victim of torture knowing that the victim's recovery may only lead to the victim's being exposed to additional torture. In addition, the victim may prefer to die rather than be exposed to further torture and risk divulging important information." He adds that psychiatrists "may be able to protect individuals from torture by cajoling such individuals into confessing or divulging the desired information."[31]

Two essential points should be made as to this last point. First, the protection that a psychiatrist may offer by cajoling potential victims of physical torture is similar to the alternating techniques used by the torturers themselves. If they wish to cajole, they surely do not need the trained expertise of a psychiatrist, but may use their own tried and tested methods. Second, when the suspect does surrender to such cajoling, there is a danger that, saved from the acute pain of immediate physical torture, he may subsequently suffer from the chronic pain of prolonged mental torture at the remorse and the sense of failure, especially in political offenses, when he may seriously undermine the cause on whose behalf he had worked and may have betrayed his former comrades.

Lippman goes on to draw attention to a serious deficiency in the declaration: it imposes no affirmative duty on doctors to report their knowledge of torture to appropriate bodies, neither national nor international, neither legal nor medical. This failure seems to echo previous examples that have been presented in other contexts, when unimpeachable statements of intent are devoid of reality or of any practical means of endorcing remedies.

It certainly is possible to conceive of a situation in which a doctor may, despite his loathing for the situation, use his medical expertise to aid a torture victim. It may be debatable whether the doctor should do so, but surely there can be no question as to the need to report, whether after helping or refusing to do so. It should be noted that in child abuse cases, doctors, together with other professionals—teachers, social workers, nurses—may be obliged to report suspicions of child abuse.[32] Why should there not be a similar obligation in law, by international convention or by professional decree?

Lawyers may confront a similar situation, complicated by their need to act in the best interests of their client, whose prospects may actually be harmed by such reporting—for example, a vindictive, heavier sentence may result if he is not believed, or further increased torture may occur on his return to the secrecy of prison. Yet a joint declaration drafted by Amnesty International and the International Commission of Jurists obligates lawyers to report "fully and fearlessly" to responsible authorities, to their professional organization, or to the mass media.[33]

Medical personnel encounter similar delicate problems in a prison setting when dealing with the possibilities of performing research on prisoners. To what extent can they ensure that an agreement to be a subject for such research flows from informed consent and is offered without duress or coercive overtones, when the result of such volunteerism is liable to be improved conditions in prison and enhanced prospects for early release? The problem is certainly rendered more complicated by virtue of the fact that in the past there have been serious abuses of the limited liberty and rights of prisoners and their consequent susceptibility to tempting propositions.

Yet the problematics of the situation do not lead necessarily to an absolute prohibition. In some respects the prisoner volunteering for medical research is under no worse constraints than a patient—terminally ill or in acute pain—who is desperately anxious to be a guinea pig in the sanguine expectation that he will gain a respite or a cure. For all the strict standards as to informed consent, some patients will possibly put aside lingering doubts in their eagerness to clutch at any possibility.

Richard Titmuss describes the altruism of many patients willing to be the subjects of medical experimentation in order for medical progress to take place.[34] Why should similar utilitarianism or similar altruism be denied to prisoners? In fact, the possibility of volunteering for medical research is often, far from being coercive and under duress, one of the most autonomous decisions that a particular prisoner can make, especially because by so doing he has the capacity to directly affect his personal fate, both as to living conditions (including remuneration) and as to parole prospects.[35] Further, outside of prison there are those who offer to participate in research under conditions that are often coercive; people of poor economic background may be enticed by pecuniary reward or the hope of receiving better treatment to expose themselves to potential health risks in the framework of medical research.

Related to this issue, but even more complicated and delicate, is the right and the ability of persons condemned to death to take part in such research and related procedures. Can any expressed desire to be part of a research program be considered legitimate? What if the condemned person was seeking a means of expiation for his crime?

Recently, a woman sentenced to death underwent a religious conversion while she and her family and lawyer battled desperately till the last moment to gain a pardon (much of it based on her own rehabilitation through religion); she also offered, impelled by the same religious commitment, that her body should be used for medicine.[36] Should her request have been denied because it might be considered to be given under duress, or because, in the past, there were so many instances of the abuse of an executed person's body? The donation of organs after death certainly seems prima facie to be easier to accept than volunteering for research while yet alive, for it seems to be totally devoid of any irrelevant motives. Yet here, too, problems lurk. For the shortage of organs and the advances of medical technology raise the possibility of determining dates and places of executions to suit the needs of medical treatment. Almost simultaneously with the woman prisoner's request, a doctor made a suggestion of this type in a leading professional journal, *MD*.[37] He claims that he has had about thirty verbal and written offers by prisoners to donate organs, and argues that when a condemned person volunteers to donate organs, the medical profession should be prepared to accept them, though at present they seem unwilling to do so.

Once again, it seems to me that the solution for these kinds of issues is that of choice. There seems to be no reason why the possibility of such donation of organs or of participation in research should not be made known to the condemned person. But, as with all other choice possibilities in the penal system, care will have to be taken to avoid coercion—perhaps the agreement could be made contingent on judicial approval.

In the past there have been instances of serious abuse. Thus, in France, King Louis XI had argued, according to George Bishop, that there was "no reason . . . why a condemned criminal's life should be taken without allowing the man to make some contribution to science."[38] This much is perhaps acceptable, at least contingent on consent. However, Bishop goes on to relate that the king would sometimes go to visit a condemned prisoner in the company of a physician who would dissect the prisoner and explain anatomy to the king in the process. Similarly, in Britain there were occasional scandals arising from the attempts of hospitals to get hold of bodies of condemned persons before the family could, so that they could use them for the purpose of dissection.[39] It should, however, be noted that there were also instances of body-snatching from graves in cemeteries and of the use of bodies of the poor or of orphans; and there was one instance in which two people in Scotland committed murders in order to provide bodies for anatomy to hospitals and universities.[40]

Abuses of the past and of more recent times[41] of prisoners exploited for the purposes of research, some of them contracting illnesses induced in them, should make us cautious and wary—but need not deny outright the possibility of properly regulated contributions by prisoners, including those condemned to death. Medical research requires close monitoring at all times to avoid abuse; the Helsinki Declaration imposes limits and guidelines. There seems no reason why an even stricter interpretation of these rules, perhaps done under judicial surveillance, or at least by an ombudsman authority, should not provide sufficient protection for prisoners.

Let it be emphasized that the advantages to be derived for science, for medicine, and for humanity are only a part of the considerations. Other aspects are the right of the prisoner to make a utilitarian calculation for his own benefit and his right to be free to be altruistic if he so desires.

13

REVENGE AND RETALIATION

IN THE BEGINNING was revenge. The most primitive societies—or perhaps pre-societies—were characterized by the fact that harm-doing generally provoked a like response by the victim or his closest kin. Sometimes, especially when the precipitating act was a killing, acts of retaliation would burgeon into an ongoing and escalating vendetta, with loss of life on both sides. Some of the strongest pressures for setting up an ordered society arose from the need to curb and control these deep-seated impulses. Indeed, although the general picture of primitive socities is of a society in which the blood-feud is the norm, there is much historical data to indicate that, at a very early stage, more viable measures were sought for resolving problems of harm-doing.[1]

Long before centralized organs were set up to impose order, fairly clear normative patterns were laid down as to how redress was to be exacted for harm inflicted, ranging from a fixed rate of monetary compensation to rituals of expiation, forgiveness, and peace-making. In general, blood money was preferred to blood letting, reconcilation to retaliation.

From a theoretical point of view, social contract theories, for instance, of Hobbes, are based on hypothetical descriptions of people voluntarily surrendering part of their freedom in order to ensure their security.[2] Freud's controversial explanation of the origins of society is based on his applying an oedipal perspective to describe a hypothetical situation in antiquity in which the primal sons conspire and join together to kill their father; then, fearful of mutual recriminations for this crime, they band together again, this time for mutual protection, to avoid potential fratricidal strife.[3] Modern minimalistic theories of the state[4] generally concede that one of the few unavoidable functions of a state is its policing activities and the administration of criminal justice. (Some libertarian writers, however, are seeking to minimize even these functions, and certain recent developments—of private police, of alternative dispute resolution frameworks, of commercial corrective institutions—make for inroads into state functions.)[5]

Emerging out of these various developments and conceptions, revenge is widely regarded as a relic of primitive times and is rejected as a legitimate aim of modern penal theory; indeed, retributionist theorists are at great pains to show that their theory is based on a clear-cut perception of what justice is and does not pander to the demands for revenge.[6] Yet there can be no doubt that the need for revenge runs very deeply through society, and finds outlet and expression ranging from military measures undertaken by total societies against their enemies, to the isolated acts of groups, or even individuals, self-righteously arrogating to themselves the right and duty to put evildoers in their place.

A recent example occurred in New York City. Bernhard Goetz, on being accosted in the subway by four youths demanding money, drew a gun and shot each of them, injuring all, one of them severely, an act debatedly done in self-defense, or as seems more likely, conceived and planned beforehand as a counter to any contingencies.[7] Goetz himself had formerly been a victim of a street mugging, and since then had gone around armed with a gun; his antagonists, it transpired, had criminal records.

In may respects this incident, and the intense publicity it aroused, resembles a similar, though basically contrary, incident from some twenty-one years earlier in the same city—the Genovese incident. A young woman was attacked, raped, and murdered while at least thirty-eight bystanders heard her scream for help in the middle of the night and did nothing. Ever since then a host of research in various disciplines has tried to determine the rational, humane, and effective response in such circumstances, attempting to draw a line somewhere

athetic indifference on the one hand and zealous
on the other.[8]

ioetz incident it was the victim himself who acted,
lear that he was responding to more than his particular victimization at that moment and was really expressing
his overall dissatisfaction as a citizen and bystander to the rising rate of crime. Certainly, the public response of sympathy
for his action and even identification with it (exemplified by
letters to the editor and the decision of a grand jury originally
not to indict him on a charge of attempted murder or even
aggravated assault) is indicative above all else of how deep the
antipathy to the violent criminal goes. As in the Genovese case,
this later incident serves as a benchmark indicator of public
sentiment, imposing itself upon the collective awareness of
society, touching off a public debate, exposing the undercur-
rents of fear and hostility, and forcing a personal confrontation with one's conscience.

Above all, it shows how widespread and how deep are
the demands for revenge, how low is the value of the human
life of a known or presumed criminal, how casually the public
may accept his death. One of the injured assailants was known
to be struggling for his life and likely to be paralyzed for life;
yet there was in the beginning no let-up in support for Goetz's
action.[9] Indeed, the fate of Goetz, acting basically, for all his
prior preparation, in the heat of the moment, is less significant
than the reactions of many of the public in the coolness and
knowledge of hindsight and in the quiet and protection of their
homes.

Translated into the terminology and procedures of an
organized criminal justice system, those supportive of Goetz
would have wished for the equivalent of a death penalty on
these four youths—or of the mutilation that they actually suffered; this, not even for an act of murder or attempted murder,
nor even for an actual assault, but only for threateningly ac-
costing a citizen in public. Such an act should certainly be

punished, but surely not with death or maiming—or is this what the public would really want? The support for Goetz by large sectors of the public certainly represents widespread fear and anger, as well as for some of those who are white, racist hostility. And the public, in New York at least, seem not to be getting what they want—at least for murder. For over the last few years, several attempts to pass a law in the state legislature have been frustrated by the veto of Governor Cuomo.[10]

A further insight into the attitudes of some people may be gleaned from the fact that, several years prior to the Goetz incident, "in April 1977 a pistol and rifle group in New York City announced that it was offering a $200 award and citation to any victim of a robbery or an assault who killed his or her attacker."[11] Svend Ranulf has explained the kind of social background that leads to these punitive responses. He explains how "indignant denunciation of a certain kind of behavior in others is not a guarantee that the denunciators themselves will find it impossible to indulge in exactly the same kind of behavior with a perfectly good conscience."[12]

At a larger level, certain questions inevitably arise. If the sentiments expressed about the Goetz affair reflect a broad stratum of current public opinion, then this must have some bearing on determining penal policy. In brief, how does one take cognizance of these feelings without surrendering to them?[13] For there is a great and grave danger that when too large a gap is engendered between official response and the desires of the population at large, the latter are liable to resort increasingly to extra-legal measures such as lynching, or to quasi-legal measures, such as overreacting to a crime situation or, in the case of the police, of shooting a fleeing felon. There are no easy answers or magic formulas to these questions—but we ignore them at our peril. The aberrations in larger political terms, as discussed in part 3, have their parallels in daily activity. Fear of crime and perceived ineptness of officialdom are liable to lead to a climate in which vigilante-style justice becomes tolerated.

One does not expect abolitionists to forgo their viewpoints because the public is liable to react with vigilantism if its appetite for revenge is not satisfied; but there is a pressing need to at least be aware of public sentiments and of the possible outcomes. If anything, they indicate clearly how much educational work is still to be done. As the New York situation so clearly shows, it is not enough to set up a legal prohibition on capital punishments. Abolitionists must also work to create a social climate accepting of that position—otherwise their achievements in legislative activity may be frustrated by the actions of the public and the police on the street.

In a related context, in South America a number of civil rights activists, who might in normal circumstances be presumed to be abolitionist, have come out in favor of the death penalty specifically because this gives the accused person some form of protection and some prospect for a judicial verdict, whereas in its absence the authorities may resort to any means to achieve the result that they want, the death of the accused.[14]

In the United States, vigilante activities were a common feature of the frontier society moving west, and lynchings were a common feature in the South, with the figures showing tens of people killed each year, most of them black, the victims not just of vindictive actions but of racist prejudices. In ancient Rome it was an accepted tenet of the law that a thief caught red-handed could be beaten to death, sometimes after a hasty trial conducted on the spot in the presence of neighbors. Although not legal, similar manifestations have plagued some of the countries of Africa, where sometimes tribal hostilities act as a catalytic agent for similar vigilante killings. United Nations conferences dealing with problems of crime and its prevention have devoted some consideration as to how such phenomena can be eradicated.[15]

In some societies the need for revenge subsists as a normative prerogative, where the blood feud may break out unless the feelings for revenge are assuaged in the manner provided by cultural norms. Of most interest in this context is that even the severest penalty of organized society may not be sufficient (whether a death penalty or life imprisonment) to prevent the feud. What is required for the protagonists to desist from their violence is an application of the accepted formula of rituals of reconcilation involving compensatory payments and traditional ceremonies.[16]

Indeed, in some respects it is the very norms that would on the one hand justify acts of revenge that also, on the other hand, generally precipitate earnest and dedicated attempts to seek the alternatives of rituals of reconciliation and the compensation. We have here the possibility of interesting and valuable insights into how deep the need for a vengeful death penalty really goes, as well as how to offset it; for, after all, those prepared to personally commit a murder in order to save the honor of their family or out of respect for the victim's memory may be presumed to have far stronger personal feelings and far stronger animosity to the culprit than the public at large. Yet when a culture has over the years developed norms that allow for alternative means of pacifying the harmed group, it is the latter that are sought.

This alternative is generally far more moderate than the penal provisions of modern organized society and involves basically compensation and forgiveness, and not punishment. It is of particular interest to note what happens when these older norms overlap or clash with the official penal provisions of modern organized society. In effect, often two parallel systems operate—sometimes in conflict, sometimes in cooperation—in which, after a murder for instance, police and prosecution attempt to gain a conviction, while leading members of the families of the victim and culprit attempt to bring about a reconciliation between the rival family groups. These may involve protracted negotiations, including the use of go-betweens to mediate; and, in some cases, the authorities themselves may participate in the full knowledge that the formal penalty of the criminal law (be it a death sentence or life imprisonment) will not satisfy the victimized family nor appease its anger. Release of tension will only emerge after compensation is paid and ritual forgiveness is requested and given.[17]

On this basis, it might be possible to conceive of creating norms in which harsh punishment would be moderated. In all discussions of the responses to extreme crimes there is a need that goes beyond society at large. This relates directly to the victim or his family. In the abovementioned procedures for reconciliation, it is the victim's family that is directly involved and whose viewpoint and needs become paramount. This is clearly a delicate matter, and no researcher has tried to assess what kind of societal response and what kind of penalty victimized persons would prefer, even though there has in recent years been renewed focus on the needs of the victim.[18] There is some independent and scattered evidence, none of it consistent. On the contrary, it is diverse enough to support both the abolitionist and retentionist points of view.

On the one hand, there is evidence of insistent efforts being made by the family of a victim to ensure that the death penalty is carried out or their expressing a willingness to be present at the execution.[19] Further, where there is no capital punishment, members of the victim's family have been known to argue for the need for legislation of this nature. On the other hand, there are examples of families of victims speaking in moderating fashion and rejecting the death penalty as merely adding to the carnage that characterizes modern life without aiding them in their grief.[20] Responses in these circumstances are obviously intensely personal expressions of belief and philosophy; but they are also surely influenced by the surrounding social environment, by public opinion, normative practices, dominant philosophies, and polemical debate. It should indeed be possible to create a climate of public opinion through enlightened debate that will help people—whether themselves directly affected or as part of the larger public— to crystallize their ideas in such a way as to conquer their gut reaction of harsh punishment and substitute more moderate responses.

Public opinion is also a factor in determining the meaning of injunctions against cruel and unusual punishment or similar phraseology. Yet it should be remembered that in the critical *Furman* decision Justice Marshall preferred to by-pass the many indications that the majority of the population favored the death penalty and opted instead for the knowledgeable opinion of the experts, who were mostly opposed. In so doing, he suggested that if only the public were to know what the experts know, they might also be in agreement as to abolition.[21] Part of the fault in this argument is that whereas the experts focused on deterrence, the public are probably swayed by retribution. As long as retribution remains an acceptable goal of penology, the research showing that capital punishment does not deter is not likely to make much impact on public opinion.[22] Justice Marshall had noticed this fact but had dismissed it as ''senseless vengeance.''

But there is a further factor and a greater danger in public opinion favoring the death penalty in cases where the law has abolished it, or even where court precedent is reluctant to impose it or pardoning authorities are willing to pardon; for in these circumstances there is a real danger that retributive (or vengeful) acts will be resorted to by individuals and condoned by the public at large, as was the case with Goetz's action.

Most particularly, though, there is one specific group capable of giving expression to the needs for capital punishment when there is officially no capital punishment. The most problematic group is the police—both because of the power that they have and because of the punitive philosophies that some of them tend to hold. Most obvious are situations in which the killings take place deliberately and in cold blood, as has, on occasion, certainly been the case in some countries of South America, where what is perceived by the police as being a too tolerant approach to criminals has led to their own clandestine operations against criminals, in which hit teams composed of policemen in their off-duty hours kill known criminals.[23] This is not necessarily the revenge of primitive socities, but often it is carried out with the same kind of passion, anger, self-righteousness, and dedication that characterized the more personal responses of primitive societies. This is simplistic justice, aimed at law and order, stemming from frustration at the uncertainties and procrastinations of the criminal justice system, often acquiesced in and connived at by the higher authorities, and supported and condoned by the public at large. In some countries these activities against criminals serve as a prelude for the later excesses against political rivals, as in the "disappearing" in countries such as Argentina and Chile.

Similar in consequences, though different in the circumstances, are instances of people killed either in police custody, in clashes with the police, or in attempts to elude capture. In the first two cases, when people are killed while inc ustody or in self-defense, the problem focuses chiefly on the empirical evidence, for in principle there is no doubt that the police have no right to kill people in the first instance, but may have a limited right to do so in the second instance, subject to the standards laid down—for example, legitimate self-defense. (Self-defense, however, will not be recognized when the empirical evidence shows that the killing in "self-defense" arose out of a deliberately contrived situation by the police in order to provide the pretext for shooting.)

The third situation is the most problematical, for the theoretical position is both uncertain and debatable. It deals with one of the most difficult problems of law enforcement and criminal justice—the right to kill a fleeing felon, or even the right to open fire when there is a strong likelihood that the person fleeing might be killed, or seriously hurt. In South America this is known officially as the Ley de Fuga, an acknowledgment of the right to kill a suspect in flight.[24]

In fact, these shootings may be regarded as deprivations of life without due process of law. When they take place in a jurisdiction which has no death penalty, they accord to the police a form of power that is denied to judges; they allow consequences that are totally unavailable in the measured and calm atmosphere of a judicial hearing to arise out of a risky and hasty decision in tense circumstances. Let me stress the key point. The right to shoot a fleeing felon when there is no immediate danger to the police or passers-by constitutes an absolute power for life-and-death decisions when the demand of law enforcement clearly takes precedence over the dictates of the sanctity of life. If the old legal adage is true that it is better for ten guilty persons to go free rather than have one innocent person unjustly punished, surely similar considerations apply in the case of a fleeing felon. Surely it would be better to allow him to escape rather than risk the dire possibilities of his being accidentally or even purposely killed.

To get an idea of what is involved, it should be noted that in an average year in the United States more people are killed by the police than are sentenced to death by courts of law, and vastly more than are actually executed. Of these, a few are even completely innocent of any crime or are innocent bystanders accidentally hit by a stray bullet.[25]

These figures also provide an interesting light on deterrence arguments, for it may well be that the greatest threat to a criminal's life may be from a police bullet and not from a judicial decision. The mere chance of being shot while engaged in criminal activity (and the number injured or maimed is greater than the number actually killed) should serve as a significant deterrent factor. Does the lack of a statute authorizing the right to kill a fleeing felon adversely affect the crime rate? Of course, there is a real danger that if police perceived that there was a deterrent factor linked to the willingness or reluctance to shoot to kill, they might even subconsciously be more prone to activate this right to shoot when it exists or to lobby for such a right when legislation prohibits it.

One wonders also whether or not the existence of a death penalty in a particular state might also not have some impact on the tendency to shoot, that is, that there might be a greater likelihood of police using their right to shoot to kill where there was no death penalty.[26]

Ostensibly, in the United States, the debate over the fleeing felon may have become a moot point as a result of a recent
Supreme Court decision declaring unconstitutional the right
to use deadly force against a fleeing felon.[27] This case is of
particular interest because it was brought in the form of a
tort action for damages by the deceased's father alleging violation of constitutional rights, after an initial police inquiry
had determined that the police officer had acted legally and
within his authority in shooting at the suspect. The suspect
was presumed to have committed a night burglary and to be
unarmed; it transpired that both presumptions were correct.
The officer himself admitted that the use of deadly force was
occasioned solely because of his desire to effect an arrest,
not because he, or any bystanders, were in any danger. The
trial court held that the officer's actions were legitimate and
were authorized both by a state statute allowing the police
to use all necessary means to effect an arrest when a suspect
was attempting to escape, as well as local police regulations,
which, though slightly more restrictive, allowed the use of
deadly force in cases of burglary.[28] This decision was overruled by the United States Court of Appeals for the Sixth Circuit, holding that the statute which authorized "the killing
of an unarmed, nonviolent fleeing felon by police in order to
prevent escape" was unconstitutional.[29]

The Supreme Court, in a 6–3 decision, upheld the court of
appeals. Justice White, speaking for the majority, stated that "the
use of deadly force to prevent the escape of all felony suspects,
whatever the circumstances, is unconstitutionally unreasonable.
It is not better that all felony suspects die than that they escape. . . . A police officer may not seize an unarmed, nondan-
gerous suspect by shooting him dead." In terms of the Fourth
Amendment strictures on unreasonable seizure of suspects, the
law was declared unconstitutional inasmuch as it related to
suspects like the accused, that is, neither dangerous nor armed.
The Court's decision was welcomed as finally laying down

guidelines restricting the use of deadly force as well as reflecting similar legislative developments in about half of the states.[30]

However, the actual restrictions specified in the Court judgment are themselves extremely limited in their compass and seem to be based less on overriding principles than on the specific facts in the case. It might have been more advisable to go beyond the narrow purview of the Fourth Amendment—involving mainly the manner in which the officer attempted to bring about the arrest—and seek a more comprehensive philosophical and practical basis for the decision.

Although superficially basing itself on the suspect's right to life, the Court does so in no more than a cursory manner in the laconic statement: "The suspect's fundamental interest in his own life need not be elaborated upon." In fact, the Court did not deal at all with other constitutional issues that had been raised by the complainant, namely, that the violation of the deceased's constitutional rights related not only to the Fourth Amendment, but also to the Fifth, Sixth, Eighth, and Fourteenth Amendments.

In her dissenting opinion, Justice O'Connor (joined by Chief Justice Burger and Justice Rehnquist) held that the police officer's action was constitutional, and specifically referred to each of these amendments, rejecting the arguments for each, including that there had not been deprivation of life without due process of law. It is this issue that seems to go to the heart of the matter and that requires deeper analysis. Simply put, when a police officer engaged in arresting for the purposes of investigating a crime, with the intention of eliciting evidence for the purpose of committing the suspect to trial, opens fire with the intent to kill (and the resort to shooting is generally meant for this purpose and not to warn, maim, or hinder), then it seems that the split-second decision, made in the heat of the tensions associated with arrest, could hardly be seen to involve the kind of deliberate and considered reflection that is an integral aspect of due process.

In this context, it should be stressed that whereas the Fifth Amendment refers to due process in the context of a criminal trial, the Fourteenth Amendment has no such restrictive reference—here the protection provided of not being deprived of life without due process of law must obviously be read in the broadest context as referring to all those who act on the authority of the state. It seems irrational, in fact, to impose strict procedures for the purpose of protecting life only in respect to the trial, where there is a greater likelihood that full protection will indeed be provided, but, in contrast, to allow flexible regulations and lax rulings to govern the authoritative utilization of life-and-death power by low-ranking police officers.

Justice O'Connor argues that "a person's interest in his life" does not encompass "a right to flee unimpeded from the scene of a burglary." With due respect, there is no connection whatsoever between these two factors—for although a suspect does indeed have an interest in his own life, he does not have any right at all to flee from the scene of an attempted arrest. In so doing he is breaking the law and subjecting himself to possible further penalties; but these are surely not the ultimate ones. Nor for that matter is he entitled to be unimpeded in his quest for freedom; the police are entitled to impede him in every way imaginable—short of depriving him of his life in so doing. It is not his interest in his life and his so-called right to escape that is at issue, but his (and, for that matter, society's) interest in his life and whether the police have a right to violate that interest, in the process of trying to arrest him.

In any event, the only case that Justice O'Connor bases her decision upon (*Payton* v. *New York*)[31] is not at all relevant for the purpose of this issue. The Court in that case suggested that "the policeman's hands should not be tied," but it was dealing with an entry into a suspect's home without a warrant, which it sanctioned because it was done with probable cause. There is surely a vast difference between not tying the hands of the police and letting their fingers freely pull the trigger.

However, the approach of the minority justices makes even more explicit the fact that it was not so much the Fourth Amendment rights dealing with arrest that was at stake, but the Fourteenth Amendment rights of due process.

Indeed, a closer reading of the majority opinion indicates clearly that it was largely the empirical facts of the case—a youth, aged fifteen, small of stature and slight of build, unarmed and thought by the policemen so to be, fleeing a burglary from which he had netted some ten dollars—that were of paramount importance in the Court's reasoning. It should be stressed also that the Court held the Tennessee statute itself constitutional for other purposes, some of which they spelled out; not just for self-defense, or to avert immediate or perhaps more remote danger, but also when "there is probable cause to believe that he has committed a crime involving the infliction or threatened infliction of serious physical harm." In other words, because the Court evaded the issue of due process, it willingly conceded the right for the police to shoot to kill when a suspect has, for instance, verbally threatened to commit a physical assault—without relevance, according to their guidelines, as to imminent danger or even the prospect of capturing him in some other manner, even if this were to involve more time and effort by the police.

It is interesting to note that the Court makes reference to an article critical of the right to shoot, in which the author claims that most fleeing felons do get caught later.[32] The Court disagrees with this conclusion, though without adducing evidence.

The Court also stressed the need for stricter standards in the case of burglary since historically the law relating to the fleeing felon was created when a *felony* meant mainly a crime for which there was the sentence of death. Quoting from the American Law Institute's Model Penal Code, the Court approvingly states: "Though effected without the protection and formalities of an orderly trial and conviction, the killing of a resisting or fleeing felon resulted in no greater consequences than those authorized for punishment of the felony of which the individual was charged or suspected."[33] Since the death penalty is no longer applicable for most offenses initially called felonies, and since many former misdemeanors are now ranked as felonies, the Court argues that "these changes have undermined the concept, which was questionable to begin with, that use of deadly force against a fleeing felon is merely a speedier execution of someone who has already forfeited his life."

Yet the Court's decision has not really resolved this issue. Though commendably disallowing deadly force in the case of an unarmed burglary, it has, by ignoring the issue of due process of law, allowed by default the use of deadly force in other fleeing felon situations; and this, unlike the historical situation, when there may be no death penalty—certainly, by dint of recent Supreme Court decisions, in all those instances in which no one has been killed,[34] or the use of force for fleeing convicted prisoners, no matter what their crime, since the Fourth Amendment would not apply. However, even if the crime is a capital offense, it is still the courts that ought to determine guilt, and then, after appropriate consideration of the facts and the background, impose the penalty. To paraphrase the Court, it is still better for the felon to escape, even if more than an unarmed burglar, than to die. To allow otherwise is to condone the irreversible act of the taking of life without the protection that a compassionate society, a civilized comity, and a wise constitution, would provide.

More than this, and worse than this, the problem is not only that the police may act on their own with consequences equivalent to a penalty that is in any event provided by the law, but that they also may so act when, and perhaps because the law does *not* provide for such a penalty.

The failure of the Court to decide in a clear and unambiguous manner is all the more deplorable since many individual states already have legislation severely limiting the situations in which the police may resort to deadly force, in some cases more strictly allowing it only when there is immediate danger, in others more flexibly, when the projected danger is in the future.[35] The Court could well have used these laws as an indication of evolving standards of decency as well as an empirical proof of the ability of the police to function effectively, even without a broad power to open fire.

In the final analysis, a nation's attitude to life and its value is expressed not only in the punishment that its courts impose, but also in the procedures that are used to arrest and indict. The dangers of vindictive vengeance are not resolved merely by setting up court systems and law enforcement agencies, nor is the sanctity of life guaranteed by focusing only on the operating procedures of the former; on the contrary, it can only be assured if the protections of due process are provided against the ongoing practices of the latter.[36]

14

SUPRA-NATIONAL
DUE PROCESS

CAPITAL PUNISHMENT has always been a problematic aspect of the law, not just in terms of punishment or of consititutional issues, but in terms of the substantive criminal law and the rules of procedure and evidence. Some aspects of the criminal law have developed specifically in order to provide a means of evading the assigned capital punishment, especially when it was mandatory.

The original distinction (so important to later developments of the law) between a felony and a misdemeanor was based on those crimes for which the death penalty was imposed and those for which lesser penalties were available.[1] In England, a parallel court system developed—that of the ecclesiastical courts—in which those entitled to "benefit of clergy" would be tried in a church jurisdiction that lacked the power to impose capital penalties.[2] At first intended, as the name implies, only for the clergy, it was later expanded as a means of allowing many others to evade the ultimate penalty of death. Similar evasive procedures were adopted in Roman Palestine and in talmudic times to evade the death penalty set out in the Bible.[3]

Some of the defenses incorporated into the criminal law—especially provocation and insanity—arose out of a desire to introduce more flexibility into the criminal law as a result of the severity of its mandatory sentencing implications for capital crimes. The defense of provocation itself is to this day available only in the case of murder, the claim serving as partial excuse for a killing and leading to a conviction on a lesser charge of manslaughter or culpable homicide.[4] In fact, these lesser crimes arose partly to provide an alternative that would allow for a conviction without the consequence of a compulsory death sentence. There is, it should be noted, no similar alternative to, for instance, a charge of battery and assault, since a defendant may always refer to any provocative behavior in such cases as a relevant mitigating factor in his punishment.

The defense of insanity is particularly interesting, for whereas its development (since the exposition of the well-known McNaghten rules in the nineteenth century) was oriented mainly to avoid the unacceptable prospect of executing the insane (it is almost never used for other than capital trials), it led to consequences that were not the most desirable—the permanent institutionalization of the accused person in a mental institution, with possibly less prospects of being releaased than of attaining commutation of a life sentence. Compromise and flexibility in this instance led to the legal recognition of a new degree of mental infirmity—diminished responsibility.[5]

The original use of the pardoning power stemmed also from the desire to provide the executive the right to grant grace and individual consideration to a criminal, a right which the legislature had denied the judiciary. Pleas would be made to the king to save the life of a family member or friend; the pragmatic solution was to invest the king with the constitutional power of pardon.[6]

In the course of trials, judges occasionally give expression to the fact that the severity of the potential punishment, especially when mandatory, obligates the court to be extra cautious in determining whether there is any lingering doubt as to the guilt of the accused. Such factors, on occasion, also have an impact on jurors. Here, jurors may exercise jury nullification—a dubious aspect of the law denied by many—whereby they deliberately ignore their instructions from the judge, which would perhaps have led to a guilty verdict, in order to reach a decision compatible with their deepest sense of justice.[7] This includes the situation in which the jury is unwilling to accept the consequences of a mandatory death sentence, or even a minimum penalty—such as the choice between death and a life sentence.

In recent years it has been argued in the United States that the whole criminal justice system is being overly weighed down by the accumulation of death penalty cases—with their inevitable appeals and pleas for stays of execution—and that these cases constitute an inordinate amount of the time and resources of the court. This phenomenon, it is argued, can only be avoided by ending the death penalty, since the prisoners and their lawyers will always pursue any legal possibility available to them.

All these manifestations and developments reflect the ambivalence toward the death penalty that has been described in earlier chapters. Society wants the death penalty, yet also shirks from performing it. It is not just its finality that is the issue, but also perhaps its futility. For deep down, despite all the talk about possible deterrence, there is a more abiding awareness that what motivates its use is not really a determined belief that an execution will save lives in the future, but rather a desperate desire to react for the life already lost. There is a dull awareness that the particular penalty being imposed is too late to prevent the harm done, and probably too ineffective in preventing future occurrences.

The dilemma and doubts that I expressed at the outset remain still partly unresolved, mainly because they are intrinsically not susceptible to total solution. The limitations on penological practice are a reflection not only of the ideological and political factors that so often impinge on discussion and adjudication, but by the very nature of the problem, the very evil to which penology is a response. It is not easy to be rational and humanistic when dealing with acts that are irrational or inhumane.

In a larger sense, penology suffers from the malaise that has affected most of the social sciences in this century. They have been unable to fulfill the sanguine expectations and aspirations originally held out for them. The hopes of the early social scientists that objective analysis and rigorous research would lead to the planned progress of social engineering, and the dreams of the nineteenth-century ideologists that commitment to sublime values would lead to the utopian advance of an enlightened humanity have not been achieved.

The early criminologists presumed that, shorn of philosophical encumbrances, they would be able to fathom the causes of crime and thereby ensure its eventual elimination. But as the emphasis has moved from biology to psychology and then sociology, the elixir has remained beyond grasp; a compromise of multi-variable causality has provided only a partial explanation for crime but not the means to prevent or control it.[8] In addition, some criminologists have argued that it is largely the political struggle which determines the nature of criminality.[9] Crime is thus endemic to and inherent in the social structure; further, some of the most extreme crimes stem from the most deplorable political and social conditions or are committed in the name of an ideology or belief.

Criminology deals with the causes, penology with the consequences. But the frustation of the former leads to the futility of the latter. Even at the lowest level, for crimes of a minor nature, it is not clear what penological policy is most just and effective, though innovative practices such as probation, parole, community service, treatment programs, compensation, and restitution are to be welcomed. But they bear little relevance to major crime (although as noted in the previous chapter, rituals of forgiveness and offers of compensation may be accepted in some societies, and although James Avery Joyce does argue that rehabilitation is the most desirable goal even for the most dangerous criminals).[10] In fact, as was indicated earlier, some of the most innovative approaches of today, such as decarceration, deliberately exclude the perpetrators of major crime and often insist on especially harsh penalties for them—such as life imprisonment.[11]

Till now, in fact, life imprisonment has been seen almost as a panacea for abolitionists, the one penalty that can be guaranteed to provide assurances that major crime will be duly and adequately punished. In fact, abolitionists perhaps proclaim too much—for the very severity that they attribute to life imprisonment is what from a human rights perspective makes it so problematical. The fact is that abolitionists are at their best when arguing against the death penalty but at their most vulnerable (because they are so convincing) when singing the praises of an alternative.

In any event, the struggles over abolition of capital punishment in the United States in the years since *Furman* have elicited many new arguments and given older ones added import. For, ever since *Gregg* the courts have been confronted with a series of cases whose overall inconsistency and illogic has furnished abolitionists with new points of law to pursue in specific cases, and added empirical proof of the inability—or unwillingness—of achieving the aims of the Supreme Court's guidelines.[12]

It is partly a certain sensibility of the guidelines that really exposes the intractibility of the problem. The guidelines are superficially quite clear—there should be no capriciousness nor arbitrariness in the decision-making process, and there should be no mandatory death penalty. Yet the cases that are accumulating show how almost impossible it is to prevent such capriciousness and arbitrariness. Further, it is probably no mere coincidence, but more likely an echo of past practices, that so many of the executions that have taken place have been in southern states.

What the decisions of the Supreme Court have done is to expose the inability to implement the rules relating to the death penalty in a fair and equitable manner. Whatever the faults of the *Gregg* decision, it contains a clear-cut and unambiguous commitment to the ending of arbitrary and capricious decisions on the death penalty. Yet the very Court that instituted this ruling has shown itself unable to apply it fairly and consistently. Underlying personal propensities and preferences continue to render the goal of standard and objective decision-making totally elusive.

In a perceptive critique of the present position, William Geimer argues that the Court's retreat from its commitment to a stringent due process standard has been "so complete that, perversely, the phrase 'death is different' has come in many respects to mean that a prisoner whose life is at stake is due less rather than more process than an ordinary litigant."[13] He spares no words in his argument that there has been an abandonment of due process standards, which marks

a low point in American jurisprudence for at least two reasons. First, the Supreme Court has acted deceptively. Ostensibly seeking to monitor the fair administration of the death penalty the Court has in fact operated under conclusive presumption that despite the implications of the post–1976 decisions demonstrating the difficulty in administering the death penalty, it is to be administered nonetheless. . . . Evidence which threatens the existence of the death penalty is to be rejected out of hand or distinguished away by vapid logic. Second, some members of the Court have sought to place the blame for the deplorable situation on attorneys who represent the condemned. Chief Justice Burger has accused these attorneys of turning death penalty litigation into a "sporting contest." In truth, as scrutiny of its recent decisions will show, it is the Court itself which has helped return the law of death to the same roulette wheel proposition it was at the time of *Furman,* and even that game is rigged.[14]

But the issues of inconsistent and insensitive decision-making, the derogatory comments on defense lawyers, and the deep rift within the Court itself, have larger implications. At the outset, I indicated the importance of the abolition struggle in the United States for the fate of the worldwide struggle against the death penalty. If the United States, with its democratic structure, liberal ethos, constitutional protections, persevering lawyers, judicial guidelines, media coverage, and concerned public, is unable to implement fairly the agonizing and critical decisions in regard to the death penalty, then the larger picture becomes ever clearer—people throughout the world are subjected to the hazards of various degrees of injustice, from kangaroo courts through military and revolutionary tribunals to the faults and failings of regular courts. In all parts of the world, no doubt, rash and unfair decisions are being made as to the fate of people, who even if guilty of heinous crimes are still entitled to the full protection of due process of law; indeed, it is the extremity of the crime, raising the prospect of the severity of the punishment, that obligates the strictest standards of judicial protection. The faults and failings of the Supreme Court in the United States are of particular relevance because they point to the pervasiveness of human fallibility, not just in questions of fact relating to the commission of the crime (a classic traditional argument), but in questions of logic relating to the implementation of guiding principles.

Although so much of the opposition to the death penalty is—rightly—based on the possibility of error, it seems to me that the impact of the recent years of judicial activity is not the errors of fact (that in any event are beyond appeal and beyond the purview of the Supreme Court) but the errors of judgement. Even in such factors as compassionate understanding for the plight of the accused, the Court has been remiss. As Geimer notes, "when the court speaks so poorly on issues of life and death," it is the duty of legal scholars to speak out, not just against capital punishment, but against such adjunct phenomena as Chief Justice Berger's "outrageous statement about defense attorneys turning death penalty litigation into a 'sporting contest'"; this in a case in which the adverse decision of the Court led to the execution taking place shortly afterwards. Geimer adds also that "capital defense attorneys work under intense stress, usually without pay, rendering valuable assistance to courts grappling with death penalty issues."[15] In fact, far from lawyers gleefully seeking a sporting contest, recent reports indicate an increasing reluctance to undertake such cases because of the tensions and the responsibility.[16]

But if such aberrations from the desired standards take place at the highest court levels when a person's life is immediately at stake, and before the potential full exposure of media coverage, what, one wonders, is happening in the lower courts, in lesser cases, removed from intense outside scrutiny? When a distinguished jurist of the caliber of Ramsey Clark describes in full and embarrassing detail the unbelievably casual manner in which judges responded to his efforts to act on behalf of a person sentenced to die—through a multiparty telephone hook-up, from which one of the three judges was absent, but who subsequently provided the crucial vote adverse to the defendants—then larger issues of criminal justice arise.[17] How, for instance, do such judges conduct their trials in lesser offenses, when "only" a person's liberty is at stake, when the defendant lawyer is a lesser personage than a former attorney-general and the son of a former Supreme Court justice, and when there is little likelihood of later damaging reportage of the travesty?

For the purposes of my argument, these questions are critical—first, since even some of the lesser offenses occasionally involve as much as life imprisonment; second, since some of the major offenses often involve "only" life imprisonment. Geimer ends his article with a plea to all lawyers, especially those who "may receive the unwelcome notice of their appointment by a court to represent a capital defendant," to be thorough in their efforts and to utilize the "high quality assistance . . . available to attorneys assigned to capital trials,"[18] such as from organizations like the American Civil Liberties Union, which, together with other organizations, is making a concerted effort to help fight capital cases.

Given this involvement by the ACLU and other bodies, given the concern by large sectors of the public, and given the determination shown by many abolitionist lawyers, there is a good prospect that those facing capital punishment will at least receive the legal aid that they need, and that, within the general limitations of the judicial system, they will have their day in court. In Florida, in fact, a special public unit of lawyers has been set up to handle death penalty appeals.

But what of those facing the lesser penalties, or those perceived so to be, such as life imprisonment? Will they, too, have their day in court? Will they, too, be given the legal assistance that they need and are entitled to; will they, too, be shown the public concern for their fate? Or will their life sentence be seen perhaps even as a victory for the abolitionist cause? Alternatively, will there be those—such as lawyers and public-spirited citizens—prepared to embark on the struggle for their rights and their liberty over time?[19]

Truth to tell, in terms of traditional arguments of deterrence and retribution, for some of the most heinous crimes, neither a life nor a death sentence may be an appropriate response. That is why there is no completely satisfactory solution to the dilemma I posed. Organized society is intended to be capable of answering to the needs of its members in many areas—from assuring protection against external enemies, through facilitating economic relationships, to providing educational and social facilities. Debate may range, ideological and practical in nature, as to the degree of desired involvement, or as to the allocation of resources.

But in the realm of penology, even a theoretical solution for many of its problems is beyond the realm of the possible. For society has no answer to the worst aberrations of human conduct, the worst depravations of the human soul, the worst machinations of the human mind. This is why, for instance, the terrorist has such a great advantage over organized society. The best deterrence and retribution is simply not available to civilized society. Life and death sentences, for all their severity, are often inadequate for the purposes that they are designed to serve. And yet, conversely, in too many cases in which they are actually used, they are too harsh for the human values of the society. As Patrick Hubbard points out in a recent thought-provoking article, society is faced with a "tragic choice" in seeking an apt punishment for the most serious crimes. "Every culture," he notes, "has issues that are unanswerable within the context of its view of the moral order."[20]

There is a possible solution to such dilemmas, but, as Hubbard concedes, it is by no means a satisfying one. Drawing on the work of Guido Calabresi and Philip Bobbitt,[21] he suggests that tragic choices ought to be made by an "aresponsible agency," that is, one which makes basically ad hoc decisions, without the need to give reasons for it and without laying down binding precedent for subsequent cases. According to Hubbard, the jury is perhaps "the paradigm of an aresponsible decision-maker," and thus "it is not surprising that the jury plays a central role in death penalty schemes."[22] Other aresponsible decision-makers in capital punishment cases are the prosecutor and the pardoning authority; but, of course, these latter, unlike the jury, may become institutionalized—yet even so, their processes generally remain too arbitrary to fulfill the guidelines of the Supreme Court. Hubbard himself answers this criticism in the very title of his article: "Reasonable Arbitrariness." Arbitrariness may often be reasonable, but surely not when what is at stake is a person's life. Can a person accept with equanimity the fact that in the process of reasonable arbitrariness—by prosecutor, jury, pardoning authority—he was the one for whom the choice becomes tragic in a decision for execution (assuming he wishes to live)? And what if, in that minority of cases when the prisoner prefers to die, the choice becomes tragic, as it is a decision for life imprisonment without parole?

The concept of an aresponsible person making the tragic choice does, however, provide a theoretical framework consistent with the thesis I have put forward—namely, that the accused person himself make the choice—this time on the assumption that both capital punishment and life imprisonment are ultimate penalties of similar severity. Society would transfer the tragic choice to the recipient of the punishment. Society's obligation would be to ensure that the threshold decision, to offer the tragic choice, would be one of utmost significance, to be made only after careful consideration and deliberation.

Prior to making such a decision, exhaustive probings would be undertaken to determine whether there was a penultimate penalty that would satisfy penological needs. Such penultimate penalties would require deep and probing analysis, in which the needs of a severe societal response to a major crime would be tempered by continuing respect for the dignity of the accused person. The possibilities here lie beyond the scope of this work, and I can only note attempts to humanize incarceration, such as allowing conjugal relations, furlough visits home, recreational, training, and educational facilities, adequate protection of all residual rights retained by a prisoner, from regular correspondence and reading material, to sufficiently nutritious food and medical services. Possibilities should be pursued to extend the practice of self-contained prisons, where—separated from society—the inmates may maintain their own inner community, including heterosexual contacts.[23]

Cultural norms can also be explored and encouraged for using all forms of mediation and reconciliation between the criminal and his victim (or the surrogate victim in the form of the family) when appropriate, with reconciliation, expressed through compensation, for instance, to serve as a legitimate mitigating circumstance when imposing the penalty. Medical treatment—ranging from drugs and psychosurgery to various forms of therapy—may provide assurances for the concerns of future deviation, though clearly raising serious issues of basic civil rights, including informed consent under conditions of coercion.[24] As some condemned persons may prefer death over a sentence of life imprisonment, some prisoners may prefer a longer period of incarceration rather than treatment of any type. Once again, the concept of autonomous choice for the prisoner provides a solution. Society's obligation is primarily then to ensure that the alternatives are reasonable ones, proportionate to the penological needs, fit for the crime and apt for the criminal. In fact, the same principle of autonomous choice that I have used as a reasonable (but by no means ideal) solution to the dilemma of which ultimate penalty to impose could be applied on a regular basis for prenultimate and lesser penalties.

To return to the ultimate penalties, they must obviously be imposed without torture. For the death penalty, this means that careful monitoring must be made of the conditions of death row and serious reconsideration given to all the defects of present practices—including both undue haste and unseemly procrastination in carrying it out as well as the means used.

For life imprisonment, no less careful monitoring of prison conditions must be ensured, particularly when lengthy solitary confinement is used or other severe restrictions imposed on this special category of prisoners. This might include regular visits by observers from international organizations, which would ensure the independence needed for critical response when necessary.

Finally, there is the question as to whether limits must be placed on the period of incarceration; the procedures used in many countries of routine and recognized procedures for making a life sentence into a fixed term sentence seems to be a minimum requirement unless very special reasons exist for denying such procedures. There are countries that follow this approach, but, once again, there is no country-by-country survey that has been undertaken, although the survey by the United Nations on the death penalty does contain some limited and sketchy information.[25] Such procedures allow generally for commutation to a period of about twenty years with the possibility of partial remission of sentence for good behavior, allowing for an actual period of incarceration of fifteen to twenty years—with both the commutation and release being dependent on an assessment of future behavior. For the most part, the dangers of recidivism seem to be minimal, although there have occasionally been errors of judgment, when a prisoner with a known propensity to violence was released and later committed further serious crimes.

Given all the problematics associated with ultimate penalties, including the use of choice between them, there is also a need for overall surveillance of the total procedures in order to ensure a just disposition in such cases. Given, further, the excesses that presently exist in so many countries and the inadequacies that exist in others, given the political overtones of many of the trials, and given the underlying involvement with basic human rights, it would seem that such surveillance would best be provided by a supra-national body.

If the international community is serious about its various statements and documents relating to capital punishment, it must seek means of enforcing its provisions and monitoring the procedures of its members. The deficiencies of the present position are well brought out by R. Sapienza.

It would be inappropriate to make cynical comments on the attitude that the International Community holds towards capital punishment. . . . What happens with capital punishment is not different from what happens with any other human rights obligation.. . . . One cannot rely . . . on a system of State to State complaints to enforce human rights obligations, or to improve their content (as would be the case with capital punishment). On the contrary, what is needed is a continous work of standard-setting and monitoring of States' behavior. . . . That is why the action of everybody, especially of non-governmental bodies is to be welcomed as a useful means of achieving higher standards of protection of the right to life, even against capital punishment.[26]

As an addendum to these possibilities—of state to state communications or the pressures of nongovernmental bodies—is the idea of a supra–national judicial body.

Most suggestions for an international criminal court are based on its being a trial court of first instance. Indeed, generally no suggestions are even made for appeal procedures, and none were available for the Nuremberg and Tokyo trials nor those that took place subsequently under the aegis of the various Allied occupying powers, though pleas for pardon were, of course, available. My suggestion is that the initial framework of an international criminal court be for appeal and review purposes.

On the assumption of the universal importance of human rights transcending national boundaries, and on the assumption that ultimate penalties require strict control by such human rights standards, I would suggest that any death sentence or life sentence imposed in a national court be subject to the monitoring procedures of an impartial international judicial body, which would examine all aspects of the criminal justice process—from arrest and interrogation through the trial and appeal procedures to the sentencing and pardon stages. This would be a court or commission that would be in constant session, on a similar basis as the European and Latin American Commissions and Courts of Human Rights.[27] They would be invested with all the powers, authority, and dignity befitting their onerous task and equipped with all the facilities and personnel to fulfill their mandate.

Hopefully, in the course of time, in the framework of calm and measured debate, norms and standards would be laid down that would obligate member states of the world community and its constituent organizations, and would serve as a guide in momentous judicial decisions as to the sentences of life and death. Such a process would prevent political exploitation of judicial authority, would provide a recognized procedure for automatic and compulsory review of all ultimate penalties, and would ensure that the "least" of the world's human beings, its hardened and depraved criminals, as well as some of its most noble persons, those who are victims of political justice, would be assured of the highest protection of the world community.

Such a court or commission could also undertake additional functions. It could serve as a judicial framework for investigating charges of torture and deviations by governmental and police authorities, and in this respect would be similar to the kind of procedures that Luis Kutner has proposed as the only means of ensuring the protection of human rights.[28] It could also be an extension of the work of the Committee Against Torture.[29] Further tasks could include all cases of genocide or humanicide that had been adjudicated in national courts, even when a lesser penalty had been imposed. This would both emphasize the international nature of the violation and ensure that the penalty was relative to the crime—neither too severely or too leniently disproportionate, the latter perhaps because of efforts on the part of the national court to cover up the full extremity of humanicidal actions on the part of its officials or nationals.

Basically, an overall approach of this type would offer respect for the individual, while not evading the need for adequate punishment in extreme cases; it would offer recognition of the need for limitations on state sovereignty in an area all too often exploited for narrow political ends, without diminishing the role of the state in one of its main functions as a judicial authority; and it would offer a guarantee that human rights would be upheld at the highest level of involvement of the world community, without its immediate embroilment in the whole paraphenalia of policing, adjudicating, and sentencing.

Extreme criminality will likely be with us as long as illness and taxes. There may well be an ideal solution to all these problems—for the meantime, however, we live in an as yet imperfect world. Of all the imperfections, few are worse than heinous crime and the harsh reaction of ultimate penalties. We must obviously try to prevent the first. But having failed to do so, we must avoid the easy resort to the second, to ultimate penalties, unless totally convinced that there is no alterantive. When possible we must seek penultimate penalties, penalties that, though appropriately strict, involve neither a death sentence or life sentence. When lesser penalties are manifestly inadequate, we must seek the most careful means of implementing the ultimate penalties—by allowing the criminal the choice of which one, and by obligating the state to subject itself to a review of its procedures and decision-making processes by official organs of the world community. And if the sentence be confirmed, with reluctance and regret, without joy or vengeance, in a spirit of humility and in recognition that human limitations provide no alternatives, we must proceed with the implementation of the unpleasant task.

I am well aware of all the difficulties involved in these suggestions—but surely these difficulties are not more than those that have arisen from other breakthroughs in the field of international human rights. Little thought was given when the Red Cross was originally set up that its role would one day involve all of the activities it performs today, for example, participating as a go-between in negotiations for the release of hostages held by terrorist groups. Soldiers, though retaining the force of their oath of allegiance to a particular nation-state, have found the capacity to transfer their allegiance to the new need for an international peace-keeping force run by the United Nations. In Europe and Latin America, countries have voluntarily conceded a restriction in some respects of their sovereignty, including that of monitoring their adherence to human rights.

Penological issues have, it should be noted, increasingly become the concern of the world community—from references to capital punishment in international conventions, through conferences organized by the committee of social defense setting out minimum standards for prisoners, to bilateral treaties between various states allowing non-citizens sentenced to prison to serve out their period of confinement in their own country, near family and friends, with language and customs familiar to them. The chief difference between these various developments and the suggestion of an international monitoring system for life sentences and death sentences is that the former seems to have so many positive and attractive aspects, serving noble humanitarian causes and without direct involvement, whereas the latter entails dealing with disputable categories of punishment and the unpleasant task of accepting partial responsibility for their implementation.

Nevertheless, whether the world community wishes it or not, these categories of punishment exist. Executions do take place, life sentences are being served. To refuse to be involved is to abdicate responsibility. It is true that by granting approval, even reluctantly, to these punishments—through monitoring procedures—the world community would be granting legitimacy to them.

This may, however, be exactly what is required. For by recognizing the unfortunate existence of ultimate penalties, it may be possible to impose desirable controls. As it is, there is already recognition of the existence of the death penalty by the world community. The International Convention on Civil and Political Rights refers to the use of capital punishment in certain cases. Article 6 states that if a country does have capital punishment, it "may be imposed only as a penalty for the most serious crimes pursuant to the sentence of a competent court and in accordance with the law." In many respects this is a compromise. Many abolitionist states would have preferred— and argued for—total abolition. But having conceded the compromise, the need surely exists to control the manner of its implementation.[30]

The language alone provides for far too much flexibility. What are to be considered "the most serious crimes," or what is a "competent court"? It is specifically in the case of the most serious crimes that the protective devices of the law are most liable to break down. The United States experience has surely shown how tenuous is the framework of the law—both the consititutional provisions of due process and the judicial guidelines of arbitrariness and capriciousness. The abolitionist countries of Europe have shown in the wake of World War II how tempting it is to resort to the death penalty, even retroactively, when the most serious crime is collaboration with a vicious conquering enemy. In China the indignation of the masses can so easily serve to prove that a serious crime deserving of death has been committed. In fundamentalist Islam countries, historical and religious justification exists for the definition of how serious is the crime and the imposition of capital and corporal punishment. In communist countries in Eastern Europe and in some developing countries in Africa and Asia, the serious harm caused to the society at large by deviation from the norms of commercial procedures may be used to justify execution or lengthy and harsh incarceration.

It is not clear to what extent a supranational judicial body could overcome these differing approaches, the consequences of ideological commitment, and the exigencies of social reality. Changes in the substantive law may be still in the realm of an eschatological dream. But intervention at the procedural level, ensuring a super due process, seems to offer more realistic prospects of early action by the world community.

What a world body can do at this juncture is to ensure that no state abuses its sovereign power to rid itself—through death or incarceration—of those who have committed the most serious or most threatening crimes. In order to impose either penalty, the state should have to show proof that due process of law has been observed—some basic minimum on which universal consensus can be attained. Early experience in the realm of procedure may well lead to later success in reassessing the substantive law as well. And if certain countries refuse to subject themselves to such surveillance, let others voluntarily press ahead, as was done at the regional level in the European community and Latin America in terms of general human rights.

This seems to me both a commendable and an attainable aim. It would surely diminish and might perhaps eliminate the many injustices that at present still accompany the process of imposing ultimate sentences of life and death. It would probably—and hopefully—lead to a diminution in the use of both of the ultimate penalties. It might lead to a concerted effort to focus on alternatives for both ultimate penalties—to creatively seek penultimate penalties. It would offer the prospect of monitoring, and thereby perhaps eradicating, torture and other violations of basic human rights. It would certainly be an affirmation that the rights to life and liberty are prior to, and take precedence over, state sovereignty and thus that ultimate penalties may be imposed only after due ratification by a representative body of the world community.

An enlightened penology must strive not for abolition of capital punishment alone but for abolition of all ultimate penalties. For as long as such penalties continue to exist, it must strive to ensure that the rights of the accused are safeguarded—both through monitoring the processes of the criminal justice system and by arguing for the right of choice of penalty. An enlightened penology must realize that involvement of the world community in the unpleasant work of monitoring the ultimate penalties and reviewing the adjudication of extreme crimes is preferable to blanket denunciations of capital punishment, pious declarations of an abolitionist stance, willing acquiescence in life imprisonment, and embarrassed silence as to what to do—punitively—with those who commit torture, terror, genocide, and humanicide.

NOTES

CHAPTER 1:
BEYOND DETERRENCE
AND RETRIBUTION

1. Gregg v. Georgia, 428 U.S. 153 (1976).
2. See Marvin Frankel, *Criminal Sentences: Law without Order* (New York: Hill and Wang, 1973); and M. Moore, S. Estrich, D. McGillis, and W. Spelman, *Dangerous Offenders: The Elusive Target of Justice* (Cambridge: Harvard University Press, 1984).
3. See Margaret Radin, "Cruel Punishment and Respect for Persons: Super Due Process for Death," *Southern California Law Review* 53 (1980):1143. See also William S. Geimer, "Death at Any Cost: A Critique of the Supreme Court's Recent Retreat from Its Death Penalty Standards," *Florida State University Law Review* 12 (1985): 746. Geimer notes: "Given the expansion of due process requirements . . . for ordinary criminal cases," there was a need for " 'super due process' in the administration of this unique penalty, if its imposition were to be admitted at all." Geimer suggests that super due process has not been achieved; but more of this anon. See also the note by B. Brinkman, "The Presumption of Life: A Starting Point for a Due Process Analysis of Capital Sentencing," *Yale Law Review* 94 (1985): 351. She suggests that the burden of proof should be on the prosecution, just as at the conviction stage, to convince the jury or judge of the need for a death penalty.

4. See Thorsten Sellin, *The Death Penalty: A Report for the Model Penal Code Project of the American Law Institute* 5 (Philadelphia: The American Law Institute, 1959) for the comparative studies, and for the statistical research, see Isaac Ehrlich, "The Deterrent Effect of Capital Punishment: A Question of Life and Death," *American Economic Review* 65 (1975):397. This is the first in a series of articles by the author and sparked a controversial debate well summarized in Gordon Waldo, "The Death Penalty and Deterrence: A Review of Recent Research," in I. Barak-Glantz and C. R. Huff, eds., *The Mad, the Bad and the Different: Essays in Honor of Simon Dinitz* (Lexington, Mass.: Lexington Books, 1981). See also P. Passell, "The Deterrent Effect of the Death Penalty: A Statistical Test," *Stanford Law Review* 28 (1975):61.

5. For instance, in the well-known case of the so-called "Gang of Four," whose death sentences were commuted to life imprisonment after two years. There is a fuller discussion of the approaches to the death penalty of different countries in chap. 6.

6. See especially arguments for capital punishment in Walter Berns, *For Capital Punishment: Crime and Morality of the Death Penalty* (New York: Basic Books, 1979); and Raoul Berger, *Death Penalties: The Supreme Court's Obstacle Course* (Cambridge: Harvard University Press, 1982). For leading abolitionist arguments, see Charles Black, *Capital Punishment: The Inevitability of Caprice and Mistake* (New York: Norton, 1974); David Pannick, *Judicial Review of the Death Penalty* (London: Duckworth, 1982); Hugo A. Bedau, *The Courts, the Constitution and Capital Punishment* (Lexington: Lexington Press, 1980); Walsh S. White, *Life in the Balance: Procedural Safeguards in Capital Cases* (Ann Arbor: The University of Michigan Press, 1984); and W. Bowers with G. Pierce and J. Devitt, *Legal Homicide: Death as Punishment in America* (Boston:

Northeastern University Press, 1984). See also Jan Gorecki, *Capital Punishment: Criminal Law and Social Evolution* (New York: Columbia University Press, 1983) for an interesting attempt to link the use of the death penalty to larger societal developments. For opposing arguments in one book, see the joint work by Ernest van den Haag and John P. Conrad, *The Death Penalty: A Debate* (New York: Plenum Press, 1983), in which the former presents the pro point of view and the latter, the con.

7. Furman v. Georgia, 408 U.S. 23 (1972); Gregg v. Georgia. For good reviews of the legal aspects, see the recent collections of articles in the law journals *Journal of Criminal Law and Criminology* (Summer 1983) and *University of California Davis Law Review* (Summer 1985).

8. For fuller discussion of these issues see pt. 3.

9. Jacques Barzun, "In Favor of Capital Punishment," in Hugo Bedau, ed., *The Death Penalty in America* (New York: Anchor Books, 1967). See also Sidney Hook, "The Death Sentence," *The New Leader* 44 (1961):182.

10. See Norman Mailer, *The Executioner's Song* (Boston: Little Brown, 1979) for an account of this affair.

11. Cesare Beccaria, *On Crimes and Punishment* (1784).

12. See *Keesing's Contemporary Archives* 27 (1981):31191. See also my discussion of *in re Caulk* in chap. 12.

13. See for instance W. C. Quillin, "The Death Penalty in the Soviet Union," *American Journal of Criminal Law* 5 (1977):225; and Will Adams, "Capital Punishment in Soviet Criminal Legislation, 1922–1965," in R. F. Kanet and I. Volgyes, eds., *On The Road to Communism* (Lawrence: University of Kansas Press, 1972). For ongoing specific examples of capital punishment for white collar crime, see *Current Digest of the Soviet Press.*

14. See Edwin H. Sutherland, *White Collar Crime* (New York: Holt, Rinehart and Winston, 1961) for the classic argument as to the seriousness of white-collar crime.

15. *Political Killings by Governments: An Amnesty International Report* (London: Amnesty International Publications, 1983).
16. See for instance comment on Brazil in Amnesty International, *The Death Penalty* (London: Amnesty International Publications 1979): "Over the past 12 years, death squads have killed many political activists, but the vast majority of their victims have been petty criminals and tramps" (p. 146).
17. See *Facts on File* 43 (1983):990. See also an article on the Philippines in the *New York Times,* 13 May 1985, "Manila Plainclothes Unit is Focus of Furor After Killing 14." The article describes the work of plainclothes special marshals used to combat urban crime, but human right activists claim that they "have scant regard for due process and could be used against opponents of President Ferdinand Marcos."
18. See Lawrence W. Sherman and Robert H. Longworthy, "Measuring Homicide by Police Officers," *Journal of Criminal Law and Criminology* 70 (1979): 546; Lawrence Sherman, "Execution Without Trial: Police Homicide and the Constitution," *Vanderbilt Law Review* 33 (1980): 70; Arthur Kobler, "Figures (and Perhaps Some Facts) on Police Killings of Civilians in the United States, 1959–69," *Journal of Social Issues* 31 (1975):185. Sherman estimates the number of civilians killed in 1976 at 590 though official figures showed a lower figure of 295 such deaths. In nearly all cases, the deaths were considered to be legally justified. The number of police killed each year is about one-fifth of this figure. See also Peter Scharf and Arnold Binder, *The Badge and the Bullet: Police Use of Deadly Force* (New York: Praeger Press, 1983). Recent reports indicate a decrease in the numbers of victims in the past few years.
19. See Tennessee v. Garner, 471 U.S. 1 (1986). For a fuller discussion of this case, see chap. 13.

20. See for instance Marc Ancel, *Suspended Sentence* (London: Heinemann, 1971); Daniel Glaser, *The Effectiveness of a Prison and Parole System* (Indianapolis: Bobbs-Merrill, 1964); United Nations, *Short-term Imprisonment* (New York, 1954).

21. For personal accounts, see for instance Tom Runyon, *In for Life* (New York: Norton, 1953); and Peter Renick, *In Constant Fear* (New York: Dutton, 1975). For a perceptive analysis by outside research observers, see Stanley Cohen and Laurie Taylor, *Psychological Survival: The Experience of Long Term Imprisonment* (New York: Pantheon Books, 1973).

22. See for instance K. C. Horton, "Life Imprisonment and Pardons in the German Federal Republic," International and Comparative Law Quarterly 29 (1980): 530. See my discussion in chap. 5.

23. United Nations, *Draft Convention against Torture and Other Cruel, Inhuman or Degrading Treatment or Punishment* (E./CN. 4/1984 L. 2 Annex 1984); United Nations, General Assembly, *Unilateral Declaration Against Torture and Other Cruel, Inhuman, or Degrading Treatment or Punishment* (32/64), 8 December 1977.

CHAPTER 2:
IDEOLOGY AND PENOLOGY

1. For discussion of the "free vote" see James B. Christoph, *Capital Punishment and British Politics: The British Movement to Abolish the Death Penalty 1945–57* (Chicago: Chicago University Press, 1962)

2. For the initial leading case in this area, see Witherspoon v. Illinois, 391 U.S. 510 (1968). Forty-nine venirepersons were excluded from the jury because of their opposition to the death penalty. For a discussion of this and later cases, see Welsh White, *Life in the Balance: Procedural*

Safeguards in Capital Cases (Ann Arbor: The University of Michigan Press, 1984), pp. 55–154. These are updated versions of earlier articles published by the author. He particularly discusses the question of possible bias by jurors in the course of their deliberations. For the most recent case see Grigsby v. Mabry, 758 F.2d 226 (1985), cert. granted *sub nom* Lockhart v. McCree, decided in May 1986, allowing continued use of death-qualified juries.

3. See for instance a discussion of Justice Marshall's overall approach in N. Daniels, "Thurgood Marshall and The Death Penalty," *Texas State University Law Review* 4 (1976): 243.

4. See for instance "Debate over the Death Penalty May Cost Top California Judge Her Job," *Philadelphia Inquirer,* 26 October 1986, p. 21.

5. George Rusche and Otto Kirchheimer, *Punishment and Social Structure* (New York: Columbia University Press, 1939); and Thorsten Sellin, *Slavery and the Penal System* (New York: Elsevier, 1976).

6. Svend Ranulf, *Moral Indignation and Middle Class Psychology* (New York: Schocken Books, 1964); and Stanley Cohen, *Visions of Social Control: Crimes, Punishment and Classification* (Cambridge, Eng.: Polity Press, 1985).

7. Walter Berns, *For Capital Punishment: Crime and the Morality of the Death Penalty* (New York: Basic Books, 1979).

8. Cesare Beccaria, *On Crimes and Punishment* (1784).

9. For a brief discussion, see Leon Sheleff, "The Relevance of Classical Criminology Today," in I. Barak-Glantz and C. R. Huff, eds., *The Mad, the Bad and the Different: Essays in Honor of Simon Dinitz* (Lexington, Mass.: Lexington Books, 1981), p. 3.

10. See Arthur Koestler, *Reflections on Hanging* (New York: MacMillan, 1956). One of Koestler's novels deals with Stalin's purges in the 1930s—see *Darkness at Noon* (New York: McMillan, 1941). His experience as a condemned prisoner during the Spanish Civil War, which he was

covering as a war correspondent, is described in his book, *Dialogue with Death* (London: Hutchinson, 1966).

11. John Stuart Mill in *Hansard's Parliamentary Debates*, 21 April 1868, reprinted in G. Ezorsky, ed., *Philosophical Perspectives on Punishment* (Albany, N.Y.: State University of New York Press, 1972).

12. For some more of the nuances in Mill's work, see Leon Sheleff, "The Limitations of Liberalism: A Response to Raz," to be published in R. Gabizon, ed., *Proceedings of the International Conference in Honor of H. L. H. Hart* (held in Jersualem in 1984).

13. See Thorsten Sellin, *The Death Penalty* (Philadelphia: The American Law Institute, 1959); and Hans Zeisel, "The Deterrent Effect of the Death Penalty: Facts v. Faith," *Supreme Court Review* (1976): 317.

14. For the situation in Canada, see C. H. S. Jayewardene, *The Penalty of Death: The Canadian Experiment* (Lexington, Mass.: Lexington Books, 1977), pp. 33–47, 85–91. Note also the article in the *New York Times*, "Pressure for Death Penalty Grows in Canada," 12 November 1984.

15. See for example A. J. Kringel, "The Death Penalty as an Inciter of Criminal and Self-directed Violence on Execution Eve and Execution Day," *Georgia Journal of Corrections* 3 (1974): 85; D. R. King, "The Brutalization Effect: Execution Publicity and the Incidence of Homicide in South Carolina," *Social Forces* 57 (1978): 683; and W. Bowers and G. Pierce, "Deterrence or Brutalization: What is the Effect of Execution?" *Crime and Delinquency* 26 (1980): 453.

16. See Immanuel Kant, *The Philosophy of Law* (Edinburgh: T. T. Clark, 1887).

17. See G. W. F. Hegel, *The Philosophy of Right* (London: Oxford University Press, 1969).

18. See Phil Harris, "A Rational Mask: Public Attitudes toward the Death Penalty," *Life Lines: Newsletter of the National Coalition Against the Death Penalty,* March 1985, p. 1.

19. For Ehrlich, see "The Deterrent Effect of Capital Punishment: A Question of Life and Death," *American Economic Review* 65 (1975): 397. For Sellin, see *The Death Penalty.*

20. Kant, *The Philosophy of Law,* p. 198.

21. Andrew Von Hirsch, *Doing Justice: The Choice of Punishments* (New York: Hill and Wang, 1976); Ernest van den Haag, *Punishing Criminals: Concerning a Very Old and Painful Question* (New York: Basic Books, 1975), specifically on capital punishment, see pp. 208–28; Walter Berns, *For Capital Punishment;* Frank Carrington, *Neither Cruel Nor Unusual* (New Rochelle, N.Y.: Arlington House, 1978). But see C. Thorn, "Retribution Exclusive of Deterrence An Insufficient Justification for Capital Punishment," *Southern California Law Review* 57 (1983): 199.

22. See F. Zimring, *Perspectives on Deterrence* (Washington, D.C.: U.S. Government Printing Office, 1971); Johannes Andenaes, "The General Preventive Effects of Punishment," *University of Pennsylvania Law Review* 114 (1966): 949; and F. Zimring and G. Hawkins, *Deterrence: The Legal Threat in Crime Control* (Chicago: University of Chicago Press, 1973).

23. Robert Martinson, "What Works? Question and Answers about Prison Reform," *Public Interest* 24 (1974): 25. But for strong support of rehabilitation, especially for long-term prisoners, see James Avery Joyce, *Capital Punishment: A World View* (New York: Nelson, 1961), chap. 7, "In Place of Fear." For a general discussion, see Francis A. Allen, *The Decline of the Rehabilitative Ideal: Penal Policy and Social Purpose* (New Haven: Yale University Press, 1981).

24. See for example Norval Morris, *The Future of Imprisonment* (Chicago: The University of Chicago Press, 1974).

25. See for instance Stephen Schafer, "The Victim and Correctional Theory: Integrating Victim Reparation with Offender Rehabilitation," in W. F. McDonald, ed., *Criminal Justice*

and the Victim (Beverly Hills: Sage Publications, 1976), p. 227.

26. But see the discussion on ritual resolutions of the blood feud involving a reconciliation between the offender and victim or victim's family, discussed in chap. 13.

27. See my final chapter for a development of this theme.

28. See especially chap. 4 and chap. 5.

29. Recently a convicted person in his early twenties, Terry Roach, was executed in South Carolina for a murder committed when he was a minor despite pleas from all over the world and efforts by his lawyers to have the case taken to an international body. (See "Young Crime, Old Punishment," *Time,* 20 January 1986, p. 22). An adult accomplice was also executed, whereas a younger accomplice was given a life sentence after turning state's evidence. There are presently on death row over thirty condemned people who were juveniles when they committed the offense. As of 1985, there were three condemned persons who had been fifteen when their crime was committed. (See Victor Streib, "Juveniles on Death Row," *Lifelines,* August 1985, p. 1.)

30. See articles in the *New York Times:* Judith Miller, "Sudan Publicly Hangs an Old Opposition Leader," which appeared on 19 January 1985, two days after an article entitled "Texas Execution is Third in the Nation in a Week." The article on the Sudan notes that the execution was a shock as it had been presumed that "the United States and Egypt had persuaded President Nimeiry to back away from decisions and harsh measures."

31. Furman v. Georgia, 408 U.S. 238 (1972); Gregg v. Georgia, 428 U.S. 153 (1976).

32. See for example Pulley v. Harris, 104 S. Ct. 871 (1984); and note by Marvin Moyell, "Eighth Amendment—Proportionality Review of Death Sentences not Required," *Journal of Criminal Law and Criminology* 75 (1984): 839.

CHAPTER 3 :
FOR LIFE

1. Hugo Bedau, preface to P. Mackey, ed., *Voices Against Death: American Opposition to Capital Punishment, 1787–1975* (New York: B. Franklin and Co., 1976), p. vi. Bedau adds that in the selections in the book "most of the abolitionists . . . have kept their answers [as to alternatives] to themselves or have no answers at all." He suggests that today abolitionists are more careful "not to attack executions only to end defending 'life imprisonment' without any possibility of parole." But he provides little documentation for this claim, which seems unfounded. It is worth noting that Bedau acknowledges also that abolitionists have ignored larger issues of terror, genocide, etc. He writes: "Whether the death penalty is legitimate in extreme or unusual circumstances—under martial law, for example, or in dealing with a Quisling or an Eichmann—is not something on which abolitionists have ever had a fixed position"—or for that matter, even generally expressed an opinion.

2. Cesare Beccaria, *On Crimes and Punishment* (1784); sec. 28, "Of the Punishment of Death."

3. Albert Camus, "Reflections on the Guillotine," in *Resistance, Rebellion and Death* (New York: Knopf, 1960), p. 231.

4. California v. Ramos, 103 S.Ct., p. 3464, Marshall, J., dissenting.

5. See Thorsten Sellin, "Beccaria's Substitute for the Death Penalty," in S. Landau and L. Sebba, eds., *Criminology in Perspective: Essays in Honor of Israel Drapkin* (Lexington, Mass.: Lexington Books, 1977).

6. See "Life Sentence Means Much Less, Study Says," *Philadelphia Inquirer,* 24 September 1984, p. 8. These figures

will be examined critically later on in this chapter. See note 60 and related text.

7. But see C. H. S. Jayewardene, *The Penalty of Death: The Canadian Experiment* (Lexington, Mass.: Lexington Books, 1977), chap. 8, "The Alternative of Life Imprisonment."

8. See Leon Sheleff, "The Mandatory Life Sentence—A Comparative Study of the Law in Israel, Great Britain, the United States and West Germany," *Tel Aviv University Studies in Law* 5 (1980–82): 119.

9. Ibid., p. 133; see chap. 5.

10. See Connecticut Board of Pardons v. Dumschat, 452 U.S. 458 (1981).

11. There is no category at all for life imprisonment in leading abstract services such as *Abstracts in Criminology* and *Criminal Justice Abstracts.* In contrast, there are many entries under the heading of "capital punishment." Similar disparities appear in almost all the leading textbooks in criminology and criminal justice. The following leading textbooks contain no references to life imprisonment at all but have separate references to capital punishment as well as other special kinds of punishment, such as fines, probation, etc. See for example Edwin Sutherland and Donald Cressey, *Criminology* (Chicago, Lippincott, 1970); Robert Caldwell *Criminology* (New York: Ronald Press, 1956); Herbert A. Bloch and Gilbert Geis, *Man, Crime and Society,* 2d ed. (New York: Random House, 1970); Elmer Johnson, *Crime, Correction and Society* (Homewood, Ill.: Dorsey, 1974); Walter C. Reckless, *The Crime Problem* (New York: Appleton-Century-Crofts, 1961). Barnes and Teeters do make one passing reference to life imprisonment, but this in the context of a discussion of habitual criminal laws (Harry Barnes and Negley Teeters, *New Horizons in Criminology* [Englewood Cliffs, N.J.: Prentice-Hall, 1959], p. 59). They do, however, also note an article by Alfred Harries, "How Long is a Life Sentence for Murder?" *Proceedings of American Correctional Association*

(1939): 518. For discussion of the use of solitary confinement for long-term prisoners, see T. McDade, *The Annals of Murder* (Omaha: University of Oklahoma Press, 1961), pp. 357–59. For a recent article on life imprisonment, see John P. Conrad, "The Society of Lifers," *The Prison Journal* 62 (1982): 125. The article deals mainly with problems of discipline in managing large populations of lifers, but it also contains useful information about the lifers, to be discussed later in this chapter (see note 62 and related text). It should also be noted that during the 1970s several articles appeared in the *British Journal of Criminology* addressing largely the psychological aspects of long-term imprisonment, but they did not related specifically to the unique problems of lifers. See, for instance, T. Flanagan, "The Pains of Long-Term Imprisonment," *British Journal of Criminology* 20 (1980): 148. The article contains in its bibliography a list of the earlier articles. See also Renee Short, *The Care of Long-Term Prisoners* (London: MacMillan, 1979) which compared the prison conditions for such prisoners in seven different countries. The heightened interest in long-term prisoners during this period was partly sparked by the initial temporary ban on capital punishment during part of that time. Finally, it should be mentioned that a check of the catalog at the main and law libraries of Temple University and University of Pennsylvania shows that there is no category of "life imprisonment."

12. Marvin Wolfgang, Arlene Kelly, and Hans Nolde, "Comparison of the Executed and the Commuted Among Admissions to Death Row," *Journal of Criminal Law, Criminology and Police Science* 53 (1962): 301.

13. Furman v. Georgia, 408 U.S. 238 (1972).

14. There are, to the best of my knowledge, no published data on the number of "lifers" who die in prison each year, or how many years they served until their death. In Pennsylvania, for example, the figures seem to be five to ten

per year—but these figures are not published in annual reports. Individual factors, such as cause of death, age, and time served are also not readily available. In a personal communication from the Pennsylvania Board of Corrections, the figures for the three most recent years indicate that 22 life prisoners died, 2 from suicide. The average length of time that they spent in prison was 10 years, but almost none reached the biblical span of 70. Most were in their 50s and had died of a wide variety of illnesses. The oldest was 83. It should be noted that during the seven-year term of Governor Thornburgh, although about 70 life prisoners died in prison, only 7 were released from prison.

15. Thus, for instances James Avery Joyce writes: "There is no case on record, as far as the author has been able to discover, where an individual has *chosen* to die at the hand of the State rather than to live" (*Capital Punishment: A World View* [New York: Thomas Nelson, 1961], p. 236). As noted, there are now several cases on record in the United States, and no doubt elsewhere as well.

16. See National Council of Civil Liberties, *Death in Prison* (1980), as reported in Penal Policy File No. 4; "Suicides in Prison," *Howard Journal of Penology and Crime Prevention* 20 (1980): 41; David A. Jones, *The Health Risks of Imprisonment* (Lexington: Lexington Books, 1976), pp. 68–72. See also Commonwealth v. Chester, 337, Mass. 702 at 709, 710:914 N.E.2d 914 (1958), in which the accused specifically asked for death penalty and then, after being granted it, committed suicide.

17. See for instance Commonwealth of Pennsylvania v. McKenna, Pa. 383 A2d., 174 (1978). The court held that "the waiver concept was never intended as a means of allowing a criminal defendant to choose his own sentence. Especially is this so where, as here, to do so would result in a state-aided suicide." However, it would appear that the real issue was not the condemned person's right to

exercise a waiver, but the fact that there were meaningful constitutional issues that his lawyer wished to raise, with the concomitant danger that an illegal execution might take place. This fact was stressed in a separate opinion by one of the judges, Dix, who argued that in principle the court "could not *sua sponte* intervene against defendant's wishes."

18. See especially George Solomon, "Capital Punishment as Suicide and as Murder," *American Journal of Ortho-psychiatry,* 45 (1975): 701. See also Hugo Adam Bedau, *The Courts, the Constitution and Capital Punishment* (Lexington: Lexington Books, 1977); and Norman Mailer, *The Executioner's Song* (Boston: Little Brown, 1979). For a study of several persons who have attempted suicide in prison in the United States, see Hans Toch, *Men in Crisis: Human Breakdowns in Prison* (Chicago: Aldine 1975), pp. 205–80.

19. There is a detailed account of such deliberate harshness in the October 1984 issue of *Lifelines.* The note, written by Bill Menza, suggests "a calculated plan" by government and prison officials "to break the spirit and will and mental health of all death row prisoners . . . as quickly as possible so that they will choose to be killed as planned by Virginian government officials." Among the methods being used are total confinement in four-by-five-foot cells (except for three five-minute showers per week), severe restrictions on contacts with prisoners, attorneys, clergy, family, and friends, and harassment for those visitors who do come for visits. See the work by Robert Johnson, "Warehousing for Death: Observations on the Human Environment of Death Row," *Crime and Delinquency* 26 (1980): 545; and *Condemned to Die: Life under Sentence of Death* (Washington, D.C.: Elsevier, 1981). See also Doug Magee, *Slow Coming Dark: Interviews on Death Row* (New York: Pilgrim Press, 1980); and Bruce Jackson and Diane Christian, *Death Row* (Boston: Beacon Press, 1980).

20. See the recent case of Groseclose v. Dutton, U.S.D.C. M. Tenn. No. 3-84-0579 (17 August 1984), as reported in the *Criminal Law Reporter* 36 (3 October 1984): 2019. It was held that conditions in Tennessee state penitentiaries were so poor that they nullify a condemned inmate's waiver of his right to postconviction remedies since it was the adverse conditions that had prompted the waiver. By analogy to the area of criminal guilty appeals a decision to forego due process protection created for a criminal defendant demands a voluntary relinquishment of constitutional rights.'' The court referred to the problems of cramped, hot cells, inadequate lighting and ventilation, cold food, and lack of regularly scheduled religious services. It should be noted that on occasion conditions such as this have led to a directly opposite response, not a waiver of rights, but the argument that the condemned person is being subject to cruel and unusual punishment. See case pending in Pennsylvania, Peterson et al. v. Thornburgh (Civ. A. No. 83-0304); as discussed also in "Life On Death Row: Can It Be Unconstitutional?" *Philadelphia Inquirer,* 16 June 1986, sec. C, p. 1. Sometimes, however, there is a third alternative, where adverse conditions may be seen as providing a justification for foregoing an appeal: "In view of the allegations in the case of *Jacobs v. Locke,* the death row conditions of confinement case presently pending in this Court, it may well be that [he] has made the more rational choice" (Betty Evans, as next friend of John Evans v. Bennet, 467 F. Supp. 1108, 1110 [S.D. Ala., 1979]).

21. Hugo Bedau, *The Courts, the Constitution and Capital Punishment,* p. 124.

22. See for instance Bessie Gilmore, as next friend of Gary Gilmore v. Utah, 429 U.S. 1012 (1976); Lenhard, as next friend of Bishop v. Wolff, 100 S. Ct. 3 (1979); Betty Evans, as next friend of John Evans v. Bennett, 440 U.S. 1301 (1979); Coppola v. Commonwealth, cert.denied, 444 U.S. 1103 (1980).

23. Lenhard, as next friend of Bishop v. Wolff, 603 F.2d 91 (1979), p. 94.

24. Melvin Urofsky, "A Right to Die: Termination of Appeal for Condemned Prisoners," *Journal of Criminal Law and Criminology* 75 (1984): 568. Karen Quinlan was the comatose patient whose family applied to the court for permission to remove her from life-sustaining devices. Her doctor claimed that such a procedure would lead to her early death. The court decided to allow the family's request. She then lingered on in a comatose state, never recovering consciousness, for almost another ten years, being fed intraveneously.

It should be noted that Urofsky's arguments in favor of allowing a condemned person to be executed are based on the difficult conditions in death row; he does not discuss the issue of death as a chosen alternative to life imprisonment. See also G. R. Strafer, "Volunteering for Execution: Competency, Voluntariness and the Propriety of Third Party Intervention" *Journal of Criminal Law and Criminology* 74 (1983): 860; "The Death Row Right to Die: Suicide or Intimate Decision?" *Southern California Law Review* 54 (1981): 575.

25. For a graphic description of torture throughout history, see George R. Scott, *The History of Torture Throughout the Ages* (London: Luxor Press, 1940). See also Harry Barnes, *The Story of Punishment: A Record of Man's Inhumanity to Man* (Montclair: Patterson Smith, 1972); L. A. Parry, *The History of Torture in England* (Montclair: Patterson Smith, 1975); James Heath, *Torture and English Law: An Administrative and Legal History from the Plantagenets to the Stuarts* (London: Greenwood Press, 1982); and M. Ruthven, *Torture: The Grand Conspiracy* (London: Wiedenfeld and Nicholson, 1976).

26. United Nations, General Assembly, *Declaration on the Protection of All Persons from Torture and Other Cruel,*

Inhuman or Degrading Treatment or Punishment, 9 December 1975; General Assembly, *Unilateral Declaration Against Torture and Other Cruel, Inhuman or Degrading Treatment or Punishment* (32/64), 8 December 1977.

27. Amnesty International, *Torture in the Eighties* (London: Amnesty International Publications, 1984); Amnesty International, *Report on Torture* (New York: Farrar, Straus and Giroux, 1975).

28. An execution is not the only situation in which the moment of death is predetermined. In the cases of suicide and euthanasia it is also predetermined, although there is, of course, a big difference in that in the latter instances death is usually the result of a voluntary decision. However, when a choice is given an accused person, a certain degree of voluntariness can be considered to be present.

29. K. C. Horton, "Life Imprisonment and Pardons in the German Federal Republic," *International and Comparative Law Quarterly* 29 (1980): 530.

30. For a fuller discussion, see chap. 12.

31. John Stuart Mill, "Parliamentary Debate on Capital Punishment Within Prisons Bill," in *Hansard's Parliamentary Debates,* 3d series, 21 April 1868 (London: Hansard, 1868). Reprinted in Gertrude Ezorsky, ed., *Philosophical Perspectives on Punishment* (Albany: SUNY Press, 1972), p. 271.

32. Ibid., pp. 272–73. Mill might also have noted that he was also parting company with his liberal predecessor, Bentham, who had favored life imprisonment with harsh conditions. But this difference actually stems from an agreement as to the harshness of life imprisonment. Thus Bentham writes: "It appears, however, to me, that the contemplation of perpetual imprisonment, accompanied with hard labor and occasional solitary confiment, would produce a deeper impression in the minds of persons in whom it is more eminently desirable that that impression should be produced, than even death itself" (John Bowring, ed.,

The Work of Jeremy Bentham [New York: Russell and Russell, 1962], 1: 450).

33. Many rulers at the time, for instance, Catherine the Great of Russia, evinced real interest in his ideas, and several attempts were made to implement some of them. See James A. Farrer, *Crimes and Punishments; Including a New Translation of Beccaria's "Dei Delitti E Delle Pene"* (London: Chatto and Windus, 1980) for a discussion of Beccaria's influence on legislation and the problems of penology. See also Leon Sheleff, "The Relevance of Classical Criminology Today," in I. Barak-Glantz and C. R. Huff, eds., *The Mad, the Bad and the Different: Essays in Honor of Simon Dinitz* (Lexington: Lexington Books, 1981), pp. 8-12.

34. Sellin, "Beccaria's Substitute," p. 8. For examples of penal servitude in practice, see Ruth Pike, *Penal Servitude in Early Modern Spain* (Madison: University of Wisconsin Press, 1983). Pike discusses work in galleys, mines, naval yards, public works, etc.—some of the examples, though, predate Beccaria.

35. George Bernard Shaw, *The Crime of Punishment* (New York: The Philosophical Library, 1946).

36. Ibid., p. 9.

37. William Tallack, *Penological and Preventive Principles* (London: Wertheimer, Lea and Co., 1888), chap. 4, "Perpetual or Life Imprisonment," pp. 151-64.

38. Ibid., p. 152.

39. Ibid., pp. 152-53.

40. Ibid., p. 160.

41. Sidney Hook, "The Death Sentence," *The New Leader* 44 (1961): 182; and Jacques Barzun, "In Favor of Capital Punishment," in Bedau, ed., *The Death Penalty.*

42. Camus, *Resistance,* p. 233. For a discussion of lethal injection, see Martin Gardner, "Execution and Indignities—An Eighth Amendment Assessment of Methods of Inflicting Capital Punishment," *The Ohio State Law Journal* 39 (1978): 110.

43. This is discussed in more detail at the end of this chapter.

44. Michel Foucault, *Discipline and Punish: The Birth of the Prison* (New York: Pantheon Books, 1977), p. 32.

45. Michael Ignatieff, *A Just Measure of Pain: The Penitentiary in the Industrial Revolution 1750–1850* (New York: Pantheon Books, 1978), p. 15. See also Barnes, *Story of Punishment,* p. 114.

46. Negley K. Teeters, *The Cradle of the Penitentiary: The Walnut Street Jail at Philadelphia 1773–1835* (Philadelphia: Pennsylvania Prison Society, 1955), p. 1.

47. Ibid., p. 2.

48. Foucault, *Discipline and Punish,* p. 74.

49. See Leon Radzinowicz, *A History of English Criminal Law* (London: Stevens and Sons, 1948); on jury nullification, see Thomas Green, *Verdict According to Conscience: Perspectives on the English Criminal Trial Jury 1200–1800* (Chicago: University of Chicago Press, 1985); on pardoning, see Fenton Bresler, *Reprieve; A Study of a System* (London: Harrap and Co., 1965); on benefit of clergy, see Ignatieff, *A Just Measure,* p. 18.

50. Ignatieff, *A Just Measure,* "Preaching Walls: The Penitentiary in Practice," pp. 80–113.

51. Ibid.

52. Ibid., p. 202. Note also the contemporaneous comment of William Paley, writing in 1785, claiming that transportation, "the sentence second in the order of severity," was an unsatisfactory substitute for the death penalty, and therefore the reason for the continued use of the death penalty. See extracts from his writings in James Heath, *Eighteenth Century Penal Theory* (Oxford: Oxford University Press, 1963). For a general discussion of transportation, see George Rude, *Protest and Punishment: The Story of the Social and Political Protestors Transported to Australia, 1788–1868* (Oxford: Oxford University Press, 1978).

53. Ignatieff, *A Just Measure,* pp. 202–3.

54. Ibid., p. 201.

55. See Teeters, *Cradle of the Penitentiary;* and Barnes, *Story of Punishment.*

56. Foucault, *Discipline and Punish,* p. 9.

57. Ibid., p. 10.

58. Ibid., p. 11.

59. Lewis Lawes, *Man's Judgement of Death* (Montclair: Patterson Smith, 1969.)

60. *Prison Admissions and Releases* (Washington, D.C.: The Department of Justice, 1984).

61. *Prison Admissions and Releases* (Washington, D.C.: The Department of Justice, 1985).

62. John P. Conrad, "The Society of Lifers," p. 128.

63. Information provided by the Pennsylvania Correctional System and the Pennsylvania Board of Probation and Parole (in personal communication).

64. The legal issues are discussed in chap. 5.

65. One interesting possibility also exists if parts of the argument made by constitutional lawyer Raoul Berger are ever accepted. Focusing specifically on the constitutional aspect and arguing from a strict interpretation perspective, he maintains that since the death penalty was an accepted punishment at the time of the Constitution was written, it cannot be declared unconstitutional now (*Death Penalties* [Cambridge: Harvard University Press,1982]). If this argument is ever accepted, then by the same token it may be claimed that since life imprisonment was almost unknown at that period, it cannot now be considered constitutional. For an important description of the historical background to the Eighth Amendment, see P. Granucci, " 'Nor Cruel and Unusual Punishment Inflicted': The Original Meaning," *California Law Review* 57 (1969): 839. For an extensive survey of its use in the United States, see Larry Berkson, *The Concept of Cruel and Unusual Punishment* (Lexington: Lexington Books, 1975).

CHAPTER 4:
THE ARBITRARY
"ARBITRARY" RULE

1. For a full list of executions in the United States from 1864 to 1967, see William J. Bowers, *Executions in America* (Lexington, Mass.: Lexington Books, 1974).
2. Witherspoon v. Illiniois, 391 U.S. 510 (1968).
3. Gerald H. Gottlieb, "Testing the Death Penalty," *Southern California Law Review* 34 (1961): 268. Arguments as to the unconstitutionality of the death sentence based on discriminatory practices had been used unavailingly in 1967 by the last person to be executed before the moratorium began. See B. Wolfe, *Pile-up on Death Row* (New York: Doubleday, 1976), p. 85.
4. Furman v. Georgia, 408 U.S. 23 (1972).
5. For a good description of the way in which the legal struggle for abolition was planned and implemented, written by one of the participants in the struggle, see Michael Meltsner, *Cruel and Unusual: The Supreme Court and Capital Punishment* (New York: Random House, 1973). He especially praises the work of Anthony Amsterdam. For the views of Amsterdam, see his article, "Capital Punishment," *The Stanford Magazine* (Fall 1977): 42.
6. Gregg v. Georgia, 428 U.S. 153 (1976).
7. Charles Black, Jr., *Capital Punishment: The Inevitability of Caprice and Mistake* (New York: Norton, 1974). For a similar approach, see the earlier LL.M. thesis by Alan Harland, *Capital Punishment in America: An Analysis of the Position Following the U.S. Supreme Court Decision in Furman v. Georgia* (Philadelphia: University of Pennsylvania LL.M. thesis, 1973).
8. See for instance the work of Neil Vidmar and Phoebe Fellsworth, "Public Opinion and the Death Penalty," *Stanford Law Review* 26 (1974): 1245; and Neil Vidmar and

T. Dittenhoffer, "Informed Public Opinion and Death Penalty Attitudes," *Canadian Journal of Criminology* 23 (1981): 43.

9. Hugo A. Bedau, "Challenging the Death Penalty," *Harvard Civil Rights–Civil Liberties Law Review* 9 (1974): 624.

10. Gregg v. Georgia; Woodson v. N. Carolina, 428 U.S. 280 (1976); Roberts v. Louisiana, 428 U.S. 325 (1976); Profitt v. Florida, 428 U.S. 242 (1976); Jurek v. Texas, 428 U.S. 262 (1976).

11. Gregg v. Georgia, p. 198.

12. Lockett v. Ohio, 438 U.S. 586 (1977). See also Hill v. State, 229 S.E. 2d 737 (1976), a death sentence case in which Judge Ingram, in a dissenting judgment, commented that "one cannot find a more similar case to compare than the case of the perpetrator co-defendant." Here, too, the life sentence given to the codefendant emerged after a plea bargain.

13. Enmund v. Florida, 458 U.S. 782 (1982). Doug Magee, who has interviewed many prisoners on death row, claims that in many instances an accomplice of the condemned person had turned state's evidence and received a short sentence. See *Slow Coming Death* (New York: Pilgrim Press, 1980). But the position of the accomplice still seems confused, for instance, as to which mental state would justify imposition of the death penalty. See Douglas Schwartz, "Imposing the Death Sentence for Felony Murder on a Non-triggerman," *Stanford Law Review* 37 (1985): 857.

14. Barclay v. Florida, 463 U.S. 939 (1983).

15. See Pulley v. Harris, 465 U.S. 37 (1984). For a critique of this case, see M. Mayell, "Eighth Amendment— Proportionality Review of Death Sentences Not Required," *Journal of Criminal Law and Criminology* 75 (1984); 839.

16. See especially William S. Geimer, "Death at any Cost: A Critique of the Supreme Court's Recent Retreat from its Death Penalty Standard," *Florida State University Law*

Review 12 (1985): 737. See also special issues of *Journal of Criminal Law and Criminology* (Summer 1983); *University of California, Davis, Law Review* (Summer 1985); and *Crime and Delinquency* (1980). See also my article "The Arbitrariness of the 'Arbitrary Rule' in Death Penalty Cases in the United States," *Israel Yearbook on Human Rights* 11 (1981): 217. Some of the ideas expressed in this article have been incorporated into this chapter.

17. See Geimer, "Death at any Cost," p. 739, discussing the case of Sullivan v. Wainwright, 104 S. Ct. 450 (1983). See also my later reference in chap. 14.

18. Zant v. Stephens, 462 U.S. 862 (1983); Pulley v. Harris. In *Zant* the Court allowed a death sentence to stand, despite finding one of three aggravating circumstances to be invalid. It seems clear that had the jury not taken account of this circumstance, they may well have concluded that a death sentence was too severe a punishment. Yet the Court ignored such a likely supposition.

19. Lockett v. Ohio, p. 605.

20. Ibid., White, J., dissenting, p. 623.

21. Ibid., pp. 624–25.

22. See Regina Reid, "Liability of an Aider and Abettor for Aggravated Murder in Ohio: *State v. Lockett,*" *Ohio State University Law Journal* 39 (1978): 214; Schwartz, "Imposing the Death Sentence."

23. Enmund v. Florida.

24. Gregg v. Georgia, p. 199.

25. Ibid., p. 199.

26. Ibid., p. 199.

27. Ibid., p. 200, n. 50.

28. Brodenkircher v. Hayes, 434 U.S. 357 (1978).

29. Ibid., pp. 368–69.

30. Roberts v. Louisiana.

31. Gregg v. Georgia, p. 200, n. 50.

32. Roberts v. Louisiana, pp. 334–35.

33. Beck v. Alabama, 447 U.S. 625 (1980).

34. Barclay v. Florida. It should be noted that as of late 1984, there had been 83 cases in which the trial judge had overruled a recommendation of life imprisonment by the jury and imposed a death penalty. Of these, 39 had been overruled by the Florida Supreme Court, 21 had been confirmed, and the rest are pending or have other outcomes. For details, see J. Weller, "Eighth Amendment—Trial Court May Impose Death Sentence Despite Jury's Recommendation of Life Imprisonment," *Journal of Criminal Law and Criminology* 75 (1984): 828, n. 133, quoting the petitioner's brief in Spaziano v. Florida, 468 U.S. 447 (1984). See also Michael Mello and Ruthann Robson, "Judge Over Jury: Florida's Practice of Imposing Death Over Life in Capital Cases," *Florida Law Review* 13 (1985): 31.

35. Barclay v. Florida, Marshall J., dissenting opinion, p. 981.

36. Ibid., p. 984. There had been four defendants; two had been given the death sentence and the other two, life sentences. Their joint responsibility, in a premeditated murder with political and racial overtones, seemed to be equal. Inasmuch as a differentiation could be made, it would seem that Barefoot's role was closer to that of the two who received life than the one who was given the death sentence.

37. Green v. State, 272 S.E. 2d 475.

38. Ibid., Hill, J., dissenting, p. 485. There was a further problem relating to another juror, which raises additional suspicions as to the validity of the decision-making process of the jury and the review by the court of this process. In the majority opinion, there is the following description of what transpired in the lower court: "After the verdict and sentence of the court, and after asking if he was excused, defense counsel requested a poll of the jury. During the poll, a juror replied to the question, 'Is this your verdict now?' by stating, 'No, it's not, your Honor. I cannot do it.' The juror previously had responded that the verdict was his verdict in the jury room. The judge took a

three-minute recess and then upon information that the juror had misunderstood the question, called the jurors back and explained what was meant by the question asked. The jury was then polled and the formerly reluctant jurior answered that it was his verdict. We find no error" (p. 483).

39. Gregg v. Georgia, p. 200, n. 50.

40. See Bessie Gilmore, as next friend of Gary Gilmore v. Utah, 429 U.S. 1012 (1976).

41. Roberts v. Louisiana, White, J., dissenting.

42. Marvin Wolfgang, Arlene Kelly, and Hans Nolde, "Comparison of the Executed and Commuted Among Admissions to Death Row," *Journal of Criminal Law, Criminology and Police Science* 53 (1962): 301.

43. See Hugo A. Bedau, "Murder, Errors of Justice and Capital Punishment," in Bedau, ed., *Death Penalty in America* (Chicago: Aldine, 1964). See the forthcoming book on this topic by C. Ronald Huff, Aryeh Rattner, and Edward Sagarin, *Convicted but Innocent: Wrongful Conviction and Public Policy* (Columbus: Ohio State University Press). Included in the research are some cases of capital punishment.

44. Connecticut Board of Pardons v. Dumschat, 452 U.S. 458 (1981).

45. See Leslie Sebba, "Pardon and Amnesty—Judicial and Penological Aspects," (Ph.D. diss., Hebrew University, 1978). It is in Hebrew with an English summary.

46. See reference in Hugo A. Bedau, *The Courts, the Constitution and Capital Punishment* (Lexington, Mass.: Lexington Books, 1977).

47. In Pennsylvania there has been an opposite situation where the outgoing governor, Governor Thornburgh, has signed a death warrant with a date of execution due to take place after he relinquishes office. There were suggestions that this, too, might be challenged in the courts. In any event, there has been no execution in Pennsylvania since the early 1960s. For interesting views of a governor's dilemma,

see former Ohio Governor Michael DiSalle's book, *The Power of Life or Death* (New York: Random House, 1965).

48. People v. Morse 388 P. 2d 33 (1984).

49. California v. Ramos, 463 U.S. 992 (1983).

50. Ibid., Marshall, J., dissenting judgment, p. 1020.

51. Ibid., p. 1023.

52. Ibid., majority opinion, p. 1011.

53. William B. Huie, *The Execution of Private Slovik* (New York: The New American Library, 1954).

54. Bedau, *The Courts,* p. 118.

55. Barefoot v. Estelle, 463 U.S. 880 (1983).

56. Per Stewart, Powell, and Stevens, JJ., in Gregg v. Georgia.

CHAPTER 5:
LIFE IMPRISONMENT
AND HUMAN RIGHTS

1. For a list of cases decided in lower courts, see Joseph Cook, *Constitutional Rights of the Accused: Post-Trial Rights* (Rochester, New York: The Lawyers Co-operative Publishing Co., 1976), pp. 26–27.

2. Furman v. Georgia, 408 U.S. 238 (1972).

3. Lockett v. Ohio, 438 U.S. 586 (1977), p. 605.

4. Weems v. United States, 217 U.S. 349 (1910).

5. Workman v. Commonwealth, 429 S.W. 2d 374.

6. This phrase was first used in the case of Trop v. Dulles, 356 U.S. 86 (1958).

7. See Leon Sheleff, "Mandatory Life Sentences: A Comparative Study of the Law in Israel, Great Britain, the United States and West Germany," *Tel Aviv University Studies in Law* 5 (1982): 116–43. Parts of this article have been incorporated into this chapter; the article itself was published before the leading case of Solem v. Helm, 463 U.S. 277 (1984); see note 24 and related text.

8. Hart v. Coiner, 483 F. 2d 136 (1973); cert. denied, 415 U.S. 983 (1974).
9. Hart v. Coiner (1973), p. 139.
10. Ibid, p. 141.
11. Ibid., pp. 140–44.
12. Rummel v. Estelle, Director, Texas Department of Corrections, 445 U.S. 263 (1980). The relevant statute was article 63 of the Texas Penal Code: "Whoever shall have been three times convicted of a felony less than capital, shall on such third conviction be imprisoned for life in the penitentiary." For a discussion of this case, see Archibald Cox, "Supreme Court, 1979 Term: Freedom of Expression in the Burger Court," *Harvard Law Review* 94 (1980): 87; Charles Schwartz, "Eighth Amendment Proportionality Analysis and the Compelling Case of William Rummel," *Journal of Criminal Law and Criminology* 71 (1980): 378.
13. Rummel v. Estelle, 587 F. 2d 651 (1978).
14. Rummell v. Estelle (1980), p. 272.
15. Ibid., pp. 291–92.
16. Ibid., p. 307.
17. See Coker v. Georgia, 433 U.S. 584 (1977). Where the maximum penalty for murder is life imprisonment, penalties for other crimes should obviously be less. That is, for as long as the guidelines of the Court remain operative—namely, that the death penalty is a uniquely severe penalty and can only be used for the taking of life—then, conversely, whatever lesser penalty is given for murder (for instance, life imprisonment), penalties for other crimes should be less than that.
18. Wanstreet v. Bordenkircher, 276 S.E.2d 205 (1981).
19. Bordenkircher, Penitentiary Superintendent v. Hayes, 434 U.S. 357 (1978).
20. Hayes v. Cowan, Warden, 547 F. 2d 42 (1977).
21. Bordenkircher v. Hayes, p. 365.

22. Ibid., p. 371. For support of the dissenting approach and criticism of the majority opinion, see Howard Abrams, "Systematic Coercion: Unconstitutional Conditions in the Criminal Law," *Journal of Criminal Law and Criminology* 72 (1981):128.

23. Connecticut Board of Pardons v. Dumschat, 452 U.S. 458 (1981).

24. Solem v. Helm. See C. Olsen, "The Requirement of Proportionality in Criminology Sentencing: *Solem v. Helm,*" *New England Journal on Criminal and Civil Confinement* 11 (1985):243. For an earlier court of appeal case in which life imprisonment without parole was held to be within the terms of the Constitution, see Green v. Teets, 244 F.2d 401 (1957). In this case the prisoner convicted of murder had originally been sentenced to death but had had the penalty commuted to life without parole.

25. Ibid., p. 302.

26. Ibid., p. 297, n. 22. Helm "is not a professional criminal. The record indicates an addiction to alcohol, and a consequent difficulty in holding a job. His record involves no instance of violence of any kind. Incarcerating him for life without possibility of parole is unlikely to advance the goals of our criminal justice system in any substantive way."

27. Ibid., dissenting opinion (per Burger, C.J.), p. 304.

28. Ibid., p. 306.

29. Ibid., p. 298, quoting *Los Angeles Times,* 16 November 1980, p. 1, col. 3.

30. Ibid., dissenting opinion, p. 317, quoting *Chicago Tribune,* 15 November 1980, p. 2, col. 3. It is interesting to note that the majority stress the fact of Rummel's release within eight months of the Supreme Court decision, whereas the minority stress the reason for his release by writ of habeas corpus, noting that it could not ever be known when or whether he would have actually been released by parole.

31. Hutto v. Davis, 454 U.S. 370 (1981).

32. Davis v. Davis, 646 F.2d 123 (Ca. 4, 1981).

33. Hutto v. Davis, p. 372.
34. Ibid. (Powell, J., concurring in the judgment), pp. 375, 380, 379.
35. Ibid., dissenting opinion, p. 381.
36. Ibid., p. 388.
37. Weems v. U.S.
38. Solem v. Helm, p. 313 (italics in original).
39. Ibid., p. 316.
40. Ibid., pp. 316–17.
41. Ibid., p. 302, as expressed in the majority opinion.
42. Ibid., p. 317.
43. Thorsten Sellin, "Beccaria's Substitute for the Death Penalty," in S. Landau and L. Sebba, eds., *Criminology in Perspective: Essays in Honor of Israel Drapkin* (Lexington, Mass.: Lexington Books, 1977).
44. See Norman Mailer, *The Executioner's Song* (Boston: Little Brown, 1979).
45. See People v. Harman, 333 N.W. 2d 591 (1983); see also State v. Hopkins, 351 So.2d 474 (La., 1977); People v. Ward, 351 N.W.2d 208 (Mich. Ct. App., 1984). In all these cases the courts upheld a mandatory life sentence for drug offenses.
46. For fuller details, see K. C. Horton, "Life Imprisonment and Pardons in the German Federal Republic," *International and Comparative law Quarterly* 29 (1980): 530.
47. Ibid.
48. Ibid., p. 532.
49. Ibid., p. 533.
50. See Amnesty International, *The Death Penalty* (London: Amnesty International Publications, 1979).
51. See for example Calvert Dodge, *A World Without Prisons: Alternatives Throughout the World* (Lexington, Mass.: Lexington Books, 1979), which contains articles about attempts throughout the world to minimize the use of prison by the use of alternative means of punishment or of procedures

such as mediation and restitution. But the book fails to deal with the problem of violent offenders, guilty of extreme crimes. See also Robert Somer, *The End of Imprisonment* (New York: Oxford University Press, 1976). See also the comment by Judge Doyle in a Wisconsin case dealing with mail censorship in the prisons (Morales v. Schmidt, 340 F. Supp. 544 [1972]): "I am persuaded that the institution of prison probably must end. In many respects it is as intolerable within the United States as was the institution of slavery, equally brutalizing to all involved, equally toxic to the social system, equally subversive of the brotherhood of man, even more costly by some standard, and probably less rational." See also Philip Hirschkop and Michael Millemann, "The Unconstitutionality of Prison Life," *Virginia Law Review* 55 (1969):795. The argument of unconstitutionality is based on what the authors see as the accumulated consequences of judicial decisions dealing with prison conditions, in which various specific situations, such as overcrowding, unnecessary restrictions, severe living conditions, etc., are declared unconstitutional. However, the total demise of prisons based on these adverse decisions seems an unlikely outcome. In most instances, it is the intention of the court only to redress the specific grievance; to this end the court sometimes appoints a special master to monitor its directives to the prison authorities. Once corrected, the pressures for change diminish.

52. *Instead of Prisons: A Handbook for Abolitionists* (Syracuse, N.Y.: Prison Research Education Action Project, 1976), p. 135. See also Eugene Natale and Cecilia Rosenberg, "And the Walls Come Tumbling Down: An Analysis of Social and Legal Pressures Bearing on the American Prison System," *New York Law Forum* 19 (1974):609. Here, too, the authors concede that there must remain "a small segment of offenders that must be kept in custody; they are 'dangerous.' It is the general consensus that society must

ensure that as long as such offenders pose this serious threat, they should be effectively isolated from us."

53. Margaret Radin, "The Jurisprudence of Death: Evolving Standards for the Cruel and Unusual Punishment Clause," *University of Pennsylvania Law Review* 126 (1978):989.

54. Ibid., p. 1022, n. 132.

55. Ibid., p. 1015.

56. Arthur Goldberg and Alan Dershowitz, "Declaring the Death Penalty Unconstitutional," *Harvard Law Review* 83 (1970):1773. See also articles in *South Texan Law Review* 27 (1986): Robert Marsel, "Mr. Justice Arthur J. Goldberg and the Death Penalty," 467; and Arthur J. Goldberg, "Memorandum to the Conference Re: Capital Punishment," 493.

57. Trop v. Dulles, 356 U.S. 86 (1958).

58. Goldberg and Dershowitz, p. 1787.

59. Ibid., p. 1788.

60. For general discussion of rights of prisoners, as determined by extensive litigation since the 1960s, see I. R. Robbins, ed., *Prisoners and the Law* (New York: Clark Boardman, 1985), especially sec. 2, "Litigating and Enforcing the Rights of Prisoners." See also, on medical experimentation, Richard Singer, "Consent of the Unfree: Medical Experimentation and Behavior Modification in the Closed Institution," *Law and Human Behavior* 1 (1977):1–44, 101–62; and on the denial of the right to marry, the Florida case of Bradbury v. Wainwright, as reported in *Criminal Law Reporter* 34 (1983):1031.

61. Herbert Packer, "Making the Punishment Fit the Crime," *Harvard Law Review* 77 (1964):1081.

62. Rudolph v. Alabama, 375 U.S. 889 (1963), cert. denied.

63. Coker v. Georgia. For a critical analysis of this judgment, see Dennis McMahon, "Rape, Recidivism and Capital Punishment: Time for the Supreme Court to Re-examine its Interpretation of the 8th Amendment," *Ohio Northern University Law Review* 9 (1982):99. McMahon argues that

the circumstances in *Coker* were such that the court should have considered the aggravating facts as justifying a death penalty even if no one had actually been killed. (The accused had a criminal record of two previous rapes and a murder; he had escaped from prison while serving a life sentence, and within four hours had entered the home of a young teenage couple with a three-week-old baby; after forcing the wife to tie her husband up, robbing him, and threatening to kill them, he then raped the wife, and kidnapped her, driving away in the couples' car.) This article raises two important issues—first, which is worse, torture without a killing or a killing without torture? The court basically ignored this issue by noting that the victim (the wife) had been "unharmed." Second, the author notes the inconsistency in the logic between the *Coker* and the *Rummel* decisions. McMahon writes: "In *Coker,* the Court completely disregarded petitioner's criminal record . . . going to the opposite extreme, the *Rummel* Court overemphasized the petitioner's past criminality" (113), presumably since the court was "only" dealing with life imprisoment. See also dissenting opinion by Chief Justice Burger in *Coker,* p. 604.

64. Note, "The Cruel and Unusual Punishment Clause and the Substantive Criminal Law," *Harvard Law Review* 79 (1966):635.

65. Ibid., p. 642, n. 43.

66. People v. Anderson, 6 Cal. 3d 628, 493 P. 2d 880 (1972). The Court held that "capital punishment is impermissibly cruel. It degrades and dehumanizes all who participate in its processes. It is unnecessary to any legitimate goal of the State, and is incompatible with the dignity of man and the judicial process" (per Wright, J., p. 899).

67. Solem v. Helm, Wanstreet v. Bordenkircher, Rummel v. Estelle.

68. Mims v. Shapp, 744 Fed. 2d 946 (1984). See also Kostal v. Tinsley, 377 F. 2d 845 (1964); and Sorte v. McGinnis,

442 F. 2d 178 (1978). As noted, soitary confinement has often been suggested as an alternative where there is no capital punishment. Historically, leading reformers, such as John Howard in England, were in favor of using it extensively. Indeed, in Howard's case, there is biographical evidence to indicate that he used it in the home as a disciplinary punishment for his son. See discussion in Michael Ignatieff, *A Just Measure of Pain: The Penitentiary in the Industrial Revolution, 1750–1850* (New York: Pantheon, 1978), pp. 48–49.

69. Hewitt et al. v. Helms, 459 U.S. 460 (1983). Yet this case dealt with a temporary situation created by emergency conditions. The prisoner was being held in what the court termed administrative segregation, while an enquiry into a jail riot was being undertaken.

70. See Roberts v. Louisiana, 428 U.S. 325 (1976).

71. People v. Smith, 468 N.E. 2d 879 (1985). See A. Scarfone, "The Mandatory Death Penalty for Murder by Lifers: Foregoing Procedural Safeguards on the Illusory Promise of Deterrence," *Syracuse Law Review* 36 (1986):1303. A case from Nevada dealing with mandatory death sentences for life prisoners is presently before the Supreme Court.

72. State v. Garcia, as reported in *Criminal Law Reporter* 35 (1984):1062. The court took into account the special status of the offender as a prisoner in allowing the mandatory provision.

73. In re Caulk, 480 A. 2d 93 (N.H., 1984).

74. Ibid., p. 94.

75. Ibid., pp. 94–95.

76. Ibid., dissenting opinion, p. 97.

77. Ibid., p. 99.

78. Ibid.

79. Ibid., p. 100.

80. Ibid.

CHAPTER 6:
GLOBAL SCALES OF JUSTICE

1. See especially William G. Sumner, *Folkways* (Boston: Ginn, 1906).
2. See for example Norval Morris and Gordon Hawkins, *The Honest Politician's Guide to Law Enforcement* (Chicago: University of Chicago Press, 1970).
3. A. S. Diamond, *Primitive Law: Past and Present* (London: Methuen, 1971).
4. Israel Kazis, "Judaism and the Death Penalty," in H. Bedau, ed., *The Death Penalty in America* (Garden City, N.Y.: Anchor, 1964), pp. 171–75; Haim H. Cohn, "The Penology of the Talmud," *Israel Law Review* 5 (1970):53. Even the statement in an early chapter of the Bible (Gen. 9:6), "Whoso sheddeth man's blood, by man shall his blood be shed," often taken as a justification for capital punishment, may be interpreted in a broader context of a rationale for pacificism.
5. See John Lawrence, *The History of Capital Punishment* (New York: The Citidel Press, 1960), p. 7. This book gives a good general description of the various uses and abuses of the death penalty, and the various manner and circumstances in which it has been carried out. See also George Bishop, *Executions: The Legal Ways of Death* (Los Angeles: Sherbonne Press, 1965).
6. One of the reasons given for legislating for lethal injections was to forestall the projected possibility of televised electrocutions. See Scott Christianson, "Execution by Lethal Injection," *Criminal Law Bulletin* 15 (1979):73, which also contains a list of newspaper articles dealing with the issue of the televising of executions. See for instance "24 States Fight U.S. Court Order Permitting Televised Executions," *New York Times,* 29 May 1977. A further reason was to avoid the possibility of the defense drawing on the sympathy of jurors by describing the alternative violent

means of execution. The sponsor of a bill for lethal injections in Delaware clearly indicated that the death of the
criminal was his major concern and not the means used.
Certainly, in suggesting lethal injection, the sponsors of
the bill suggested it would make it easier to obtain convictions in capital-murder cases. The majority leader in the
Delaware Senate, Thomas Sharp, said: "I'm not too concerned about the method they use to execute people
because once they've reached this point, they damn well
should be executed. I don't care if we hang them . . . run
them over or shoot them," as quoted in the *Philadelphia
Inquirer,* 16 May 1986, sec. B, p. 8.

7. See In re Kemmler, 136 U.S. 436 (1890) for discussion on
the use of electrocution, the Supreme Court holding it to
be constitutional. For the first challenge to lethal injection, see *ex parte* Granviel, 561 S.W. 2d 503 (1978).

8. For description of crowd behavior at executions, see
Michael Ignatieff, *A Just Measure of Pain: The Penitentiary in the Industrial Revolution 1750–1850* (New York:
Pantheon, 1978), pp. 23–24, Michel Foucault, *Discipline
and Punish: The Birth of the Prison* (New York: Pantheon,
1977, pp. 59–60. Note that Arthur Koestler claims that
there were also occasions when the condemned person
would be revived and then hanged again (see *Reflections
on Hanging* [London: Victor Gallancz, 1956], p. 17).
Foucalt also confirms this; see p. 52.

9. See Louisiana ex rel. Francis v. Resweber, 329 U.S. 459
(1947). The decision was on a 5–4 vote. For a discussion
of this case, see B. Prettyman, *Death and the Supreme
Court* (New York: Harcourt, Brace and World, 1961). The
Court argued basically that since the officials had acted
in good faith, there was no legal prohibition on a further
attempt of execution. The accused was apparently no more
than the unfortunate victim of an unfortunate occurrence.
"The situation of the unfortunate victim of this accident
is just as though he had suffered the identical amount of

mental anguish and physical pain in any other occurrences, such as, for example, a fire in the cell block."

10. See for example "Louisiana Marchers Support and Protest a Killer's Execution," *New York Times,* 5 January 1985.

11. For details in these various geographical and cultural areas, see Amnesty International, *The Death Penalty* (London: Amnesty International Publications, 1979).

12. See Lawrence, *History of Capital Punishment,* especially chap. 6.

13. See Wilkerson v. Utah, 99 U.S. 130 (1879), in which the Supreme Court held that a public shooting was constitutional.

14. See Harry Barnes and Negley Teeters, *New Horizons in Criminology* (Englewood Cliffs, N.J.: Prentice-Hall, 1959), p. 308. There is a picture of the crowd taken at Owensboro, Kentucky on 14 August 1936. The crowd was estimated at 20,000.

15. See *The Death Penalty,* pp. 154–55.

16. David Brick, "Decision of Death: The Capital Punishment Lottery," *The New Republic,* 12 December 1983, p. 24.

17. See for example Peterson et al. v. Thornburgh (Civ. A. No. 893-0304, Eastern District of Pa., 18 June 1984). This case is still being ajudicated in higher courts.

18. With the present reluctance to carry out death penalties and with ever increasing numbers of condemned prisoners spending ever increasing periods of time on death row, the major immediate consequence of a death sentence is to allow a justification for particularly harsh conditions of confinement, which may last for years.

19. For a probing discussion of conditions in death row, based on interviews, see Robert Johnson, *Condemned to Die: Life Under Sentence Of Death* (Washington, D.C: Elsevier, 1981).

20. See their monthly bulletin, *Lifelines: Newsletter of the National Coalition Against the Death Penalty.*

21. See Egon Larson, *A Flame in Barbed Wire: The Story of Amnesty International* (New York, Norton, 1979); and Johnathan Power, *Against Oblivion: Amnesty International's Fight for Human Rights* (Douglas, Isle of Man: Fontana, 1981). See also *Amnesty International 1961– 1976: A Chronology* (London: Amnesty International Publications, 1976), and also its monthly newsletter, which provides ongoing reports for the number of executions it has monitored.

22. "Declaration of Stockholm, December 1977," *The Death Penalty,* p. 199.

23. For the convention, see General Assembly Resolution 2200A (XXI), 21 UN GAOR, Supp. 16, p. 49.

24. See *The Death Penalty,* app. C, p. 203.

25. Council of Europe, "Protocol to the Convention for the Protection of Human Rights and Fundamental Freedom Concerning the Abolition of the Death Penalty," Strasbourg, April 1983, in *International Legal Materials* (1984):539.

26. See for instance W. C. Quillin, "The Death Penalty in the Soviet Union," *American Journal of Criminal Law* 5 (1977):225. For ongoing reports, see occasional items in *Current Digest of Soviet Press.* For a historical survey, see Will Adams, "Capital Punishment in Imperial and Soviet Criminal Law," *American Journal of Comparative Law* 18 (1970):575.

27. See Marcello Maestro, *Cesare Beccaria and the Origins of Penal Reform* (Philadelphia: Temple University Press, 1973); and Coleman Phillipson, *Three Criminal Law Reformers: Beccaria, Bentham, Romilly* (London: Pent and Sons, 1913).

28. See Alexander Solzhenitsyn, *The Gulag Archipalego* (New York: Harper and Row, 1973), chap. 11, "The Supreme Measure," pp. 432–55. However, it should be noted that according to Solzhenitsyn, capital punishment was abolished only for nonpolitical offenders, whereas Catherine

"found capital punishment entirely appropriate to defending herself, her throne and her system"; basically, of course, this is an approach that is still followed in many countries, which retain capital punishment only for political crimes.

29. Alicja Grzeskowiak and Georges Sliwowski, "The Death Penalty in the New Polish Criminal Legislation," in Marjorie Kravitz, ed., *International Summaries: A Collection of Selected Translations in Law Enforcement and Criminal Justice,* vol. 2 (Washington, D.C.: Washington Law Enforcement Assistance Administration, 1978), p. 1.

30. Zvonimir Separovic, "Yugoslavia," in E. H. Johnson, ed., *International Handbook of Contemporary Developments in Criminology* (Westport, Conn.: Greenwood Press, 1983).

31. Charles Fenyvesi, "Indecent Burial: Budapest's Unquiet Dead," *The New Republic,* 11 July 1983, p. 14. Fenyvesi writes: "The executed were interred in unmarked graves, probably in a place known as 'the prisoner's cemetery' in a Budapest suburb. It is surrounded by barbed wire and guarded by soldiers and no visitors are allowed. The graves are marked only by numbers. Only top officials have access to the ledger that identifies who is buried in which gravesite." See also "Sec. 301: Where Hungary's Past is Buried," *New York Times,* 23 June 1986, p. 1.

32. Ignacio Berdugo Gomez de la Torre, "The Death Penalty in Current Latin American Law," in Kravitz, *International Summaries,* p. 19.

33. Ibid., p. 24.

34. Ibid.

35. This is a document of the Organization of American States, O.A.S. Doc. OEA/Ser. A/16 (1970).

36. The fourteen countries were Costa Rica, Uruguay, Columbia, Ecuador, El Salvador, Panama, Honduras, Dominican Republic, Guatemala, Mexico, Venezuela, Nicaragua, Argentina, and Paraguay.

37. Inter-American Court of Human Rights—3rd Advisory Opinion (8 September 1983), No. 003183—Restrictions to the Death Penalty.
38. See the report of the case in *Human Rights Law Journal* 4 (1983):339.
39. Ibid., p. 354.
40. *The Death Penalty,* pp. 143–44. For individual examples, see reports in *Human Rights: The Inter-American System* (Oceana Publications). For the use of a "Repressive-Punitive Approach" to combat terrorism in preference to traditional legal sanctions, see Mark Baker, "The South American Legal Response to Terrorism," *Boston University Law Journal* 3 (1985):67, and especially 74–77.
41. For a description of these years, see John Simpson and Jana Benner, *The Disappeared: Voices from a Secret War* (London: Robson Books, 1985). See especially "Afterword" for a summary of the fate of some of those responsible for the human rights violations. See also E. F. Mignone, C. L. Estland and S. Issacharoff, "Dictatorships on Trial: Prosecution of Human Rights Violators in Argentina," *Yale Journal of International Law* 10 (1984):118. See further discussion in chap. 9.
42. Tibamanya Mwene Mushanga, "The Death Penalty and Its Alternatives" (paper presented at Amnesty International Conference on the Abolition of the Death Penalty, 1977).
43. Ibid.
44. Ibid.
45. See Leon Sheleff, *The Bystander: Behavior, Law, Ethics* (Lexington, Mass.: Lexington Books, 1978), p. 5; and the report in *International Review of Criminal Policy* 27 (1969):66.
46. *The Death Penalty,* pp. 143–56. See also Rhoda E. Howard, *Human Rights in Commonwealth Africa* (Totowa, N.J.: Rowman and Littlefield, 1986), especially chap. 7, "Civil Rights and the Rule of Law," pp. 151–88. Comprehensive as this book is, it makes, however, no mention of capital

punishment, and discusses prison only in the context of preventive detention.

47. "U.S. Businesswomen Acquitted in Nigerian Oil Case," *Christian Science Monitor,* 28 February 1985, p. 2.

48. See "Drug Shots," *New African* (June 1985):38. See also, in the same issue, Eddie Troh, "To Die or Not To Die," p. 16. Subsequently there has been a further important and positive development with the establishment of the Nigerian Council of Human Rights. It is not clear what their attitude to capital punishment is, but they do plan to involve themselves with prison reform. (Ben Etaghere, "Human Rights Agency Launched," *African Concord,* 3 April 1986, p. 16). Note also the adoption by the African Organization of Unity in 1981 of the African Charter of Human and People's Rights.

49. Kayoda Oluyemi, "Nigeria," in Johnson, *International Handbook,* p. 483. See also M. Clinard and D. Abbot, *Crime in Developing Countries* (New York: Wiley, 1983), p. 248.

50. See Barendt van Niekerk, "Hanged by the Neck," *South African Law Journal* 86 (1969):457, and (1970):60. See also James Midgley, "Public Opinion and the Death Penalty in South Africa," *British Journal of Criminology* 14 (1974): 345. See also the report in the London *Times,* 20 September 1985.

51. Donald Woods, *Biko* (New York: Paddington Press, 1978).

52. See *Facts on File,* 7 February 1986, p. 85. The offer to free Mandela was made publicly in a speech by President Botha on 31 January 1986.

53. Dhlamini and Others v. Carter N.O. and Another, Case 2 (1968), *Rhodesian Law Reports,* p. 157.

54. Dhlamini and Others v. Carter N.O. and Another, Case 3 (1968), *Rhodesian Law Reports,* p. 162.

55. For brief general discussion of Islamic Law, see Adda B. Bozeman, *The Future of Law in a Multicultural World* (Princeton: Princeton University Press, 1971), pp.50–84.For a specific analysis of penal provisions, see Graeme Newman,

"Khomeini and Criminal Justice: Notes on Crime and Culture," *Journal of Criminal Law and Criminology* 23 (1982):561.

56. See *Keesing's Contemporary Archives* 31 (1985):33700. See also the prescient comments in an article by Judith Miller, "The Sudan: An Inquisition," *New York Times,* 26 Janaury 1985. The article deals with a public hanging of an opposition leader (see my earlier reference in chap. 2) during Numeiri's rule and a television recantation by some of his closest supporters in order to avoid the death penalty. A European diplomat commented: "The hanging and recantations were morally repugnant to his people, even to his dwindling supporters. We may look back and say that it signaled the beginning of the end for him." Shortly after he was indeed deposed.

57. *The Death Penalty,* pp. 171–72.

58. See John Wright, *Libya: A Modern History* (London: Croom Helm, 1982), especially pp. 197, 276.

59. See *Keesing's Contemporary Archives* 30 (1984):3304–5.

60. Gull Hassan Khan v. Gov. of Pakistan and Another, P.L.D. (1980), Peshawar, p. 54, as quoted in David Pannick, *Judicial Review of the Death Penalty* (London: Ducksworth, 1982).

61. *The Death Penalty,* p. 130.

62. Ibid., p. 102.

63. Ong Ah Chuon v. Public Prosecutor (1981), A.C. 648.

64. Pannick, *Judicial Review.*

65. *The Death Penalty,* p. 98.

66. For Indonesia, see Brian May, *The Indonesian Tragedy* (London: Routledge and Kegan Paul, 1978), pp. 120–25. For Cambodia, see Craig Etcheson, *The Rise and Demise of Democratic Kampuchea* (Boulder, Col.: Westview Press, 1977).

67. *The Death Penalty,* p. 81.

68. Ibid., p. 85. Other countries follow a similar policy of secret executions and either no official announcement or one

made much later. See "Indonesia Reports Execution of a Militant Moslem Leader," *New York Times,* 15 February 1985.

69. "Court Refuses to Free a Death Row Japanese," *New York Times,* 31 May 1985.

70. Eugene B. Block, *When Men Play God: The Fallacy of Capital Punishment* (San Francisco: Cragmenot Publications, 1983).

71. For a brief discussion of the trial in the larger context of changes in the criminal justice system, seen mainly as positive, see Shao-chuan Leng, "Criminal Justice in Post-Mao China," *The China Quarterly* (1981):440. See also Tien-Wei Wu, *Lin Biao and the Gang of Four* (Carbondale, Ill.: Southern Illinois University Press, 1983).

72. See Brian E. McKnight, *The Quality of Mercy: Amnesties and Traditional Chinese Justice* (Honolulu: The University Press of Hawaii, 1981).

73. See Derk Bodda and Clarence Morris, *Law in Imperial China* (Cambridge: Harvard University Press, 1967). They write: "There is abundant evidence that by the Han dynasty the restriction of executioners and serious legal proceedings to autumn and winter was not only an idea but an accepted practice," though there were apparently violations of the rule (p. 45).

74. "Official Explanation on Criminal Law and Criminal Procedure Law," presented by Pery Zhen, Director of Commission for Legal Affairs of National People's Congress Standing Committee, at the Second Session of the 5th National People's Congress, 26 June 1979, in Hungdah Chiu, "Certain Problems in Recent Law Reform in the People's Republic of China," delivered at the Eighth Sino-American Conference on Mainland China, Institute for International Studies, University of South Carolina, May 1979.

75. Simon Leys, *The Burning Forest: Essays on Chinese Culture and Politics* (New York: New Republic / Holt, Rinehart and Winston, 1983), p. 124. Among human rights violations,

he cites "five million exeuctions (conservative estimate, advanced by one of the most cautious and respected specialists of contemporary Chinese history, Jacques Guillerman in *Le Parti Communist chinois au pouvoir* [Paris: Payot, 1972], p. 33, n. 1)."

76. Judith Shapiro and Liang Heng, "China: How Much Freedom?" *New York Review of Books,* 24 October 1985, p. 16.

77. Ibid. See also the article in the *New York Times,* 3 January 1984, in which China claims a 40% reduction in crime as a result of these measures. See also the picture on 18 January showing Chinese residents looking at photographs of mass executions of criminals.

78. *The Death Penalty,* p. 74.

79. For recent developments, see James B. Christoph, *Capital Punishment and British Politics: The British Movement to Abolish the Death Penalty 1945–57* (Chicago: University of Chicago Press, 1962), especially pp. 116–24, where results of public opinion polls are discussed. For analysis of earlier debate, see David Cooper, *The Lesson of the Scaffold: The Public Execution Controversy in Victorian England* (Athens: Ohio University Press, 1974).

80. For a concise overview of historical developments, see Leon Radzinowicz, *The History of English Criminal Law and Its Administration from 1750* (London: Stevens, 1968), vol. 4, chap. 8, "Relinquishing an Unenforceable Code," pp. 303–53.

81. For an argumemt of this nature, see the speech by John Stuart Mill, in *Hansard's Parliamentary Debates,* 21 April 1868, reprinted in G. Ezorsky, ed., *Philosophical Perspectives on Punishment* (Albany: State University of New York Press, 1972). A relevant extract is in photocopy form in James Avery Joyce, *Capital Punishment: A World View* (New York: Nelson, 1981), p. 116.

82. See references to the activities of Sidney Silverman in Joyce, *Capital Punishment;* Christoph, *The British Movement;*

and Arthur Koestler, *Reflections.*

83. See Fenton Bresler, *Reprieve: A Study of a System* (London: Harrap, 1965).

84. See Christoph, *The British Movement,* p. 122.

85. Ibid., pp. 48–107. See also F. T. Jesse, *Trials of Timothy John Evans and John Reginald Christie* (London: Hodges, 1957).

86. "Death Penalty Return Rejected," *Facts on File* 43 (1983):531.

87. See Hugo A. Bedau, "Challenging the Death Penalty," *Harvard Civil Rights–Civil Liberties Law Review* 9 (1974):624.

88. Editorial, *Times,* 17 July 1983.

89. See Rene MacColl, *Roger Casement: A New Judgment* (London: 1956). It is of interest to note that Casement had, several years earlier, been knighted for his services in divulging atrocities committed by employees of a British-owned company in South America.

90. *Keesing's Contemporary Archives* 27 (1981):31191.

91. "IRA Stages Mass Jailbreak," *Facts on File* 43 (1983):765. There have been occasional reports of more of the escapees being captured over the years. See for instance *Keesing's Contemporary Archives* 32 (1986):34318 for a report on two escapees who were arrested in January 1986 in Amsterdam, and who were to be extradited back to Britain.

CHAPTER 7:
GENOCIDE

1. Although noting that German officers and officials who were involved in atrocities in particular places would be returned to those self-same countries for trial by national courts, the Moscow Declaration also provided that "German criminals whose offenses have no particular geographical location . . . will be punished by joint decision of the governments of the Allies." The declaration

contains a warning that the guilty will be pursued "to the uttermost ends of the earth . . . in order that justice may be done." For the full text of the declaration, see R. Falk, G. Kolko, and R. J. Lifton, eds., *Crimes of War: A Legal, Political-Documentary and Psychological Inquiry into the Responsibility of Leaders, Citizens, and Soldiers for Criminal Acts in Wars* (New York: Random House, 1971), p. 73.

2. For a description of the background to the London Agreement, signed on 8 August 1945, and a description of its terms, see Bradley F. Smith, *Reaching Judgment at Nuremberg* (New York: Basic Books, 1977), pp. 46–73.

3. During the course of the war, Prime Minister Winston Churchill had publicly intimated his approval of such a course. Speaking on 4 October 1944, he had argued that the Nazi leaders should be punished and added that "it should not be assumed that the procedure of trial will be necessarily adopted." In the United States, Secretary of the Treasury Henry Morgantheau had spoken of the need for "a dreadful retribution to be visited on Germany." He suggested that "the names of major criminals should be issued to the Allied Forces. As the men were captured, they would be identified and shot." See Ann Tusa and John Tusa, *The Nuremberg Trial* (London: McMillan, 1983), p. 50.

4. Sheldon Glueck, *War Criminals: Their Prosecution and Punishment* (New York: Knopf, 1944), p. 8. See also Raphael Lemkin, *Axis Rule in Occupied Europe* (Washington, D.C.: Carnegie Endowment for Peace, 1944). Lemkin was the first to use the term "genocide."

5. Glueck, *War Criminals,* p. 9. For a further statement as to the possibility of postwar trials, see Hans Kelsen, "Collective and Individual Responsibility in International Law with Particular Regard to the Punishment of War Criminals," *California Law Review* 33 (1943):530.

6. For key excerpts from the judgments in the Nuremberg, Tokyo, and Eichmann trials, see Falk et al., *Crimes of War,*

pp. 88–137. The full official proceedings of the Nuremberg trial have been published in 42 volumes as have those of many of the lesser trials, in 15 volumes. A full English translation of the judgement in the Eichmann trial has also been published. Of the Tokyo trial, the State Department, in 1946, published the majority opinion, the indictment, and the prosecutor's opening statement.

7. See especially Robert K. Woetzel, *The Nuremberg Trials in International Law* (New York: Praeger, 1962); Quincy Wright, "Legal Positivism and the Nuremberg Judgment," *American Journal of International Law* 42 (1948):405; Eugene Davidson, *The Trial of the Germans* (New York: McMillan, 1966).

8. Smith, *Reaching Judgment*, pp. 143–265. See also Robert Canot, *Justice at Nuremberg* (New York: Harper and Row, 1974). This latter book contains details of how the verdicts were announced and how they were received by the accused (pp. 492–507). See also Tusa and Tusa, *The Nuremberg Trial*, pp. 456–72.

9. "Explosion Set Off Near Hess' Prison," *Philadelphia Inquirer*, 24 October 1986, p. 17.

10. See Barry Dubner, *The Law of International Sea Piracy* (London: Martinus-Nijhoff, 1980). For a brief historical account, see Gerhard O. W. Mueller and Freda Adler, *Outlaws of the Ocean* (New York: Hearst Marine Books, 1985).

11. See for example Gerhard O.W. Mueller and E. Wise, eds., *International Criminal Law* (South Hackensack, N.J.: Rothman, 1965); Cherif Bassiouni and Ved Nanda, eds., *A Treatise on International Criminal Law*, vol. 1, *Crimes and Punishment* (Springfield, Ill.: Thomas, 1973); Cherif Bassiouni, *International Criminal Law: A Draft International Criminal Code* (Alphen aan den Rijn, Netherlands: Sijthoff and Noordhoff, 1980).

12. See Bassiouni, *International Criminal Law* for the analysis of the law on drugs, pp. 95–96; and Bassiouni and Nanda, *Crimes and Punishment*, pp. 533–56.

13. For a fictional account of such a possible trial, written during the war, see Michael Foot, *The Trial of Mussolini, Being a Verbatim Report of the First Great Trial for War Criminals Held in London Sometime in 1944 or 1945* (London: Gollanz, 1943).

14. For text of the London Agreement, see 59 Stat 1546.

15. For American figures, see *Trials of War Criminals* (Washington, D.C.: U.S. Government Printing Office, 1946–49), vol. 15, p. 1142. It may be noted that the clemency decisions sometimes contained reasoned statements based on the recommendations of a special board (see pp. 1176–91).

16. See Ibid., vol. 7, *The Hostage Trial,* pp. 1230–1319.

17. See Paul Hayes, *Quisling: The Career and Political Ideas of Vidkun Quisling (1887–1945)* (Newton Abbot, Devon: David and Charles, 1971); and Herbert Lottman, *Petain: Hero or Traitor: The Untold Story* (New York: Morrow, 1984). It should be noted that Petain voluntarily returned to France to stand trial, though for the most part refusing to participate in the proceedings. Later, Pierre Laval, who had been Petain's prime minister, was also sentenced to death and executed. Both he and his lawyers walked out of the trial, which was basically conducted in absentia. Other members of the Vichy cabinet were also executed.

18. See Peter Novick, *The Resistance versus Vichy: The Purge of Collaborators in Liberated France* (New York: Columbia University Press, 1968), p. 186, and especially app. D, p. 209.

19. Novick, *Resistance versus Vichy,* pp. 71-72. A *milicien* is a militiaman. Some estimates of the executions were much higher, ranging from 10,000 to 100,000. There were purges also carried out in other countries against collaborators. Jewish groups also were responsible for similar actions against Nazis involved in the holocaust. See Michael Bar-Zohar, *Ha-Nokmim (The Avengers)* (Tel Aviv: Levin-Epstein, 1968), in Hebrew. See also Michael Elkins, *Forged*

in Fury (New York: Interbook, 1971). Bar-Zohar describes also other acts of vengeance, for instance, of a survivor, broken in spirit, who faithfully reads the German newspapers for announcements of happy events in the life of the children of Nazis, such as weddings, and then writes to them asking them at this happy moment in their lives to think of all those young people whose lives were cut short by their father's actions, and who never would know the happiness of a wedding day (p. 255).

20. See discussion in chap. 8.

21. Richard Minear, *Victor's Justice: The Tokyo War Crimes Trial* (Princeton: Princeton Univesity Press, 1971). For a recent symposium on the trial, see C. Hasayu, N. Ando, Y. Onuma, and R. Minear, eds., *The Tokyo War Crimes Trial* (Tokyo: Kudansha, 1986). For a more critical analysis of Japanese behavior, see Lord Russell, *The Knights of Bushido: A Short History of Japanese War Crimes* (London: Cassell, 1958).

22. Minear, *Victors' Justice,* pp. 90–91.

23. Ibid., p. 162. It should be noted that other judges provided thoughtful dissenting opinions, notably Judge Roling of the Netherlands and Judge Pal of India, who subsequently published his views independently, in English and Japanese, and was in favor of acquittal of all the accused. See Falk et al., *Crimes of War,* pp. 116–36; Radhabinod Pal, *International Military Tribunal for the Far East: Dissentient Judgment* (Calcutta: Sanyal, 1953); and Bert Roling, "The Nuremberg and the Tokyo Trials in Retrospect," in Bassiouni and Nanda, *A Treatise,* p. 590.

24. See Falk et al., *Crimes of War,* pp. 116–17. For an excellent account of the emperor's responsibility for the war, see David Bergamini, *Japan's Imperial Conspiracy,* 2 vols. (New York: Morrow, 1971). Judge Webb himself contributes an introduction, in which he writes: "It is Mr. Bergamini's view, implicit, if not stated, that we should have sentenced no Japanese leader to death without also

trying the Emperor. I can sympathize with this view even though I do not concur in it" (p. xiv)—meaning apparently that Judge Webb would have opposed the death penalty for the emperor also.

25. Minear, *Victors' Justice,* p. 162.
26. Hirota v. MacArthur, 338 U.S. 197 (1948).
27. Ibid., Douglas, J., concurring opinion, p. 215.
28. In re Yamashita, 327 U.S. 1 (1946). For excerpts, see Falk et al., *Crimes of War,* p. 141.
29. A Frank Reel, *The Case of General Yamashita* (Chicago: University of Chicago Press, 1949). For a similar critical approach, see Richard Lael, *The Yamashita Precedent: War Crimes and War Responsibility* (Wilmington, Del.: Scholarly Resources, 1982).
30. In re Yamashita, Rutledge, J., dissenting opinion, p. 43.
31. Ibid., Murphy, J., dissenting opinion, p. 29.
32. Reel, *General Yamashita.*
33. Lawrence Taylor, *A Trial of Generals: Homma, Yamashita, MacArthur* (South Bend, Inc.: Icarus Press, 1981), p. 218.
34. Eichmann v. Attorney-General (1962), Vol. 16(3) Piskei Din, p. 2033. For discussion of the trial, see the critical report by Hannah Arendt, *Eichmann in Jerusalem: A Report on the Banality of Evil* (New York: Viking, 1963); the response by the chief prosecutor in the trial, Gideon Hausner, *Justice in Jerusalem* (New York: Harper and Row, 1966); and an analysis of the legal issues by the official observer of the International Commission of Jurists, Peter Papadatos, *The Eichmann Trial* (London: Stevens and Sons, 1964); see also Robert Woetzel, ''The Eichmann Case in International Law,'' *Criminal Law Review* (1962), 671; and Helen Silving, *''In re Eichmann:* A Dilemma of Law and Morality,'' *American Journal of International Law* 55 (1961):307.
35. Aubrey Hodes, *Martin Buber: An Intimate Portrait* (New York: Viking Press, 1971), pp. 111–16.
36. Arendt, *Eichmann in Jerusalem.*

37. Ibid., pp. 255–56.
38. Papadatos, *Eichmannn Trial,* pp. 94–100.
39. Ibid., p. 95. Napoleon, however, escaped from the island of Elba.
40. Ibid.
41. Ibid.
42. Ibid.
43. Ibid., p. 98. For reactions to the trial in Israel, see Akivah W. Deutsch, *The Eichmann Trial in the Eyes of Israeli Youngsters* (Ramat Gan, Israel: Bar Ilan University Press, 1974). For reactions to the trial in the United States, see C. Glock, G. Selznick, and J. Spaeth, *The Apathetic Majority: A Study Based on Public Reponses to the Eichmann Trial* (New York: Harper and Row, 1966), with support for the death penalty being 37%, and for life imprisonment 43%, though there were also differences in subgroups, dependent on factors such as knowledge about the trial and the Holocaust.
44. Papadatos, *Eichman Trial,* p. 99.
45. In a recent book,, *The Prevention of Genocide* (New Haven: Yale University Press, 1985), Leo Kuper argues convincingly for an international court to deal with the problem of genocide but does not discuss the nature of the penalties that should be imposed by it.
46. See David Libai and Leon Sheleff, "Capital Punishment: The Israeli Experience," *Acta Juridica* (1975):236.

CHAPTER 8:
BEFORE NUREMBERG AND AFTER EICHMANN

1. James F. Willis, *Prologue to Nuremberg: The Politics and Diplomacy of Punishing War Criminals of the First World War* (London: Greenwood Press, 1982), p. 46.
2. Ibid., p. 61.

3. See letter of Lord Curzon to David Lloyd George, 13 November 1918, as reported in Lord Beaverbrook, *Men and Power, 1917-1918* (London: Hutchinson, 1956), p. 387. It is of particular interest to note that some eight months later, though still in favor of trial for the kaiser, Curzon was extremely dubious as to the wisdon of holding it in England. In a further letter to the prime minister, he raises a series of forseeable problems, including the unpleasantness of crowds jeeering at the kaiser, the possibility of his acquittal, the embarrassment for the king that his cousin would be on trial, and the potential harm to a rapprochement with Germany.

4. Willis, *Prologue to Nuremberg,* p. 40.

5. Willis, *Prologue to Nuremberg,* provides the text of these Articles. See also R. Falk, G. Kolko, and R. J. Lifton, *Crimes of War* (New York: Random House, 1971), p. 41.

6. See Haigazn Kazarian, "A Turkish Military Court Tries The Principal Genocidists of the District of Yozgat," *The Armenian Review* 25 (1972): 34-39; see also Willis, *Prologue to Nuremberg,* p. 155.

7. Willis, *Prologue to Nuremberg,* p. 153.

8. Ibid., p. 163.

9. Ibid., p. 173.

10. Ibid., p. 163.

11. See Gerard Chaliand and Ternon Yves, *The Armenians: From Genocide to Resistance* (London: Zed Press, 1983).

12. See Saul Friedman, *Pogrumchik: The Assassination of Simon Petlura* (New York: Hart Publishing, 1976). The defense lawyer Henri Torres referred to the earlier acquittal of the Armenian and also to a Swiss case in which a White Russian had been acquitted of an attempt to kill the Bolshevik foreign minister, Chicherin (p. 334).

13. For general survey of developments in international law, see Cherif Bassiouni, ed., *A Treatise on Interantional Criminal Law,* vol. 1, *Crimes and Punishment* (Springfield, Ill.: Thomas, 1973), pt. 4, "Common Crimes Against Mankind," pp. 455-556.

14. See Richard Minear, *Victors' Justice: The Tokyo War Crimes Trial,* (Princeton: Princeton University Press, 1971).

15. Eugene Davidson, *The Nuremberg Fallacy: War and War Crimes Since World War II* (New York: McMillan, 1973). See also Geoffrey Best, *Nuremberg and After: The Continuing History of War Crimes and Crimes Against Humanity* (Reading: University of Reading, 1984); and the recent United Nations report on genocide, prepared by Benjamin Whitaker and submitted on 2 July 1985. Eight specific examples of genocide were given, but though the report was "noted" by the United Nations Sub-Commission on Prevention of Discrimination and Protection of Minorities, it was not passed on to the parent body, the Human Rights Commission of the U.N. Economic and Social Council, since a number of countries, whose activities had been described by the report, objected.

16. Leo Kuper, *Genocide: Its Political Uses in the Twentieth Century* (New Haven: Yale University Press, 1981). See also his more recent book, *The Prevention of Genocide* (New Haven: Yale University Press, 1985).

17. Irving Louis Horowitz, *Taking Lives: Genocide and State Power* (New Brunswick: Transaction Books, 1980).

18. Israel W. Charny, *Genocide: The Human Cancer* (New York: Hearst Books, 1982). See also the newsletter he edits, *Internet on the Holocaust and Genocide* (Jerusalem).

19. See for instance Richard Quinney, *Class, State and Crime: On the Theory and Practice of Criminal Justice* (New York: D. McKay, 1977).

20. George Vold, *Theoretical Criminology* (New York: Oxford University Press, 1958), chap. 11, pp. 203–19.

21. See Semakula Kiwanuka, *Amin and the Tragedy of Uganda* (Munich: Weltforum, 1979), especially chap. 5, "Amin and Hitler: Some Comparisons of International Reactions," pp. 123–35.

22. For the most part, though, the United Nations has avoided dealing with these issues.

23. See "The 'Secret' Speech to the Twentieth Party Congress," in R. H. McNeal ed., *Lenin, Stalin, Kruschev: Voices of Bolshevism* (Englewood Cliffs, N.J.: Prentice-Hall, 1963), pp. 143–49 (extracts from speech). It is interesting to note the description by McNeal of a speech made by Kruschev in 1937 in favor of the death penalty for thirteen persons, when Kruschev organized "an extraordinary mass demonstration of an estimated 200,000 Muscovites on Red Square, justifying their purge" (p. 143).

24. Kruschev himself has been accused of excesses, for instance, the removal of his chief rival, Beria, head of the secret police. See John Reshetar, *A Concise History of the Communist Party of the Soviet Union* (New York: Praeger, 1960), p. 261. Beria was arrested in June 1953 and executed after a secret trial in December 1953, together with six of his lieutenants.

25. See for example Joseph Collins, *The Soviet Invasion of Afghanistan: A Study in the Use of Force in Soviet Foreign Policy* (Lexington, Mass.: Lexington Books, 1986).

26. See Seymour Hersh, *My Lai: A Report on the Massacre and its Aftermath* (New York: Random House, 1970); William Peers, *The My Lai Inquiry* (New York: Norton, 1979); Arthur Everett, Kathryn Johnson, and Harry Rosenthal, *Calley* (New York: Dell, 1971).

27. See Bertrand Russell, *War Crimes in Vietnam* (New York: Monthly Review Press, 1967). This was the first of several trials in which other countries were tried. See also Telford Taylor, *Nuremberg and Vietnam: An American Tragedy* (Chicago: Quadrangle Books, 1970). For an analysis of attempts to raise these issues in American courts, see Johnathan M. Fredman, "American Courts, International Law and the War in Vietnam," *Columbia Journal of Law and Social Problems,* 18 (1984):295. He writes: "In effect, the Nuremberg theory bows to the reality posed by war" (p. 344). The recent election of Kurt Waldheim to the Presidency of Austria, despite allegations of his indirect

involvement in wartime atrocities, serves as a reminder of how difficult it is to deal with these issues. For what was at issue was not whether Waldheim should be indicted or punished, but the converse—whether he should be honored with the exalted position of the President of Austria. Despite proof that he had lied about his service in the German army, and that it seems clear that at the least he had knowledge of atrocities (which is apparently why he lied), the majority of the Austrian people saw no reason why he should not become their symbolic leader.

28. See Edward Peters, *Torture* (New York: Blackwell, 1985), especially the discussion of French actions in Algeria.

C H A P T E R 9 :
H U M A N I C I D E

1. See Amnesty International, *Political Killings by Governments* (London: The Pitman Press, 1983), pp. 5–6. These political killings are unlawful, deliberate, outside the judicial process, and in violation of national law and international standards. The term *extra-judicial execution* was apparently first used in a report prepared for Amnesty International by Eddy Kaufman. See his paper "Murder Committed or Acquiesced in by Government" (presented at the Conference on the Abolition of the Death Penalty, Stockholm, 1977, organized by Amnesty International). See also E. Kaufman and W. Fagen, "Extrajudicial Executions: An Insight into the Global Dimensions of a Human Rights Violation," *Human Rights Quarterly* 3 (1981):82.

2. This is the term that was finally used in the Amnesty International report.

3. Several such reports have appeared in the international press in recent years, although it may be noted that the otherwise exhaustive survey by Gerhard Mueller and Freda Adler makes no mention of such crimes *(Outlaws of the*

Oceans: The Complete Book of Contemporary Crime on the High Seas [New York: Hearst Marine Books, 1985]). For short descriptions of several instances, see "More Stowaways Thrown to the Sharks," *New African,* November 1984, p. 18.

4. The term *humanicide* has been used by others in a similar context; for instance, see Robert A. Friedlander, "Terrorism and Political Violence: Do the Ends Justify the Means?" in Marius H. Livingston, ed., *International Terrorism in a Contemporary World* (Westport: Greenwood Press, 1978), p. 321, referring to earlier use of the term by J. J. Lador-Lederer.

5. Mortimer Kadish and Sanford Kadish, *Discretion to Disobey* (Palo Alto, Calif.: Stanford University Press, 1973). See pp. 72–94 for a discussion of "justified rule departure by officials."

6. In particular, the European Court of Human Rights and the European Commission of Human Rights have heard numerous claims of alleged violations of international law and human rights.

7. Yoram Dinstein, *The Defense of "Obedience to Superior Orders" in International Law* (Leyden: A. W. Sijthoff, 1965).

8. Barry Dubner, *The Law of International Sea Piracy* (London: Martinus-Nijhoff Publishers, 1980), pp. 42–44.

9. Ibid., app. 2 to chap. 1. Dubner cites both the *South China Morning Post* and the *Hongkong Standard,* 9 and 11 August 1977, which call piracy on the high seas around Borneo and the Southern Philippines "not uncommon." See also "Increased Attacks on 'Boat People' Reported, " *New York Times,* 19 May 1985, p. 23.

10. B. G. Ramcharan, "The Concept and the Dimensions of the Right to Life," in Ramcharan, ed., *The Right to Life in International Law* (Dordrecht: Martinus Nijhoff, 1985), pp. 1–32.

11. Ibid., p. 7.

12. David Weissbrodt, "Protecting the Right to Life: International Measures Against Arbitrary or Summary Killings by Governments," in Ramcharan, *The Right to Life,* pp. 297–314.

13. Ibid., p. 303.

14. C. K. Boyle, "The Concept of Arbitrary Deprivations of Life," in Ramcharan, *The Right to Life,* pp. 221–45.

15. *Political Killings,* pp. 109–11. The report notes that ways should be found of ensuring the implementation of the *The Code of Conduct for Law Enforcement Officials.* The report also suggests "a workshop for the military . . . intended to facilitate the development of an international organization of military officers for the promotion of human rights and of a code or codes of conduct for the military profession" (p. 110).

16. Israel Charny, *Genocide: The Human Cancer* (New York: Hearst Books, 1982). The book also goes under the title *How Can We Commit the Unthinkable?*

17. *Political Killings,* p. 113.

18. For a description of the criminal activities, see Sanford J. Ungar, *Africa: The People and Politics of an Emerging Continent* (New York: Simon and Schuster, 1978), pp. 411–15.

19. See "Condemned African Leader Seized on Return from Exile," *Philadelphia Inquirer,* 24 October 1986, p. 15; and an item in "Current Events" on Bokassa's trial, *Africa Events* (December 1986), p. 21.

20. In *Africa* Ungar claims that there were at least 50,000 people killed. See also *Political Killings,* pp. 10–11.

21. For a discussion of the situation in Equatorial Guinea, see Leo Kuper, *The Prevention of Genocide* (New Haven: Yale University Press, 1985), pp. 133–34, 136–39.

22. Amnesty International, *Report on Torture* (New York: Farras, Strauss and Giroux, 1975).

23. See the report "A Promise of Genuine Justice," *South* (January 1987), p. 31.

24. Nita Rous Monitzas, "Argentina's Hornet's Nest," *AfricaAsia* (February 1986), p. 26.

25. Ibid., p. 27.

26. Emilio Fermin Mignone, Cynthia L. Estland, and Samuel Issacharoff, "Dictatorship on Trial: Prosecution of Human Rights Violations in Argentina," *Yale Journal of International Law* 10 (1984):150.

27. For habeas corpus writs at the international level, see the work of Luis Kutner, for instance "World Habeas Corpus, Human Rights and World Community," *De Paul Law Review* 17 (1967):20; and his edited book, *The Human Right to Individual Freedom: A Symposium on World Habeas Corpus* (Coral Gables, Florida: University of Miami Press, 1970). For compensation to victims of crime and for general overview of compensation, see Burt Galaway and Joe Hudson, eds., *Offender Restitution in Theory and Action* (Lexington, Mass.: Lexington Books, 1978). A United Nations Voluntary Fund for Victims of Torture was established by General Assembly Resolution 36/151.

28. For specific international aspects dealing with people victimized because of their humanistic concerns (for instance, a journalist being punished, made to suffer, or even killed for his part in bringing information of human rights violations to the outside world), see Leon Sheleff, "Bystanders of Injustice," presented at the Fourth International Symposium on Victimology, Tokyo and Kyoto, Japan, 1982.

29. 28 U.S.C. 1350 (1982).

30. Filartiga v. Pena-Irala, 630 F. 2d 876 (1980).

31. Ibid., p. 882.

32. There have been several reports of these cases in the mass media. In the latter case, a number of allegations have been lodged that some of those being sued had links with the government officials in the White House and the CIA who are presently under investigation by Congress and a special prosecutor. For the original report on the Chilean incident, see *Facts on File* 46 (11 July 1986), p. 511.

33. See for instance United Nations, General Assembly, *Code of Conduct for Law Enforcement Officials* (34/169), 17 December 1979, in Ramcharan, *The Right to Life,* pp. 323–28.

CHAPTER 10:
TREASON AND TERROR

1. Thompson v. Whittier, 185 F. Supp. 306 (dist. Ct. D.C., 1960); sub. nom. Thompson v. Glenson, 317 F. 2d 901 (Ct. App. D.C., 1962).
2. See Federal Espionage Act 62 Stat. 737 (1948); United States v. Rosenberg, 195 F. 2d, 583 (C.C.A. 2d, 1952), cert. denied 34 U.S. 838 (1952). An earlier version of the law passed during the First World War had been used against the Socialist leader Eugene Debs for opposing the draft during that war (40 Stat. 218 [1917]). He was sentenced to ten years, but had his sentence commuted some years later (Debs v. United States, 249 U.S. 211 [1919]).
3. See Otto Kirchheimer, *Political Justice: The Use of Legal Procedure for Political Ends* (Princeton: Princeton University Press, 1961).
4. John G. Bellamy, *The Law of Treason in England in the Later Middle Ages* (Cambridge: Cambridge University Press, 1970), p. 9.
5. Ibid., especially chap. 5, "The Scope of Treason," pp. 102–38.
6. Ibid., p. 20.
7. Ibid., p. 103.
8. U.S. *Constitution,* art. 3, sec. 3.
9. James Willard Hurst, *The Law of Treason in the United States: Collected Essays* (Westport, Conn.: Greenwood Publishing, 1971), p. 5.

10. Ibid., p. 87. But there have been a few executions carried out for treason against states, the most notable being that of John Brown for levying war against Virginia, an armed insurrection to free slaves being interpreted as such. See *The Trial of John Brown,* American State Trials 6 (1916), p. 700.

11. Cramer v. United States, 325 U.S. 1 (1944).

12. See David Watson, "Trial of Jefferson Davis: An Interesting Constitutional Question," *Yale Law Journal* 24 (1915):669. See also Case of Jefferson Davis, 7 Fed. Cas. 63, No 3, 621a (C.C.D. Va., 1867–71); and Jefferson Davis, *The Rise and Fall of the Confederate Government* (New York, 1881).

13. At the time of the trial, widespread interest was aroused and protest demonstrations were held in many parts of the world in an effort to thwart their execution. Since then several books have been written on the trial, including critical analyses claiming that they were innocent. See the book by their children, Robert Meeropol and Michael Meeropol, *We Are Your Sons: The Legacy of Ethel and Julius Rosenberg* (Boston: Houghton, Mifflin, 1975); see also Walter Schneir and Miriam Schneir, *Invitation to an Inquest* (Garden City, N.Y.: Doubleday, 1965).

14. Philip Shenon, "Weinberger Backs Death Penalty for Espionage in Peacetime," *New York Times,* 13 June 1985, p. 1.

15. Bradley Chapin, *The American Law of Treason: Revolutionary and Early National Origins* (Seattle: University of Washington Press, 1964), pp. 26–27.

16. Ibid., p. 15.

17. Ibid., p. 66.

18. Ibid., p. 69.

19. Ibid., p. 70.

20. James G. Wilson, "Chaining the Leviathan: The Unconstitutionality of Executing those Convicted of Treason," *University of Pittsburgh Law Review* 45 (1983):111.

21. Ibid., p. 111. It should be noted that prior to independence a member of George Washington's personal guard was tried and executed for recruiting for the British and counterfeiting, the legal basis for such action being the crime of sedition of the Articles of War passed in 1775 by the Continental Congress (p. 108).
22. Ibid., pp. 126–29. Wilson discussed the cases of Cramer v. United States; Haupt v. United States, 330 U.S. 631 (1947); Kawakita v. United States, 343 U.S. 717 (1952).
23. Ibid., p. 169.
24. Ibid., p. 170.
25. See Menahem Begin, *The Revolt: Story of the Irqun* (New York: Nash Publishing, 1972), pp. 288–90; and Nancy Crawshaw, *The Cyprus Revolt* (London: George Allen and Unwin, 1978), pp. 180–82.
26. Georg Simmel, *Conflict* (Glencoe, Ill.: The Free Press, 1955). Kant wrote: "A state ought not during war countenance such hostilities as would make mutual confidence in a subsequent peace impossible" (Immanuel Kant, *Perpetual Peace* [1795]).
27. See *International Legal Materials,* 1983, p. 538 for text of a press release by Council of Europe on 26 January 1983.
28. See Cesare Beccaria, *On Crimes and Punishment* (1784), sec. 11, "Of Capital Punishment." He writes: "The death of a citizen cannot be necessary, but in one case. When, though deprived of his liberty, he has such power and connections as may endanger the security of the nation; when his existence may produce a dangerous revolution."
29. See the discussion in P. Novick, *The Resistance versus Vichy* (New York: Columbia University Press, 1968), app. D, "Comparative Purge Legislation and Court Systems," pp. 209–14. See also H. Mason, *The Purge of the Dutch Quislings* (The Hague: 1952); Carl C. Givskov, "Danish 'Purge Laws'," *Journal of Criminal Law, Criminology and Police Science,* 39 (1948):447. Givskov writes: "As to the security of the citizens it was found, too, that restoring the death

penalty was needed. The persons to whom it was applied had committed crimes of such extraordinary and hitherto unknown character that the community was obliged to shield itself against their being free again either by amnesty or by escape, and enabled to commit new crimes. From the point of view of the reformation [*sic*] theory it must be admitted that by the death penalty no attempt can be made to improve the condemned to make them good citizens again. The general opinion was that those persons were so raw and rugged in thoughts and manners that their 'resocialization' had to be considered vain. Whatever theoretically may be said about restoring the death penalty, no doubt it was a public claim which would have been very difficult if not impossible for the government not to answer.''

30. Paul Hayes, *Quisling: The Career and Political Ideas of Vidkun Quisling 1887–1945* (Newton Abbot, Devon: David and Chares, 1971).

31. Ibid., p. 303.

32. See Klaus Haspprecht, ed., *Willy Brandt: Portrait and Self-Portrait* (Los Angeles: Nash Publishing, 1971), including extracts from Brandt's autobiography, *My Road to Berlin* (Garden City, N.Y.: Doubleday, 1961).

33. See Haim H. Cohn, ''The Right and Duty of Resistance,'' *Revue de l'homme* 1 (1968):491.

34. See for example Paul Robinson, *Criminal Law Defenses* (St. Paul: West Publishing Co., 1984), the section entitled ''Lesser Evils Defense,'' pp. 45–68.

35. See my discussion in chap. 8.

36. John G. Bellamy, *The Tudor Law of Treason: An Introduction* (London: Routledge and Kegan Paul, 1979), p. 12.

37. Thomas Perry Thornton, ''Terrorism and the Death Penalty,'' in Hugo Bedau, ed., *The Death Penalty in America,* 3d ed. (Oxford: Oxford University Press, 1982), p. 181.

38. Ibid., pp. 181–82.

39. For text of "Convention for the Prevention and Punishment of Terrorism, Geneva, November 16, 1937," see Yonah Alexander, M. Browne, and A. Nanes, eds., *Control of Terrorism: International Documents* (New York: Crane Russak, 1979), pp. 19–29. Prior to the assassination, there had, it should be noted, been several international conferences that had dealt with the perceived problems of increased terrorist activities.

40. For text of "Convention for the Creation of an International Criminal Court," Geneva, 17 November 1937, see ibid., pp. 31–42.

41. Ibid.

42. For text of "Draft Convention for the Prevention and Punishment of Certain Acts of International Terorism, Submitted by the United States to the United Nations General Assembly, September 26, 1972," see ibid., p. 113.

43. Ibid., "Preface," p. ix. See also B. Jenkins and D. Rubin, "New Vulnerabilities and the Acquisition of New Weapons by Nongovernment Groups," in A. Evans and J. Murphy, eds., *Legal Aspects of International Terrorism* (Lexington, Mass.: Lexington Books, 1978).

44. Alexander et al., *Control of Terrorism*, p. xi. See also "Report of the International Task Force on the Prevention of Nuclear Terrorism," presented in June 1986. The twenty-six-member task force included scientists, psychologists, and experts on terrorism. It warned that "terrorists might be more willing than nations to use acquired nuclear weapons."

45. I am well aware of the controversial nature of such a statement, and how easily it can be misinterpreted; or how easily any such right could be abused. However, it is based on the recognized legal principles of necessity and justification allowing a person placed in an intolerable situation to choose between lesser evils. Factually, one could well presume that there is almost no doubt that those responsible for the safety and security of a city or a region, or

even a nation, are quite likely to resort to any means to elicit the requisite information in order to avoid the kind of catastrophe suggested by Alexander et al. It does not add to the logic of the law to ignore such a possibility or deny such a reality, nor will ignoring it prevent its use in dire and extreme circumstances. In fact, ignoring the problem will only deny those truly concerned with human rights from the guidance and the review procedures which they would genuinely welcome, while not hindering at all those for whom such respect for proper procedures is irrelevant; an unwillingness to recognize the defense of necessity in such instances will almost inevitably lead to the perpetrators of such actions seeking support for their actions from higher ranking police or political authorities, including cover-up efforts to avoid judicial scrutiny. *CBS News* (Monday, 19 January 1987) carried a report that both the United States and Great Britain have set up special secret units, designated with the task of searching for nuclear-armed terrorists. One wonders what such units would do if they found the terrorists but not the bomb that they had planted.

46. Alexander et al., *Control of Terrorism,* p. xii.
47. Thornton, *"Terrorism and the Death Penalty,"* p. 185. See also Paul Wilkinson, *Terrorism and The Liberal State* (New York: Wiley, 1977.)
48. Thornton, "Terrorism and the Death Penalty," p. 185.
49. Ibid.
50. Edward Kossoy, *Living with Guerrilla: Guerrilla as a Legal Problem and a Political Fact* (Geneva: Libraire Droz, 1976).
51. For good discussion of some of the key issues, see articles in Marius H. Livingston, ed.,, *International Terrorism in the Contemporary World* (Westport, Conn.: Greenwood Press, 1976): Yonah Alexander, ed., *International Terrorism: National, Regional and Global Perspectives* (New York: Praeger Publishers, 1976); Alona E. Evans and John F.

Murphy, *Legal Aspects of International Terrorism* (Lexington, Mass.: Lexington Books, 1978); David C. Rapoport and Yonah Alexander, eds., *The Morality of Terrorism: Religious and Secular Justifications* (New York: Pergamon Press, 1982); M. Cherif Bassiouni, ed., *International Terrorism and Political Crimes* (Springfield, Ill.: Charles C. Thomas, 1975). See also the journal *Terrorism.* Recently, Abraham Sofner has argued that because of political considerations, the distinction between guerrilla and terrorism is being obscured, and terrorism itself is being legitimized. See "Terrorism and the Law," *Foreign Affairs* 64 (1986):901.

52. For the "Hague Convention of 1907, Respecting the Laws and Customs of War on Land," see *U.S. Statutes at Large,* 36 2301; for the Geneva Conventions, see *U.S. Treaties and Other International Agreements* 6 (Washington, D.C.: U.S. Government Printing Office, 1956).

53. See Yoram Dinstein, *The Defense of "Obedience to Superior Orders" in International Law* (Leyden: A. W. Sijthoff, 1965); L. C. Green, *Superior Orders in National and International Law* (Leyden: A. W. Sijthoff, 1976); Nico Keijzer, *Military Obedience* (Leyden: Sijthoff and Nidjhoff, 1978); Peter Karsten, *Law, Soldiers, and Combat* (Westport, Conn.: Greenwood Press, 1978); and Morris Greenspan, *The Soldier's Guide to the Laws of War* (Washington, D.C.: Public Affairs Press, 1969).

54. See Morris Greenspan, "International Law and Its Protection in Unconventional Warfare," *Annals of the American Academy of Political and Social Science* 34 (1962):30.

55. Albert Camus, *The Just Assassins,* in *Caligula and Three Other Plays* (New York: Vintage Books, 1962), Act 2, pp. 252–62. See also Elie Wiesel, *Dawn* (New York: Hill and Wang, 1960).

56. For a good discussion of the advantages that accrue to sides, whether states or rebel groups, by abiding by the norms of international law and the dictates of good conscience,

see Karsten, *Law, Soldiers, and Combat,* especially pp. 161–64.

57. Kossoy, p. 328. The liberation movement of the Kurd people is of particular interest, for despite the strict limits on their struggle—generally, pitched battles with the army of either Iran or Iraq—they have been given little support by the world community, or for that matter, by partisan political and ideological groupings. Perhaps, unfortunately, it is because they have practiced restraint that they have been so ignored. It is tragic to think that they have failed to achieve with pure guerrilla tactics what they might have achieved through terror. Lack of awareness of their problem is almost a test case of which—guerrilla or terror—is the more efficacious, since the Kurds fulfill all the criteria of independence: a large population (some ten million), occupying a large defined area, with a unique and clearly defined cultural tradition of its own going back many centuries, and whose rights were given world recogniton after the First World War. It is perhaps understandable that the Iranians and Iraqis should refuse the demands of the Kurds for independence, but it is deplorable that the world community should ignore their struggle. In Turkey, it should be noted, the struggle has taken on a different, more violent, form. See G. Chaliand and A. R. Ghassemlou, *People Without a Country: The Kurds and Kurdistan* (London: Zed Press, 1980). It is also of great relevance to note that according to the Amnesty International report, hundreds of Kurds have been executed for their antigovernmental activities. As for Mao, whatever standards he might have maintained as a guerrilla leader seem to have been largely abandoned on his accession to power (see discussion in chap. 6).

58. See Linda Gerstel Feder, *"In re Doherty:* Distinguishing Terrorist Activities from Politically Motivated Acts under the Political Offense Exception to Extradition," *Temple International and Comparative Law Journal* 1 (1985):99.

See also Duane Thompson, "The Evolution of the Political Offense Exception in an Age of Modern Political Violence," *Yale Journal of World Public Order* 9 (1983):315.

59. Eain v. Wilkes, 641 F. 2d 506 (1981), cert. denied, 454 U.S. 894 (1981).

60. In re Doherty, 579 F. Supp. 270 (1984).

61. See David Libai and Leon Sheleff, "Capital Punishment: The Israeli Experience, " *Acta Juridica* (1975): 236. See also my article in *New Outlook* (1973).

62. See George Jonas, *Vengeance* (New York; Bantam, 1984); he claims that there was such a response, though official denials have been made of some of these contentions.

63. The reservist was put on trial and sentenced to several years imprisonment.

64. The information was made public by a number of journalist on the spot. An officer in the army was tried in military disciplinary proceedings for his responsibility in the killings, but was acquitted on this charge. Subsequently, in May 1986, there were more relevations, indicating that leading members of the Israeli secret service had been implicated. They were given presidential pardons without being brought to trial. Shortly afterwards, in June 1986, allegations of a similar nature were made in Britain as to killings of members of the I.R.A. by British security forces. There were also charges as to a cover-up, when the person in charge of the investigation was removed from his position before he could submit a report (*Facts on File* 46 [1986]:645).

65. See discussion of this issue in chap. 13.

66. Libai and Sheleff, "Capital Punishment."

67. The Israeli Declaration of Independence reads, *inter alia:* "The State of Israel will be based on freedom, justice and peace as envisaged by the Prophets of Israel; will uphold the full social and political equality of all its citizens, without distinction of religion, race or sex; will guarantee freedom of religion, conscience, education and culture."

NOTES TO PAGE 278 : 453

68. This kind of argument—of stricter standards to be applied against those who support one's own political platform, but sully it by the means they use—has further connotations and possibilities. For instance, as in the debate in the United States, sparked originally by Jeane Kirkpatrick, former ambassador to the United Nations, as to the difference betwen totalitarian regimes (mainly left-wing radical) and authoritarian regimes (mainly right-wing reactionary). The argument is that the latter could be supported because they were less effective than the former, both in the immediate totality of their control and in the long-range possibility of survival. There is, however, a further differentiation between them. In general the United States tends to support the latter, generally because of their anti-communist stance. This fact means that the United States, or any other country supporting so-called authoritarian regimes, bears some indirect responsibility for the atrocities—ranging from illegal arrests through torture to humanicide—that are committed by such regimes. Specifically *because* they are allies, *stricter* standards should be applied to them, because their very authoritarian activities reflect adversely on, and ultimately undermine, the democratic values of the countries that support them.

69. See for example articles by L. Kos-Rabcewicz-Zubkowski, "Essential Features of an International Criminal Court," in Livingston, *International Terrorism;* and J. Y. Doutricourt, "The International Criminal Court: The Concept of International Criminal Jurisdiction," in Bassiouni, *International Terrorism.* For the possibility of differentiating between types of violence, between terror and guerrilla, etc., see John Dugard, "International Terrorism and the Just War," in Rapaport and Alexander, *The Morality of Terrorism,* p. 77.

70. For a recent revelation of intended, but aborted, U.S. action, see "U.S. Aides in '72 Weighed Killing Officer Who Now leads Panama," *New York Times,* 13 June 1986, p. 1.

71. For some examples, see L. A. Parry, *The History of Torture in England* (London: Sampson, Law, Marston and Co., 1934; reprinted in Patterson Smith Series, 1973).
72. See James H. Chadborn, *Lynching and The Law* (Chapel Hill: University of North Carolina Press, 1933).
73. See discussion in chap. 14. Note also that Kos-Rabcewicz-Zubkowski, "Essential Features," raises the possibility of an international prison for international terrorists, suggesting that this "could perhaps be a better solution as it would be known that there is no chance that the international criminal court controlling such a prison would yield to blackmail" (pp. 338–39), though this last hope seems overly optimistic.

C H A P T E R   1 1 :
W O R S E   T H A N   D E A T H

1. But see Harry E. Barnes, *The Story of Punishment: A Record of Man's Inhumanity to Man* (Montclair: Patterson Smith, 1972), p. 16, where he notes the close parallels between third-degree techniques and medieval practices.
2. See the annual reports and occasional special reports by Amnesty International on torture and on human rights violations in various countries (London, Amnesty International Publications); see also Jonathan Power, *Against Oblivion: Amnesty International's Fight for Human Rights* (Douglas, Isle of Man: Fontana Paperbacks, 1981) Egon Larson, *A Flame in Barbed Wire: The Story of Amnesty International* (New York: Norton, 1979); the journal *International Review of the Red Cross,* (Geneva: International Committee of the Red Cross); and David Forsythe, *Humanitarian Politics: The International Committee of the Red Cross* (Baltimore: Johns Hopkins University Press, 1977); see also the *International Commission of Jurists*

Bulletin on violations of human rights and the rule of law.

3. Amnesty International, *Report on Torture* (New York: Farrar, Straus and Giroux, 1975).

4. For general descriptions, see Edward Peters, *Torture* (New York: Blackwell, 1985), pp. 165–69.

5. John Stuart Mill, "Parliamentary Debate on Capital Punishment Within Prisons Bill," in *Hansard's Parliamentary Debates,* 3d Series, 21 April 1868 (London: Hansard, 1868).

6. As quoted in P. E. Mackey, "Edward Livingston and the Origin of the Movement to Abolish Capital Punishment in America," *Louisiana History* (1975):145. Mackey adds: "Though he had numerous enlightened ideas about penology, his plans for the sentencing and imprisonment of convicted murderers will strike the modern reader as unduly harsh."

7. See Richard Gelles and Murray Straus, *Behind Closed Doors: Violence in the American Family* (Garden City: Anchor Press/Doubleday, 1980); Richard Gelles, *Family Violence* (Beverly Hills: Sage Publications, 1979); Richard Gelles, *The Violent Home: A Study of Physical Aggression Between Husbands and Wives* (Beverly Hills: Sage Publications, 1972); Richard Gelles and Claire P. Cornell, eds., *International Perspectives on Family Violence* (Lexington, Mass.: Lexington Books, 1983).

8. Gelles, *Family Violence,* p. 11.

9. See Susan Brownmiller, *Against Our Will: Men, Women, and Rape* (New York: Simon and Schuster, 1975).

10. See Graeme Newman, *The Punishment Response* (New York: Lippincott Co., 1978), chap. 4, "Punishment and Obedience: Punishing Women, Children, Slaves and Soldiers." Newman notes that in the past "children were the objects of punishment," and then adds that "the richest and most telling practice of all, which clearly demonstrates the intricate interrelationship between various punishment systems, was the widespread practice in the seventeenth century of taking children to see hangings or gibbeted

corpses and whipping them soundly on the site" (p. 62).

11. See Amnesty International, *Report on Torture.*

12. For a general analysis of prisoners, see K. Wright and D. Cingranelli, "Inhumane, Cruel and Degrading Treatment of Criminal Prisoners Throughout the World," *Justice Quarterly* 2 (1985):345.

13. See W. P. Gormley, "The Development of International Law Through Cases from the European Court of Human Rights," *Ottawa Law Review* 2 (1968):382. For specific cases, see Ireland v. United Kingdom, *Yearbook of European Convention on Human Rights* (1976), p. 512 (Application No. 5801/7151) and *Yearbook* (1978), p. 602; and Denmark, Norway, Sweden and the Netherlands v. Greece, *Yearbook* (1969), p. 186.

14. See for instance Larry Berkson, *The Concept of Cruel and Unusual Punishment* (Lexington, Mass.: Lexington Books 1975); Leonard Orland, *Prisons: Houses of Darkness* (New York: The Free Press, 1975), especially chap. 6, pp. 81–110; and Ira P. Robbins, ed., *Prisoners and the Law* (New York: Clark Boardman, 1985). In general, see the specialized journal, *New England Journal of Criminal and Civil Confinement.*

15. See the discussion on South America in chap. 6. See also Mark Baker, "The South American Legal Response to Terrorism," *Boston University International Law Journal,* 3 (1985):67, especially, sec. 4, "The Regional Response— Multinational Agreements," pp. 90–97.

16. See for example discussion of the Camargo and De Guerrero case, dealing with compensation for unjustified death, by C. K. Boyle, "The Concept of Arbitrary Deprivation of Life," in B. G. Ramcharan, ed., *The Right to Life in International Law* (Dordrecht: Nijhoff, 1985), pp. 234–39.

17. See for example Peters, *Torture,* pp. 182–83, describing the preparation of torturers in Greece during the regime of the colonels.

18. See David Matza, *Delinquency and Drift* (New York: Wiley, 1964), especially chap. 4, "The Sense of Injustice," pp. 101–51.

19. United Nations, General Assemby, *Draft Convention Against Torture and Other Cruel, Inhuman or Degrading Treatment or Punishment* (E./CN. 4/1984/L.2 Annex 1984); United Nations, General Assembly, *Unilateral Declaration Against Torture and Other Cruel, Inhuman or Degrading Treatment or Punishment* (32/64), 8 December 1977. The convention also deals with the conditions for extradition of torturers (only to countries that do not practice torture), the rights of victims to rehabilitation and compensation, and the formation of an International Committee Against Torture.

20. John Langbein, *Torture and the Law of Proof: Europe and England in the Ancient Regime* (Chicago: University of Chicago Press, 1977).

21. Ibid., p. 13.

22. Ibid., p. 14.

23. Ibid., p. 16.

24. United Nations, *Draft Convention Against Torture,* Article 12.

25. See Rupert Cross, *Evidence* (London: Butterworth, 1974), p. 546.

26. See Wong Sun v. United States, 371 U.S. 471 (1963).

27. Robert S. Gerstein, "Do Terrorists Have Rights?" In D. Rapaport and Y. Alexander, eds., *The Morality of Terrorism* (New York; Pergamon, 1982), p. 298. He warns against the possible temptation for abuse. It is interesting to note that in one of the most recent books on torture (Peters, *Torture),* the author completely ignores this problem, except for a passing reference to the use of torture to elicit information from heretics in the thirteenth century. There have also been suggestions for using a "truth serum," but this itself is seen by many authorities to be torture. Amnesty

International discusses the problem of what it calls "pharmacological torture," and claims that the potentialities of divulging the truth through their use have been greatly misconceived. "To believe that such a drug exists implies not only naivety, but also disrespect for the enormous resilience and complexity of the human brain" (*Report on Torture*, p. 55).

28. See W. L. Twining and P. E. Twining, "Bentham on Torture," *Northern Ireland Legal Quarterly* 24 (1973): 305.

29. Ibid., pp. 346–47.

30. Ibid., p. 339.

31. Ibid.

32. Ibid., p. 355.

33. Ibid., p. 356.

34. United States v. Holmes, 26 Fed. Cas. 360, No. 15, 383 (E.D. Pa. 1842); and Regina v. Dudley and Stephens (1884) 14 Q.B. 273. For an interesting analysis of the latter case in its political and sociological setting, see A. B. Simpson, *Cannabalism and the Common Law* (Chicago: University of Chicago Press, 1984).

35. Lon Fuller, "The Speluncean Explorers," *Harvard Law Review* 62 (1949):616.

36. See Katz v. United States, 389 U.S. 347 (1967). Although the wiretapping was disallowed in this case, the Court indicated the acceptability of such a practice as long as proper procedures of obtaining prior permission from the court were followed.

37. United States v. Fleming, 7 U.S.C.M.A. 543, 23 C.M.R. 7 (1957).

38. See for instance Christoph Schreuder,"Derogation of Human Rights in Situations of Public Emergency: The Experience of the European Convention on Human Rights," *Yale Journal of World Public Order* 9 (1982):113.

39. See Ronald Melzack and Patrick Wall, *The Challenge of Pain* (New York: Basic Books, 1983); and an earlier version by Melzack, *The Puzzle of Pain* (New York: Basic

Books, 1973), particularly pp. 22–24. See also M. Zborowski, "Cultural Components in Responses to Pain," *Journal of Social Issues* 8, no. 4 (1952):16.

40. Ireland v. United Kingdom, European Court of Human Rights (1978), reported in *International Legal Materials* 17 (1978):680. But there was a dissenting minority, which would have found that torture had been practiced.

41. See Matthew Lippman, "The Protection of Universal Human Rights: The Problem of Torture," *Universal Human Rights* 1 (1979):43.

42. See *Report on Torture.*

43. Graeme Newman, *Just and Painful: A Case for the Corporal Punishment of Criminals* (London: McMillan, 1983).

44. Ibid., pp. 15–16.

45. Ibid., pp. 123–24. In fact, some of the torturous activity may be at the hands of other inmates, including the possibility of a fatal attack, or at least an injurious one.

46. Ibid., p. 141.

47. Ibid., p. 124.

48. See for example Jackson v. Bishop, 404 F. 2d 571 (1968). For historical discussion, see George R. Scott, *The History of Corporal Punishment* (London: Werner Lourie, 1938).

49. Newman, *Just and Painful,* p. 125.

50. See Ingraham v. Wright, 430 US 651 (1977). The Court held that corporal punishment in the schools did not constitute a violation of the Eighth and Fourteenth Amendments. It should be noted that recently Sweden imposed a total ban on any kind of corporal punishment, including spanking of children by their parents. For a discussion as to how paternalistic reasons are advanced for policies and practices that are sometimes harmful to the young, see Leon Sheleff, *Generations Apart: Adult Hostility to Youth* (New York: McGraw Hill, 1981), chap. 8, "In Loco Paternalism," pp. 213–40.

51. Giles Playfair and Derrick Sington, *Crime, Punishment and Cure* (London: Secker and Warburg, 1965), p. 254. In a

discussion over several pages (pp. 254–58), they refer to the situation at various prisons. See also Georg Sturrup, *Treatment of Sexual Offenders in Herstedvesten, Denmark* (1968).

52. Ibid., p. 256.
53. Ibid.
54. Fred Grimm, "Three Convicted Rapists Request Castration," *Philadelphia Inquirer,* 8 January 1985, p. 1.
55. See Susan Brownmiller, *Against Our Will.*
56. It should, however, be noted that in an earlier decision the Supreme Court did allow coercive sterlization, when it was carried out for feeblemindedness: see Buck v. Bell, 274 U.S. 200 (1927). As Nicholas Kittrie notes (*The Right to be Different: Deviance and Enforced Therapy* (Baltimore: Johns Hopkins Press, 1971), twenty-six states in the United States still have coercive sterlization laws, although they are rarely used. They are generally applicable only in institutions for the mentally deficient and generally require the consent of a guardian. Although it is a milder procedure than castration, there are clear possibilities of abuse, especially in those jurisdictions where the guardian's consent is not required.
57. See for instance Anthony M. Scacco, Jr., ed., *Male Rape: A Casebook of Sexual Aggression* (New York: AMS Press, 1982).
58. James Jacobs and Eric Steele, "Sexual Deprivation and Penal Policy," *Cornell Law Review* 62 (1977):312.
59. Robert Mendelsohn, *Mal(e) practice: How Doctors Manipulate Women* (Chicago: Contemporary Books, 1981). Mendelson's work is controversial both within the medical profession and beyond. The book itself is aimed at the general public, and so there is not always specific and detailed references for all of his figures.
60. Ibid., p. 97.
61. Ibid., p. 100.
62. Ibid., p. 102.

63. Dennis Rainear, "The Use of Depo-Provera for Treating Male Sex Offenders: A Review of the Constitutional and Medical Issues," *Toledo Law Review* 16 (1984): 181–230.
64. Ibid., pp. 205–6.
65. Sidney Wolfe, "Depo-Provera for Sex Offenders Criticized," *Criminal Justice Newsletter,* 12 September 1983, p. 6.
66. Rainear, "Use of Depo-Provera," especially, pp. 196–99.
67. Ibid., p. 209.
68. See Arizona v. Christopher, 652 P.2d 1031 (1982).
69. Rainear, "Use of Depo-Provera," pp. 226–27.

C H A P T E R 1 2 :
T H E M E D I C A L M O D E L

1. Erving Goffman, *Asylums: Essays on the Social Situation of Mental Patients and Other Inmates* (New York: Anchor Books, 1961). For an attempt to do away with total institutions, dealing with prisons and mental hosptials, see Andrew Scull, *Decarceration: Community Treatment and the Deviant: A Radical View* (Englewood Cliffs, N.J.: Prentice-Hall, 1977).
2. See for instance Jessica Mitford, *Kind and Usual Punishment: The Prison Business* (New York: Knopf 1973), pp. 138–68. For a general overview, see Richard Singer, "Consent of the Unfree: Medical Experimentation and Behavior Modification in the Closed Institution," *Law and Human Behavior* 1 (1977):1.
3. See my discussion, pp. 349-50.
4. See for example Bishop v. Stoneman, 508 F. 2d 1224 (1974); and Thomas v. Pate, 493 F. 2d 151 (1974), pp. 157–59. See also Estelle v. Gamble, 429 U.S. 97 (dissenting opinion by Justice Stevens, pp. 108–17). In the last case the petitioner apparently spent a year in solitary confinement for refusing to work after injuring his back in a work accident and not receiving the medical help he requested.

5. Nicholas Kittrie, *The Right to be Different: Deviance and Enforced Therapy* (Baltimore: Johns Hopkins Press, 1971).

6. Gabriel Tarde, *Penal Philosophy* (Boston: Little Brown, 1912), pp. 555–56.

7. Margaret Radin, "Proportionality, Subjectivity, and Tragedy," *University of California Davis Law Review* 18 (1985):1176. My own ideas on capital punishment have been directly affected, as will as shown later in this chapter, by my positive attitude to euthanasia. This in turn flows from my desire to avoid a situation in which prolongation of life by extraordinary medical means results in the infliction of pain, both physical and emotional, on the helpless and the vulnerable. Thus the court in Satz v. Perlmutter spoke of enforced medical treatment against a patient's will as "inflicting never ending physical torture on his body until the inevitable, but artificially suspended, moment of death" (362 So. 2d 160 [1978], aff'd 379 So. 2d 359 [1980]).

8. Samuel Butler, *Erewhon* (New York: E. P. Hutton, 1917), especially chaps. 10–12.

9. See Liora Navon, Ph.D. diss. in sociology and anthropology, Tel Aviv University (in progress.).

10. As quoted in Melvin I. Urofsky, "A Right to Die: Termination of Appeal for Condemned Persons," *Journal of Criminal Law and Criminology* 75 (1984):559. For the failed appeal in this case, see Coppola v. Commonwealth, 257 S.E. 2d 797 (1979).

11. George Annas, "When Suicide Prevention Becomes Brutality: The Case of Elizabeth Bouvia," *Hastings Center Report* (1984):20. For reports of the case, see Bouvia v. County of Riverside, No. 159780, Sup. Ct. Riverside Co., Cal. (16 December 1983), Tr. 1238–50. It should, however, be noted that between the first and second decisions, there was a decision of the New Jersey Supreme Court that allowed life-sustaining treatment, including feeding tubes, to be

withdrawn from terminally ill patients, whether competent or incompetent. See In re Conroy, 98 N.J. 321, 486 A.2d 1209 (1985). In the case at issue, the patient, eighty-four-year-old Claire Conroy, was considered mentally incompetent but was not comatose or in a vegetative state. She died before the decision was handed down, but Karen Quinlan was still alive at this stage, some nine years after the court had allowed life-sustaining equipment to be removed, and she had been kept alive by feeding tubes. After the decision in the Conroy case, the lawyer representing Quinlan's parents indicated that he would not seek to have the tubes removed ("'Right to Die' Rule in Terminal Cases Widened in Jersey," *New York Times,* 18 January 1985). Karen Quinlan died several months later.

It should be added that there are problematics in the *Bouvia* case that go way beyond the issues that I am dealing with in this chapter, namely, the rights of handicapped and disabled people, the negative stereotypes that many in society have of them, the often incorrect presumptions that people have of their limited prospects to function in society and experience satisfaction and happiness in their lives. These issues and their legal implications have been well discussed in a note by Belinda Stradley, *"Elizabeth Bouvia v. Riverside Hospital:* Suicide, Euthanasia, Murder: The Line Blurs," *Golden Gate University Law Review* 15 (1985):407. She is particularly concerned that the widespread coverage given to Bouvia's problems and the sympathy evoked for her may serve to reinforce existing negative, and incorrect, stereotypes about disabled people. She stresses that quadriplegics may lead meaningful lives, and that the legislation aimed at eliminating discrimination against them should not be used (as was done in the *Bouvia* case) to argue for her right to be helped to put an end to her life. But she ignores the fact of Bouvia's unrelenting pain. For the purposes of my thesis, the key issue becomes one of autonomy, the need to respect a clearly expressed wish on the part of someone who is apparently incapable of ensuring consummation of that wish. Recently a man was sentenced to fifteen years imprisonment for the mercy killing of a neighbor who was a quadriplegic, done at her request. His own effort at committing suicide immediately afterwards failed. Her family and their neighbors were, according to the press reports, understanding and supportive of his action, and considered the punishment to be unnecessarily severe. ("New Jersey Man Gets Fifteen Years in Prison in Mercy-killing," *Philadelphia Inquirer,* 30 May 1986, sec. B, p. 4).

12. Andrew Malcolm, "Right to Die Dispute Focuses on Californian," *New York Times,* 20 October 1984.

13. Bettyruth Walter, "A Little Music," *The Pennsylvania Gazette* 81 (April 1983). She sums up the experience: "The most extraordinary thing about my father was probably not his life, but his death. And he had to do it twice. Contrary to popular opinion, you can die more than once. But it's also true that you must be 'brought back' quickly, because if too much time elapses, the result can be something quite horrible. I know whereof I speak, because I witnessed it with my own eyes. My father deserved a better death. We all do." For a further personal and moving account of a mother's death, see Arthur Waskow, "To Catch a Breath," *Moment* (April 1986):46. In referring to his mother's reactions to the respirator and his own sense of what she was undergoing, he uses the term "torture."

14. See Doris Portwood, *Common-Sense Suicide: The Final Right* (New York: Dodd, Mead & Company, 1978), who argues from a feminist perspective that since women tend to outlive their husbands, they are more condemned to the consequences of loneliness. She accordingly argues that there is a need for the women's movement to investigate the problem of euthanasia. In her words, "senior women have a unique opportunity to promote a long overdue social

reform" (p. 9). She notes that there is almost no subject which remains taboo with the exception of "rational suicide for the older person. It needs to be talked about and American women of social security age are the ones to start the talking. . . . Senior American women have wealth and power yet hundreds of thousands end their lives in baffled misery in the near imprisonment of nursing homes or hospitals" (p. 10). It could, of course, be argued that the loneliness that she refers to is not an inevitable concomitant of old age or widowhood, but part of society's failure toward the old, with euthanasia merely compounding the failure. Thus, communities may be set up to cater positively for the needs of the old, family ties may be reinforced, empathetic succour may be provided for the disabled elderly.

Yet such arguments have only a limited validity for Portwood's thesis. They are important inasmuch as they stress the need for reform—but they ignore the right of the individual to an autonomous decision even if there is reform, and ignore the fact of ongoing misery of institutionalization, which Portwood describes, for as long as there is no reform.

Portwood also quotes a statement by Horace Kallen, who says: "Safeguarding a person's right to die when and as he chooses, so long as this right works no violence on the rights of others seems to me a proper function for the laws of a free society of free and educated men" (p. 56). See also Milton Heifitz with Charles Mangel, *The Right to Die* (New York: G. P. Putnam, 1975); A. B. Downing, ed., *Euthanasia and the Right to Death: The Case for Voluntary Euthanasia* (London: Peter Owen, 1969); W. Steele, Jr. and B. Hill, Jr., "A Plea for a Legal Right to Die," *Oklahoma Law Review* 29 (1976):328; Bonnie Steinbock, ed., *Killing and Letting Die* (Englewood Cliffs, N.J.: Prentice-Hall, 1980). Steinbock herself claims that present practices of withdrawing medical treatment are by no means euthanasia, but only the recognition of the patient's right to refuse treatment; see "The Intentional Termination of Life" (p. 69). See also the articles by Michael Tooley, "An Irrelevant Consideration: Killing versus Letting Die," and James Rachels, "Active and Passive Euthanasia."

15. See Lucius Annaeus Seneca, *The Workes of Lucius Annaeus Seneca, both Morrall and Naturall* (London: William Stansby, 1614); and Norman Gulley, *The Philosophy of Socrates* (New York: St. Martin's Press, 1968).

16. For a case in which a doctor was acquitted, see Barber v. Superior Court, 195 Ca Rptr. 484 (1983). In England, too, a doctor was indicted, but acquitted, for allowing a Down's Syndrome infant to die from lack of food, with the consent of the parents. See Helen Beynon, "Doctors as Murderers," *Criminal Law Review* (1982):17; and M. Gunn and J. Smith, *"Arthur's* Case and the Right to Life of a Down's Syndrome Child," *Criminal Law Review* (1985):705. The case of a Down's Syndrome infant seems to be substantively different from other cases of euthanasia primarily because there is no possibility of fulfilling the condition of consent; and the consent of the parents will in many cases be suspect. Problems of this nature are part of a research project by Varda Ben-Schachar. See her Ph.D. diss. in criminology, Tel-Aviv University (in progress).

17. Peter MacKinnon, "Euthanasia and Homicide," *Criminal Law Quarterly* 26 (1983–84):495. In the *Arthur* case, too, the "judge treated the distinction between act and omission as crucial" (Gunn and Smith, *"Arthur's* Case," p. 707).

18. See Leon Sheleff, *The Bystander: Behavior, Law, Ethics* (Lexington, Mass.: Lexington Books, 1978), especially chap. 6, "The Duty to Rescue," pp. 101–22. See also Aleksander W. Rudzinski, "The Duty to Rescue: A Comparative Analysis," in James M. Ratcliffe, ed., *The Good Samaritan and the Law* (New York: Anchor Books, 1966).

19. Elisabeth Kubler-Ross, *On Death and Dying* (New York: MacMillan, 1970).

20. MacKinnon, "Euthanasia and Homicide," p. 484. See also Bernard Dickens, "The Right to Natural Death," *McGill Law Journal* 26 (1980–81):847; Bernard Freamon and Linda Mehling, "A Review of the Right to Die for Terminally Ill Patients," *Yale Law and Policy Review* 1 (1982):80.

21. This was recognized by one of Becarria's biographers, Marcello Maestro, in his book *Caesare Beccaria and the Origins of Penal Reform* (Philadelphia: Temple University Press, 1973), where he writes: "It is clear that Beccaria's opposition to the death penalty would be weakened by his recognition that man does have the right to take his own life" (p. 31).

22. A concurring opinion by one of the judges in the latest Bouvia case basically accepts this positon. Judge Compton adds that Elizabeth Bouvia "has made a conscious and informed choice that she prefers death to continued existence in her helpless and, to her, intolerable condition. I believe she has an abolute right to effectuate that decision. This state and the medical profession instead of frustrating her desire, should be attempting to relieve her suffering by permitting and in fact assisting her to die with ease and dignity. The fact that she is forced to suffer the ordeal of self-starvation to achieve her objective is in itself inhumane.

"The right to die is an integral part of our right to control our own destinies so long as the rights of others are not affected. That right should, in my opinion, include the ability to enlist assistance from others, including the medical profession, in making death as painless and quick as possible. . . . Whatever choice Elizabeth Bouvia may ultimately make, I can only hope that her courage, persistence and example will cause our society to deal realistically with the plight of those unfortunate individuals to whom death beckons as a welcome respite from suffering." The opinion also refers to the humiliating and dehumanizing aspects of her helplessness.

No other judge joined in Judge Compton's opinion. This approach remains unique—but possibly portends future developments. See also a perceptive analysis by Andrew Malcolm, "To Suffer a Prolonged Illness or Elect to Die: A Case Study," *New York Times,* 16 December 1984. He describes how the patient undergoing euthanasia bade farewell to family and friends, how she listened to her favorite music and poetry, and then how, at the last moment, she opened her eyes and whispered "thank you." See the companion article dealing with the general issue, "Negotiated Death: An Open Secret," describing help afforded by lawyers in coping with the legal aspects. A recent New Jersey decision has also shown the need for sensitive consideration of the manner of dying. The hospital had refused the terminal patient's request not to be put on a feeding tube when her degenerative disease would lead to such a situation. However, they were willing to transfer her to another nearby hospital which was prepared to comply with her request. She opposed the transfer because she was satisfied with the quality of her care and had become emotionally attached to her medical attendants and caregivers. The court found in her favor, holding that a transfer against her will would cause her emotional and psychological strain and would lead to feelings of rejection. Despite being aware that their decision would offend the sensibilities of the hospital staff, the court felt that it was more important that the patient not "experience suffering over and above the grim suffering necessarily inherent in her disease and in her choice of no artificial feeding." See Superior Court of New Jersey, Appellate Division, A-442-86T5 (6 October 1986).

In any event, pending litigation may preempt legislation. See the symposium in *Issues in Law and Medicine* 2, no. 2 (September 1986): especially the lead article by John R. Connery, "The Ethical Standard for Withholding/Withdrawing Nutrition and Hydration," pp. 87-98.

There are two pending appeals on this matter before higher courts. One is in New Jersey, where the trial court held that the provision of food and fluid is elective therapy and therefore could be refused by the patient or his guardian (in this case at the request of the patient's family, since she, though conscious, is incapable of communicating her wishes, not even by eye-blinking). The other is in Massachusetts, where the trial court came to an opposite conclusion, and the family's petition to obligate the hospital to desist from feeding was denied (here, the patient was unconscious for over three years). In both cases the patient's major organs were functioning normally, and both patients had a long life expectancy. See In the Matter of Nancy Jobes, No. C-4971-85E (N.J. Super. Ct. Ch. Div.) and Brophy v. New England Sinai Hospital, No. 85E009G1 (Mass. Trial Ct. P. and Fam. Ct. Dept., Norfolk Div.). See also Patrick Derr, "Nutrition and Hydration as Elective Therapy: Brophy and Jobes from an Ethical and Historical Perspective," *Issues in Law and Medicine* 2 (1986):25. These cases deal ultimately with the willingness of the courts to allow a patient who is in a terminal, comatose, or vegetative state to be starved to death, with the consent of the guardian. If this passive euthanasia, an omission, were to be allowed, it seems that simple logic and compassionate sensitivity will then lead to an acceptance of active euthanasia, a commission, which would have the one big advantage of avoiding starving a helpless being to death.

23. See "Right-to-Die Initiative Urged in California," *Public Administration Times,* 1 November 1986, p. 3.

24. See for example W. Curran and W. Carscella, "The Ethics of Medical Participation in Capital Punishment by Intraveneous Drug Injection" *New England Journal of Medicine* 302 (1980):226. See also Stephen Cornman, "*Chaney v. Heckler* and Lethal Injection: Attacking the Drugs to Invalidate the Punishment," *Criminal Justice*

Journal 7 (1984):363. In several cases the Food and Drugs Administration has been challenged to declare use of lethal drugs for executions illegal.

25. John Lawrence describes the case of William Taylor, who, in 1893, was rendered unconscious by the initial current. The chair holding him then broke and he fell forward. He was given morphine in the hope of keeping him unconscious until the chain was fixed, just over an hour later. Lawrence, *A History of Capital Punishment* (New York: The Citadel Press, 1960), p. 65. A recent execution in Indiana took three applications of current, over more than a quarter of an hour, before the doctor was able to pronounce the person dead (see *New York Times,* 17 October 1985). Lethal injections have also not been without mishap—but the injections in such cases were administered by medically untrained personnel.

26. Burton Wolfe, *Pile-up on Death Row* (New York: Doubleday, 1973), pp. 85-95.

27. Albert Camus, "Reflections on the Guillotine," in *Resistance, Rebellion and Death* (New York: Knopf, 1960).

28. Alfred Heijder and Herman van Geuns, *Professional Code of Ethics* (London: Amnesty International Publications, 1976).

29. The Declaration of Tokyo, unanimously passed at the 29th World Medical Assembly of the World Medical Association on 10 October 1975. Earlier that year, the International Council of Nurses also adopted a resolution condemning torture. For an excellent discussion of the problems of doctors and other medical personnel when confronted with torture in confinement situations, see Eric Stover and Elena Nightingale, eds., *The Breaking of Bodies and Minds: Torture, Psychiatric Abuse and the Health Professions* (New York: W. H. Freeman, 1985).

30. Matthew Lippman, "The Protection of Universal Human Rights: The Problem of Torture," *Universal Human Rights* 1 (1979):48.

31. Ibid.

32. See Monroe Paulsen, Graham Parker, and Lynn Adelman, "Child Abuse Reporting Laws: Some Legislative History," *George Washington Law Review* 36 (1966):482; Henry H. Foster and Doris Jonas Freed, "The Battered Child: Whose Responsibility, Lawyer or Physician?" *Trial* 3 (December–January 1966–67):33.

33. *Draft Principles for a Code of Ethics for Lawyers, Relevant to Torture and Other Cruel, Inhuman or Degrading Treatment or Punishment;* see the report "Lawyers Against Torture," *Review of the International Commission of Jurists* 15 (1976):29.

34. See Richard M. Titmuss, *The Gift Relationship: From Human Blood to Social Policy* (New York: Pantheon Books, 1971).

35. See "Inmates Sue to Keep Research in Prisons," *Science* 212 (1981):650. Often officials stress that prospects for parole will not be enhanced by volunteering, so as to avoid complaints of duress.

36. See the article in the *New York Times,* 20 September 1984.

37. Jack Kervokian, "Why is the Medical Profession Against Condemned Criminals as a Source of Transplant Organs?" *MD* (October 1984):28. See also his *Medical Research and the Death Penalty* (New York: Vantage, 1960). But the possible exploitation of the condemned may be noted in the practice in Iran, where medical personnel have reportedly drained blood from prisoners just prior to their execution so that it could be given to wounded soldiers fighting in the Iraq-Iran war, presumably without the prisoner's permission. See Stover and Nightingale, *The Breaking of Bodies,* quoting from the article, "Iran Reportedly Draining Blood from Prisoners," *American Medical Association Newsletter* (14 October 1983).

38. George Bishop, *Executions: The Legal Ways of Death* (Los Angeles: Sherbourne Press, 1965), p. 187.

39. E. Cadogan, *The Roots of Evil* (London, 1937), p. 147, as quoted in Arthur Koestler, *Reflections on Hanging* (London: Victor Gollanz, 1965), p. 18.

40. See George McGregor, *The History of Burke and Hare* (1884). McGregor suggests that the bodies provided by these murders helped make Edinburgh a leader in medical studies.

41. Mitford, *Kind and Usual Punishment,* chap. 9, "Cheaper Than Chimpanzees," pp. 138–68. For cases dealing with medical experimentation, see Clay v. Martin, 509 F.2d 109 (1975); Mackey v. Procunier, 477 F.2d 877 (1973); Bailey v. Lally, 481 F.2d Supp. 203 (1970). In the latter case the court noted that the conditions in the particular prison were not so harsh as to coerce the prisoners to seek an altnerative option, nor were the rewards unfairly enticing. Full explanations were provided of the nature of the research, and participants were entitled to withdraw at any time. The court also mentioned that the daughter of one of the experimenters had volunteered for a similar research program at college in order to earn money. In regard to remuneration, the court also made note of the fact that the ACLU "had complained that prisoners received less than civilian volunteers and that the pay to prisoners should be raised" (p. 224, n. 31).

CHAPTER 13:
REVENGE AND RETALIATION

1. See A. S. Diamond, *Primitive Law: Past and Present* (London: Methuen, 1971), chap. 18, "Before the Evolution of Courts," pp. 185–93, especially, p. 192. See also Leon Sheleff, "A Critique of the Criminal Law," *Tel Aviv University Studies in Law* 3 (1978):113.

2. Thomas Hobbes, *Leviathan* (Baltimore: Penguin, 1968).

3. Sigmund Freud, *Totem and Taboo* (1913) in James Strachey, ed., *The Standard Edition of the Complete Psychological Works,* 24 vols., (London: Hogarth Press, 1953–66), vol. 13.

4. See, in general, articles of this nature in the *Journal of Libertarian Studies.*

5. Commercial corrective institutions have been set up in a number of states in the United States. Much concern has been expressed as to the potential for abuse and exploitation, and there have been moves in some states to prohibit them.

6. See for instance Andrew Von Hirsch, *Doing Justice: The Choice of Punishments* (New York: Hill and Wang, 1976).

7. For a description and analysis of this affair, including the backgrounds of the protagonists, see Lillian Rubin, *Quiet Rage: Bernie Goetz in a Time of Madness* (New York: Farrar, Straus and Giroux, 1986).

8. For a discussion of the Genovese case, see A. M. Rosenthal, *38 Witnesses* (New York: McGraw Hill, 1964). For a survey of research in this area, see Leon Sheleff, *The Bystander: Behavior, Law, Ethics* (Lexington, Mass.: Lexington Books, 1978).

9. See for instance Sidney Schanberg, "The Bernhard Goetz Mailbag," *New York Times,* 19 January 1985. He states that the mail that he received was running five to one in support of Goetz's action. See also the letter by the senator from New York, Alfonse D'Amato, "New York's Empathy for Bernhard Goetz," in *New York Times,* 8 February 1985.

10. It might be noted that New York did retain the death penalty for murder committed by those serving a life sentence. It was a mandatory punishment and on this basis was declared unconstitutional. See People v. Smith, 479 N.Y.S. 2d 706 (CC. App. 1984). For recent discussion of this issue, see Andrea Galbo, "Death After Life: The Future of New York's Mandatory Death Penalty for Murder Committed by Life-term Prisoners," *Fordham Urban Law Journal* 23 (1985):597.

11. J. L. Barkas, *Victims* (New York: Scribners, 1978), p. 201.

12. Svend Ranulf, *Moral Indignation and Middle Class Psychology* (New York: Schocken Books, 1964), p. 77.

13. The fact of these kind of sentiments have other implications. Is there perhaps an opposite to an abolitionist stance, not just of being a retentionist, but of being actively vindictive. If an absolute abolitionist (one who would be incapable of returning a guilty verdict when there would then be a chance of a death penalty) can be kept off a jury, could people whose support of violent responses to violent crimes could be proved be kept off similarly? Are they capable of dispensing justice fairly in a capital trial? Given the sophisticated jury challenges that have developed in the last few years, this approach might profitably be pursued in the future by the defense.

14. See discussion in chap. 6.

15. See "Preparatory Meeting of Experts in Social Defense (African Region) for the Fourth United Nations Congress on the Prevention of Crime and the Treatment of Offenders," *International Review of Criminal Policy* 27 (1969):66. For vigilante action in the United States, see James H. Chadborn, *Lynching and the Law* (Chapel Hill: University of North Carolina Press, 1933); for ancient Rome, see A. W. Lintott, *Violence in Republican Rome* (London: Oxford University Press, 1968). p. 16.

16. See for example Margaret Masluck, "The Albanian Blood Feud," in Paul Bohannan, ed., *Law and Warfare* (New York: The Natural History Press, 1967).

17. See for instance the paper presented by Abdul Karim on the blood feud and rituals of reconcilaition among Arabs in Israel (presented at the fourth meeting of the Israeli Criminological Society, 1980).

18. Much of this has been represented in the development of victimology as an academic field of study. For moving personal accounts, see Barkas, *Victims,* and Alice R. Kaminsky, *The Victim's Song* (Buffalo, N.Y.: Prometheus Books, 1985).

19. See for instance "Relatives of Murder Victim Urge No Clemency for Carolina Killer," *New York Times,* 20 September 1984.

20. See for example the note by Doug Magee, "Victim's Family Opposes More Execution," *Lifelines: Newsletter of the National Coalition Against the Death Penalty* (July–August 1984):4.

21. Furman v. Georgia, 408 U.S. 238 (1972), per Marshall, J., pp. 362–63.

22. For a report on some of the latest research on public attitudes to capital punishment, see Phil Harris, "A Rational Mask: Public Attitudes Toward the Death Penalty," *Lifelines: Newsletter of the National Coalition Against the Death Penalty* (March 1985):1. He notes that "a 1981 ABC/*Washington Post* poll found that deterrence was less often a reason given for favoring the death penalty than revenge." For further examples of public opinion, see P. C. Ellsworth and L. Ross, "Public Opinion and Capital Punishment: A Close Examination of Views of Abolitionists and Retentionists," *Crime and Delinquency* (1983):116.

23. Amnesty International, *The Death Penalty* (1979), p. 143: "Para-military groups, the existence of which are condoned or actively supported by the authorities, as well as units of official security forces, carry out murders and illegal detentions in a number of Latin American countries."

24. Ibid., p. 144.

25. See for instance Paul Tappan, *Crime, Justice and Corrections* (New York: McGraw-Hill, 1960), p. 286. For an example of two innocent people killed while fleeing a policeman, who they thought was an armed robber since he was in plain clothes and had used an unmarked car to block their passage, see Commonwealth v. Duerr, 45 A.2d 235 (1946). The policeman was originally acquitted of murder but was found guilty in a second trial of involuntary manslaughter.

26. I offer these as speculative possibilities. Research in these matters would obviously be difficult. For a general discussion of the use of deadly force by the police, see Peter Scharf and Arnold Binder, *The Badge and the Bullet: Police Use of Deadly Force* (New York: Praeger Press, 1984). See also J. Fyfe, "Observations on Police Deadly Force," *Crime and Delinquency* 27 (1981):376; Note, "Constitutional Law," *Cincinnati Law Review* 52 (1983):1157.

27. Tennessee v. Garner and Memphis Police Dept. v. Garner, 471 U.S. 1. See John Blume III, "Deadly Force in Memphis: *Tennessee v. Garner,*" *Cumberland Law Review* 15 (1985):89.

28. The regulations stated, *inter alia:* "Under certain specified conditions, deadly force may be exercised against a fleeing felon," but no attempt is made to define those specified conditions. Research done over the years had indicated a disproportionate number of blacks among the shooting victims—see James Fyfe, "Blind Justice: Police Shootings in Memphis," *Journal of Criminal Law and Criminology* 73 (1982):707. In the research it was noted that half of the shootings involved only property crimes.

29. 710 Fed. 2d 240, 246 (CA 6 1983).

30. See the editorial, "A Welcome Curb on Deadly Force," *New York Times,* 29 March 1985.

31. Payton v. New York, 445 U.S. 573 (1980).

32. See Lawrence Sherman, "Execution Without Trial: Police Homicide and the Constitution" *Vanderbilt Law Review* 33 (1980):71.

33. Tennessee v. Garner, p. 14.

34. See Coker v. Georgia, 633 U.S. 584 (1977).

35. For approaches of different states, see Paul Mogin, "The Policeman's Privilege to Shoot a Fleeing Suspect: Constitutional Limits on the Use of Deadly Force," *American Criminal Law Review* 18 (1981):533, especially pp.

538–40. Mogin argues strongly by analogy that the restrictions on the use of the death penalty must lead to similar controls over the use of deadly force.

36. A newspaper article by the lawyer for Garner (Steven Winter, "A Setback for Deadly Force,"*New York Times,* 11 April 1985) points out the interesting juxtaposition in time that the decision in *Tennessee* v. *Garner* was announced on the same day, 27 March 1985, that the Manhattan district attorney decided (after a second grand jury hearing) to indict Bernhard Goetz for attempted murder. This later reassessment of Goetz's position serves to emphasize the rash judgment of Goetz's earlier supporters. This decision of the grand jury was subsequently nullified by court decision based on errors made by the prosecution in presenting the facts of the case. It was suggested that evidence was suppressed indicating the intention of the youths to physically harm Goetz. Still later, a third grand jury was constituted, which again indicted him.

CHAPTER 14: SUPRA-NATIONAL DUE PROCESS

1. For general development of the criminal law, see Leon Radcinowicz, *History of English Criminal Law and Its Administration* (London: Stevens and Sons, 1956).

2. See "Benefit of Clergy" in Arthur A. Leff, "The Leff Dictionary of Law: A Fragment," *Yale Law Review* 94 (1985):2151.

3. See *Encyclopedia Judaica,* s.v. "Capital Punishment."

4. See Paul H. Robinson, *Criminal Law Defenses* (St. Paul: West Publishing Co., 1984) vol. 1, sec. 102.

5. See George P. Fletcher, *Rethinking Criminal Law* (Boston: Little, Brown, 1978), pp. 250–53.

6. See N. Hurnard, *The King's Pardon for Homicide Before 1307* (Oxford: Oxford University Press, 1969); and Fenton Bresler, *Reprieve: A Study of a System* (London: Harrap, 1965).

7. See Mortimer Kadish and Sanford Kadish, "The Institutionalization of Conflict: Jury Acquittals, *Journal of Social Issues* 27 (1971): 199; and Thomas A. Green, *Verdict According to Conscience: Perspectives on the English Criminal Trial Jury, 1200–1800* (Chicago: University of Chicago Press, 1985).

8. See Walter C. Reckless, *The Crime Problem* (New York: Appelton-Century-Crofts, 1961) chap. 3, "The Search for Causes," pp. 233–362.

9. See George Vold, *Theoretical Criminology* (New York: Oxford University Pres, 1958); and Ian Taylor, Paul Walton, and Jock Young, *The New Criminology* (New York: Torch, 1974), especially chap. 8, "The New Conflict Theories," pp. 237–67.

10. James Avery Joyce, *Capital Punishment: A World View* (New York: Thomas Nelson, 1961), p. 329. Joyce's view deserves serious consideration, but his model may be overly sanguine, and his perception of human behavior and social reality is not always reliable. Thus he approvingly quotes a conversation between the Chinese leader, Mao, and one of the leaders of the Algerian rebellion against the French, Ferhat Abbas. Apparently Mao "lectured Ferhat Abbas on the need of persuading and re-educating the people opposed to him. They should not be killed, Mao is said to have insisted. The Algerian rebels had been carrying out a policy of terrorism and assassinations, not only against the French, but also against pro-French or rival Algerian nationalist groups. Mao is alleged to have said: 'It is a mistake to believe that by physically eliminating traitors or enemy prisoners, you can serve the revolutionary cause.'" One does not know which is the most disturbing: Mao's hypocrisy, in volunteering this advice when

his regime was not just re-educating, but engaging in wholesale executions, or Joyce's naivete in quoting this story years after Mao's excesses were widely known. For a reference to some of the excesses of Mao's regime, see my brief discussion in chap. 6.

11. See for instance Graeme Newman, *Just and Painful* (London: McMillan, 1983).

12. See especially William S. Geimer, "Death at Any Cost: A Critique of the Supreme Court's Recent Retreat from its Death Penalty Standards," *Florida State University Law Review* 12 (1985):737. Among the more recent cases discussed are: Eddings v. Oklahoma, 455 U.S. 104 (1982); Godfrey v. Georgia, 446 U.S. 420 (1980); Enmund v. Florida, 458 U.S. 782 (1982); Barefoot v. Estelle, 463 U.S. 880 (1983); Zant v. Stephens, 462 U.S. 862 (1983); Barclay v. Florida, 463 U.S. 939 (1983).

13. Geimer, "Death at Any Cost," pp. 738–39.

14. Ibid.

15. Ibid., p. 779.

16. See "Death Row Inmates Find a Scarcity of Lawyers for Appeals," *New York Times,* 22 September 1986, p. 1.

17. Ramsey Clark, "Spenkelink's Last Appeal," in H. A. Bedau, ed., *Death Penalty in America,* 3d ed. (New York: Oxford University Press, 1982).

18. Geimer, "Death at Any Cost," p. 779. For the importance of effective counsel at the sentencing stage, see Gary Goodpaster, "The Trial for Life: Effective Assistance of Counsel in Death Penalty Cases," *New York University Law Review* 58 (1983):299.

19. In some places life prisoners have banded together to seek to preserve their rights and advance their interests, but little publicity or support is given to this phenomenon.

20. F. Patrick Hubbard, "Reasonable Levels of Arbitrariness in Death Sentencing Patterns: A Tragic Perspective on Capital Punishment," *University of California, Davis Law Review* 18 (1985):1113.

21. Guido Calabresi and Philip Bobbitt, *Tragic Choices* (New York: Norton, 1978).

22. Hubbard, "Death Sentencing Patterns," p. 1152.

23. See for example Erick Andersen, "Rings: A New Maximum-Security Prison for Young Men and Women in Denmark," in D. Ward and K. Schoen, eds., *Confinement in Maximum Custody: New Last-Resort Prisons in the United States and Western Europe* (Lexington, Mass.: Lexington Books, 1981), p. 159. The author concedes that rehabilitation is not the aim; rather, it is to ensure that prison life will be made "less negative." The prison is based on the principle of giving "the inmates as much responsibility for their own lives as possible" (p. 161). This prison was still in an experimental stage at the time of the writing of the article. It should be noted that the period of imprisonment is generally for a few years, though one inmate has been sentenced to fourteen years. But for a balanced analysis of the Swedish system, pointing out how some incorrect stereotypes as to its presumed benefits have been facilely accepted, see David Ward, "Sweden: The Middle Way to Prison Reform?" in M. Wolfgang, ed., *Prisons: Present and Possible* (Lexington Mass.: Lexington Books, 1979). Ward also notes that inasmuch as the Swedish system has made achievements, they are generally part of a more comprehensive human services policy and social welfare program.

24. See especially Nicholas N. Kittrie, *The Right to be Different: Deviance and Enforced Therapy* (Baltimore: John Hopkins Press, 1971). See also H. Soldman, "The Limits of Clockwork: The Neurobiology of Violent Behavior," in J. Conrad and S. Dinitz, eds., *In Fear of Each Other* (Lexington, Mass.: Lexington Books, 1977), p. 63.

25. United Nations, *Capital Punishment Developments 1961-1965* (New York: United Nations, 1967) pp. 29–35. See also my article "Mandatory Life Sentences: A Comparative Study of the Law In Israel, Great Britain, the United States and West Germany," *Tel Aviv University Studies*

in Law 5 (1982):115; and D. A. Thomas, *Principles of Sentencing* (London: Heinemann, 1970), especially p. 55.

26. R. Sapienza, "International Legal Standards on Capital Punishment" in B. G. Ramcharan, ed., *The Right to Life in International Law* (Dordrecht: Martinus Nijhoff, 1985), p. 294.

27. For other work in human rights done through the auspices of the United Nations, see Ton Zuijdwijk, *Petitioning the United Nations: A Study in Human Rights* (New York: St. Martin's Press, 1982); and J. Moller, "Petitioning the United Nations," *Universal Human Rights* 1 (1979): 57.

28. See for instance Luis Kutner, "World Habeas Corpus, Human Rights and World Community," *De Paul Law Review* 17 (1967):20; and Kutner, ed., *The Human Right to Individual Freedom: A Symposium on World Habeas Corpus* (Coral Gables, Florida: University of Miami Press, 1970). The United Nations Human Rights Commission and the Committee Against Torture partially answer to such needs, though lacking judicial status and the power to enforce. It should, however, be noted that recently a group of United States organizations has lodged a protest with the commission as to the cruel, inhuman, and degrading treatment being inflicted on a group of 1,800 Cuban refugees being held in prison on suspicion of having criminal backgrounds; they had been released to the United States by the Cuban authorities some six years earlier as a part of a larger release of over 100,000 Cubans. The groups involved, including the American Civil Liberties Union and the Americas Watch Committee, had chosen to take the issue to an international forum after unsuccessfully exhausting all their legal options in United States courts (see "Cubans Mistreated in U.S. Prison, Groups Say," *Philadelphia Inquirer,* 30 May 1986). For overall involvement of the world community on issues of life and death, including capital punishment, see B. G. Ramcharan., ed.,

The Right to Life in International Law. See also Leon Hurwitz, *The State as Defendant: Governmental Accountability and the Redress of Individual Grievances* (Westport, Conn.: Greenwood Press, 1981).

29. Article 17 of the U.N. *Convention Against Torture;* see *The Review of the International Commission of Jurists,* December 1985, p. 58.

30. For the background to this article and the working out of the compromise formula, see B. G. Ramcharan, ''The Drafting History of Article 6 of The International Covenant on Civil and Political Rights,'' in *The Right to Life in International Law,* p. 42.

SUBJECT INDEX

INDEX OF NAMES

INDEX OF U.S. CASES